BRITISH PACIFIC LOCOMOTIVES

BRITISH PACIFIC
LOCOMOTIVES

By
CECIL J. ALLEN
M.INST.T., A.I.LOCO.E.

LONDON

IAN ALLAN LTD

First published 1962
Second edition 1971
This impression 1990

ISBN 0 7110 0261 4

Published by Ian Allan Ltd, Shepperton, Surrey; and printed by Ian Allan Printing
Ltd at their works at Coombelands in Runnymede, England

CONTENTS

FOREWORD BY T. C. B. MILLER 7

PREFACE TO THE FOURTH EDITION 8

AUTHOR'S PREFACE 9

I 'THE GREAT BEAR', GREAT WESTERN RAILWAY . . 11

II THE RAVEN PACIFICS, NORTH EASTERN RAILWAY . 15

III THE GRESLEY PACIFICS, GREAT NORTHERN AND
   LONDON & NORTH EASTERN RAILWAYS . . 19

   1 The Emergence of 'Great Northern' 19
   2 The 'A1' Pacifics 21
   3 Pacific versus 'Castle' 28
   4 The 'A3' Pacifics 31
   5 No. 10000 37
   6 Preparing for the Streamliners 41
   7 The 'A4' Pacifics 48
   8 The Silver Jubilee 54
   9 126 Miles per Hour 61
   10 Everyday Pacific Performance 67
   11 Numbers, Names and Notes 77
   12 The Gresley Conjugated Motion 81
   13 The Final Years 83

IV THE THOMPSON PACIFICS, LONDON & NORTH EASTERN
   RAILWAY 94

   1 The Revolt from Gresley 94
   2 The Rebuilding of Great Northern 99
   3 The Thompson 'A2s' and their Work 100

V THE PEPPERCORN PACIFICS, LONDON & NORTH
   EASTERN RAILWAY 106

   1 The Standard 'A2' Class 106
   2 The 'A1' Class 109
   3 Some 'A1' Performances 110

VI THE STANIER PACIFICS, LONDON, MIDLAND &
   SCOTTISH RAILWAY 119

   1 The Princess Royal and her Sisters 119
   2 Glasgow to Euston in 5¾ Hours 123
   3 The 'Turbomotive' 127
   4 Coronation, the 'Duchesses' and the 'Cities' 131
   5 The Coronation Scot on Trial 136
   6 'Duchess' Pacifics under Test and in Service . . . 141
   7 Coronation across the Atlantic 148
   8 Names, Locations and Casualties. 150

VII THE BULLEID PACIFICS, SOUTHERN RAILWAY . . 156

  1 A Revolutionary Design 156
  2 The Valve-Motion and other Novelties 159
  3 The Lightweight Pacifics 163
  4 Teething Troubles 165
  5 The All-Welded Boilers 168
  6 The 1948 Locomotive Exchanges 170
  7 Under Test at Rugby 174
  8 The Rebuilding 176
  9 On the Footplate 180
  10 Day-to-day Performance 182

VIII THE STANDARD PACIFICS, BRITISH RAILWAYS . . 195

  1 The Principles of Design 195
  2 The 'Britannias', Class '7' 197
  3 The 'Britannias' on Test 201
  4 Defects and their Correction 202
  5 The 'Britannias' in Service 205
  6 Some 'Britannia' Speed Achievements 209
  7 The 'Clans', Class '6' 218
  8 The 'Duke of Gloucester', Class '8' 220

IX BRITISH PACIFIC DESIGNS THAT WERE NEVER BUILT 227

APPENDIX: SOME RECENT PERFORMANCES OF BULLEID
    PACIFICS 234

INDEX 238

FOREWORD

By the Assistant General Manager, formerly Chief Mechanical and Electrical Engineer, Eastern Region, British Railways

Even before the first Pacific type locomotive in Great Britain emerged from Swindon Works in 1908 there had begun a period which has lasted well over half a century, throughout which Cecil J. Allen has faithfully recorded and reported British locomotive practice and performance. Who, therefore, could be better qualified than he to write the story of those locomotives which embody the ultimate development of steam traction in this country? For almost forty years Pacifics have reigned supreme on express passenger trains. In this book Mr Allen has combined in the most readable way a mass of information on the design and dimensions of these locomotives with accounts of their outstanding performance, and with tales of triumph and disaster. Here will be found the smell of warm oil and burning brake blocks, the flicker of the speedometer needle and the eager click of stop watches, intermixed with the sober facts of building and testing, of power output and physical characteristics.

Whether the reader seeks details of design, of numbering or naming, of historical runs in the quest of speed, of successes or failures, all will be found in these pages. Such a comprehensive account has surely never before been written of one type of locomotive.

It is fitting that such an account should have been made available to students of railways, and, indeed, to all who have an interest in them, for in setting down the history of these locomotives Mr Allen has embraced the whole field of express passenger train performance in this country over four decades. The particular value of his book is that it brings together for the first time, and in such a way that they may be compared, the achievements of the Group Railways, as well as recording what has been accomplished since they were amalgamated into British Railways in 1948.

This is the tale of the finest hour of the steam locomotive in Great Britain, and although the age of steam is drawing to a close, let it always be remembered that the steam locomotive – and above all the Pacific – has been ready and able to the very end to put up a performance as fine as any described in this book.

29th March, 1962   T. C. B. MILLER

PREFACE TO THE FOURTH EDITION

Of all the books which my late father wrote postwar, this is one of the two — the other was his masterly survey of railways in his beloved Switzerland — which I think he would be happiest to see revived. It encapsulated the style and authority he had brought to more than four decades of reporting and analysing British locomotive practice and performance, month in and month out. One mark of that authority is that CJA was the only lay observer invited to ride on all the record performance attempts of the 1930s. A personal letter from Gresley would have seen him present at *Mallard's* 126mph in July 1938 had this exploit not been staged on a Sunday, which my father insisted he must reserve for spiritual affairs.

Since this book was written other publications have reviewed in intimate detail the mechanical history of individual Pacific types and their class members. But *British Pacific Locomotives* is still unique as a definitive compendium of the finest feats of all the country's biggest steam passenger locomotives.

The book was written at the start of the 1960s, when Pacific withdrawals had barely begun. Both publishers and I agree that no point would have been served either by revision to take account of subsequent knowledge — for instance, the explanation for *Duke of Gloucester's* initially uninspiring performance — or addition to take the story through scrappings to preservation. The text is best left wholly reflecting the personality of the author and the sentiment of its period, the twilight of British steam.

Blockley, Glos   GEOFFREY FREEMAN ALLEN
June 1990

AUTHOR'S PREFACE

Between eleven and fourteen years ago I was responsible for the production of three small books, one describing the Stanier Pacifics of the London Midland & Scottish Railway, a second the Gresley Pacifics of the London & North Eastern Railway, and a third, jointly with Mr S. C. Townroe, the Bulleid Pacifics of the Southern Railway. Since then much has happened. The Gresley Pacifics have been succeeded by those of Thompson and Peppercorn; most of the Bulleid Pacifics have been completely rebuilt; and a product of nationalisation has been the standard Pacifics of British Railways. To complete the Pacific list, there have been the Raven Pacifics of the former North Eastern Railway, and, first of them all, *The Great Bear* of the Great Western Railway, Churchward's solitary contribution.

Steam locomotive building for the railways of Britain now having ended, the time has come to set out British Pacific history in full, which this volume essays to do. The three books mentioned above have provided a nucleus, but in large measure they have been rewritten, and much has been added to the original matter, especially as to changes in the original designs that have been prompted by experience, and as to runs of note which have been made by the various types concerned. Indeed, it can be claimed that the many runs tabulated in full give the most complete survey yet published of the maximum performance capabilities of British Pacific locomotives of all types, and the way in which they have been handled.

All the remaining matter is entirely new. The complete lists of names, numbers, building dates and dimensions will, it is hoped, prove of service to many readers for reference purposes; and the extensive series of photographs will provide a visual reminder of the appearance of the many 4-6-2 types at all stages of their development.

Grateful acknowledgement is needed of the help of a number of gentlemen whom I have consulted in putting this book together. In particular I would mention Mr T. C. B. Miller, Assistant General Manager, Eastern Region, British Railways, who has read through the proofs and made many helpful suggestions, and has also most kindly contributed a Foreword. To Mr G. C. Gold, Mechanical & Electrical Engineer (Workshops), Mr J. C. Spark, Works Manager and Mr F. Horne, Chief Draughtsman at Doncaster Works. I am indebted for much help concerning the Gresley, Thompson and Peppercorn Pacifics; to Mr R. N. H. Hardy, District Running & Maintenance Engineer, Great Eastern Line, and Mr D. W. Harvey, Depot Master at Norwich, for their experience in working and maintaining the 'Britannia' Pacifics; and to my former collaborator, Mr C. S. Townroe, District Motive Power Superintendent, Eastleigh, and Mr R. G. Jarvis, Chief Technical Assistant at Brighton Works, for all the information I sought about the Bulleid Pacifics. Last but not least there is Mr Ronald I. Nelson, with the help of whose most carefully compiled records of his many footplate journeys I have been able to give a much more complete survey of Pacific handling than would otherwise have been possible.

Some readers of my monthly articles on locomotive practice and performance, and particularly those who are older, during recent years have inclined to be critical that so much attention is now being devoted to diesel power. This, however, is inevitable; we cannot always live in the past. But the fact that I have been able to compile a book devoted exclusively to steam should show them where my heart has always been and still is.

April, 1962   CECIL J. ALLEN

I

'THE GREAT BEAR', GREAT WESTERN RAILWAY

To the former Great Western Railway and its eminent Chief Mechanical Engineer, George Jackson Churchward, goes the credit for having built, as far back as 1908, Britain's first Pacific express locomotive, No. 111 *The Great Bear*. Why a locomotive of such size and power should have been thought necessary at that date is still obscure. H. Holcroft, in his *Outline of Great Western Locomotive Practice*, thinks it probable that the fine performance of the Great Western 'Star' class 4-6-0s had prompted the G.W.R. directors to seek even higher standards, though as the 'Stars' could handle the longest trains that could be accommodated at Paddington such a decision might seem premature, to say the least.

Had its ability to raise steam been proportionate to its size, the larger boiler might have given the 4-6-2 a bigger reserve than a 'Star', and so might have permitted faster timings, but there is no evidence that the Pacific had any such reserve. In all the half-century of writing *British Locomotive Practice and Performance* I described only one run behind her, and that of no particular merit. In brief, though the appearance of what was, in the first decade of the century, an outsize in British locomotives certainly brought prestige to the Great Western Railway, *The Great Bear* was one of the very few locomotive types that Swindon has produced, and in particular among Churchward designs, to which the word 'failure' could be applied.

The reason for this lack of success was probably the fact that Churchward designed his 4-6-2 merely as an enlargement of a 'Star' rather than working out an entirely new design. Thus the cylinders, wheels, motion and bogie were all those of a 'Star', and 'Star' frames also were incorporated, with the necessary extension at the rear end, in the form of slabs, for the trailing axle. In view of the length of the engine, the throw-over at the leading end was greater than that of the 4-6-0; and as sufficient clearance had to be allowed for side play of the rear bogie wheels, no enlargement of the cylinders was possible, so that the 15-in. diameter of the 'Star' cylinders was adhered to. A fraction might have been added to the cylinder diameter if the 5¾-in. width of the bogie wheel tyres had been reduced to the 5½ in. and even 5¼ in. common on other railways at the time, but Holcroft, who was engaged in the Swindon drawing office at that time and was responsible for the cylinder design, relates in his book how Churchward would not agree to any such reduction. Like the 'Stars', the 4-6-2 had inside Walschaerts motion, the outside piston-valves being operated by horizontal rocking levers.

A special boiler, classed by Swindon as No. 6, was designed for *The Great Bear*, with the barrel in three rings, tapering through the second ring only from the 5 ft 6 in. diameter of the front ring to the 6 ft of the rear ring; no combustion chamber was provided, and to the unusual length of the barrel – 23 ft – coupled with the absence of a combustion chamber, the engine's indifferent steaming may in part be attributed. The wide firebox was unique in Swindon practice; it was 8 ft long, 6 ft 6 in. wide at the front end and 5 ft 9 in. wide at the rear end, giving 41·75 sq ft of firegrate area. Another unusual feature for the G.W.R. was the support of the brick arch by three 3-in. diameter cross water-tubes; later on, however, these burned out and from then onwards a normal brick arch was used. As usual in Churchward's engines, the seven-element superheater provided for no more than steam-drying rather than high temperature superheat; it had a heating surface of 545 sq ft only. The evaporative heating surface of the firebox was 182 sq ft and that of the tubes 2,673 sq ft, a total of 2,855 sq ft; working pressure was 225 lb per sq in.

Churchward always liked to brake all wheels, but such difficulty was experienced in arranging for the braking of the trailing axle, owing to its 4½-in. side play either way (which prevented the use of ordinary fixed brake hangers), that this pair of wheels had to dispense with brakes. A separate vacuum cylinder was even considered, but was ruled out because it added too much weight. In service this radial axle gave more trouble than any other part of the engine, for its inside bearings were difficult to lubricate properly and the wearing surfaces were exposed to cinders and dust from the ashpan and grit thrown up from the track, so that they frequently overheated. It might have been a different story had the design incorporated a radial truck with outside axleboxes, as in every other British 4-6-2 design with the sole exception of the first two Raven Pacifics of the North Eastern Railway.

With an eye to appearance, Churchward decided to match the length of his Pacific with a bogie tender rather than the standard six-wheel type. This also had inside bearings, but all wheels were braked. The capacity of 6 tons of coal and 3,500 gallons of water was no greater than that of the standard six-wheel tender of the 4-6-0s, but the bogie construction put the full weight up from 40 to 45¾ tons. The weight of the engine in working order was at first announced as 96 tons, but the revised later figure was 97¼ tons.

The weight imposed on each coupled axle was shown on the official diagram as 20 tons, but Ahrons and Holcroft both give a figure of 20 tons 9 cwt. This restricted *The Great Bear* solely to the Paddington–Bristol main line, as the strengthening of underline bridges on the West of England main line to carry axle-loads up to 22½ tons at that time was far from complete. It is very doubtful, also, how the 34 ft 6 in. wheelbase of the 4-6-2 would have taken to the curvature of the West of England line, and in particular to the sharp reverse curves beyond Newton Abbot; a notice in the cab of the engine warned drivers to exercise the utmost caution in running through cross-over roads and other sharply curved connections.

In 1950 K. J. Cook, at that time the Mechanical Engineer of the Western Region, presented a paper to the Institution of Locomotive Engineers on the work of G. J. Churchward at Swindon, the last of a series which had described the course of locomotive development on the former London Midland & Scottish, London & North Eastern and Southern Railways. But whereas the three earlier contributors had been extremely frank about happenings on the L.M.S.R., L.N.E.R. and S.R., nothing ever appears to have gone wrong at Swindon. A single paragraph sufficed to deal with *The Great Bear*, and of its performances we read: 'Although the engine ran satisfactorily and worked very exacting services, its weight and length restricted it severely to a small number of routes, and consequently it was not perpetuated', followed by the polite fiction that 'No. 111 was converted to take a No. 8 boiler and became standard with the "Castles" '.

To the best of my knowledge, however, no published record exists to show that the performance of *The Great Bear* ever equalled one of the best efforts of a 'Star', let alone improved on it. As to the 'very exacting services', No. 111 was used to some extent on the 11 a.m. two-hour express from Paddington to Bristol, which in those days was a substantial train working through to Plymouth and with a slip portion for Bath; later on, the heavy Bristol train

TABLE I
LEADING DIMENSIONS OF *THE GREAT BEAR*

Cylinders (4), diameter	15 in.
,, stroke	26 in.
Driving wheels, diameter . . .	6 ft 8½ in.
Wheelbase, rigid	14 ft 0 in.
,, total	34 ft 6 in.
Heating surface, tubes and flues . .	2,673 sq ft
,, ,, firebox	182 sq ft*
,, ,, total	2,855 sq ft
Superheating surface	545 sq ft
Firegrate area	41·75 sq ft
Working pressure, per sq in. . . .	225 lb
Tractive effort (85 per cent) . . .	27,970 lb
Adhesion weight	61½ tons
Engine weight (working order) . .	97¼ tons
Engine and tender weight . . .	143 tons
Length over buffers	71 ft 2 in.

* Including water-tubes in firebox.

starting variously at 6.30 and 6.40 p.m., first stop Bath, became a regular duty, with a return to London on a fast night freight. Five years after entering service the engine returned to Swindon for general overhaul, and a two-row superheater was substituted for that previously fitted, reducing the superheating surface to 399 sq in.; adjustments also were made to the weight distribution.

For fourteen years *The Great Bear* remained Britain's only Pacific, until the emergence in 1922 from Doncaster Works of the Great Northern Railway of Gresley's first Pacific; and the story has often been told of Churchward's remark on his first hearing news of Gresley's production: 'What did that young man want to *build* a Pacific engine for? We could have sold him ours!'

But, one imagines, at nothing more than scrap value, for this was the fate of No. 111 just over a year later, at the beginning of 1924, when the boiler was needing heavy repairs. It was announced as a rebuilding in the form of a 'Castle' 4-6-0, which retained the same number but was renamed *Viscount Churchill*. The 'rebuilding', however, was a paper transaction only, for little more than the front end of the main frames, cylinders and coupled wheels – and the number-plates! – remained of what could hardly be regarded as Churchward's masterpiece.

II

THE RAVEN PACIFICS,
NORTH EASTERN RAILWAY

CHRONOLOGICALLY, the next Pacific design to be dealt with in this book should be Gresley's first 4-6-2 on the Great Northern Railway, but as the rival North Eastern Railway design which appeared a few months later was so relatively short-lived, we may dispose of the latter first. The year was 1922, and by the passing of the Railways Act in 1921 the Grouping of the railways was destined to come into effect at the beginning of 1923. Out of the constituent companies of the future London & North Eastern Railway it would become necessary to choose a Chief Mechanical Engineer for the new system. The North Eastern Railway would be the biggest, wealthiest and most influential constituent, and would provide the Chief General Manager. For the direction of locomotive affairs there might well, therefore, be a species of competition, and chiefly between Doncaster and Darlington.

It is difficult to find another reason for an almost unprecedented happening in July, 1922. It was the publication, in both the *Locomotive Magazine* and the *Railway Magazine* of that month, no less than five months before the engine actually appeared, of the drawings and leading dimensions of the Pacific locomotive which was being built for the N.E.R. to the designs of Sir Vincent Raven. The reason, it might seem, was that Gresley's first Great Northern Pacific was already in service, and the Chief Mechanical Engineer of the North Eastern felt it essential to show that his company was not lagging behind in the race for power. However, the Great Northern had got in first, and not only was Gresley chosen to become Chief Mechanical Engineer of the London & North Eastern Railway, but his Pacific design, even in its original form, proved definitely superior in performance to its North Eastern rival.

The parallel between Raven's N.E.R. Pacific and *The Great Bear* of Churchward's design on the G.W.R. is in many ways a striking one. In both cases prestige rather than a real need was the predominant consideration. Both were long-drawn-out versions of existing types – the N.E.R. engine of the Raven three-cylinder Atlantics and the G.W.R. engine of the Churchward 'Stars' – rather than being designed as completely new motive power units, like Gresley's *Great Northern*. It may well have been, also, that because of the competitive element that I have mentioned, Sir Vincent Raven's design was produced in some haste, so that he might not lose in the race. But such a conclusion is merely speculative.

Like his 'Z' class three-cylinder Atlantics, Raven's Pacific had its three cylinders in line, forming, with their piston-valve chests, a single massive casting that supported the smokebox. All cylinders drove on the leading coupled axle, which meant undesirably short connecting-rods. As the motion was of the Stephenson type, six eccentrics had to be accommodated with the middle big-end on the crank axle, which also was not a good arrangement as it cramped the bearings. The very lengthy wheelbase of 40 ft 5 in., due to the drive on the leading pair of coupled wheels, compared with the 35 ft 9 in. of a Gresley Pacific and the 34 ft 6 in. only of *The Great Bear*. It is interesting also that Raven made the same error as Churchward in providing inside bearings to the rear pair of wheels in his first two Pacifics. The remaining three, for which components had been prepared at Darlington, came out after the Grouping and therefore under the *aegis* of Gresley, and were modified to take sliding rear axleboxes of the Cartazzi type, like Gresley's Pacifics.

The Raven Pacifics shared with the Gresley 'K3' Moguls the distinction of having the largest parallel-boiler diameter in the country, that is, 6 ft. This gave the engines an extremely massive appearance, as also did their enormous length; this, with the three 'pop' safety-valves mounted in line at the rear end, earned for them the *soubriquet* of 'Skittle Alleys'. Actually the length between tubeplates, 21 ft, was 5 ft less than the barrel length of 26 ft, for the firebox was well recessed into the barrel to form a combustion chamber, and the smokebox also was of considerable length. The firebox was the first of the wide type to be seen on the North Eastern Railway; 8 ft long and 6 ft 5 in. wide, it provided a grate area of 41·0 sq ft and a heating surface of 211 sq ft. Tube heating surface was 2,211 sq ft, making a total of 2,422 sq ft, and the superheating surface was 696 sq ft.

While the working pressure of 200 lb per sq in. gave the Raven Pacific an advantage over the Gresley Pacific's 180 lb, this was countered by the fact that Raven's 19-in. cylinder diameter was 1 in. less than Gresley's 20-in. As both types had the same driving-wheel diameter, 6 ft 8 in., the two tractive efforts were almost identical – Raven's 29,920 lb as compared with Gresley's 29,835 lb. Preliminary calculations gave the adhesion weight of the North Eastern Pacific as 60 tons, but in actual fact it turned out to be 59 tons; the engine weight was 97 tons, as estimated, equal to that of the Great Western *Great Bear* but 4½ tons more than the 92½ tons of Gresley's *Great Northern*. A standard North Eastern six-wheel tender was provided, in appearance distinctly out of proportion to the immense length of the engine, with accommodation for 5½ tons of coal and 4,125 gallons of water.

When Gresley became Chief Mechanical Engineer of the London & North Eastern Railway, at the beginning of 1923, two of his Pacifics were at work and two of Sir Vincent Raven's design. The former could, of course, have decided to standardise his own design without further ado, but he did not do so without a comparative trial of the two types, the fairness of which was emphasized by the fact that the North Eastern Railway dynamometer car and staff were used for the tests. These took place in the summer of 1923 between ex-North Eastern 4-6-2 No. 2400 *City of Newcastle* and the third of the ex-Great Northern 4-6-2s to leave Doncaster Works, the famous No. 4472 *Flying Scotsman*. The trains selected were the two hardest locomotive turns on the Great Northern main line at that time, the 10.51 a.m. from Doncaster to Kings Cross and the 5.40 p.m. back, carrying Leeds, Bradford and Hull portions and, between Kings Cross and Grantham, a Lincoln coach as well.

Tom Blades, a well-known Gateshead driver, was in charge of No. 2400, with Fireman Fisher, and though he did as well as was possible with her over what was to him a strange road, the issue was never in doubt. *City of Newcastle*'s average coal consumption, as compared with that of *Flying Scotsman*, was 4·29 against 3·94 lb per drawbar-h.p.-hr, or 58·7 against 52·6 lb per mile; water was being used at the rate of 40·4 as against 38·3 gallons per mile, or 31·7 against 31·0 gallons per drawbar-h.p.-hr. Owing to the running of relief trains on certain days, No. 4472's average tare load coming up was 415 tons to No. 2400's 434 tons, and 519 tons going down to 527 tons (on one evening the North Eastern Pacific was loaded to no less than 546 tare tons); the N.E.R. engine therefore had slightly the higher average drawbar h.p. output during the trials, 673 compared with 663.

This, of course, was several years before Gresley had learned the lessons of the exchange of 1925 with a Great Western 'Castle' 4-6-0, and neither his engine nor Sir Vincent Raven's had the benefit of long-lap, long-travel piston-valves. The average cut-off working therefore was as high as 40 per cent on both engines, but both the regulators were partly open only for most of the time, as is clear from the low steam-chest pressures. The North Eastern fireman kept up the better boiler pressures, with his average of 197 lb per sq in. – practically blowing-off point – whereas *Flying Scotsman*'s average pressure was 164 lb only. But the average steam-chest pressure on No. 2400 was no more than 106 lb per sq in., and No. 4472 was not much better off with an average of 118 lb.

Even up a continuous climb like that from Kings Cross to Potters Bar, where No. 4472 was being worked in from 44 to 45 per cent cut-off and No. 2400 from 40 to 49 per cent, and boiler pressure on both was not far from the blowing-off point, the steam-chest pressure of *Flying Scotsman* averaged no more than 141 lb per sq in. and of *City of Newcastle* 135 lb. But even if falling short of the much higher thermal efficiency of later years, the Great Northern engine was doing the better work, with an average drawbar h.p. of 928 compared with the 875 of its North Eastern rival. Such superiority fully justified Gresley in deciding to standardize his own Pacific design.

As with *The Great Bear*, no records remain of any outstanding performances by the Raven Pacifics. The fastest run that I ever timed with one of them was behind No. 2402 *City of York* from Darlington to York; we passed Northallerton, 14·15 miles, in 15 min. 11 sec., and after a signal check from 70 down to 45 m.p.h. at Otterington reached the only 80 m.p.h. maximum that I ever recorded with one of these engines, at Alne, keeping up an average of 75 m.p.h. on the level for just over 20 miles. But this was with an eight-coach load of 245 gross tons only and, like most other runs with these engines, the times and speeds could have been paralleled without much difficulty by one of Raven's 'Z' class three-cylinder Atlantics. I remember particularly one run from Newcastle to York behind No. 2401 which was probably the best of the bunch, hauling a trivial load of under 300 tons, when the driver, who for some obscure reason rejoiced in the nickname of 'Sandrod', excitedly exclaimed to me when I went up to the engine to speak to him: 'I canna haud her in! I canna haud her in!' Actually he had been dropping time steadily by some dismal running. Towards the end of 1929, in order to see if the steaming of these engines could be improved, Gresley fitted No. 2404 *City of Ripon* with the same standard boiler as one of his original Class 'A1' Pacifics, reducing the working pressure from 200 to 180 lb per sq in. As there was no alteration in the cylinder dimensions, the tractive effort came down from 29,920 to 26,925 lb. Later on this locomotive acquired a standard eight-wheel tender also. But there was no improvement in performance sufficient to justify a similar modification of the other four engines of the class, and a rebuilding of the front end similarly to that of the Gresley Pacifics when they acquired their long-lap, long-travel valves would have been a very expensive business. The Raven engines suffered from heating troubles also, particularly with the inadequate surface of the driving axle bearings, and it was no surprise that when in the middle 1930s heavy repairs had become due, the decision was reached to scrap them. So, after a relatively short life, the Raven Pacifics all went to the scrap heap in 1936 and 1937.

TABLE II (A)
LEADING DIMENSIONS OF RAVEN PACIFICS

	As built	No. 2404 after rebuilding
Cylinders (3), diameter . . .	19 in.	19 in.
,, stroke	26 in.	26 in.
Driving wheels, diameter . . .	6 ft 8 in.	6 ft 8 in.
Wheelbase, rigid	15 ft 0 in.	15 ft 0 in.
,, total	40 ft 5 in.	40 ft 5 in.
Heating surface, tubes and flues . .	2,211 sq ft	2,715 sq ft
,, ,, firebox . . .	211 sq ft	215 sq ft
,, ,, total	2,422 sq ft	2,930 sq ft
Superheating surface	696 sq ft	525 sq ft
Firegrate area	41·0 sq ft	41·25 sq ft
Working pressure, per sq in. . .	200 lb	180 lb
Tractive effort (85 per cent) . .	29,920 lb	26,925 lb
Adhesion weight	59 tons	59 tons
Engine weight (working order) . .	97 tons	98 tons
Engine and tender weight . . .	143 tons	144½ tons
Length over buffers	72 ft 4½ in.	71 ft 10 in.

TABLE II (B)
NUMBERS, NAMES AND BUILDING DATES,
RAVEN PACIFICS

No.	Name	Built
2400	City of Newcastle . . .	1922
2401	City of Kingston-upon-Hull .	1923
2402	City of York . . .	1924
2403	City of Durham . . .	1924
2404*	City of Ripon . . .	1924

* Rebuilt in 1929 by Gresley with standard 'A1' Pacific boiler.

III

THE GRESLEY PACIFICS – GREAT NORTHERN AND LONDON & NORTH EASTERN RAILWAYS

1 – *The Emergence of 'Great Northern'*

ONE afternoon in the spring of 1922, when returning from my usual round of weekly travel to Barnet, where I then lived, I was making my way to the 'Local' station at Kings Cross by way of the principal departure platform at the terminus – then No. 1 – when my progress was suddenly arrested. In those days the island platform on the departure side of the main station had not been built, and the space between the present Nos. 6 and 10 platforms was occupied by sidings and a short loading dock for horses, carriages and motors at the inner end. On this never-to-be-forgotten day a new articulated sleeping car was standing alongside the loading dock, and beyond that – shining, stately and strikingly impressive – the most massive locomotive that I had ever set eyes on in Great Britain until then. It was No. 1470 *Great Northern*, Gresley's first Pacific, brought to London to be exhibited to the directors of his company, the Great Northern Railway.

For months previously rumours had been going the rounds as to what Gresley was 'doing' at Doncaster. The successful running of his Moguls, first introduced in 1912 and culminating in the 'K3' three-cylinder design of 1920, prompted the idea that the new engine would be a 2-6-2; actually a 2-6-2 design had been considered seriously. The 'K3' class engines had shown themselves capable of speeds well in excess of 70 m.p.h., notwithstanding driving wheels of no more than 5 ft 8 in. diameter, and with the first-class maintenance of Great Northern track their pony trucks had given no trouble at speed, so that a 2-6-2 might have proved suitable for express passenger work. As events proved, however, we were to wait another fourteen years, until 1936, for the materialization of the first Gresley main line 2-6-2; and the new Great Northern engine of 1922 turned out to be a Pacific. So it was that with No. 1470 Gresley initiated a series of locomotives which more than any other of his designs has qualified him to take a place among the immortals of British locomotive history.

The late Sir Nigel Gresley in every sense of the word was a 'big' man. The bigness of his physical frame matched the breadth of his vision. Although, as we shall see later, he could be a traditionalist when he chose, possibly even to the disadvantage of his engines, in general he was receptive to all ideas, from wherever they might come, and he was never small-minded enough to consider that his reputation might suffer if he were to acknowledge the source of any inspiration. Whether as Chief Mechanical Engineer of the Great Northern

Railway or, later, of the London & North Eastern Railway, he had the great advantage of being master in his own house and of having a free hand in the development of his ideas, without any interference from operating officers whose notions as to what was required might be cast in a less heroic mould.

The bigness of the Gresley mind equally was reflected in the bigness of his locomotives. More than any other British locomotive engineer he specialized in a 'big engine' policy; instead of letting his locomotives catch up on events, he built for the future, as with No. 1470, which he proclaimed would be adequate for the haulage of 600-ton trains at a time when a 400-ton load on the Great Northern main line was regarded as very heavy indeed. Bit by bit, as new Pacifics were added to the London & North Eastern stock and the 'A3' and 'A4' classes later joined the original 'A1s', Gresley provided the London & North Eastern Railway with a stud of powerful locomotives which had ample reserve to meet every possible extreme of load or weather without needing pilot assistance, or, on the other hand, losing time.

Another feature of Gresley's work as a designer is worth emphasis. When he had designed and built a new locomotive class, the engines went straight out on to the road and began to earn dividends from the word 'go'. There were normal teething troubles with the new Pacifics, in particular with lubrication, but nothing of serious moment. Each design had been thought out with the utmost thoroughness in the drawing office, and with his engines most subsequent alterations that must have made certain other new British locomotive classes very costly to their owners have been unnecessary. So it was with No. 1470 and her successors, and in one respect only, as was to be proved in striking fashion three years later, did Gresley allow conservatism to enter into his design in a way which affected, not the ability of the engines to pull, but the efficiency with which they used their fuel.

Throughout its independent history, from 1850 to 1922, the Great Northern Railway was fortunate in having no more than four Locomotive Superintendents – Archibald Sturrock, Patrick Stirling, H. A. Ivatt and H. N. Gresley – so that there was a continuity in locomotive design policy of a rarity seen elsewhere only on the Great Western Railway. In the principal Great Northern express locomotive designs, therefore, there was a logical development from Stirling's 8 ft 1½ in. 4-2-2 of 1870 to Ivatt's large-boilered 4-4-2 of 1902 and finally to Gresley's 4-6-2 of 1922.

There was one feature of design, however, in which both Ivatt and Gresley differed radically from Stirling. The last-named was inclined to over-cylinder his engines, particularly his last series of 4-2-2s, in which he followed the dubious course of trying to obtain increased tractive power merely by increasing cylinder dimensions, without any increase in the capacity of his boiler to raise steam. In the last of these, Nos. 1003 to 1008 inclusive, the diameter and stroke of the cylinders were increased to no less than 19½ in. and 28 in. respectively; by contrast, the diminutive 4-ft diameter boiler which had to supply them with steam contained no more than 1,031 sq ft of heating surface and 20 sq ft of firegrate area, though the grate was certainly bigger than the 17·6 sq ft of the original Stirling 8-footers.

In the first Ivatt large-boilered Atlantics the change in these proportions was revolutionary indeed, for cylinders of 18¾ in. diameter and 24-in. stroke were mated to a 5 ft 6 in. diameter boiler providing no less than 2,500 sq ft of heating surface and 31 sq ft of grate. Ivatt's *dictum* has often been quoted that the measure of a locomotive's success is its 'ability to boil water", and this was exemplified to a remarkable degree in Atlantic No. 251. That is to say, whereas Stirling's No. 1003 had 106 sq ft of heating surface and 2·07 sq ft of firegrate area to every cubic foot of cylinder volume, in No. 251 these proportions had changed to 326 to 1 and 4·00 to 1 respectively.

Gresley's first Pacific took a position midway between these two extremes. With three 20 in. by 26 in. cylinders, 3,455 sq ft of heating surface (including superheater) and 41·25 sq ft of firegrate, the proportion of heating surface to cylinder volume had come down again to 165 sq ft to 1 cu ft, and firegrate area to cylinder volume was now a shade less than 2·00 sq ft to 1 cu ft. Where the Pacific scored heavily over both its predecessors, however, was in the matter of adhesion. The driving axle of the Stirling 8-footer carried 19 tons of the engine's weight; in No. 251 the adhesion weight went up to 36 tons; in No. 1470 the weight available for adhesion had risen to 60 tons. The Stirling 8-footers, in the days of light, non-corridor stock, largely six-wheelers, had been just about equal to their work, with little reserve; the Ivatt Atlantics, after superheating, could do splendidly, even with heavy trains, in every respect other than starting up steep grades; the Gresley Pacifics, on their introduction, were far ahead of all the traffic demands of that time.

2 – *The 'A1' Pacifics*

SOME facts not previously made public concerning the inception of the Gresley Pacific have come to light recently in F. A. S. Brown's book entitled *Nigel Gresley – Locomotive Engineer*. In the first place, this was not his first Pacific design. As described later in Chapter IX, four years after his appointment in 1911 as Chief Mechanical Engineer of the Great Northern Railway the heavy tasks that were being imposed on the Ivatt Atlantics after the outbreak of the First World War convinced Gresley that a considerably more powerful express locomotive type was now being called for, and by 1915 a four-cylinder 4-6-2 was on the drawing board at Doncaster. Why matters went no further at that time is not revealed; probably wartime conditions were responsible. Which is just as well, for what has emerged about this design suggests a drawn-out version of an Ivatt Atlantic, and had it been built, Gresley might have fallen into the same error as Raven with his elongated Class 'Z' Atlantic and Churchward with his elongated 'Star' 4-6-0.

But the first Gresley Pacific, when No. 1470 appeared in 1922, although a completely new design, had been influenced from another quarter altogether. The receptiveness of Gresley to new ideas, no matter from where they came, I have described already; and here was a classic example. In the United States several locomotive building firms had amalgamated in 1904 to form the

American Locomotive Company – the famous 'Alco' of later years – in much the same way as our own North British Locomotive Company was formed. As has not been unusual in American locomotive history, the new firm decided to try its hand at designing, and in 1910 turned out an experimental Pacific to which it gave the number 50000, and which it was prepared to loan for trial purposes to any interested railway, in the hope of securing orders. It was claimed for No. 50000 that the engine was the first to have 'rationalized proportions of boiler, firebox and cylinders' – that is, optimum ratios between these parts – and that it was, therefore, a 'maximum capacity' Pacific.

The Pennsylvania Railroad was impressed by these claims, and in 1911 ordered a slightly heavier version of the new design. In the same year that the American Locomotive Company was formed, the Pennsylvania had completed one of the world's first locomotive testing plants at its Altoona locomotive works, and so was in a position exhaustively to test its purchase on the plant as well as on the road. The result was the evolution of the Pennsylvania 'K4' Pacific design, probably the most competent and efficient type of locomotive of its size ever known in the United States, perfectly proportioned, and with a boiler capable of supplying steam to two 27 in. by 28 in. cylinders for indefinite periods at cut-offs exceeding 50 per cent. In 1916 a series of articles was published in *Engineering* describing the design and performance of the 'K4s', and there is little doubt that these had a strong influence on the design of Gresley's No. 1470.

While the engine embodied various features which were to be expected, from the practice already developed by Gresley, other details were new to the G.N.R. Of the expected features, the use of three cylinders, with the Gresley derived motion for the inside cylinder, was, of course, one. Another was the wide type of firebox, which had proved so successful with the Ivatt Atlantics; and the engine-crews had become so accustomed to firing the square type of grate of the latter, rather than the long narrow grate in general use elsewhere, that no undue difficulty in firing needed to be foreseen in the increase of fire-grate area from 30·9 to 41·25 sq ft.

But the chief novelty was the use of a tapered boiler barrel. The 'K3' Moguls had shown that a parallel boiler up to 6 ft diameter could be accommodated within the confines of the British loading gauge; in No. 1470 it was seen that Gresley, starting with a diameter of 5 ft 9 in. at the smokebox end, had tapered the barrel out to no less a diameter than 6 ft 5 in. at the firebox end. The crown-plate of the firebox, on the other hand, tapered downwards towards the cab, so providing the maximum cross-sectional area immediately adjacent to the barrel, where the heat values are greatest. Also the firebox was arranged to taper inwards on both sides towards the cab, thus giving an unusually fine look-out with a boiler of such large size. These were all features of the Pennsylvania 'K4' firebox; but though they were also standard G.W.R. Belpaire practice, Gresley was the first to apply the same principle to a round-topped firebox. The boiler was pitched with its centre-line 9 ft 4 in. above rail level.

Gresley was careful to avoid excessive length in his boiler-tubes, and therefore mounted the smokebox of the engine with its centre-line well in rear of the bogie centre-line. The distance between tubeplates was further reduced to 19 ft by the projection of the firebox for a short distance into the barrel; this alteration also had the effect of increasing the firebox heating surface and providing the firebox with a small additional volume to serve as a combustion chamber and so to assist in complete combustion of the fuel. Some complicated flanging work was needed at Doncaster in shaping both the inner and outer fireboxes and the throat-plate.

At the front end, the lay-out of so large an engine within the confines of the British loading gauge called for most careful planning, and in some respects the engine suffered from its size. In his multi-cylinder engines Gresley would go to considerable lengths in order to secure undivided drive – that is, to drive with all three cylinders on the same axle. He had a strong objection to driving on a leading coupled axle, as this made it impossible to give the latter the lateral play that he thought essential, and he was influenced also by his individualistic ideas on balancing, which are discussed in Section 7 of this chapter. To obtain undivided drive on No. 1470, it was necessary to raise the middle cylinder, and to incline it sharply at an angle of 1 in 8, so that the leading coupled axle might be cleared.

In this location Gresley's derived motion for the inside cylinder played a useful part. By eliminating the crosshead connection of an independent valve-motion for the inside cylinder, the designer could bring his inside crosshead down close enough to the leading axle to keep the inclined cylinder well clear of the base of the smokebox; and in any event there would not have been room enough to fit a Walschaerts gear to a cylinder inclined at such an angle. But there was plenty of space available in which to mount the 2-to-1 levers of the derived motion across the front of the engine, ahead of the three cylinders. A disadvantage of mounting the three cylinders in line, however, was that it limited the size of the piston-valves to 8 in. diameter – a feature that evoked some criticism at the time, as these valves were required to supply 20-in. cylinders, and it was held that so small a diameter might restrict the steam flow.

The conservatism to which reference has been made previously was seen in the boiler pressure and the valve-setting. With the former, notwithstanding the known and obvious success of Churchward's 225 lb per sq in. on the Great Western, Gresley decided to stick to 180 lb, though he would find some justification, of course, in the reduced costs of maintaining boilers at the lower pressure. As to the valve-setting, $1\frac{1}{4}$ in. lap, $\frac{1}{4}$-in. exhaust clearance, $\frac{3}{16}$-in. lead, and a maximum valve-travel of $4\frac{9}{16}$ in. at 65 per cent cut-off meant that most of the work of the engine necessarily would be done with a relatively long cut-off and the regulator no more than partially open.

But Gresley was not alone in his attitude. Little ever leaked out of Swindon as to either the design details of Great Western locomotives or their effect on performance, and the influence that Swindon valve-setting had on the outstanding feats of the G.W.R. 4-6-0 *Polar Star* on London & North Western metals, in the 1910 exchange, seems to have been lost on other locomotive engineers. Equally the radical improvement brought about by the substitution of piston-valves for slide-valves in making possible increased valve-travel without increase in wear and tear appeared to be ignored, while very possibly so much had been gained in reduced coal consumption by the introduction of superheating that these engineers considered little further could be gained by abandoning their traditional designs of cylinders and valve events. Thus it was that Gresley, so progressive in other matters, curiously stuck to tradition in his first Pacific design, and was not to be shaken until he had had experience of the working of a Great Western locomotive over his own line three years later, as described in Section 3 of this chapter.

The limitation of maximum cut-off to 65 per cent was for a reason revealed by B. Spencer in his paper 'The Development of the L.N.E.R. Locomotive Design, 1923–41', read to the Institution of Locomotive Engineers on 19th March, 1947. When the first 'K3' 2-6-0, No. 1000, was being tested on express passenger trains, it was found that the cover of the centre piston-valve chest had been damaged by the crosshead spindle of the centre valve. Apparently the latter had overrun – *i.e.* its travel had increased beyond the theoretical maximum – by the engine having been put into the full 75 per cent cut-off when coasting with the regulator shut. The 'whip' under strain of the long 2-to-1 lever, or of the stay supporting its fulcrum, or both, had been largely responsible. It was discovered, too, that at high speeds, with the regulator full open, the middle cylinder was doing more than its proper one-third share of the work. At that time the 'K3' had $6\frac{3}{8}$ in. valve-travel at 75 per cent cut-off, with $1\frac{1}{2}$ in. lap, $\frac{1}{8}$ in. exhaust clearance and $\frac{1}{8}$ in. lead.

For these reasons the Pacific cut-off limitation to a maximum of 65 per cent was decided on, reducing the maximum valve-travel by about 1 in. In one respect at least the Gresley Pacifics have suffered from this restraint, because it has made them somewhat deficient in tractive effort when the maximum effort is needed, as when getting away with a heavy train from a sharply curved platform; the deficiency is more pronounced, also, with a three-cylinder than with a two-cylinder or four-cylinder engine. Many readers no doubt have seen one of these engines in considerable difficulties when starting weighty trains out of Newcastle or northwards out of York. At one time, rear-end assistance out of Newcastle became a regular procedure with the principal East Coast trains.

The light and graceful details of the rods and motion of No. 1470 were due to the use of heat-treated nickel-chrome steel for these parts, as in the Pennsylvania 'K4' Pacific. Both connecting and coupling-rods were milled out to form an I-section, and the deep web of the connecting-rod was no more than $\frac{5}{16}$ in. thick. This reduction of weight was made possible by the tensile strength of the heat-treated alloy being some 50 per cent greater than that of ordinary mild steel, and was helpful in reducing hammer-blow and other stresses set up by the unbalanced forces of the reciprocating motion. Another beneficial effect has been to assist the extremely smooth riding of these engines, which has always been good since the substitution of uncompensated plate springs for the helical springs fitted at first to the middle pair of coupled wheels.

For the Great Northern Railway the cab fitted by Gresley to his Pacific was an entirely new departure, with its high arched roof and two windows in either side. Its level floor and general spaciousness made it an immeasurable advance on the cabs of the Ivatt Atlantics, and to drivers and firemen the exchange of the violent antics of the latter on the road for the smooth and easy travel of the bigger machines must have been a most welcome improvement. The pull-out type of regulator so long standard on the G.N.R. was retained, but with operating handles on both sides of the cab; a distinctive Gresley feature of the cab equipment was the vertical reversing column, working in conjunction with a vacuum-operated clutch on the reversing shaft. A very clear type of cut-off percentage indicator, moving vertically on the back of the firebox, coupled with the provision of a steam-chest pressure gauge, enabled the driver of a Pacific to follow the working of both his regulator and valve-motion with a precision not possible before on the G.N.R., or, for that matter, on any other British railway.

A novelty for the Great Northern Railway was the first use of an eight-wheel tender. Unlike the double bogie tenders of the London & South Western, Caledonian and Glasgow & South Western Railways, and the tender built by Churchward for *The Great Bear*, however, the tender of No. 1470 was carried on four rigid axles. At the time this arrangement caused some surprise, but it has proved perfectly successful in practice, and has been the standard for all L.N.E.R. Pacifics since. The first Pacific tenders had spoked wheels, but at a later date the solid disc type of wheel was introduced, and subsequently became standard practice. Incidentally, the use of an eight-wheel in place of a six-wheel tender added to the problem of length which had been set by the change from the 4-4-2 to the 4-6-2 wheel arrangement; the increase was from an engine and tender wheelbase of 48 ft $5\frac{3}{4}$ in. and an over-all length of 57 ft $10\frac{1}{4}$ in., with the Atlantic, to 60 ft 10 in. and 70 ft 5 in. respectively with the Pacific, and the latter could not be turned on anything less than a 65-ft turntable.

At the start two of the new Pacifics were built: No. 1470 appeared in April, 1922, and No. 1471 followed three months later, No. 1471 at first without name. Two months after the latter's emergence from Doncaster Works a test run was arranged from Kings Cross to Grantham and back to substantiate Gresley's contention that the new engines would find no difficulty in handling 600-ton trains. The train actually made up consisted of twenty vehicles, and weighed 610 tons. It took $7\frac{1}{2}$ min. to get through Finsbury Park, 24 min. to Potters Bar, 30 min. to Hatfield and 46 min. to Hitchin, but the next 26·95 miles to Huntingdon were run in 23 min., and Peterborough was cleared in 86 min. The climb of 23·75 miles from Peterborough to Stoke was accomplished in exactly half-an-hour, with an average speed of 45 m.p.h. up the final 1 in 178, and Grantham, 105·45 miles, was reached in 122 min. from London. Compared with Gresley Pacific performances in later years this run, though excellent, would excite no special comment, of course; but back in 1922 it was an eye-opener indeed.

On the strength of the performances of Nos. 1470 and 1471, ten more

Pacifics were put on order in the same year, but when the first of this batch, No. 1472 *Flying Scotsman*, appeared in January, 1923, there was no longer any Great Northern Railway; the G.N.R. had become merged in the London & North Eastern Railway. The ten new Pacifics were all completed during 1923 and were numbered 1472 to 1481 inclusive; their names were as set out in Table III(G), which gives the numbers and names borne by all the Gresley Pacifics at the various stages of their history.

Early in the summer of 1923 I was permitted to ride on the footplate of No. 1473 *Solario* from Doncaster to Kings Cross, and the handling of the engine, as on the comparative test runs with No. 1472 and North Eastern Pacific No. 2400, already dealt with in Chapter II, furnishes a striking contrast to the way in which they have been worked in later years; nothing could illustrate more clearly the effect of a valve-gear laid out with the traditional short lap and short valve-travel of bygone days. The train was the same 10 a.m. from Leeds to London, leaving Doncaster at 10.51 a.m. and with stops at Retford, Grantham and Peterborough due in Kings Cross by 1.55 p.m. With its normal formation of thirteen coaches from Doncaster and fourteen from Grantham, the load was about 440 tons and 475 to 480 tons over each stage.

There was no question as to the ability of *Solario* to keep time. Despite a little loss at the start through brakes dragging on, we ran the 17·35 miles to Retford in 21 min. 15 sec., start to stop, with a top speed of 70½ m.p.h. at Scrooby troughs; then we attained 48 m.p.h. on the climb from Retford to Markham, reached 80½ m.p.h. by Crow Park and after crossing the wide level of the Trent Valley were still doing 68 at Newark, but only to be stopped dead by adverse signals at a small box called Balderton. The 21·5 miles from Retford to Balderton took 23 min. 25 sec. start to stop, and the 11·65 uphill miles from there to Grantham 16 min. 30 sec.; net time from Retford to Grantham was about 36 min. for the 33·15 miles, as against a booking of 38 min.

From Grantham, now with the full 480 tons, we did finely to climb the 5·35 miles at 1 in 200 to Stoke in 9 min. 10 sec. from the start; then came a spell of fast running, with a maximum of 82 m.p.h., which brought us into Peterborough in 30 min. 25 sec. for the 29·1 miles, scheduled 33 min. Out of Peterborough the engine lost 1 min. 20 sec. to Huntingdon – 21 min. 20 sec. for the very sharply timed 17·5 miles – but easily recouped the loss, more especially after Hitchin, where we topped the lengthy 1 in 200 to Stevenage at 48 m.p.h., and finished with a rousing 18 min. 5 sec. for the final 17·7 miles from Hatfield into Kings Cross, including 77½ m.p.h. through Wood Green. This made a total of 81 min. 25 sec. for the 76·35 miles from Peterborough, against 84 min. scheduled. In all, the engine had gained about 7 min.

But how was this done? For the major part of the journey the cut-off was fixed at 45 per cent. On the easy and downhill stretches the regulator was about one-half open; up the banks three-quarters open and 50 per cent, or four-fifths and 45 per cent, were the normal settings. Starts, of course, were on the full permissible 65 per cent cut-off. Never once did I see the regulator full open. The pressure in the boiler varied a good deal. In climbing from Retford to Markham it rose from 160 to 170 lb; by Newark it had dropped to

140 lb; for most of the journey about 160 to 170 lb was the figure. By the look of the tender on arrival, we had burned perhaps 3¼ tons on the 156-mile run, which would work out at nearly 47 lb per mile; normally the original Gresley Pacifics could be reckoned on as consuming an average of 50 lb to the mile on all their duties. Two years were to pass before the extravagance of such a coal consumption was to be made apparent; meantime the engines were able to handle any load, and as thoroughly reliable machines were giving every satisfaction. No. 1475, indeed, ran some 110,000 miles before being sent to Doncaster for her first general overhaul.

It was well on in 1923 before the last of Gresley's initial batch of 'A1' Pacifics, No. 1481 *St Simon*, appeared from Doncaster Works. The loading gauges of the northern constituents of the L.N.E.R. group, and in particular of what had been the North British Railway, were not so generous as that of the Great Northern, and it was realized that if the Pacifics were to work through to Edinburgh, clearances north of the Border were too scanty for them to pass in comfort. *St Simon* therefore emerged in a cut-down form, with a maximum height of 13 ft 1 in. above rail instead of the previous 13 ft 4 in. This affected the chimney, which was shortened and reduced in diameter, and the high arched roof of the cab had to be reduced similarly, with a perceptible change in the appearance of the engine. All subsequent 'A1' Pacifics appeared in the same form as *St Simon*, and the previous eleven engines were cut down correspondingly.

Up to the important developments following the L.N.E.R.–G.W.R. locomotive exchange of 1925, as described in Section 3 of this chapter, the fact that a new Gresley design was so well thought out as to need little modification after entering service was well exemplified in his 'A1' Pacifics. Little in the way of alteration was needed. The change from helical to plate springs for the driving axle has been mentioned already. Early heating troubles with bearings and inadequate clearances with some of the pins of the motion were soon cured. The stiffness of the pull-out regulator caused considerable criticism from North Eastern drivers (who were accustomed to the smoothly working Lockyer balanced regulator) when the first Pacifics were drafted to that Area, and steps were taken to improve matters. But these were minor troubles in a first-class design which was destined to make British locomotive history.

By 1924 the first all-L.N.E.R. system of engine numbering had been settled, with 3,000 added to the Great Northern numbers, so that Pacifics Nos. 1470 to 1481 now became Nos. 4470 to 4481 inclusive. Moreover, the success of the design was by now so firmly established that in the same year the building of forty more 'A1' Pacifics was decided on, twenty by Doncaster Works and the remaining twenty by the North British Locomotive Company in Glasgow, the former numbered from 2543 to 2562 and the latter from 2563 to 2582. All the Scottish-built series were turned out during 1924, but Nos. 2555 to 2562 appeared from Doncaster in 1925.

Nos. 2563 to 2582 were fitted with the Westinghouse brake, as they were intended for the North Eastern Area, on which air-brakes until then had been standard. Before 1924 was out the first Scottish-built Pacific, No. 2563

William Whitelaw, had made its way as far north as Aberdeen, and in the following year the first Pacific trials were made between Marylebone and Manchester with No. 4473 *Solario*, foreshadowing the wide range of action that these engines eventually would enjoy.

3 – *Pacific versus 'Castle'*

ONE immediate result of the Grouping was greatly to intensify the competitive nature of railway advertising in Great Britain. Each of the four new main line systems now could afford to spend a good deal more on publicity than had been possible with most of the individual railways previously, and the newly established publicity departments lost no time in exploiting these possibilities. An urge arose to lay claim to records in every realm of railway equipment and operation – the biggest, the fastest, and so on – and all kinds of figures and statistics came under scrutiny in the interests of prestige and publicity. Among these rivalries, possession of the most powerful locomotive was thought to be a strong advertising point, and this particular competition was destined to have some startling results.

In the year 1924, to mark the recovery from the effects of the First World War, the British Empire Exhibition was opened at Wembley. As one of the most spectacular railway exhibits in the Palace of Engineering, the London & North Eastern Railway installed on its stand 'A1' Pacific No. 4472 *Flying Scotsman*, superbly finished with various embellishments in brass, polished steel and colour not possessed by other engines of the same type. Not to be outdone, the Great Western Railway brought to its immediately adjacent stand No. 4073 *Caerphilly Castle*, first of a new series of enlarged 'Star' class 4-6-0s that had emerged from Swindon in the previous year: the 'Castle' design thus was one year younger than the Gresley Pacific.

At first glance the Great Western engine, with its lower-pitched boiler, of much smaller diameter at the smokebox end, shorter wheelbase and length overall, and six-wheel as against eight-wheel tender, seemed much the less imposing of the two engines. But visitors to the stands were intrigued by the notice which the G.W.R. exhibited in a prominent position in front of their engine claiming it to be 'the most powerful express passenger locomotive in Great Britain'. On the face of it the claim seemed absurd, but on the basis of the tractive force formula it was, of course, justified. For *Caerphilly Castle*, with a working pressure of 225 lb per sq in., could put out a tractive effort of 31,625 lb (at the usual 85 per cent of the boiler pressure), while the Pacific, though with the larger cylinder volume of the two engines, was tied down by Gresley's conservatism in boiler pressure to a maximum of 29,835 lb.

But could the 'Castle' boiler produce steam at the rate necessary to make the Great Western claim effective? This was the question which was to be answered in the following year, and with such emphasis as eventually to effect a radical change in the Gresley Pacific design. It has been asserted, though without proof, that the outcome of the Wembley Exhibition was a challenge –

in precisely what terms it was made or from what precise quarter it came was never revealed – by the London & North Eastern Railway to the Great Western Railway to prove which company really was entitled to claim 'the most powerful engine'. But it may equally have been that Gresley asked for the loan of a 'Castle' for test purposes, or that Sir Felix Pole, the Great Western General Manager, offered him one.

The upshot, in any event, was the famous exchange of locomotives between the two companies, which took place towards the end of April, 1925. I was a passenger on a number of the trial runs, and they were indeed experiences to be remembered. However the owners of the two engines may have attempted to represent the trials as nothing more than a friendly exchange of information, the public, and railway enthusiasts in particular, regarded it as a sporting event of the first magnitude; the test routes were lined with excited spectators, and great crowds watched the starts and finishes of the test runs, especially at the London terminals.

From the L.N.E.R. there went over to the G.W.R. No. 4474 *Victor Wild*, in charge of Driver Pibworth and Fireman Birkwood, and the engine could not have had a more competent crew. As with the 1948 exchanges, the tests covered a fortnight, one week for learning the road and the next week with the stiffest test the Great Western could produce – the 10.30 a.m. down 'Cornish Riviera Limited' non-stop from Paddington to Plymouth one day, and the corresponding up express on the next, a round three times repeated from Monday to Saturday. To master a tricky road like the Western, with its alluring stretches of level and then its sudden and formidable obstacles, such as the climb to Whiteball in Somerset and finally the fearsome gradients west of Newton Abbot, is something that no driver could possibly do in no more than a week of preliminary running, and in such conditions the exactitude with which Pibworth succeeded in maintaining his point-to-point times was a masterly feat indeed. No late arrivals in either direction were booked against him in either direction of the test week proper.

His fireman had an even more difficult task. Firing the 41 sq ft of a Pacific firegrate with soft Welsh coking steam coal, which had been loaded on the tender in very large lumps, was a different proposition entirely from using the normal hard Yorkshire coal, and required a totally different technique, but with friendly assistance from the Great Western pilotman, Birkwood was able to adapt his methods with such skill as to bring No. 4474's coal consumption on the three eastbound journeys down from 50·9 lb per mile on the first trip to 45·2 lb on the second and 40·4 lb on the third. On the far harder westbound workings the consumptions were 50·0, 48·8 and 52·4 lb per mile, the increase on the third run being due to a very high wind on that day which caught the train broadside most of the way from Paddington to Taunton.

The down 'Limited' was booked through Westbury, 95·55 miles from Paddington, in 97½ min., with a load of just under 500 tare tons (530 tons gross); slipping two coaches there and two more at Taunton, the train had fallen to 361 tare tons in weight from Taunton, which meant 385 gross tons to get over Whiteball summit; Exeter, 173·7 miles, had to be passed in 179 min.; and after the loss of a third slip portion, the load remaining to be worked up the 1 in 40 to Dainton and the 1 in 50 of Rattery bank was 292 tons tare and 310 tons gross. On the run which I made behind *Victor Wild*, we lost nearly 3 min. to Westbury because of the wind (100 min. 20 sec. to this point), but by fine running from there passed Taunton, 142·95 miles, 1 min. early in 147 min. exactly; there was another loss of nearly 2 min. to Exeter, but notwithstanding permanent way checks on either side of Newton Abbot and on the approach to Plymouth, *Victor Wild* stopped triumphantly at North Road in 246 min. 45 sec. from Paddington, 15 sec. ahead of time.

But the Pacific's competitor on Great Western metals, No. 4074 *Caldicot Castle*, was in charge of the redoubtable Edward Rowe, a driver of sporting temperament who, given the road, worried little about any restraint the time-table might lay on the movements of his train. And the Great Western authorities, with publicity in mind, took great care to see that Rowe *should* be given the road. The upshot was that two of the journeys made by *Caldicot Castle* in this test week were two of the most astonishing feats for which 'Castles' have ever been responsible.

On 2nd May Rowe took the 'Limited' down to Plymouth, with the same loading as the Pacific, in 231 min. 58 sec., passing Westbury in 94 min. 40 sec. and Exeter in 169 min. 10 sec.; on 27th April, with one coach more than the Pacific, 358 tons tare and 380 tons gross, he came up from Exeter in 164 min. 1 sec. start to stop for the 173·7 miles. In both directions, therefore, Rowe had gained precisely 15 min. on schedule. Moreover, despite the cost in coal consumption of such brilliant running, the 4-6-0 burned no more than 44·1, 45·6 and 46·8 lb of coal to the mile going down, and 40·6, 36·8 and 37·9 lb per mile coming up, the highest figure in each case being on the day when the gain of 15 min. was being made. In both time and coal consumption, therefore, the 'Castle' had beaten her rival handsomely on Great Western metals.

In qualification of these results, it may be added that the Pacific had to be restrained in her downhill speeds over the winding stretches of line from Reading onwards, due to her longer wheelbase (a matter which equally had barred *The Great Bear* from the West of England main line years before), and that Rowe took some of his speed restrictions, Reading in particular, at a speed considerably over the prescribed limits. Moreover, some of the Pacific's uphill work, notably a minimum speed of 32 m.p.h. over Dainton summit coming east with 310 tons and, with the full 345 tons, the fine times of 22 min. exactly from Exeter up the hill to Whiteball summit, and of no more than 26 min. 5 sec. for the 25·45 miles from Westbury up to Savernake (both exceptionally fast), was outstanding, even by Great Western standards. But with every allowance for these points, the 'Castle' performance was well ahead of that of the Pacific.

To everyone's astonishment, the same took place on London & North Eastern metals, with Yorkshire coal. Certainly the L.N.E.R. made an unlucky choice of both engine and driver to compete with the 'Castle' out of Kings Cross. No. 4475 *Flying Fox* was the engine originally selected and prepared, but one of her axleboxes ran hot on the very first day, on the climb to Stoke

Summit, and No. 2545 *Diamond Jubilee* had to be substituted. On this engine's first trip something went wrong with the steam sanding gear, and 9 min. were dropped on the ascent from Kings Cross to Potters Bar. Moreover, the choice of driver does not appear to have been of the happiest, and doubtless he was under restraint in the matter of coal consumption. So the result was that, although the running times were closer than those of the contestants between Paddington and Plymouth, over the Great Northern main line also *Pendennis Castle* had the best of it in both time and coal consumption.

Though the blast and draught arrangements of a 'Castle' are designed for Welsh coking coal, and the strong blast inevitably must increase coal consumption with a hard coal, Fireman Pearce mastered the art of firing with this unaccustomed fuel to such a degree as to keep his consumption with the 480-ton test loads to an average of 57·0 lb per mile between Kings Cross and Grantham, and 49·8 lb per mile between Kings Cross and Doncaster. Against this, No. 2545 *Diamond Jubilee* was burning an average of 59·0 lb per mile between London and Grantham and 55·3 lb per mile between London and Doncaster. This gave the 'Castles' an average advantage of 6 lb per mile with Welsh coal and 3·7 lb per mile with the Yorkshire product.

Moreover, Driver Young, with *Pendennis Castle*, again was winning in time with such feats as passing New Barnet, 67·2 miles from Peterborough, in 67 min. 45 sec. with a 485-ton train and reaching Kings Cross in 77¾ min. net; or in running from Kings Cross to Peterborough, 76·35 miles, with 480 tons in 78 min. 50 sec. start to stop. The perfectly clean starts of the 'Castle', especially up through the two greasy-railed tunnels out of Kings Cross, were viewed with amazement by the L.N.E.R. authorities; who would have dreamed that this moderately dimensioned 4-6-0 could lift 480-ton trains from Kings Cross out through Finsbury Park in times of between 5¾ and 6 min., day after day, without the least suspicion of a slip? So the contest ended; the Great Western Railway had substantiated up to the hilt their claim at the Wembley Exhibition, and did not fail to make all the capital they could in the *Great Western Railway Magazine* of the fact that their engine had 'won', presenting the case in such terms as to end in friction what should have been a friendly exchange of knowledge.

4 – The 'A3' Pacifics

It might well be thought impossible for such an interchange trial as that of 1925 to take place without its results having some influence on subsequent L.N.E.R. locomotive practice. But this could not be regarded as a foregone conclusion. As mentioned already, the only previous exchange in which a Great Western engine had participated, when the four-cylinder 4-6-0 *Polar Star* ran over London & North Western metals in 1910, and in which the Swindon engine had proved devastatingly superior in capacity and efficiency to any L.N.W.R. express locomotive at that time, had had no influence whatever on L.N.W.R. locomotive design, so far as concerned front-end design or valve-setting. Even Gresley, big man though he was, still seemed disinclined to move after the results of the 1925 exchange had been made public, until his chief technical assistant, B. Spencer, succeeded in persuading him to experiment with an improved valve-setting.

Actually, a year before all this happened, Gresley, as the result of suggestions by Spencer, had given serious consideration to fitting the 'A1' Pacifics with a long-lap valve-motion in order to permit early cut-off working. Spencer's claim was that while the engines were reliable enough, and more than competent to handle any task given them, their coal consumption was excessive. When designs were prepared for a modified gear, however, the scheme was dropped because of the expense involved in altering all the engines concerned; no more was done at that time than to give an additional lap of $\frac{1}{16}$ in. to the centre valve to counteract the over-running effect at high speed. Had the valve-gear change been made in 1924, the whole story of the famous exchange of 1925 might have been different; after the exchange was over, little excuse could remain for failing to make it.

As a first step, 'A1' Pacific No. 4477 *Gay Crusader* was provided with valves having $1\frac{1}{2}$-in. in place of $1\frac{1}{4}$-in. lap, and though a minimum of alteration to the valve-gear had been made, the results were so satisfactory that the full modification envisaged in the 1924 design was now at last decided on. Pacific No. 2555 *Centenary* was the first to be given the redesigned valve-motion, with $1\frac{5}{8}$-in. lap, $\frac{1}{8}$-in. lead, and an increase in maximum valve travel from $4\frac{9}{16}$ in. to $5\frac{3}{4}$ in., still with a limitation of maximum cut-off to 65 per cent; the additional $\frac{1}{16}$ in. of lap for the valve of the middle cylinder also was retained. The results were astonishing. As compared with the average coal consumption of the remaining 'A1' Pacifics, *Centenary*, with the short cut-off working now made possible, brought the figure down from 50 to 38 lb per mile, which meant an economy of 33 cwt on a single round trip from Doncaster to Kings Cross and back. Eventually, all the other 'A1' Pacifics were modified in the same way as they came into 'Plant' for heavy repairs, and the redesigned gear became the standard for future Pacific construction.

But the other lesson of the 1925 exchange – that of high working pressures, one of the secrets of the Great Western success – had yet to be applied, and in this matter Gresley did not move until 1927. In that year two of the 'A1' Pacifics emerged from Doncaster Works with new boilers in which the pressure was increased from 180 to 220 lb per sq in. With this alteration came the provision of a larger superheater, forty-three elements instead of thirty-two, which increased the superheating surface from 525 to 706 sq ft, while the tube heating surface was reduced from 2,715 to 2,477 sq ft. Other boiler dimensions remained unaltered, except for an increase in the thickness of the boiler-plates and a closer pitching of the firebox stays, to withstand the higher pressure. The two engines concerned were No. 2544 *Lemberg* and No. 4480 *Enterprise*.

While *Enterprise* retained her 20-in. diameter cylinders, *Lemberg* had hers lined up to $18\frac{1}{4}$ in.: the former thus had her tractive effort increased to 36,465 lb, while in the latter the reduction in cylinder diameter roughly balanced the

Above, Churchward's No. 111 The Great Bear, *Great Western Railway, as built in 1908.* [*British Railways*

Below, The Great Bear *as later modified with top-feed, heading a down Cheltenham express past Kensal Green.* [*F. E. Mackay*

Raven 4-6-2 No. 2400, (later named City of Newcastle), *North Eastern Railway, about to leave Kings Cross with the 5.40 p.m. Leeds express on a trial against Gresley Pacifics.*
[*Colling L. Turner*

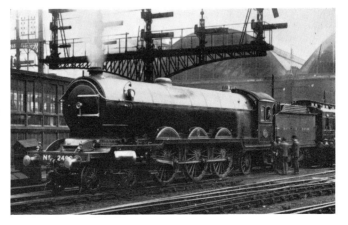

Above, Raven N.E.R. Pacific No. 2403 City of Durham *with outside bearings to the trailing wheels.* [*F. R. Hebron*

Above, on a rare visit to London – Raven N.E.R. 4-6-2 No. 2400 City of Newcastle *passing New Southgate with the up 'Norseman'.*
[*F. R. Hebron*

Below, as rebuilt with Gresley boiler and equipped with standard 8-wheel tender – Raven 4-6-2 No. 2404 City of Ripon.

Above, Gresley's first Pacific, No. 1470 Great Northern *of the former Class 'A1', as originally built, with G.N.R. numbers and letters.*

Right, the famous No. 4472 Flying Scotsman, *w i t h L.N.E.R. letters and numbers, as specially embellished for the 1924 Wembley Exhibition.* [W. J. Reynolds

Below, on 'foreign' metals – No. 4474 Victor Wild *passing Sonning box with the 1.30 p.m. from Paddington to Penzance, Great Western Railway, in the 1925 exchange trials.* [M. W. Earley

Above, No. 2568 Sceptre, *former Class 'A1', with Westinghouse brake-pump for working in the North Eastern Area.*

No. 2544 Lemberg, *one of the first 'A1' Pacifics to be fitted with 220 lb boiler, at speed with an up express.* [*P. Ransome-Wallis*

Historic occasion – No. 4472 Flying Scotsman *sets out from Kings Cross on the first non-stop run of the 'Flying Scotsman' express to Edinburgh, May 1st, 1928.* [*British Railways*

Above, a photograph of No. 4471 Sir Frederick Banbury *in original form, climbing Holloway bank with a down Newcastle express, which contrasts with that of (below) No. 2550* Blink Bonny *with cut-down chimney and cab, passing New Southgate with the down midday 'Scotsman'.*

[*Both, F. R. Hebron*

Experiments in smoke deflection. Above, 'A3' 4-6-2 No. 2747 Coronach in 1932, with cut-away smokebox front and opening on top behind the original chimney.

Right, 'A3' 4-6-2 No. 2751 Humorist, also with opening in smokebox front, fitted with flared double chimney.
[C. A. Gostling

Below, the next stage – Humorist with the upper part of the smokebox completely cut away, stovepipe chimney and small deflectors.
[P. Ransome-Wallis

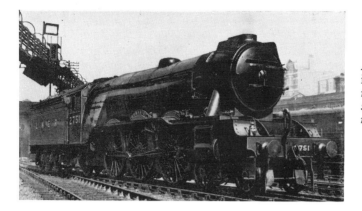

Left, No. 2751 Humorist *with the smokebox restored to normal, stovepipe double chimney and small deflectors.*
[*P. Ransome-Wallis*

Right, 'A3' 4-6-2 Humorist, *now No. 60097, with the penultimate modification—stovepipe double chimney, banjo dome and full-size deflectors. The final change was to a rimmed double chimney.*
[*P. Ransome-Wallis*

Left, 'A3' 4-6-2 No. 60055 Woolwinder *with flared double chimney and small deflectors.*
[*J. B. Bucknall*

Right, the latest development, now being applied generally 'A3'. 4-6-2 No. 60049 Galtee More *with flared double chimney and German wing type deflectors*
[*P. Ransome-Wallis*

increased boiler pressure, and left the tractive effort at much the same level as before, actually now 30,360 lb. Between the work of the two engines there was little difference; only on starting, or at other times when exceptional effort was required, did the larger cylinders of *Enterprise* give her the advantage. On the other hand, in those days I always found *Lemberg* to be an exceptionally fast engine when sustained high speed was needed. The alterations to *Enterprise* put the weight of the engine up from $92\frac{1}{2}$ to $96\frac{1}{4}$ tons, and to maintain the previous ratio of tractive effort to adhesion, the weight distribution was modified to increase the adhesion weight from 60 to $66\frac{1}{4}$ tons. Later in 1927 Nos. 2573 *Harvester*, 2578 *Bayardo* and 2580 *Shotover* were rebuilt similarly to *Enterprise*, retaining their 20-in. cylinders.

Soon after the conversion of *Enterprise* I had the opportunity of making some trips on the footplate with her, and the change in driving method from the handling of 'A1' Pacific *Solario*, as described in Section 2 of this chapter, was striking indeed. Going north on the 5.45 p.m. from Kings Cross, with a 460-ton train, we had come down to 30 per cent cut-off by the top of the 1 in 105 at Holloway, and this was enough to get us through Finsbury Park in $5\frac{1}{2}$ min. exactly. By Hornsey we were down to 15 per cent, and the driver then gradually advanced to 20 per cent up the long 1 in 200 to Potters Bar; for most of the distance from here on to Peterborough, 13 to 15 per cent instead of *Solario*'s 45 per cent was the working position, with the regulator partly closed on the downhill lengths, and the Peterborough stop was reached easily in 83 min. 50 sec.

Much the same thing happened on the 10.10 a.m. from Kings Cross, with a 440-ton train; again we cleared Finsbury Park in $5\frac{1}{2}$ min., this time with 40 per cent cut-off at the top of Holloway bank; 22 per cent was used up to Potters Bar and 15 per cent for most of the remainder of the run. In the up direction, similar methods of working brought a 315-ton train through New Barnet, 96·3 miles from Grantham, in 99 min. 10 sec., with no maximum speed higher than $72\frac{1}{2}$ m.p.h., and we reached London in 109 min. 30 sec., or $108\frac{3}{4}$ min. net for the 105·5 miles. On this run the steam-chest pressure gauge showed that whenever the engine was working hard, the pressure in the steam-chest was within about 90 per cent of the actual boiler pressure – a testimony to the care that had been bestowed on the design and layout of the steam passages.

In February, 1928, comparative tests were carried out with the dynamometer car between Kings Cross and Doncaster in which *Lemberg* was pitted against No. 4473 *Solario*, the former with 220 lb pressure and $18\frac{1}{4}$-in. cylinders and the latter with 180 lb pressure and 20-in. cylinders. Each was tested for a full week, with average tare loads of 428 and 435 tons respectively on the up journey, 506 and 491 tons from Kings Cross to Peterborough, and 348 and 331 tons from Peterborough to Doncaster. Average coal consumptions were 35·37 and 38·83 lb per mile in favour of the high-pressure Pacific, and water consumption 288·8 against 317·5 lb per mile, while *Lemberg* also was making the higher average speeds, 56·84 against 54·93 m.p.h. coming up and 52·54 against 50·73 m.p.h. going down. But *Solario* had to battle with bad weather conditions, with the result that the average coal consumptions per drawbar-h.p.-hr were almost identical, 3·11 lb with *Lemberg* and 3·07 lb with *Solario* – a curiously inconclusive outcome. It is difficult to understand why *Enterprise*, with the larger cylinders, was not included in these comparative trials.

In any event, the working of the 220-lb Pacifics was regarded as sufficiently satisfactory to justify the introduction of the higher working pressure and enlarged superheater, though opinions at Doncaster were divided as to whether the higher pressure or the higher superheat were responsible for improved performance. For all new construction, a reduced cylinder diameter was decided on, but the higher pressure certainly gave the Pacifics an increased starting tractive effort to compensate in a measure for what they lost by the limitation of maximum cut-off to 65 per cent. So the building of the first 'A3' Pacifics was decided on, and now it could be claimed that the lessons of the 1925 exchange had been applied in full. Yet in one respect the new Gresley practice was diametrically opposed to that of the G.W.R. In 1927 Collett, who had completed at Swindon his first 4-6-0 'King', with working pressure raised still further to 250 lb, had retained the same sixteen-element superheater – or, more precisely, steam-dryer – that had been used in his previous 'Castles', carrying no more than 225 lb pressure. Gresley, on the other hand, in increasing his working pressure from 180 to 220 lb per sq in., had increased his superheater at the same time from thirty-two to forty-three elements, and, so far as concerned the Yorkshire coal normally used, the working of the 'A3' Pacifics has fully justified his high temperature superheat.

It may be added that in 1926 Gresley experimented on No. 2562 *Isinglass* with an even larger 'E' type superheater having no fewer than sixty-two elements, but as compared with 'A1' Pacific No. 2570 *Tranquil*, which had a thirty-two-element superheater, the gain in average superheat temperature was no more than 31°F. The forty-three-element superheater finally standardized in 1928 for the 'A3' Pacifics therefore was regarded as adequate. Its presence became apparent externally by the large patch on each side of the smokebox, housing the outer ends of the superheater header.

The first new Pacifics to be built with 220-lb boilers, to the 'A3' design, were headed by No. 2743 *Felstead*, which emerged from Doncaster Works in August, 1928; they were numbered from 2743 to 2752 inclusive. Six were completed in 1928 and the remaining four in 1929. Gresley had decided to split the difference between the 20-in. cylinders of *Enterprise* and the 18¼-in. cylinders of *Lemberg* and to standardize on 19 in. with the new 'A3' series. This gave a tractive effort, at 85 per cent of the boiler pressure, of 32,910 lb. The 5¾-in. valve-travel and 1⅝-in. lap remained standard, as also the 8-in. piston-valves. In common with a change which was now taking place all over the country, the driving position was altered from the right-hand to the left-hand side of the cab.

Another development about this time was the equipment of some of the Pacifics with corridor tenders. One phase of the inter-group competition already referred to had been as to which group could run the longest distance without stop. In 1927 the L.N.E.R. had begun by working the 9.50 a.m. relief

'Scotsman' non-stop over the 268·35 miles between Kings Cross and Newcastle, while the L.M.S.R. was running the 236·25 miles from Euston to Carnforth non-stop with the 'Royal Scot'; on receipt of its new 'Royal Scot' 4-6-0 engines the L.M.S.R. had extended its run from Euston through to Carlisle, 299·1 miles; and the L.N.E.R., from 1st May, 1928, had countered by booking the 'Flying Scotsman' non-stop over the 392·8 miles between Kings Cross and Edinburgh – a feat, incidentally, which would have been difficult, if not impossible, of accomplishment but for the economical engine working made possible by the valve gear modifications that followed the 1925 locomotive exchange.

For the run of nearly 400 miles it became necessary to provide means whereby the engine-crew could be changed midway, just north of York, without stopping the train; and this was the genesis of Gresley's unique corridor tender. Space in the tender was naturally precious, and the corridor was therefore of very limited dimensions. The immortal story is told of how Gresley was discovered by one of his daughters crawling on all fours between a row of dining-room chairs ranged at a distance of 18 in. from the wall, to test whether this distance would be adequate! In order that no inkling might reach the L.M.S.R. of what was going on, the first corridor tender was built under conditions of the utmost secrecy at Doncaster, and when it went out on trial for the first time, it was attached not to a Pacific but to an Ivatt Atlantic.

The first five Pacifics to be provided with corridor tenders were No. 4472 *Flying Scotsman*, No. 4476 *Royal Lancer*, No. 2573 *Harvester*, No. 2577 *Night Hawk* and No. 2580 *Shotover*. Each of these tenders is 25 ft 10 in. long and is provided with a passage 18 in. wide and 5 ft high running along the right-hand side. At the rear end of the tender there is a Pullman vestibule connection exactly similar to that of a coach; starting from this the corridor turns sharp right, and then sharp left at the corner of the tender, which is fitted with a circular window to provide light. When fully charged with 9 tons of coal and 5,000 gallons of water, each of these massive tenders weighs 62½ tons, increasing the weight of an 'A3' Pacific with tender to 158¾ tons. More corridor tenders were built after the introduction of the 'A4' Pacifics, to a total of twenty.

In the year 1929, when the A.C.F.I. feed-water heating apparatus was under trial on ex-Great Eastern 4-6-0 engines of the 'B12' class and on ex-North Eastern Atlantics of the 'C7' class, Gresley decided on a similar experiment with Pacifics, two of which were fitted, 'A1' class No. 2576 *The White Knight* and 'A3' class No. 2580 *Shotover*. As with boilers of this size there was no room for the heaters in the usual position on both sides of the boiler barrel between chimney and dome, a special type of heater was designed to occupy part of the smokebox and project as a kind of half-moon above it almost up to the height of the chimney, giving the engines concerned a curiously massive appearance at the front end. Tests proved that the apparatus could deliver feed into the boiler (by means of a feed-pump, of course) at temperatures up to 225°F. The two engines carried the apparatus for some years, but nothing came of the experiment.

The value of the 220-lb boiler of the 'A3' Pacifics in promoting more efficient working now became so well established as to prompt the decision to rebuild all the fifty-two 'A1' Pacifics into Class 'A3' as reboilering became necessary. This conversion included the reduction in cylinder diameter to 19 in. Reconstruction was held up for a time during the Second World War; and after the war, with the emergence of new Pacific types under Gresley's successors, the remaining engines of Class 'A1' by then had been re-classified as 'A10'. The last conversion from Class 'A10' to Class 'A3', that of *Sir Visto* (originally No. 2567, later No. 68 and finally No. 60068) did not take place until 1949. *Enterprise* and *Lemberg* in due course received the standard 19-in. cylinders of the 'A3' class.

In 1930 eight more 'A3' Pacifics made their appearance; all were built at Doncaster, and the numbers were 2595 to 2599 inclusive and 2795, 2796 and 2797. With these engines there was introduced a new type of tender, with curved tops to the side-sheets, like those of the corridor tenders, and high curved rear ends. This was one only of various tender modifications of later years, such as the streamlined tenders built for the 'A4' Pacifics, to which pattern all the corridor tenders were altered eventually, and the streamlined version of the non-corridor tenders that appeared at a still later date. The last of the 'A3s' were built in 1934 (except No. 2508 *Brown Jack*, which appeared in 1935), nine in all, numbered from 2500 to 2508 inclusive, bringing the total of 'A3' engines built as such to twenty-seven, and of all the Pacifics up to that date to seventy-nine.

The final batch, beginning with No. 2500 *Windsor Lad*, had their domes replaced by a new type of steam collector, shaped like a banjo, into which steam passes through transverse slots in the top of the boiler barrel rather than through the usual circular opening, with a view to the prevention of priming. The slots intercept moisture in the steam, and tend to cause this to fall back into the boiler barrel. This 'banjo dome', which has since become a standard fitting for all the Pacifics, was shifted back from the usual dome position astride the joint between the second and third rings of the boiler barrel to the middle of the third ring, with quite a perceptible effect on the appearance of the engines. In fact, this change began a deterioration in the fine external lines of the original 'A1' series which has continued apace with each successive modification.

The derailment at speed in March, 1931, of the down L.M.S.R. 'Royal Scot' on a cross-over at Leighton Buzzard, attributed in part to steam obscuring the driver's vision through the front spectacle of his cab, drew attention to the dangers of drifting exhaust. Engines with taper boilers had rarely suffered in this way in the same degree as the L.M.S.R. 'Royal Scot' 4-6-0s, one of which was involved in this accident, with their parallel boilers and extremely short chimneys, but the much softer blast brought about with short cut-off working prompted certain experiments with the Gresley Pacifics. The engines selected were No. 2747 *Coronach* and No. 2751 *Humorist*. In 1932 the former had the upper part of the smokebox cut away in a wedge shape, with the deepest portion pointing forwards; the bottom of this opening was formed by an inclined plate which blocked off the remainder of the smokebox and carried air upwards to a vent behind the chimney. The smokebox wrapper plate remained, so that from the front the change appeared merely as a large aperture at the top of the smokebox.

In the case of *Humorist*, however, the part of the wrapper plate above the aperture went also, so that the top of the smokebox itself now sloped downwards; small deflector plates also were fitted on both sides of the chimney. Rather curiously, although the *Coronach* arrangement was intended to compress the air entering the cavity at the front so that its pressure and velocity might increase until it emerged from the aperture behind the chimney and lifted the exhaust, the modified arrangement on *Humorist* proved the more effective of the two, and remained in use for some five years.

Then, in 1937, a more important experiment was made with the latter engine. It was the fitting of a double blast-pipe of the Kylchap type, with its concentric petticoats, inside a smokebox of the normal type, together with a flared double chimney. With the still lower terminal exhaust pressures now made possible, however, drifting exhaust became so troublesome that a stovepipe chimney had to be substituted, with the previous small deflector-plates on both sides of it. The change proved helpful, and No. 2751 remained in this condition until standard smokebox deflector-plates were fitted by Gresley's successor in 1947. So excellent a reputation was established by *Humorist* for free steaming and free running that it is surprising that Gresley did nothing to equip other 'A3' Pacifics with double blast pipes and chimneys. Not until many years later did this become standard equipment for all the Gresley Pacifics, 'A3' and 'A4' alike.

5 – *No.* 10000

Before we carry on the story to the streamlined 'A4' Pacifics, brief reference is necessary to another Gresley product which strictly, from the wheel arrangement point of view, has no place in a book devoted to Pacific locomotives. For No. 10000, which emerged from Darlington during 1929, was a Pacific with an extra pair of wheels. It was not actually of the 4-6-4 or Baltic type, for the rear two pairs of wheels were not arranged as a bogie; the leading pair had the normal Cartazzi axleboxes of the Gresley Pacifics, while the rear pair were mounted in a Bissel truck, to give the necessary flexibility of wheelbase. This was therefore a 4-6-2-2 locomotive.

The outstanding feature of No. 10000 was, of course, the boiler. At the time experiments were proceeding in different countries with super-pressure boilers of several types, coupled with compound propulsion, in order to make better use of the expansive properties of the steam and thereby to increase thermal efficiency. Gresley therefore joined forces with H. E. Yarrow, of the well-known firm of that name, specialists in marine water-tube boilers, in designing a water-tube boiler suitable for mounting on a locomotive chassis. As it was clear that the boiler casing would have to be built out to the extreme limits of the loading gauge, and that there would be no possibility of the chimney projecting above it, a close study had to be made of the external contour of the boiler clothing to ensure that the exhaust steam would be lifted clear of the cab. In this matter Professor W. E. Dalby of the City and Guilds Technical College collaborated with Gresley in making tests with a wind tunnel in which steam, simulated by powdered chalk, was ejected from a model of the proposed locomotive.

The boiler comprised one upper steam drum of 3-ft diameter, 27 ft 11½ in. long; two water drums, 1 ft 6 in. diameter and 11 ft 0½ in. long, one on either side of the firebox; and two further water drums, ahead of and at a slightly higher level than the latter, each of 1 ft 7 in. diameter and 13 ft 5¾ in. long. Connecting the upper drum with the two firebox drums were 238 tubes of 2½ in. diameter, arched over the firegrate; and the upper drum was connected with the forward lower drums by 444 2-in. diameter and 74 2½-in. diameter tubes. There was also a screen of 12 2½-in. diameter tubes at the back of the firebox. Under test at the makers' works this boiler gave a continuous evaporation of 20,000 lb of steam per hour for four hours continuously, at the full pressure of 450 lb per sq in. at which No. 10000 was intended to work. The whole was enclosed by a casing which began at the front end in the form of smoke deflectors and extended back to the cab, curved inwards in a series of steps over the cylinders and the coupled wheels, and below the firebox.

As previously mentioned, No. 10000 was designed for compound propulsion. The outside cylinders, 20 in. by 26 in., were of the standard type used in Gresley's original 'A1' Pacifics, and were the low-pressure pair; they had 8-in. diameter piston-valves with a maximum travel of 6 $\frac{11}{16}$ in. and a maximum cut-off of 75 per cent. The inside high-pressure cylinders were 12-in. diameter (later reduced to 10-in.) by 26-in. stroke, with 6-in. piston-valves having a maximum travel of 6 $\frac{13}{16}$ in. and arranged for a maximum cut-off of 80 per cent. The ratio of h.p. to l.p. cylinder volume thus was 1 : 2¾. Two sets only of Walschaerts motion were fitted, operating the outside cylinder piston-valves in the usual way, but Gresley devised an ingenious arrangement whereby the cut-off of the inside cylinder piston-valves, which were worked by rocking-shafts, could be independent of the outside cylinder cut-off.

This was done by slotting the inner arm of the rocking-shafts and fitting a movable die-block, attached to the valve-rod, in each slot. By moving the die-block towards or away from the centre of oscillation of the rocking-shaft, the travel, and so the percentage of cut-off, could be lessened or increased. It was thus possible to provide two sets of reversing gear, one to shift the radius rods in the links in the usual way, and the other to actuate the die-blocks of the h.p. cylinder motion. For starting, arrangements were made for admitting h.p. steam direct to the l.p. cylinders by a special regulator, but for the first few moments only; a special safety-valve was fitted to ensure that the pressure in the l.p. cylinders should not rise above 200 lb per sq in.

Special boiler fittings had to be obtained suitable for the high working pressure of 450 lb per sq in., including safety-valves, regulator, water-gauges, and one of the injectors. The other injector took its steam from a manifold which reduced the pressure to 200 lb, in order to supply steam to the whistle, ejector, sanding gear, train heating and other details. The driving wheels were 6 ft 8 in. diameter and carried an adhesion weight of 62½ tons out of the total engine weight of 103½ tons; the length of engine and tender over buffers was 75 ft 4 in.

No. 10000 was built at Darlington Works and stationed at Gateshead shed, where she worked in the ordinary Pacific link and shared in all the ordinary Pacific turns. These included one which involved working the 11.17 a.m. from Newcastle to Edinburgh, the 5.25 p.m. from Edinburgh to York (the present-day 'North Briton') and a night express back to Newcastle, or 410 miles in the 24 hours. At the end of July, 1930, also, she worked the 'Flying Scotsman' non-stop from Edinburgh to Kings Cross and returned on the following day with the same train, keeping time with both, but this was on the very easy original schedule of 8¼ hours.

In 1931 Gresley reported in a paper to the Institution of Mechanical Engineers that No. 10000 had worked 'trains of over 500 tons weight for long distances at express speeds with consistent success and reliability' and that 'there is every indication that it will prove more economical in fuel consumption than express engines of the latest types'. But this proved an over-optimistic forecast. Actually a paper to the Institution of Locomotive Engineers in 1947 by B. Spencer, who had been Gresley's personal assistant and was reviewing the course of L.N.E.R. locomotive development from 1923 to 1941, proved that the very opposite had been the case.

At first the evaporative heating surface of the boiler was found to be on the small side, with the result that No. 10000 steamed satisfactorily only when developing high outputs at long cut-offs with a smokebox vacuum in the region of 6 in. But at this figure the smokebox temperature was too high, while the superheat temperature rose to as much as 900°F. Some improvement was effected by fitting a double blastpipe, and a shortening of the superheater elements reduced the smokebox temperature to a maximum of 700°F.

With this lowering, however, condensation occurred in the l.p. cylinders, and an intermediate superheater was then fitted which added some 100°F. to the l.p. steam temperature and also helped to reduce the smokebox temperature. Even so, the engine was weak when working compound and accelerating from a stop, for the superheat took time to build up, and meantime the l.p. cylinders were contributing little work because of condensation. It proved difficult, also, to keep the boiler walls airtight, because of variation in the temperature of the plates, and this again led to steaming troubles due to air being drawn through the defective joints instead of through the grate.

Considerable alterations were made to the baffles, to ensure that the hot gases as far as possible came into contact with the whole of the water tubes, but without the result hoped for. Thus, despite the originality of the design and the admirable workmanship, No. 10000 in her original form could not be regarded as a success; the engine was proving expensive to maintain and in general was burning considerably more coal than the standard Pacifics.

In the end, therefore, Gresley decided on a complete reconstruction as a three-cylinder simple with a boiler of conventional type, which was completed in 1937. From then on No. 10000, apart from her 4-6-2-2 wheel arrangement, closely resembled one of the streamlined 'A4' Pacifics, described in Section 7 of this chapter. But there were important differences, and chief among them the fact that No. 10000's three cylinders were of 20-in. diameter as compared with the 'A4's' 18½-in., which on a tractive effort basis – 41,440 lb at 85 per cent of the working pressure of 250 lb per sq in. – made the former the most powerful express locomotive in the country. Also the firegrate area was 50 sq ft, as in Gresley's 'P2' 2-8-2 engines, compared with the 'A4's' 41·25 sq ft. This increased the evaporative heating surface to 3,347 sq ft, slightly more than the 3,325 sq ft of an 'A4' boiler, though the superheating surface, 749 sq ft, was the same in each case. With the extra pair of wheels No. 10000 was, of course, the heavier of the two, 107¾ tons in working order as against the 103 tons of an 'A4'.

The equipment of the rebuilt No. 10000 included double blast-pipe and chimney, corridor tender, and turbo-generator to supply current for head and tail lamps, cab lighting and lamps under the skirting and between the frames to facilitate engine examination. At night the wheels could be floodlit while the engine was running.

Although I never travelled behind No. 10000 in her original form, I did so after she had been rebuilt, and found her a very capable performer. In a table of runs on the up 'Flying Scotsman' which I included in a 'British Locomotive Practice and Performance' article in 1938, this engine figured in two with very heavy loads which showed her to be the equal of, if not superior to, an 'A4' Pacific. At this time the 'Scotsman' was allowed no more than 105½ min. for the 105·45 miles from Grantham to Kings Cross, and with loads of fourteen bogies and more of the heaviest stock this was a tough proposition.

On one run with a load of 461 tons tare and 490 tons gross No. 10000 made the best start from Grantham up the 1 in 200 to Stoke summit of all the twelve runs in the table, taking no more than 8 min. 7 sec. start-to-pass for the 5·35 miles and attaining no less than 52 m.p.h. up the grade. Later on came a sudden acceleration along the level past Holme to 85½ m.p.h. at Connington, and a minimum of 63½ m.p.h. up the 4½ miles of Abbots Ripton bank, uniformly at 1 in 200. On another run, with 446 tons tare and 470 tons gross, I timed No. 10000 to maintain an average speed of 72·2 m.p.h. from Huntingdon to Hitchin – 26·95 miles in 22 min. 27 sec. – the climb of 12·5 miles from Biggleswade up to Stevenage, including 2¼ miles at 1 in 400, 1¼ at 1 in 330, 2¼ at 1 in 264, and finally 4¾ at 1 in 200, being completed at an average of 67·2 m.p.h. The net times from Grantham to Kings Cross on these two runs, including stretches taken under easy steam to avoid too early an arrival, were 103 and 99¼ min. respectively.

In her later years No. 10000, which was never honoured with a name, became No. 60700 in the British Railways numbering, and the lone example of Class 'W1'. In 1955 her cylinders were lined up from 20-in. to 19-in. diameter. She was stationed at Doncaster, her regular duty being to work the

Leeds express which in successive years left Kings Cross at various times between 3.50 and 4.05 p.m. It was when working this train, on the evening of 1st September, 1955, that No. 60700 sustained the only serious mishap of her career. The thirteen-coach train was starting northwards out of Peterborough when the engine became derailed at Westwood Junction as the result of the complete fracture of the right-hand bogie frame-plate, the engine and the leading coach both turning over, though happily without any serious injury either to crew or passengers. Nearly four-fifths of the failed frame-plate was found to be flawed. The engine had travelled some 138,819 miles since her last general overhaul, without any defective condition betraying itself. It was a mercy indeed that the failure occurred when the speed was no more than 20 m.p.h.; had it occurred on a high-speed stretch the results might have been disastrous.

The accident, which was of an unprecedented description, was the subject of an extremely detailed investigation by the Ministry of Transport Inspecting Officer, Lt.-Col. G. R. S. Wilson. After it had occurred the bogie frames of the whole of the Gresley Pacifics on the Eastern, North Eastern and Scottish Regions were closely examined, but no similarly defective condition was discovered. New methods of bogie examination at specified intervals, however, were instituted at all motive power depots in the Regions concerned, so that the mishap certainly had beneficial results from the safety point of view. No. 60700 was taken to Doncaster and had slightly longer frame-plates fitted, with considerably stronger fabricated stretchers, and continued in service until she went to the scrap-heap in 1960.

6 – Preparing for the Streamliners

THE period between 1930 and 1939 marked a sudden and startling advance in railway speed all over the world. In Great Britain it began, in 1932, with the abandonment by the L.M.S.R. and L.N.E.R. of the long-standing agreement which had tied down the minimum times between London and both Glasgow and Edinburgh to the 8 hours 15 min. laid down after the Race to Aberdeen in 1895. How absurd such a limitation had become had been abundantly clear when in the summer of 1928 all intermediate stops had been taken out of the run of the 'Flying Scotsman' between Kings Cross and Edinburgh, but the engines had still been compelled to dawdle along at a much reduced speed in order to fill out the unchanged $8\frac{1}{4}$ hours allowance. In the very first year of the acceleration, the non-stop timing was cut by no less than 45 min. at one stroke, bringing it down to $7\frac{1}{2}$ hours, and this was reduced successively to $7\frac{1}{4}$ hours in 1936 and 7 hours in 1937. At the same time the speeds of other expresses were being increased considerably, and runs timed at a mile-a-minute and more from start to stop were beginning to appear in the time-tables.

Meantime the development overseas of other forms of motive power for the working of high-speed passenger services was coming prominently under notice. By 1932 the German State Railways had introduced their *Fliegende Hamburger* two-car streamline train, and by 1933 they were running it every day from Berlin to Hamburg at an average speed of 77·4 m.p.h. – 178·1 miles in 138 min. – a schedule which, with allowance for speed restrictions, required regular running speeds up to 100 m.p.h. In the United States in 1934 similar and more capacious diesel streamliners, the 'Pioneer Zephyr' of the Chicago, Burlington & Quincy Railroad and the 'City of Portland' of the Union Pacific, had taken the whole of that country by storm and had set on foot a change in motive power on American railways which has resulted in the by now almost complete substitution of steam by diesel traction. It is not surprising, therefore, that, with a British public now speed-conscious, questions began to be asked as to why we could not see some similar enterprise in this country.

The answer was that Great Britain, with abundant supplies of the best steam coal in the world, would be foolish to abandon this fuel in favour of imported oil for the running of its trains. But Gresley did not leave the matter there. In 1934 he obtained estimates from the German builders of the 'Flying Hamburger' unit as to the time which, in their estimation, would be needed to travel between London and Newcastle by a three-car train with similar diesel-electric power, taking all speed restrictions into account. After a study of the physical characteristics of the route, the time stated by the German firm, for a train of 115 tons weight, seating 140 passengers, was 4¼ hours. Gresley, convinced that a similar time could be maintained reliably by steam power, decided to make some preliminary experiments with Pacifics in order to prove his point; for one of these, between Kings Cross and Leeds, an 'A1' Pacific was turned out, and for the other, over the full Kings Cross–Newcastle course, an 'A3'.

So it was that on a dull and misty November morning in 1934 – actually 30th November – I found myself in the 'Local' Station at Kings Cross, in company with a few officials, stepping into a four-coach train which had been marshalled for the run to Leeds. At the head of it was No. 4472 *Flying Scotsman*, and on the footplate the famous Bill Sparshatt with his Fireman Webster, about to give us a run of a speed quality undreamed of even over L.N.E.R. metals up to that time. In retrospect, it is, perhaps, remarkable that we got any further than the mouth of Gasworks Tunnel that morning. For the engine, with so short a train, was well back along the platform, and Sparshatt opened up with such vigour that when we reached the sharp and awkward connections leading from the platform out on to the main line, the engine was travelling at such a speed as to leave flange-marks on rails in positions where flanges certainly are not expected to run. Mercifully, however, nothing worse happened, and so we were away.

With a load of no more than 147 tons, *Flying Scotsman* now treated us to a display of unprecedented brilliance. Little notice was taken of the tentative schedule prepared; the engine was given her head, and the operating authorities played the game magnificently by keeping the road ahead of us perfectly clear. What a thrill it was! We were through Finsbury Park in just over 4 min. and Hatfield in just over 17 min.; 71½ m.p.h. was the speed through Wood Green and 67 to 68½ m.p.h. all the way up the 1 in 200 to Potters Bar; next followed 83 through Hatfield and 93½ through Hitchin; and then 86 to 95 all the way until we eased for the Offord curves. So we were through Hitchin in 28 min. 22 sec., Huntingdon in 46 min. 31 sec., and Peterborough in no more than 39 sec. over the even hour – for the first 76·35 miles! Sparshott had not allowed his engine to exceed 95 m.p.h., which was reached just after Hitchin.

After recovery from the Peterborough slack, which was rigidly observed, right down to 21 m.p.h., there came an ascent to Stoke summit which, mile by mile as we made it, seemed completely unbelievable. We were to get used to these things later on, as the streamliners came into regular service, but on this first 80-m.p.h. flight on record 'up the hill', it might well have been thought that the grade had flattened out to zero, for all the notice Sparshatt and his engine took of it. By Werrington Junction we were doing 71½ m.p.h. and by Tallington 79; up the 1 in 440 and 264 to Essendine speed increased to 84; the minimum up the 4½ miles at 1 in 200 to milepost 95½ was a steady 82¼; and after a momentary increase to 83 on the easier 1½ miles to Corby Glen, we stormed the last 3 miles of 1 in 178 to the summit, now with *Flying Scotsman* cutting off at 40 per cent, at an absolute minimum of 81 m.p.h. The 10 miles' climb between the 90th and 100th mileposts had been made at an *average* speed of 82½ m.p.h.!

So the special was whirled over the 29·1 miles from Peterborough to Grantham in 23 min. to the dead second. The schedule had allowed us 26 min., and on passing Grantham, 105·45 miles, in 83 min. 39 sec. from Kings Cross, we were nearly 8½ min. ahead of time. Still the road remained clear. From here the running was perhaps a shade easier; otherwise I verily believe we should have been through Doncaster in a 'record-of-records' time of 2 hours from London; as it was, we were passing the 153¾ milepost at the precise end of the second hour. Two independent stages of the journey had been completed at average speeds of over 80 m.p.h. – the 70·05 miles from Wood Green to Fletton Junction at 80·8, and now the 71·3 miles from Helpston to Black Carr Junction – Stoke summit included – at 80·3 m.p.h. Doncaster, 156·0 miles, was passed in 122 min. 27 sec. from Kings Cross.

Relatively to the steepness of the gradients, Sparshatt treated us to some more amazing speed after Doncaster; 2¾ miles at 1 in 150 up past South Elmsall dropped the speed no more than from 80 to 77½ m.p.h., and the final 1¼ miles at the same inclination to Nostell summit from 81 to 77½ m.p.h., while to finish the 1 in 100–122 to Ardsley summit at 55½ m.p.h. was another extraordinary experience. Up several uphill lengths on which minimum speeds were a full 50 per cent and more higher than those normally run, we experienced lurches on curves of which we had barely suspected the existence previously. Who would have conceived possible a time of no more than 17 min. 1 sec. for the 19·85 miles from Doncaster to Wakefield, begun at 40 m.p.h. and ended at 35? Finally, after the usual 10 m.p.h. slack through Holbeck, *Flying Scotsman* drew up in Leeds Central 2 hours 31 min. 56 sec.

after leaving Kings Cross. As previously indicated, Sparshatt would have had little difficulty in cutting this to the even 2½ hours; as it was, we had pared our 2¾-hour schedule by a full 13 min.

The seating accommodation on the down journey (had a third-class brake replaced the dynamometer car) would roughly have equalled the 102 seats in the twin-unit German *Fliegende Hamburger*, but our train had a proper restaurant car as compared with the German train's cold buffet only. From Leeds to London, however, in order to simulate a train of the accommodation that might be needed for a high-speed London–Leeds or London–Newcastle service, two corridor thirds were added, bringing the seating up to more than double that of the *Fliegende Hamburger*. We were booked out of Leeds at 2 p.m., and this fact brought back vivid memories of Great Northern days, when Ivatt Atlantics used to leave Leeds Central at precisely the same hour with the famous 'Special Express' that was due in Kings Cross at 5.27 p.m. That was with five coaches; today we were destined to bring six coaches into the London terminus 50 min. earlier!

In Table III (A) I have given the principal details of the up run, as of the down. The engine seemed just as much at home with the heavier train, and there were some even more brilliant exploits, as, for example, the way in which we recovered from 35 m.p.h. through Doncaster to 77½ by Rossington, took Piper's Wood 'hump' at 73, and were up to 88 by Scrooby troughs – all in 10 miles! Minima of 74 m.p.h. over Markham summit (following 81¼ over Retford level crossing!), 69 at Peascliffe Tunnel, and 68½ at Stoke summit were all excellent with a 207-ton load. To Grantham we ran the 80·25 miles from Leeds, including the steep climb from the start and the Wakefield and Doncaster slacks, in 70 min. 18 sec.; the test schedule was 74 min.

Now *Flying Scotsman* went like the wind. Down from Stoke summit the fastest quarter-miles that I 'clocked' were two at 97½ m.p.h., and this was the figure quoted in a hurriedly prepared broadcast of the day's events that I gave that evening as part of the B.B.C. 'nine o'clock news'. But closer examination of the dynamometer car roll showed that for a very short distance, between Little Bytham and Essendine, the magic '100' line had been reached – a climax indeed to the engine's exploits. On passing Peterborough, in 92 min. to the second from Leeds, we were 8 min. ahead of time.

By now Fireman Webster was tiring, and small wonder! In the whole of this strenuous day he shovelled all but 9 tons of coal into the firebox of the engine, with no more rest between the two 2½-hour continuous spells of firing than the two hours we had spent in Leeds. So, between Peterborough and London, Sparshatt held pretty closely to his point-to-point bookings, and eventually we came to a stand in Kings Cross at just after 4.37 p.m., in 2 hours 37 min. 17 sec. from Leeds. Our amazing engine and her crew had spent exactly 250 miles out of a single day's duty travelling at a mean speed of 80 m.p.h.! Their return journey of 371·5 miles had occupied 9 min. 13 sec. over 5 hours. This made it clear that steam was capable of equalling any diesel-electric performance up to that date.

TABLE III (A)
L.N.E.R. KINGS CROSS–LEEDS
Test Runs, 30th November, 1934
Engine: Original 'A1' 4-6-2 No. 4472, Flying Scotsman

145 tons tare, 147 tons gross					205 tons tare, 207 tons gross			
Dist.	Sched.	Actual	Speeds		Dist.	Sched.	Actual	Speeds
miles	min.	min. sec.	m.p.h.		miles	min.	min. sec.	m.p.h.
0·00	0	0 00	—	KINGS CROSS	185·70	165	157 17	—
2·50	—	4 04	55	FINSBURY PARK	183·20	—	153 22	—
4·95	—	6 25	71½	Wood Green	180·75	—	151 13	81
9·15	—	10 07	68½	New Barnet	176·55	—	148 08	80
12·70	—	13 16	67	Potters Bar	173·00	—	145 16	70
17·70	19	17 03	83	HATFIELD	168·00	148	141 11	85
23·50	—	22 06	†60/68½	Woolmer Green	162·20	—	136 48	72
28·55	—	26 05	80	Stevenage	157·15	—	132 37	70/76
31·90	30	28 22	93½	HITCHIN	153·80	137	129 50	72½
37·10	—	31 40	95/86	Arlesey	148·60	—	125 38	75/76¼
41·15	—	34 27	92	Biggleswade	144·55	—	122 00	62
44·15	—	36 24	92½	Sandy	141·55	—	118 33	*40
47·50	—	38 38	93	Tempsford	138·20	—	115 55	81
51·75	—	41 29	85	St Neots	133·95	—	112 38	71½
55·95	—	44 24	90/*78	Offord	129·75	—	109 08	eased
58·85	50	46 31	82	HUNTINGDON	126·85	116	106 42	80½
62·00	—	48 58	72½	Milepost 62	123·70	—	104 13	72
69·35	—	54 28	83	Holme	116·35	—	98 31	83
75·00	—	58 57	—	Fletton Junction	110·70	—	93 52	—
76·35	66	60 39	*21	PETERBOROUGH	109·35	100	92 00	*25
79·50	—	64 20	71½	Werrington Junction	106·20	—	89 00	80
84·85	—	68 26	80	Tallington	100·85	—	85 10	86½
88·65	—	71 13	84	Essendine	97·05	—	82 38	100
92·25	—	73 47	84	Little Bytham	93·45	—	80 25	95½
97·10	—	77 21	82	Corby Glen	88·60	—	77 11	86
100·10	—	79 33	81	Stoke	85·60	—	74 54	68½
105·45	92	83 39	87/*62	GRANTHAM	80·25	74	70 18	73¾
109·70	—	87 16	—	Barkstone	76·00	—	66 45	69
115·35	—	91 24	90	Claypole	70·35	—	62 13	78
120·10	103	94 38	86½	NEWARK	65·60	62	58 28	77½
126·30	—	99 10	82½	Carlton	59·40	—	53 01	82
133·75	—	104 53	76½	Markham	51·95	—	48 23	74
138·60	119	108 44	84/*69	RETFORD	47·10	47	44 28	81½
143·95	—	112 53	87	Ranskill	41·75	—	40 41	86½
149·50	—	116 50	88/79	Milepost 149½	36·20	—	36 44	73/88
153·20	—	119 31	87	Black Carr Junction	32·50	—	33 49	77½
155·95	133	122 27	*40	DONCASTER	29·75	32	30 58	*35
159·95	—	126 38	76	Carcroft	25·75	—	27 01	*72
164·60	—	130 17	80/77½	South Elmsall	21·10	—	23 25	77½/82
167·75	—	132 41	81	Hemsworth	19·95	—	20 47	74½
170·35	—	134 37	77½	Nostell	15·35	—	18 33	61½
174·15	—	137 26	83	Sandal	11·55	—	14 55	64
175·80	151	139 28	*35	WAKEFIELD	9·90	14	12 42	*39
178·20	—	141 22	57/*40	Lofthouse	7·50	—	9 46	*48
180·10	157	144 39	55½	Ardsley	5·60	9	7 46	54
183·20	—	147 46	68	Beeston	2·50	—	4 17	56
185·20	—	150 15	*10	Holbeck	0·50	—	1 36	—
185·70	165	151 56	—	LEEDS CENTRAL	0·00	0	0 00	—

* Speed restriction.   † Speed reduction by brakes leaking on slightly.

More concrete proposals soon began to emerge. History does not relate from whom the initiative came, but there is every reason to believe that Gresley was responsible; and fortunately he had a Chief General Manager and a Board of Directors who were anything but hidebound by conservatism, and were quite prepared to make any move which would enhance the prestige of the London & North Eastern Railway. Early in 1935, therefore, the decision was reached to build a steam-hauled streamline train, the first in Britain, which daily would bridge the 268·35 miles between London and Newcastle in 4 hours each way.

A second test trip therefore was planned for 5th March, 1935, on which the Kings Cross–Newcastle journey would be made in each direction non-stop in 4 hours. Whereas the London–Leeds test of the previous November had been made with an 'A1' Pacific, and 180-lb pressure, on this second run it was decided that the engine used should be a 220-lb 'A3'. No. 2750 *Papyrus* was the locomotive selected, and she was destined to have an extremely strenuous day. In the down direction, Driver Gutteridge and Fireman Wightman of Kings Cross shed would officiate; coming back, they would turn over the engine to the record-breaking Sparshatt-Webster combination. The load was six coaches, of 213 tons tare and 217 tons gross.

With recollections of the previous November's all but disastrous exit from No. 11 platform at Kings Cross, the authorities wisely switched the March special into No. 10, so that we had a reasonably straight start. Going down, Gutteridge did not allow the speed to exceed 88½ m.p.h. at any point; 80½ at Hatfield, 88½ at Three Counties, 86 at Tempsford, 81 at Tallington, 83¼ at Claypole, and 80 at both Gamston and Black Carr Junction, were the highest speeds south of Doncaster. Allowing for the heavier load, the uphill work probably equalled that of *Flying Scotsman* in the previous test, for from Essendine to Stoke speed remained steadily at between 75 and 77½ m.p.h. The running was an almost exact forecast of what would become a daily performance in the streamline era; Peterborough was passed in 63 min. 21 sec., Grantham in 87 min. 42 sec., Retford in 115 min. 18 sec., and Black Carr Junction, 153·2 miles, in 127 min. 39 sec.

Now came an unexpected incident. The approach to Doncaster was heralded by prolonged whistling, for signals were against us. Slowing down almost to walking pace, Gutteridge picked up a pilotman, who informed him that that morning a freight train had distributed itself over the track near Arksey, and that single line working was in force. At Moat Hills box (156·8 miles) we came to a dead stand, but fortunately for no more than 19 sec. From Arksey, passed at a walking pace, *Papyrus* did a fine bit of acceleration, getting up to 85 m.p.h. in no more than 8 miles of dead level track. As a result, we were through York in 165 min. 11 sec., just over a minute late. Two years later, the 'Coronation' was due to begin running to York every day in 157 minutes, with a load of no less than 325 tons against our 217 tons. Such is the march of time – and railway speed!

From York we bowled along happily over the Great Plain of York at between 79 and 85 m.p.h. all the way from Beningbrough to Northallerton, and after severe slowings past Browney Colliery, Durham and Lamesley, drew into the Central Station at Newcastle in 237 min. 7 sec. from London, 3 min. early; our net time had been 230 min. for the 268·35 miles. Here *Papyrus*, her crew and her passengers now had a rest of 2¾ hours before we started back; no decision had been reached in advance as to what engine would be used for the up journey, but our 'A3' was perfectly cool and in excellent running order, so it was decided that *Papyrus* should be used up as well as down. Prompt to time at 3.47 p.m. we started, with Sparshatt now in charge.

For Sparshatt, the going was distinctly leisurely as far as Ferryhill, to which point we lost 1¾ min., but then we were treated to some grand running; the next 55·4 miles, to Poppleton Junction, were reeled off in 41 min. 28 sec., with a sustained 80 to 88 m.p.h. for the 33 miles from Danby Wiske onwards. This took us through York in 72 min. 17 sec. from Newcastle (80·2 miles); continuing, we passed Shaftholme Junction, 108·15 miles, in 99 min. 3 sec., 4 minutes early. What of the derailed freighter? By now, fortunately, the up road was clear, though very cautious running was still needed past the site of the derailment; as a result, our gain had been all but wiped out as we passed Doncaster, once again on time.

From Doncaster to Grantham, Sparshatt was content to 'nurse' his engine in preparation for the record speed which it was certainly intended to attempt on the descent from Stoke. We ran well, keeping closely to booked point-to-point times, and so passing Grantham in 148 min. 42 sec. Now *Papyrus* was opened out. Up the long 1 in 200 to Stoke there was very little variation in speed, no more than from 71½ to 69 m.p.h. Down the far side we accelerated like a rocket; by Little Bytham we were well over the '100' line; and finally there came the 'peak' of 108.

This was no mere sudden spurt; for more than 2 miles I was reading 105 m.p.h. or over, and we averaged 105·4 m.p.h. from Little Bytham to Essendine and 100·6 on to Tallington; indeed, for 12·25 miles, from Corby to Tallington, our mean speed was 100·2 m.p.h. So we brought the Grantham–Peterborough time down to 21 min. (*plus* one second), gaining as much as 5 min. on the test schedule between these two points alone. To the recorders the thrill of such a flight, far faster than anything they had clocked before, may be imagined.

The engine stood it all magnificently, and seemed game to carry on indefinitely; from Peterborough to London the time was the fastest on record up to that date. The 76·35 miles to Kings Cross were run in 62 min. 6 sec., so that we stopped under the terminus roof in 231 min. 48 sec. from our Newcastle start. Of the tail end of the run the most remarkable feature was the time of 20 min. 17 sec. for the 26·95 miles from Huntingdon to Hitchin, largely uphill, with speed as high as 87 m.p.h. before Sandy; at the finish of the long in 200 climb, on passing Stevenage, we were doing 78 m.p.h.

What a day it had been! Our 'A3' Pacific had run 500 miles from Kings Cross to Croxdale (just south of Durham) and back in 423 min. 57 sec., or (allowing for the two Arksey delays) 412½ min. net, at an average of 72·7 m.p.h.

for the entire distance. Some 121 miles of the down journey and 179 miles of the up, 300 miles all told, had been covered at a mean rate of 80 m.p.h. Moreover, it had all been done on a coal consumption averaging no more than 43 lb to the mile. So, the two engine-crews and *Papyrus*, with the help of perfect control of the traffic over the whole length of the main line, proved that a 4-hour schedule was perfectly feasible. The stage had been set for the 'A4' Pacifics and for the streamline trains.

7 – The 'A4' Pacifics

IF ever a convincing proof were needed of my earlier contention that when Gresley designed a locomotive, it went straight out on to the line to take up, with complete success and reliability, the service for which he had evolved the design, it may be found in the *début* of his first streamlined 'A4' Pacific, No. 2509 *Silver Link*. Once again his drawing office staff had done their work thoroughly and well; all the necessary thinking and experimenting were over before the engine took the road; and this competence in design had been backed by first-class Doncaster workmanship.

For within three weeks of the emergence from Doncaster of No. 2509, the new engine had achieved by far the most dazzling feat of British railway speed up to that date, which will probably remain the British record for all time with steam power over a distance of more than 40 miles. Moreover, as no second engine of the class was ready, *Silver Link* three days later began to work the new streamline train, the 'Silver Jubilee', *in both directions daily*, five days a week, for the next fortnight without any relief – a duty which required the locomotive to make *two* 232-mile non-stop runs each day at a scheduled average speed of 70·4 m.p.h. from start to stop! To such a *première* as this British locomotive history finds no parallel whatever.

In the 'A4' Pacifics, Gresley had reached the crowning achievement of his distinguished career. Later, while on the one hand *Mallard* was to achieve a world speed record for steam by attaining a maximum speed of 126 m.p.h., other 'A4' Pacifics were to prove that the competence of the class was by no means confined to the haulage of lightweight streamline trains. Ultimately they were to be faced with such tasks as running the 'Flying Scotsman,' with a load of 550 tons and even more, over the 105·5 miles from Grantham to Kings Cross in 105½ min. every day. In the early stages of the Second World War *Silver Link* herself was to take from Kings Cross to Newcastle, un-assisted, a train of 25 bogie coaches, weighing with its crowded passenger complement fully 850 tons behind the tender.

And even up to 1960, years after Gresley's untimely death, and notwith-standing the efforts of his successors to 'improve' the master's work, if any Eastern Region engine has been needed for a major task, it is on a Gresley 'A4' that the choice has fallen. This was seen on the experimental high speed run from Kings Cross in May 1946, when it was not Thompson's rebuild of No. 4470 *Great Northern* that was selected, but No. 2512 *Silver Fox*. Again, in the extensive locomotive exchange trials of 1948, when the Eastern Region had available both the rebuilt *Great Northern* and the new 'A2' Pacific designs, Gresley 'A4' Pacifics, unaltered from the original 'A4' design in any respect other than Gresley's addition of the Kylchap exhaust and double chimney, were the engines chosen to uphold the reputation of the Eastern Region of British Railways.

We come now to the details of the 'A4' design. While the general layout, including wheelbase, motion details, boiler diameters, and so on, was identical with that of the 'A1' and 'A3' Pacifics, there were notable differences. Of these the most striking, of course, was appearance. Notwithstanding the successful trial with *Papyrus* on the proposed 4-hour schedule between London and Newcastle, Gresley realised that, to maintain such speeds in all weathers, a margin of power would be needed, and that any assistance which it was possible to give the engine, by reducing both internal and external resistance, would be of value. Streamlining both locomotive and train immediately suggested themselves as an aid in this direction, in view of the high continuous speeds contemplated; and such an addition would have publicity value also.

In the typical atmospheric conditions of these islands, it would be vitally necessary so to design the streamlining that when the locomotive was working at high speed, on a short cut-off, the smoke and exhaust steam would be lifted clear of the cab windows. Exhaustive wind tunnel experiments were carried out at the City and Guilds of London Engineering College, and resulted in the decision to build the front end of the locomotive in the form of a horizontal wedge. The original intention, as has been revealed by B. Spencer in his paper to the Institution of Locomotive Engineers, to which I have referred previously, was to provide a casing level on top from the chimney back to the cab. But the experiments showed that, while in a head wind this plan would work, in a side wind the increased wind pressure on the windward side of the boiler and the reduced pressure on the lee side would tend to draw the exhaust down and obscure the driver's view.

Additional trials led to the evolution of the now familiar rimless chimney, pear-shaped in plan, projecting well above the sloping smokebox front at the front corner, and then curved downwards to merge with the boiler top at the point of the pear. Further assistance in smoke-lifting was given by louvres in each side of the chimney. No modification of this arrangement has ever been needed, and it has proved completely effective in service at all speeds, except with the double-chimney 'A4s', mentioned later, which have given some trouble with drifting exhaust when running with short cut-offs.

Experiments next were conducted, at the National Physical Laboratory, with scale models of the proposed 'A4' and of an 'A3' Pacific, to determine of what value the streamline casing would be in overcoming air resistance at high speed. These showed a reduction of from 40 to 640 h.p., with the streamline casing, in the power output required to move the locomotive at speeds from 60 to 150 m.p.h. The 150 m.p.h. speed was to simulate the effect of a locomotive running at high speed into a strong headwind. The actual horsepower economies calculated from these experiments, in favour of the streamlining, were 41 h.p. at 60 m.p.h., 97 h.p. at 80 m.p.h., 138 h.p. at 90 m.p.h., 190 h.p. at 100 m.p.h., 253 h.p. at 110 m.p.h. and 639 h.p. at 150 m.p.h.

The streamlining therefore would mean an average saving of 100 h.p. continuously on a working such as that of the 'Silver Jubilee'. If internal engine resistance be included, and the resistance of the train (which worked out at an average of about 620 drawbar h.p. on the London–Newcastle journey), the 'A4' would have to put out an average of some 970 indicated h.p. as compared with the 1,070 h.p. of an 'A3'. As the average coal consumption of the 'A4' Pacifics on the 'Silver Jubilee' workings was found by experience to be 37·6 lb to the mile, the streamlining therefore was worth all but 4 lb of coal a mile, equivalent to 200 tons a year on this one train. Such a saving alone should justify any increased maintenance costs due to enclosure of the boiler and motion inside the streamline casing.

While the view of an 'A4' from the dead head-on position, with the flat face of the wedge front narrowing down to the buffer-beam, was the least attractive feature of the engine's appearance, the side elevation was one of the most beautiful and shapely examples of locomotive streamlining that the world has ever seen. With the bold upward curve of the smokebox and boiler top, merging into the pointed front of the cab, and the aerofoil curve above the cylinders and motion and their valance below, the engines have always looked as though they had been built for speed.

After Gresley's death, his successor, on the ground that the valances interfered with access to the motion, had them all cut away, through the whole series of the 'A4' Pacifics, and the engines have never looked quite so attractive since. As suggested in the previous paragraph, a penalty of streamlining is that the casing hides away much that must be seen in the course of day-to-day maintenance, so that a nice balance must be kept between what is gained in reduced resistance and enhanced appearance and what may be lost by the cost of stripping the casing in order to inspect what lies beneath.

Next we come to the internal modifications of the 'A3' design that were made in the 'A4'. Most important, of course, was the raising of the working pressure from 220 to 250 lb per sq in. In the boiler barrel, the distance between tubeplates was reduced from 19 to 18 ft, which increased the length of the firebox combustion chamber by 12 in. Very careful attention was paid to the size and shape of the steam and exhaust passages – a lesson that had been learned from the Chapelon researches in France – and care was taken, too, in the building of the engines to see that the interior of all these passages was left with a perfectly smooth surface, the aim being to give the steam as unrestricted a passage as possible from the regulator to its final ejection from the blast-pipe.

The fruit of such careful work is readily visible to any traveller on the footplate of an 'A4' who, with the help of the steam-chest pressure gauge that Gresley fitted to all these engines, will observe that when the regulator is fully opened, the steam-chest pressure and boiler pressure are almost identical. Practically none of the pressure has been lost by frictional resistance on the way down to the cylinders.

Next, and as a part result, no doubt, of experience with *Lemberg* – which, as noted in Chapter IV, had her cylinders lined up to $18\frac{1}{4}$ in. diameter when she was fitted with a 220 lb boiler in 1927, and thereafter became noted for her sustained high speed propensities – Gresley reduced the 19 in. cylinder diameter of the 'A3' engines to $18\frac{1}{2}$ in. in the 'A4'. The extra space so obtained permitted an increase in the piston-valve diameter from 8 in. to 9 in., so that a much better balance for maximum ease of steam-flow had been obtained between cylinders and valves. In tractive effort, the reduction in cylinder diameter was more than balanced by the increase in boiler pressure, and the 32,910 lb of the 'A3' thus was increased to 35,455 lb tractive effort in the 'A4'. The standard 'A3' valve-motion was fitted, with the usual conjugated arrangement for the middle valve, and maximum cut-off still limited to 65 per cent.

Another matter of great importance which came under consideration during the evolution of the 'A4' design was the stability of the engines at the high speeds contemplated with the streamline trains. It had been calculated that the centre of gravity of an 'A3' Pacific, in full running order, was 5 ft $11\frac{1}{4}$ in. above rail, and this was verified, with remarkable exactitude, in a test which was carried out at Doncaster Works with No. 2598 *Blenheim*. By seizing the engine with the works cranes, and tipping her up sideways, it was proved that the calculation was no more than   -in. out; in working order the centre of gravity was 5 ft $11\frac{3}{16}$ in. above the rail level, and empty 5ft $7\frac{7}{8}$ in. above. The centre-line of the 'A4' boiler, as with all the Gresley 2-6-2, 4-6-2 and 2-8-2 designs, was pitched 9 ft $4\frac{1}{2}$ in. above rail level.

It was also necessary to pay close attention to the way in which the 'A4' engines would hold the track at high speed. Originally the springs which control the lateral sliding movement of the bogie were designed to exert a force of 2 tons when first brought into action, and a maximum of $4\frac{1}{2}$ tons when the full lateral displacement of 4 in. was reached. But after the streamline trains had come into service, it was found that the flanges of the leading pair of coupled wheels were wearing more rapidly than those of the middle and trailing pair, and to correct this tendency the initial force of the bogie control springs was altered to 4 tons, and the maximum to 7 tons. At the same time an alteration was made to the slides controlling the action of the radial wheels at the rear end of the engine: to reduce their control, their inclination was modified from 1 in 7 to 1 in $10\frac{2}{3}$. The combined alteration was found to be effective.

In balancing his 'A4' engines, Gresley, as with all his three-cylinder locomotives, adopted a method which in some quarters has been criticised. With most designers it is customary to distribute the balance of the reciprocating masses of both inside and outside cylinders, up to something like 40 per cent of their weight, equally between all the coupled wheels. But Gresley, while increasing his outside cylinder balance to 60 per cent with the 'A1' Pacifics, provided balance for the inside cylinder on the driving wheels only. In the 'A4' Pacifics, however, the outside cylinder balance was reduced to the more normal 40 per cent, though inside cylinder balance still remained concentrated on the driving wheels.

In replying to the discussion following his paper on Gresley's locomotive designs, previously referred to, B. Spencer remarked that while this disproportion might result in the axle hammer-blow on the driving wheels being in a direction opposite to that from the leading and trailing coupled wheels, a considerable reduction was effected by this means in the whole engine hammer-blow. This arrangement had not resulted in excessive wear of crankpins or bushes, though those responsible for track maintenance might possibly complain of the excessive hammer-blow from individual axles, which could have an adverse effect on the rail-bearers and cross-girders of bridges.

To ensure smooth riding of the 'A4' Pacifics at speed, Gresley increased the distance between the hangers of the laminated springs of the driving wheels from 3 ft 6 in. to 4 ft, and their potential deflection – the measure of their flexibility – from 0·135 in. to 0·270 in. per ton of imposed weight. The flexibility, that is to say, was doubled. It would be generally agreed that the riding qualities of an 'A4' at speed are superb.

After having experimented in the matter with 'A1' Pacific No. 4473 *Solario*, Gresley decided to fit the spacious cabs of the 'A4s' with bucket seats for the crew, facing forwards in such a position that there would be an excellent look-out ahead from the sitting position. Though common enough in the United States, the provision of seats in the cab was a novelty for Great Britain. For accurate observance of speed restrictions, each engine was provided with a Flaman speed indicator of the self-recording type, containing a moving tape on which the speed of the journey was recorded continuously, so keeping the speed round curves and past other speed-restricted points under official observation. The only convenient location for this bulky fitting was under the fireman's seat, where, however, the speed dial was easily visible to the driver. The cab itself was of a 'wind-cutter' type, with pointed front, better adapted to aid in reducing air resistance than the flat-fronted cab of an 'A1' or 'A3'.

As with Gresley's 'P2' 2-8-2 locomotives, the only possible location for the whistle was ahead of the chimney – an interesting detail which, with the bucket seats for the crew, attracted much closer attention from the Press than any parts of the engine more intimately concerned with its ability to move a load at high speed. A chime whistle was fitted, and its beautiful tone contrasted strongly with the high-pitched note of the standard L.N.E.R. whistle. The whistle also derived from the 'P2' 2-8-2s, and resulted from a visit paid by Gresley to his friend Captain Howey and to the latter's Romney, Hythe & Dymchurch Railway. Sir Nigel was so impressed with two standard Canadian Pacific whistles about to be fitted to the model C.P.R. Pacifics *Dr Syn* and *Black Prince* that Howey presented him with one of them, to be used on one of the new L.N.E.R. 2-8-2 engines. The 'A4' whistles were a more melodious version of this type. In addition, one of the later 'A4s', No. 4489 *Dominion of Canada*, was presented by the Canadian Pacific Railway with a standard bell, which was mounted on her sloping front below the chimney.

Lastly, it was necessary to ensure adequate brake-power for high speed running. As compared with the 'A3' Pacifics, therefore, Gresley increased the brake-power of the 'A4' engines from 66 to 93 per cent of the adhesion weight, and on the tender from 53 to 62 per cent of the weight in full running order. Nevertheless, even this modification was not sufficient to cope with the problem of pulling the 'Silver Jubilee' up from a full 90 m.p.h. to a dead stand between any two of the two-aspect colour-light signals on the North Eastern Area north of York, and this fact was responsible, indirectly, for the amazing speed of the 'Silver Jubilee' trial trip which is described in the next chapter. Still more interesting, in the same connection, is the fact that it was a series of brake trials, in the year 1938, arranged to test out a quick-acting brake system which would give further protection to high speed trains, that gave the opportunity for *Mallard*'s world record speed of 126 m.p.h.

The engine last-mentioned was one of the only five Pacifics to which Gresley fitted the Kylchap exhaust, with its double blast-pipe and double chimney. As described in Section 4 of this chapter, the experiments were first made with 'A3' Pacific No. 2751 *Humorist*. No. 4468 *Mallard* was the first 'A4' Pacific to be built with the double chimney, and was followed by the last three of the thirty-five 'A4' Pacifics that Gresley built – Nos. 4901 *Capercaillie* (later renamed *Sir Charles Newton*), 4902 *Seagull* and 4903 *Peregrine* (later renamed *Lord Faringdon*). The three engines concerned are now Nos. 60005, 60033 and 60034 in the British Railways stock, and *Mallard* has become No. 60022.

Apart from *Mallard*'s epoch-making feat of speed, it is significant that in the 1948 locomotive exchange trials, out of all the 'A4' Pacifics available, the double-chimney Nos. 60022, 60033 and 60034 were the three selected to represent the Eastern Region. Indeed, the performance of the double-chimney engines always has been so markedly superior to that of the remaining 'A4s' as to excite surprise that more than twenty years elapsed before any attempt was made to equip any of the earlier 'A4' engines with this valuable aid to freedom of exhaust and improved draught.

A year after the 'Silver Jubilee' had entered service, in view of the highly successful working of the 'A4' engines the building of fourteen more of this type was put in hand, and the first of them, No. 4482 *Golden Eagle* and No. 4483 *Kingfisher*, appeared late in 1936. A certain number of these would be needed for the additional streamlined trains between London and Edinburgh and London and the West Riding of Yorkshire, as described in the next chapter, but it was also intended to use the engines interchangeably with the 'A1' and 'A3' Pacifics on the principal non-streamlined main line services. Eventually the order was increased, and from 1936 to 1938 thirty-one additional 'A4s' were turned out of Doncaster Works, bringing the total up to thirty-five.

The numbering was on curiously casual lines. Following on the original 'Silver Jubilee' engines, Nos. 2509 to 2512 inclusive, came Nos. 4482 to 4498. But before Nos. 4499 and 4500 were built, Nos. 4462 to 4469 were interposed; and finally there came another short series, completely isolated in numbers, from 4900 to 4903 inclusive. This was in accordance with L.N.E.R. numbering practice at that time, however, blocks of numbers being allocated as they became available when new engines were under construction, in sequence only when sequence was possible without re-numbering existing engines.

When No. 4498 had been completed, at the end of 1937, the one-hundredth Gresley Pacific had come into being. By the express desire of the directors, this auspicious occasion was signalised by naming the engine *Sir Nigei Gresley* – a well-deserved tribute to the fine work that this distinguished engineer had done for his company, and a recognition of the high level to which his designing enterprise had raised London & North Eastern prestige. The naming ceremony took place at Marylebone terminus on 26th November, 1937. It is not inappropriate that No. 4498 has always been one of the most capable performers of the entire 'A4' series.

The building of the last 'A4' in 1938, No. 4903 *Peregrine*, later renamed *Lord Faringdon*, completed the list of the Gresley Pacifics built during the designer's lifetime, 114 all told. Of these all are still in active service with one exception, 'A4' No. 4469. This engine, first named *Gadwall* and then renamed *Sir Ralph Wedgwood*, was unfortunate enough to catch the full force of a German bomb at York on the night of 29th April, 1942, and was so badly damaged as to be incapable of repair. The remains of the engine were therefore broken up, and the name was transferred to No. 4466, which until then had been *Herring Gull*.

Having recalled the introduction of the 'A4' Pacifics, and examined in detail the design, we must now review some of the outstanding performances of these remarkable engines, more especially on the trial runs which preceded the introduction of the streamline trains, as well as the average quality of performance demanded by these high speed schedules.

8 – The 'Silver Jubilee'

27TH SEPTEMBER, 1935, is a day which will remain firmly imprinted on my memory for as long as I live. The new 'Silver Jubilee', Britain's first stream-line train, was to make her first public appearance. Three days before the streamliner entered regular service, on 30th September, a special run to Grantham and back had been arranged, to which a large and representative company, including L.N.E.R. directors and officers, their numerous guests, and the representatives of the Press, had been invited. To me fell the task of taking the official times of the run, and I little realised what a responsibility was to fall on my shoulders!

Round about 2 p.m. we assembled on No. 6 platform at Kings Cross, where the new train was drawn up, the cynosure of all eyes. Nothing like this startling vision of silver grey and stainless steel had ever been seen on British rails before. Three articulated sets made up the formation – a triplet restaurant car set in the centre, flanked by third and first-class brake 'twins', with the first class at the rear. Flush windows and coach panelling, with the valances extending down between the bogies and flexible sheets joining coach-end to coach-end, provided a completely smooth surface from one end of the train to the other. At the head stood *Silver Link*, with her striking wedge front and revolutionary outline.

As the scheduled departure time of 2.25 approached, we took our places in the train. Directors and their friends withdrew to the seclusion of the first class at the rear, where they were destined to appreciate to the full all the extreme possibilities of 'tail swing' at high speed. I ensconced myself in a facing corner of a compartment in the leading third class brake, where I hoped to be able to work without disturbance. On the engine were Driver Arthur Taylor and Fireman Luty, who were about to make locomotive history. Accompanying them was Mr I. S. W. Groom, Locomotive Running Superintendent of the Southern Area.

Prompt to time at 2.25 we started, amid the cheers of an enormous crowd assembled on No. 10 platform. At this stage it should be remarked that although the point-to-point times of the schedule laid down for the special were those calculated for the regular 'Silver Jubilee' working from the following Monday, it was the intention to use the trial trip for the purpose of ascertaining what power the engine had in reserve. As mentioned in the previous chapter, at the last minute it had been realised that the brake-power of engine and train was insufficient to pull the 'Silver Jubilee' up from 90 m.p.h. to a dead stop between any one of the North Eastern Area colour-light signals north of York and the next, should the line not be clear. For this reason it would now be necessary to restrict the maximum speed between York and Darlington to 70 m.p.h., and to cut the schedule south of York in order to compensate for the minutes lost in this way. So *Silver Link* was to be 'given her head' on this run.

It was not long before the effect of this decision became apparent. By Wood Green we were up to 70 m.p.h., and from there, instead of dropping in speed up the long 1 in 200 to Potters Bar, the engine accelerated steadily with her 230-ton load, until we topped the summit at 75! Then, accelerating like lightning past Marsh Moor and Red Hall, we added another 20 to sweep through Hatfield at all but 95, and touched 98 at the point where the railway crosses the River Lea.

It was at the London end of Hatfield down platform, over a trailing connection from a siding, that there came the first of a series of alarming shocks that were to make this journey one of the most unnerving of my life. Gresley had devised a special system of suspension for his new stock which would cause the coach-bodies to 'float' at high speed, but, like the bogie side-control springs of the locomotive, the springs controlling lateral movement of the coach bogies also were inadequate in compression. So when, for track reasons explained in the next paragraph, centrifugal force caused the coach-bodies to make a lateral movement of any amplitude, the effect was suddenly to compress these springs to the limit, imparting a jerk to the coach-body that at times was quite unnerving. The Press representatives regarded these sensations, no doubt, as a satisfying proof that we were travelling fast; but on those of us 'in the know' the effect was rather different!

The track conditions to which I have referred were these. It would not be disputed that maintenance of the old Great Northern main line in general was of a high standard. But so far as this new service was concerned, it can hardly be claimed that *liaison* between the Mechanical, Operating and Civil Engineering Departments had been of the best. Both from the experimental runs of the previous November and March and from the schedule laid down for the 'Silver Jubilee', it must have been obvious to the civil engineering authorities what speeds would be necessary to keep time. Yet little or nothing had been done to adapt the track to regular speeds far higher than ever contemplated previously.

In general, the curves were canted for a maximum speed of 70 m.p.h., and were reasonably comfortable at 80 to 85, which until then was rarely exceeded. The 'transitioning' of curves – that is, the laying in of a spiral entry and exit, with a gradual working up of the cant to its full figure, in place of the previous direct tangenting – was in but an early stage of development. Thus the most violent shocks that we experienced on this hectic journey were from curves over which the cant was deficient at such speeds, or, through lack of transition, was too suddenly attained or lost. In this way we suffered two tremendous 'biffs' through Hatfield, one at the station and another at a curve a little later on; the engine then tore up the 1 in 200 to Woolmer Green as though it were not there, giving us another violent shake-up as we passed at 88 m.p.h. over a curve later restricted to 70. Apparently the riding of *Silver Link* herself was admirable, and those on the engine had not the slightest idea of the sensations to which they were subjecting their passengers! But the major excitements were yet to come.

It was at the 30th milepost that the speed first crossed the '100' line. From then onwards, for 25 miles on end, *Silver Link* blazed away at this enormous speed and more. To the crowd of watchers on Hitchin platforms it must have been the sight of a lifetime as we hurled ourselves through the station at 107. By Arlesey we were up to 112½; and from here onwards the engine was demonstrating her ability to keep up a steady 105 or so on little easier than level track. Indeed, at St Neots, after climbing 3¾ miles at 1 in 330 (with a short downhill break in the middle of it) we were still doing 104½ an hour!

By now there had drifted into my compartment Sir Nigel himself, completely imperturbable, armed with a chronograph watch of vast dimensions which he had had made specially for speed recording purposes. He sat down next to me, and beyond him Chas. J. Brown, Chief Civil Engineer, under whom I was serving at that time; the latter was a nervous man, and his face betrayed the fact by being some shades paler than normally. On the opposite seat sat Randolph Churchill, collecting impressions of the run for the *Daily Mail*, and in search of some facts about the speed. With every fresh lurch of our coach, the Chief Mechanical Engineer directed shafts of wit at the Chief Civil Engineer concerning the condition of the latter's track, not altogether appreciated by the recipient!

Between deference to these distinguished visitors, anxiety to concentrate on the all-important business of recording accurately the run of a century, and speculation as to whether, at all but 110 m.p.h., some one-and-one-eighth of

TABLE III (B)
L.N.E.R. KINGS CROSS–PETERBOROUGH
The 'Silver Jubilee' Trial Trip
27th September, 1935
Engine: 'A4' 4-6-2 No. 2509 *Silver Link*
Load: 220 tons tare, 230 tons full

Dist.		Sched.	Actual	Speeds
miles		min.	min. sec.	m.p.h.
0·00	KINGS CROSS .	0	0 00	—
2·50	Finsbury Park . .	—	4 42	—
4·95	Wood Green . .	—	7 11	70
9·15	New Barnet . .	—	10 43	72
12·70	Potters Bar . .	—	13 36	75
17·70	HATFIELD . .	18½	17 07	94½
20·30	Welwyn Garden City	—	18 46	98
23·50	Woolmer Green . .	—	20 52	88
25·05	Knebworth . .	—	21 55	‡93½
28·55	Stevenage . .	—	24 13	90
30·00	Milepost 30 . .	—	25 06	100
31·90	HITCHIN . .	29½	26 14	107
37·10	Arlesey . . .	—	29 03	112½
41·15	Biggleswade . .	—	31 22	§105
44·15	Sandy . . .	—	32 59	112½
47·50	Tempsford . .	—	34 50	109½
51·75	St Neots . . .	—	37 13	104½
55·00	Milepost 55 . .	—	39 03	109½
55·95	Offord . . .	—	39 41	*85
58·85	HUNTINGDON .	48½	41 41	88
62·00	Milepost 62 . .	—	43 53	83½
63·50	Abbots Ripton .	—	44 58	—
69·35	Holme . . .	—	48 50	93½
72·60	Yaxley . . .	—	51 08	80½
75·00	Fletton Junction .	—	52 55	—
76·35	PETERBOROUGH .	†63½	†55 02	*20

* Speed restriction.   † Passing time.
‡ At Langley Junction.   § At Langford.

an inch of steel flange would suffice to hold us to the rails on the Offord curves, now dead ahead, or whether we should dive straight into the River Ouse, the state of the recorder's mind can be better imagined than described!

However, Driver Taylor showed sufficient regard for Offord to touch down to 85, over curves later restricted to a maximum of 70! By now the most staggering part of the journey was over. Shall we ever repeat such times, I wonder, as 9 min. 7 sec. from Hatfield to Hitchin or 15 min. 17 sec. over the 27·0 miles from Hitchin to Huntingdon? From Hatfield to Huntingdon, 41·15 miles, we had averaged 100·5 m.p.h. throughout; between mileposts 30 and 55, where the speed had never fallen below 100, the average had been 107·5 m.p.h. and for 43 miles on end an average of 100 m.p.h. had been kept up. So it was that *Silver Link* rolled under the footbridge at the centre of Peterborough North station *fifty-five minutes after leaving Kings Cross* (*plus a paltry two seconds*)!

Having recovered from a 20 m.p.h. slack through Peterborough to 83 m.p.h. again by Essendine, we stood a good chance of reaching Grantham in 80 min. from London, but adverse signals were now sighted. We had caught up the 1.40 p.m. Harrogate express, which had left 45 min. ahead of us! Finally, we stopped at Grantham in 88 min. 15 sec. from Kings Cross. The excitement was over; although there was some very fast running in places, including a time of 20 min. 12 sec. for the 26·95 miles from Huntingdon to Hitchin, and a top speed of 94 m.p.h. at Tempsford, nothing of the extreme order of the down run was attempted on the way back.

After this, Gresley lost no time in modifying the spring suspension of the stock, and the Chief Civil Engineer at last took a revision of the track levels seriously in hand, laying down numerous slight speed restrictions – 70 or 80 m.p.h. – at points where the track could not be improved sufficiently to permit a maximum of 90 m.p.h.

With this attention the riding of the 'Silver Jubilee' soon settled down to something quite reasonably steady. 'Nevertheless,' as I wrote later in *British Locomotive Practice and Performance*, 'this and the other L.N.E.R. streamliners always had their exciting moments, especially when they were newly out of the shops after overhaul and particularly lively on their springing in consequence. Removal by the staff of the vases of flowers from the restaurant car tables, as the "Jubilee" forged its way through the tunnels from Kings Cross, was on such occasions a solemn ritual resembling the ceremony of putting the fiddles on the dining saloon tables at sea. Yet, as we pursued our uneasy course through dinner, the only nonchalant comment from Tees-side or Tyneside *habitués* in the opposite pew – for the ever-popular "Silver Bullet" as they called it, always had the atmosphere, at its first-class end, of a travelling club – would be "It's a rough night tonight", or words to that effect, and their appetites would not appear to be in the least impaired.' Generally, however, one could depend on a smooth and comfortable trip, though certain specific points, such as Shaftholme Junction, had their special liveliness which was better in retrospect than in prospect!

Seldom, if ever, before has a train swung into such immediate popularity as the 'Silver Jubilee'. From the very start it ran filled to capacity day after day, and passengers who had not booked their seats well in advance stood the risk of not getting on the streamliner at all. North East Coast business men appreciated to the full the advantage of being able to go to their offices and see their letters, then board the train at Newcastle at 10 a.m., or its connection from Middlesbrough at the same hour, be whisked into Kings Cross by 2 p.m. for an afternoon engagement in the capital, start back after 3½ hours at 5.30 p.m., and be in their home stations once again by 9.30 p.m. Moreover, these times could be relied on, for despite the almost entire novelty of a schedule at such speeds, keen engine-crews took to the idea at once, and timekeeping was exemplary.

Between Kings Cross and Darlington the allowance in each direction for the 232·25 miles was 198 min. Some of the point-to-point timings were extremely fast, in particular the 19 min. allowed for the 26·95 miles from Hitchin to Huntingdon, which demanded an *average* speed of 85·3 m.p.h. over this length. On the down journey the 'Jubilee' was booked through

Peterborough, 76·35 miles, in 63½ min, Grantham, 105·45 miles, in 87½ min., and York, 188·15 miles, in 157½ min. Later on, these times were slightly eased, after the substitution of three-aspect for two-aspect colour-light signalling north of York had made it possible to increase the maximum speed over that magnificent racing-ground from 70 to the normal 90 m.p.h. of the remainder of the route.

In view of the cut of over an hour in the best previous times between London and Newcastle, a small supplementary fare of 5s first class and 3s third class was exacted for the privilege of using the train, but it was soon demonstrated that the public had no objection whatever to paying on this modest scale for the privilege of high speed. The 'Silver Jubilee' regularly was earning gross receipts of about 14s a mile, every day that it ran, and in two years the supplements alone paid the entire cost of building the rolling stock.

Moreover, so far from high speed in itself being dangerous – notwithstanding the terrifying discomforts of the trial trip! – during the four years that the 'Silver Jubilee' ran, up to the outbreak of war in 1939, it was never involved in any major mishap. Indeed, between 30th September, 1935, and 9th October, 1937, the 'Silver Jubilee' set of coaches covered in all 277,370 miles, of which 230,200 miles were at a booked average of 70·4 m.p.h., and 162,030 miles at 75 m.p.h., and once only during this period was the train held up by a hot box. Saturdays and Sundays, with the Christmas and Easter holiday periods, gave ample time for maintenance; but even so, this was a very fine record. As previously mentioned, the speed 'ceiling' was fixed at 90 m.p.h., and in normal running, with the watchdog provided by the Flaman speed indicators and their continuous recording tapes, drivers seldom much exceeded these figures. But every now and again one would clock a '100', especially if the speed indicator happened to be out of order, and there was a speed merchant at the front end!

The second of the streamlined 4-6-2s, No. 2510 *Quicksilver*, was not ready to take a share in the working of the 'Silver Jubilee' until the third week after the service had started. There soon followed No. 2511 *Silver King* and No. 2512 *Silver Fox*. The last-mentioned was presented by the United Steel Companies with stainless steel representations of a fox in full flight, made at their Samuel Fox steelworks at Stocksbridge, which were fixed to both sides of the boiler casing, as well as stainless steel clothing bands and hand-rails to the boiler.

Silver King was stationed at Gateshead as a reserve engine, and spent most of her time running between Newcastle and Edinburgh. At weekends, when the 'Silver Jubilee' did not run on Saturdays and Sundays, the other three 'A4s' soon began to be drafted to heavy regular workings, such as the 'Flying Scotsman', and so to prove a measure of competence in such service no whit inferior to their work on the high speed lightweight train.

Precisely eleven months after the historic 'Silver Jubilee' trial trip, on 27th August, 1936, it was decided to make a run from Newcastle to Kings Cross with the dynamometer car added to the seven-car 'Jubilee' set. This brought the weight for the first time up to 254 tare tons, or 270 tons including the passenger complement. It was the official intention to do something out of the ordinary down the long descent southwards from Stoke, and representatives of *The Times* and other papers were invited to be in attendance at Kings Cross on our arrival in order to obtain 'hot news' of what had happened. I was permitted to join the staff in the dynamometer car, and this was another occasion that I am never likely to forget.

The train ran normally as far as Grantham. The driver was Haygreen of Kings Cross, and his work at the regulator was not very impressive; there was very little of the full regulator, and much of the engine's work was being done with 130 to 180 lb pressure in the steam-chest out of the rated 250 lb. Even up the hills the regulator was not opened more than to give 200 to 220 lb or so at the pistons.

At last, at Grantham, the regulator was opened to full. But now the boiler pressure itself was only 215 to 225 lb, so that with 25 per cent cut-off we fell from $71\frac{1}{2}$ to $68\frac{1}{2}$ m.p.h. on the 1 in 200 up to Stoke. Once over the summit Haygreen notched up to 15 per cent, but then had gradually to open out to 25, 30, and finally 35 per cent to reach the 113 m.p.h. which eventually was touched, not on the 1 in 200 past Little Bytham, where speed had flattened out to 106, but on the easier strips of level and 1 in 264 down after Essendine. Had the boiler pressure been up to the full 250 lb at Stoke, we could have reached the same speed and more without having to flog the engine to an extent that was to have unfortunate results.

It was after we had passed Peterborough that a very slight periodic irregularity began to show itself in the drawbar pull curve on the dynamometer car roll. Nothing untoward happened, however, until we had roared through Hatfield at about 85 m.p.h.; to this point we had taken 177 min. 52 sec. for the 214·55 miles from Darlington, and were about 4 min. ahead of time. Suddenly a rain of fragments hit the underside of the dynamometer car, with little doubt stone ballast thrown up by something which had dropped from the engine. Speed began to fall, and an anxious colloquy as to what had happened started over the 'inter-com' between car and footplate, punctuated by one or two further bombardments from below.

Nevertheless it was decided to proceed; and the next 24 min. were among the most nerve-racking that several of us at the front end had ever spent. Speed gradually dropped; there had been a sharp reduction at Brookman's Park, and for most of the distance down from Potters Bar we ran without steam. It had to be put on again to get into the platform at Kings Cross, and with *Silver Fox* roaring like a wounded bull, and steam shooting straight out at the front end, we dragged our way up the platform finally to come to rest a bare 7 min. late.

It was found that the middle big-end bearing metal had melted; the big-end itself, with additional play, had disintegrated completely; both cylinder-ends had been pushed off; and it is a miracle indeed that we escaped a much more serious casualty, if not disaster. A train-load of passengers, some of them taking lunch at the time, had been moved at the highest speed ever attained by a British passenger train in ordinary service – a record which still holds – but we had had a reminder that very high speeds are not unattended by risk.

Notwithstanding these excitements, it was decided to carry on with the return dynamometer trip that day as planned, and for this *Silver Link* was assigned, in charge of Bill Sparshatt. Our late friend had been solemnly warned that there were to be no fireworks, and his observance, whether of the overriding speed limit of 90 m.p.h. south of York and 70 m.p.h. beyond, or of all service slacks, was meticulous in the extreme. But the engine was handled to perfection, and inclusive of all slacks he ran the 160·3 miles from Potters Bar to Brayton Junction, Selby, at an average of 77·2 m.p.h.

From the start the full 65 per cent cut-off was in use, reduced to 45 per cent by Holloway and 25 per cent at Finsbury Park, which Sparshatt continued to use as far as Potters Bar, as steam pressure was down to 205 lb along this stage. After that 18 per cent was the cut-off generally in use, and at this figure, with full regulator, and a pressure of 230–235 lb in the steam-chest when the boiler pressure was at 235–240 lb – again a tribute to the design and layout of the steam passages – the uphill work was grand, especially when we attained 90 m.p.h. with 270 tons up the 1 in 440 beyond Tallington, climbed 1¾ miles at 1 in 264 at a minimum of 86½, reached 88 again on the easier stretch beyond, mounted 4½ miles of 1 in 200 at a minimum of 78½, and finally, after re-attaining 80½ on the easy 1½ miles past Corby, carried the final 3 miles at 1 in 178 by storm at a minimum of 75 m.p.h. This gave us the fine average of 82·4 m.p.h. with 270 tons of train, for the whole of the 15·25 miles from Tallington up to Stoke. Times and speeds of this run as far as York are set out in detail in Table III(C), Section 10. Finally we reached Darlington in 194 min. 43 sec. from London (232·25 miles), and Newcastle 4 min. early at 9.26 p.m., another feather in the cap of *Silver Link*, pioneer engine of the 'A4' series.

9 – 126 *Miles per Hour*

STREAMLINE service having proved so extremely popular with the public, the London & North Eastern management, probably not without stimulus from Gresley, began to look around for fresh fields to conquer. Just as the 'Silver Jubilee' had been so named in order to commemorate the fruitful twenty-five years of the reign of King George V, it was decided to mark the year of coronation of King George VI by the introduction of a second stream-line train called 'Coronation'. This would run at such a time as to provide Tyneside with an evening flight to London in addition to the morning 'Silver Jubilee'. But the main purpose was to bring the capitals of England and Scotland, London and Edinburgh, within the unprecedented time of 6 hours of one another daily, and, moreover, to give patrons of the train up to the late afternoon of the day – 4 p.m. in London and 4.30 p.m. in Edinburgh – before having to start their journeys.

The working of the 'Silver Jubilee' had provided all the information needed for the London–Newcastle stage of the run. To obtain some useful data for the Newcastle–Edinburgh stage, a special train of 252 tons' weight, dynamometer car included, was run from Newcastle to Edinburgh and back on Saturday, 26th September, 1936, with 'A4' 4-6-2 No. 2511 *Silver King*. Driver Dron made the northbound run of 124·5 miles in 118 minutes and the return journey in 114 minutes. On the southbound trip a grand effort was the ascent of the 4 miles at 1 in 96 of Cockburnspath bank, which was topped at the remarkable speed of 68 m.p.h. This required a drawbar h.p. of 1,460 and an indicated h.p. of between 2,500 and 2,600. The latter, of course, was a calculated figure, for because of the streamlined casing it has never yet been possible to indicate an 'A4' locomotive.

The inauguration of the 'Coronation' service was timed for July, 1937. Five of the latest 'A4' Pacifics were assigned to the 'Coronation' train – Nos. 4488 *Union of South Africa*, 4489 *Dominion of Canada*, 4490 *Empire of India*, 4491 *Commonwealth of Australia*, and 4492 *Dominion of New Zealand* – and these were painted in a beautiful shade of Garter blue, later to become the standard for the entire 'A4' series, with stainless steel numbers, letters and mouldings. Nos. 4488 and 4489 at first were named *Osprey* and *Woodcock* respectively, before the 'Dominion' series of names was decided on. No. 4489 appeared in grey, but was painted blue a few weeks later when renamed.

When the two new 'Coronation' trains appeared, competent observers were astonished indeed at the task which Gresley proposed to set his 'A4' Pacifics in hauling them. For whereas he had restricted the weight of the 'Silver Jubilee' to a seven-coach formation of 220 tare tons, the 'Coronation' sets were of nine vehicles each, four twin articulated sets with an observation car of novel design at the rear end. Apart from the two additional vehicles, the provision of two separate kitchen cars and of electrically-operated pressure ventilation throughout each train helped to put the total tare load up to 312 tons – 42 per cent more than that of the 'Silver Jubilee.' Moreover, the 'Coronation' was to be worked to York, 188·15 miles from Kings Cross, in no more than 157 minutes, at an average of 71·9 m.p.h. – the fastest schedule to appear in any British time-table up to that date.

At first York was the only stop on the down journey, but Newcastle was too important to be omitted, and later on a stop at Newcastle was made also, so that the run of 392·8 miles between Kings Cross and Edinburgh had to be completed in 6 hours with two intermediate stops of 3 min. duration each. In the up direction Newcastle was the only halt, and the 268·25 miles from there to London were run non-stop in 3 hours, 57 min. In both directions, as was the general custom in those days, the work exacted of the engines south of York was considerably harder than that over the North Eastern Area – a curious reversal of the practice of both earlier and later years – so that in the event of any time being dropped to York going north, there was a good chance of recovering it before Edinburgh.

Not so coming south, however; and there were one or two days at least of bad weather conditions when the entire contents of the coal bunker had disappeared from the tender of the Pacific working the up 'Coronation' well before the end of the journey, so making necessary a stop at Hitchin for help. This was partly due to the original tender coverings of the streamlined engines; while at Kings Cross shed care was taken to pack the coal into the corners under the coverings, Haymarket shed used to drop the coal on to the tenders from above, in the ordinary way, and as a result the engines might leave Edinburgh for the south without the coal space being filled to capacity. But after the unfortunate casualty at Wiske Moor, north of Northallerton, when an inspector riding on the footplate with the southbound 'Coronation' was killed because of the rush of water that came over the tender top when the two streamliners met at speed on Wiske Moor troughs, the tender coverings were removed, and there was no difficulty after that in ensuring that the engines had a full coal supply.

Nevertheless, as with the 'Silver Jubilee', the reliability of the 'A4' Pacifics, even on so onerous an assignment as this, was exceptional. From the inauguration of the 'Coronation' service, *Commonwealth of Australia* worked either the down or up train for 48 out of the first 51 days – that is, for all but three days of the first ten weeks – just as *Dominion of New Zealand* worked the non-stop 'Flying Scotsman' on 52 out of the first 54 days of its running after the schedule had been pared to 7 hours. On the 'Coronation' workings the average coal consumption between London and Edinburgh, in normal conditions, worked out at about 43 lb per mile, as compared with the $37\frac{1}{2}$ lb of the 'Silver Jubilee.' But the disproportion in the power demand north and south of York must have involved the engines in a considerably higher rate of consumption on the Kings Cross–York stage of their journeys than over the remainder.

The two 'Coronation' observation cars were interesting vehicles. At the rear end, each of them reversed the locomotive wedge front by being built in the form of a 'beaver tail' – a fine piece of coach-building craftsmanship. The idea, of course, was to reduce the rear-end resistance caused by the square end of an ordinary tail-coach creating a vacuum behind it as it moves through the atmosphere at high speed. So marshalled, the 'Coronation' trains were a perfect example of complete streamlining from head to tail – wedge-fronted locomotive with aerofoil curves and valances over the motion, and wedge-fronted cab; coaches with flush windows and side panels, with rubber sheeting joining coach to coach; and beaver tail.

During the first winter the 'Coronation' ran, however, it was realised that with starts from the two terminals as late as 4.0 and 4.30 p.m. the opportunities of 'observation' from the rear end were negligible, as nearly all the journey was being made in darkness, and the tail cars therefore were withdrawn during the winter months. By reducing the tare load to 279 tons, this gave the locomotives some welcome relief to compensate for the adverse effects of winter weather conditions. On the other hand, experience with the relatively heavy 'Coronation' formations decided Gresley to agree to provide an additional coach on the 'Silver Jubilee', which invariably ran filled to capacity. So the leading brake third 'twin' of the latter was rebuilt as a 'triplet,' bringing the number of vehicles up to eight, and the tare weight to 248 tons.

As previously with the 'Silver Jubilee,' the inauguration of the 'Coronation' service was preceded by Press trip, which took place on 30th June. Nothing like the *tour de force* of the 'Silver Jubilee' trial was attempted on the down journey; indeed, it is doubtful if such times would have been even possible with the much increased load. *Dominion of Canada* was the engine, and Driver Burfoot stuck closely to his schedule all the way to Grantham; we were a minute late through Hatfield (19 min. 29 sec.), but ¾-min. ahead at Peterborough (62 min. 50 sec.) and passed Grantham almost on the stroke of the 87½ min. allowed (87 min. 34 sec.), reaching Barkston North, 111·1 miles (where the train was to be turned round the Barkston triangle) in 93 min. 29 sec.

But on the return journey it was decided once again to whip one of the Pacifics up to a 100 m.p.h. speed. There was some incentive, moreover, as on the previous day the London Midland & Scottish Railway claimed to have wrested the speed supremacy from the London & North Eastern by touching 114 m.p.h. in the test run with their new 'Coronation Scot' on the descent from Whitmore to Crewe, though with 270 tons of train only as compared with our 320 tons. So Burfoot started *Dominion of Canada* away from Barkston with such vigour that by Grantham we were already doing 66 m.p.h., and accelerated further to 69 up the 1 in 200 to Stoke.

Then came the lightning speed down towards Peterborough to which these various tests were by now making us almost accustomed – 86½ m.p.h. by Corby, and in succession from milepost 97, miles at 90·0, 92·3, 97·3, 100·0, 102·9, 107·5 and 109·1 m.p.h. (posts 91 to 90), after which speed tailed away to 101·5 and 94·7 m.p.h. over the next two miles. The actual maximum was 109½ m.p.h., so we had failed to reach the L.M.S.R. figure by 4½ m.p.h., or even to equal the previous L.N.E.R. figure. It was a cause of acute disappointment at Doncaster that the L.M.S.R. remained unbeaten, but subsequent experience of No. 4489 showed that her performance did not equal that of the rest of the batch, so that an unhappy choice of engine had been made on this occasion. Nevertheless, in the load conditions, the failure was quite an honourable one. From Grantham to Peterborough the 29·1 miles took 20 min. 53 sec. After that we were content to stick to schedule, and ran from Grantham to Kings Cross in 86 min. 3 sec., as compared with our allowance of 86½ min.

On the following Monday I was asked to accompany the first regular down run of the 'Coronation,' to take times for publicity purposes. *Commonwealth of Australia* was our engine, and with a full complement of passengers the gross load was about 330 tons. I have vivid recollections of this trip also. The Chief Engineer of the Southern Area was a passenger, and from time to time he would rise solemnly from his pew in another part of the car to ascertain from me to what extent our driver was exceeding the precise speed limits which the Engineer's Department had now laid down.

Certainly we had some lively moments—Hatfield at 86½ m.p.h., an acceleration to 90 before Langley troughs (braked to 67 to take water), 88

Above, the former L.M.R. Holbeck shed, Leeds, is now in the North Eastern Area, and Gresley Pacifics thus have been working over the former Midland route to Carlisle and Glasgow (St. Enoch). No. 60082 Neil Gow *is seen leaving Leeds City with the northbound 'Thames-Clyde Express'.*

[*J. R. Carter*

Right, approaching Peterborough with the down 'Northumbrian' – 'A3' 4-6-2 No. 60049 Galtee More, *showing double chimney, banjo dome and German wing type deflectors.*

[*Colin P. Walker*

Running into Kings Cross – Super-pressure 4-6-4 No. 10000 in its original form.

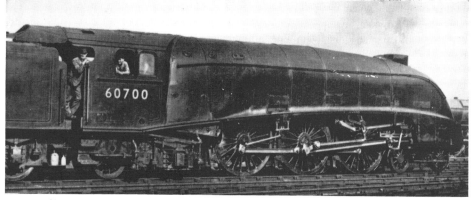

Above, No. 10000 rebuilt as a 3-cylinder streamlined 4-6-4 and renumbered 60700 in the British Railways list.   [*P. Ransome-Wallis*

Below, at speed with a 15-coach up Newcastle express – No. 60700, formerly No. 10000, as rebuilt.   [*E. R. Wethersett*

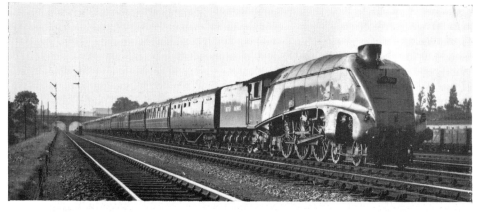

Above, 'A4' No. 4466 Herring Gull *(later* Sir Ralph Wedgwood) *draws away from
4-6-4 No. 10000 on the climb to Holloway with the down 'Coronation' streamliner;
this and the semi-fast Leeds train were both due to leave Kings Cross at 4 p.m.*
[C. C. B. Herbert

Below, No. 2509 Silver Link, *first of the 'A4' class, in her original grey livery, with
the name painted on the streamlined casing.* [British Railways

Above, 'A4' No. 4496 Golden Shuttle, *built for the 'West Riding Limited' streamline train, in blue livery with nameplate in the standard position, and raised numbers and lettering of stainless steel.*

[*British Railways*

Above, 'A4' No. 4485 Kestrel *with the original single chimney, at the head of the 'Flying Scotsman'.*   [*P. Ransome-Wallis*

Below, Double-chimney 'A4' No. 4901 Sir Charles Newton *after the removal by Edward Thompson of the valances over the motion and with the abbreviated 'NE' on the tender that was adopted for a short time.*

[*British Railways*

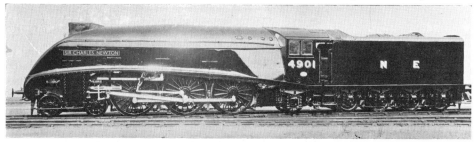

Right, with presentation North American bell - 'A4' 4-6-2 No. 4489 Dominion of Canada on the turntable at Kings Cross Motive Power Depot. The bell has since been removed.

[*C. C. B. Herbert*

Above, another 'foreign excursion' - double chimney 'A4' No. 60034 Lord Faringdon *lifts the weighty London Midland Region 'Royal Scot' up Camden bank in the 1948 locomotive exchanges. The L.M.R. dynamometer car is next the engine.* [*F. R. Hebron*

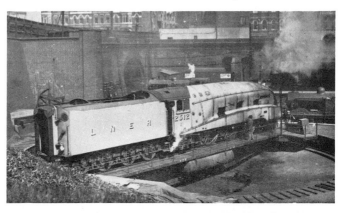

Right, 'A4' No. 2512 Silver Fox *on Kings Cross Station turntable, showing the corridor tender*

Above, the unsightly Thompson transformation of Gresley's first 4-6-2, No. 4470 Great Northern, intended to be the prototype for a new class 'A1', with stovepipe chimney and diminutive cab.
[*British Railways*

Right, No. 4470 Great Northern with the rear-end framing and normal cab restored.
[*C. C. B. Herbert*

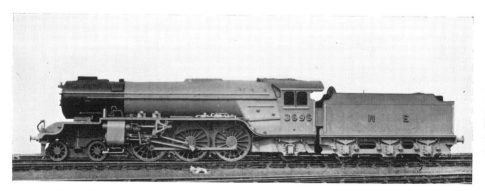

Above, No. 3696 (later No. 60507 Duke of Rothesay), first of the four 'V2' 2-6-2s redesigned by Thompson as Pacifics of Class 'A2/1', with original six-wheel tender. [*British Railways*

Left, No. 2003
Lord Presi-
dent, *one of the
six 2-8-2 loco-
motives built by
Gresley for ser-
vice between
Edinburgh and
Aberdeen, later
converted by
Thompson to
the 4-6-2 wheel
arrangement.*
[*W. J. Reynolds*

*Right, after the
conversion,
Class 'A2/2'*
Lord Presi-
dent, *later No.
60503, with
flared double
chimney, small
deflectors, and
banjo dome.*
[*K. R. Firt*

Below, Thompson Class 'A2/3' 4-6-2 No. 60519 Honeyway, *with double stovepipe
chimney and full size smoke deflectors.*   [*G. Wheeler*

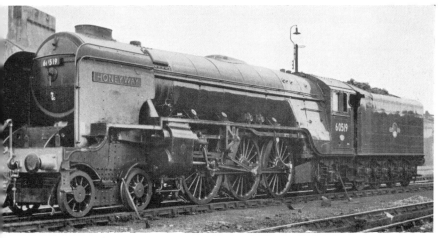

Above, Peppercorn 'A2' Pacific No. 60530 Sayajirao *passing Auchterarder with the up 'Heart of Midlothian' during the short period when that train was running through from Perth via Stirling and Polmont.* [W. J. V. Anderson

Below, Thompson 'A2/3' Pacific No. 60518 Tehran *on a fast freight train, approaching Potters Bar tunnel.* [Eric Treacy

through Hitchin and 94 beyond, 98 at Holme – these took us past Peter-borough in 61 min. 20 sec. We were through Grantham in 85 min. 17 sec., and despite a permanent way slowing immediately after, cleared Doncaster, 155·95 miles, in the fine time of 125 min. 11 sec. from Kings Cross, nearly 3½ minutes early. After that Driver Dron took things relatively easily, and we were at a stand under the great curved roof at York in 155 min. 36 sec. from London. In the first hour we had covered 75¾ miles, and in the second – allowing for the permanent way slowing – another 75½ miles, a remarkably consistent piece of high speed work. This run also appears in detail in Table III (C), Section 10.

All that needs to be said about the remainder of the journey to Edinburgh is to comment on the fact that the Engineer's Department in Scotland appeared to have learned little from what had happened on the 'Silver Jubilee' trial two years before. Other than the few normal speed restrictions, such as that through Berwick, nothing had been done to lay down any higher speed limits for curves of less severity. This fact we were to appreciate to the full going down Cock-burnspath bank, for when we struck the reverse curves below Innerwick we were doing a modest 94 m.p.h.! I was travelling at the time in the 'beaver tail,' which wagged itself with such terrific vigour as to project luggage from a rack on one side of the car in a beautifully curved trajectory clean across to the floor on the other! Nevertheless we survived this Scottish excitement, and ran into Waverley a shade after 9·59 p.m., nicely on time.

While the 'Empire' engines took the major part in working the 'Coronation' streamliner, other 'A4' Pacifics were drafted to it when necessary, and occasionally, in an emergency, even non-streamlined 'A3s' took a share, as mentioned in the next chapter. The same happened when the 'West Riding Limited,' last of the three L.N.E.R. streamline trains, made its appearance at the beginning of October, 1937. The two 'A4' engines specially named for and allocated to this service were No. 4495 *Golden Fleece* and 4496 *Golden Shuttle*, which, like Nos. 4488 to 4492 inclusive, received the new blue livery almost from the time of their construction (No. 4495 ran in green as *Great Snipe* for a week or so), but this train also was worked by other 'A4s' from time to time.

Going down, the 'West Riding Limited' was not so good a timekeeper as its two predecessors. A surprisingly late departure from Kings Cross was arranged, at 7.10 p.m., which projected this flyer into the middle of the evening down fast freights; and at the end of its journey, in addition, it was on the tail of the 5.50 p.m. from Kings Cross to Leeds, due in Leeds Central only ten minutes earlier and also not the best of timekeepers. The result was that signal checks were not as rare as they ought to have been. But on the up journey the 'West Riding Limited' trailed the up 'Silver Jubilee' at a 15-minute interval, and so could be reasonably certain of a good road. The 'West Riding Limited' was an eight-car set, exactly similar to the 'Coronation' other than having no observation car, and weighed 279 tons empty.

As with the previous streamliners, there was a Press trip, this time from Leeds Central down to Barkston, where we turned on the triangle, and back to Leeds. *Golden Fleece* was the engine, but as we had no lengthy incline to run down like the southward descent from Stoke, there were no very thrilling moments; the highest speed was $93\frac{1}{2}$ m.p.h. at Crow Park, going south. The only excitement was that of taking Retford level crossing, at a time well before its later relaying and realignment, at 75 m.p.h., which gave the party a very hearty shaking up. By now, however, many of us were getting more acclimatized to such sensations!

We come now to the most startling performance for which any Gresley locomotive was ever responsible, and it is significant, as suggested previously, that it should have been achieved by an engine equipped, not only with complete external streamlining, but also with the internal 'streamlining' resulting from the improvements in the steam passages that Gresley had effected in the 'A4s', and, above all, by the freedom of exhaust that the doubling of blast-pipe and chimney made possible. The engine concerned, of course, was *Mallard*, and the occasion was the memorable test run of 3rd July, 1938.

The nominal reason for the 1938 trials was that experiments were in progress with a type of quick-acting vacuum brake which would make it possible to pull up the streamline trains more smartly, from the maximum speeds that they attained habitually, than the standard brakes in use. As mentioned already, this problem had a direct effect on the schedule of the 'Silver Jubilee' until the two-aspect colour-light signalling north of York had been replaced by three-aspect signals.

But there is no doubt also that the sporting instincts of Sir Nigel had been aroused by the 114 m.p.h. attained by the L.M.S.R. Pacific *Coronation* in the previous year, which had transferred the blue riband of British railway speed from the L.N.E.R. to the L.M.S.R. – a fact of which the latter company had not failed to take very adequate publicity advantage! – and that he was determined, under the cloak of these tests, to give the rivals a speed challenge which they would have little chance of beating. In *Mallard* he found a perfect instrument for his purpose, and in Driver Duddington, of Doncaster, a fearless collaborator. The test train consisted of three of the 'Coronation' twin sets, *plus* the dynamometer car, seven vehicles in all weighing 240 tons. It is fortunate that the dynamometer car was in use, as its precise accuracy put the maximum speeds attained beyond the realm of doubt.

The train was started a little north of Grantham, and passed the station at a modest 24 m.p.h., with the regulator wide open, and cut-off 40 per cent. In $2\frac{1}{4}$ miles at 1 in 200 up, the train accelerated to $59\frac{3}{4}$ m.p.h.; in $1\frac{1}{2}$ miles further, with cut-off eased to 30 per cent., the speed increased to 69 m.p.h.; and up the final $1\frac{1}{2}$ miles through the tunnel to Stoke box, still at 1 in 200, $74\frac{1}{2}$ m.p.h. had been reached as the summit was passed. Due to some expert work with the shovel by Fireman Bray, the boiler continued to supply all the steam needed for an unchanged 40 per cent. as the engine swept southwards.

From milepost 100, speeds at the end of each successive mile were $87\frac{1}{2}$, $96\frac{1}{2}$, 104, 107, $111\frac{1}{2}$, 116, 119 m.p.h. (milepost 93), and then, at the ensuing half-miles, 120$\frac{3}{4}$, 122$\frac{1}{2}$, 123, 124$\frac{1}{4}$ and finally 125 m.p.h. at milepost 90$\frac{1}{4}$, while the dynamometer record for a very short distance revealed the tremendous maximum of 126 m.p.h., the figure usually quoted, and at which the 6 ft 8 in. driving wheels were doing more than 500 revolutions a minute. All this was at 40 per cent cut-off with full regulator, increased between mileposts 94$\frac{1}{4}$ and 93 to 45 per cent. Five miles (posts 94 to 89) were reeled off at an average of 120·4 m.p.h., and speed actually exceeded 120 m.p.h. for three miles continuously (posts 92$\frac{3}{4}$ to 89$\frac{3}{4}$). So the record was secure; *Mallard* had travelled faster, not only than the L.M.S.R. *Coronation*, but also than all other steam locomotives in the world whose high speed performances, properly authenticated by a sequence of passing times, are on record.

Now, once again, the price had to be paid. The over-running of the middle valve-spindle, with cut-offs as lengthy as 40 and even 45 per cent and full regulator at such enormous speeds, was bound to have been considerable, and no middle big-end of a Gresley Pacific was likely to stand up to such a punishment. Certainly the middle big-end of *Mallard* refused to do so. But with the record in his pocket, there was no need for the driver to flog the engine any further; *Mallard* was run quietly on to Peterborough, and after a visit to Doncaster Works, where it was found that the engine needed no more attention than a renewal of the bearing metal in the middle big-end, she emerged once again, covered with glory, to take up her normal duties. *Mallard* now carries above the driving wheels two small commemorative plaques, encircled with laurel leaves, to commemorate her epic achievement.

So the speed 'ceiling' had risen exactly in proportion to the gradual development of the Gresley design technique. On 30th November, 1934, 'A1' Pacific No. 4472 *Flying Scotsman* had attained 100 m.p.h. for the first time, with 180 lb steam pressure and the modifications to the valve-motion, resulting from the 1925 locomotive exchange, without which the attainment of the third figure probably would have been impossible. On 5th March, 1935, 'A3' Pacific No. 2750 *Papyrus*, with 217 as compared with 207 tons of train, had lifted the maximum to 108 m.p.h.; this with 220 lb steam pressure and a considerably larger superheater. Next came the exploits of the 'A4' Pacifics Nos. 2509 *Silver Link* and 2512 *Silver Fox*, on 27th September, 1935, and 27th August, 1936, respectively, the former with 235 tons and the latter with 270 tons, in touching 112$\frac{1}{2}$ and 113 m.p.h.; we had now come to the use of 250 lb pressure, improved steam passages, 9-inch piston-valves, and complete external streamlining. Last of all, with twin blast-pipes and double chimney, on 3rd July, 1938, the 'A4' *Mallard* raised the maximum attainable speed to 126 m.p.h. – a figure which is likely to remain the record for all time with steam power.

10 – *Everyday Pacific Performance*

To deal at all adequately with the performance of the Gresley Pacifics would need many pages of description. With the accelerations from 1932 onwards its quality went up by leaps and bounds, and it had reached a very high level in the streamline years from 1935 to the outbreak of the Second World War. Even after the war began, notwithstanding the extent by which main line schedules were decelerated, for some time the curtailment of the principal services increased train loads on so enormous a scale that exceptional performances were still the rule, until the punishment of the engines made it absolutely necessary to restrain the loadings to more reasonable figures.

From 1935 onwards, although the streamline trains were head and shoulders in speed above all other services, many of the trains needed very hard locomotive work for timekeeping, especially in the Southern Area between Kings Cross and Doncaster. Hardest of all was the 'Flying Scotsman', with the new and extremely weighty set of stock introduced by Gresley in 1938, of which the fourteen coaches, pressure-ventilated, had a tare weight of 504 tons. This had to be taken over the 105·5 miles from Kings Cross to Grantham in 110 minutes start to stop, and on from there to York, 82·7 miles, in 83 min. Coming up, the York–Grantham stretch was allowed 86½ min., and then the Grantham–London run had to be made at an average of precisely a mile a minute, often in early summer and late autumn with a load of up to 550 tons – one of the most exacting schedules in the whole country at that time.

Among other trains, the so-called 'Breakfast Flyer' from Leeds was allowed only 100 min. for the Grantham–Kings Cross stretch, though a less weighty train. I was personally responsible for getting three other schedules pared to just within the 60 m.p.h. limit. They were those of the 'Yorkshire Pullman' in each direction between Kings Cross and Doncaster, which became 156 min. down and 155 min. up for the 156 miles, and the 50-min. schedule from Grantham to Doncaster, 50·5 miles, of the 5·45 p.m. from Kings Cross. The then Superintendent of the Line, Western Area, V. M. Barrington-Ward (later Sir Michael Barrington-Ward), readily agreed to the small cuts in the timings of these trains that would add 362 miles to the L.N.E.R. mile-a-minute mileage, in view of the strong advertising point that the L.M.S.R. was making at that period of its similarly-timed runs.

The competence with which the Pacifics tackled these tasks was a perpetual delight to any recorder who, like myself, was travelling constantly up and down the East Coast main line during those halcyon years. Whether one found an 'A1', an 'A3' or an 'A4' locomotive at the head of one's train made little difference; loss of time by locomotive was a rare event. Moreover, the advent of the streamliners seemed to have put all the staff on their toes; the track had been brought up to a superb condition; the signalling had been greatly improved and adapted to high speed standards; the operating authorities, from the top downwards, took the utmost pains to see that the line was kept clear for the faster trains, even through such bottle-necks as from Greenwood to Potters Bar; and, above all, the engine-crews, whether in the streamline links or not, had caught the high speed infection, and the effect was stimulating to a degree.

It was nothing unusual, with a heavy down express of 450 to 500 tons

weight, notwithstanding the long initial climb from the terminus out to
Potters Bar, to cover the 76·35 miles to Peterborough in 75 to 77 min. A
common time for the lovely racing stretch of 26·95 miles from Hitchin to
Huntingdon would be something between 21 and 22 min., and would include
a top speed of between 85 and 90 m.p.h. past Three Counties. One typical
record of mine shows 'A3' No. 2505 *Cameronian*, on the down 'Flying
Scotsman', losing 4 min. by a very bad signal check at Hitchin, and for all
that passing Peterborough in 76 min. 19 sec. – 72¼ min. net – with speeds
of 83½ m.p.h. beyond Sandy, 72½ at St Neots, 77½ at Offord, 64½ at milepost
62, and 86½ at Holme, this with a 460-ton train. Even with 540 tons No.
4475 *Flying Fox*, after a 20 m.p.h. permanent way slowing at Knebworth,
took no more than 77 min. 50 sec., or 75¾ min. net. A run recorded by O. S.
Nock with 'A3' Pacific No. 2744 *Grand Parade* included what may have been
a record exit from Kings Cross with a load as heavy as 530 tons, for Peterborough was passed in an actual time of 73 min. 55 sec., with a maximum
of 87½ m.p.h. at Three Counties and an average of 77·8 m.p.h. over the
Hitchin–Huntingdon stretch.

One of the most amazing performances ever achieved, not by an 'A3'
but by an 'A1', is set out in the last column of Table III (C); it was recorded
by R. E. Charlewood. The train concerned was the down 'Scarborough
Flyer', allowed no more than the even three hours to run the 188·2 miles
from Kings Cross to York, and in mid-season a considerably weightier
proposition than any of the streamliners, though, of course, on an easier
timing by 23 min. than the 'Coronation'. On this occasion Driver Duddington, the renowned Doncaster expert, was at the regulator of No. 4473 *Solario*,
and received all the necessary stimulus to an exceptional effort after the
train had had to make an emergency stop at Welwyn Garden City; the roof-
board of a coach had come adrift and had been noticed by a watchful
signalman. The express had been delayed 3 min. on starting by an exceptional
rush of passengers, and as a result of this and the stop was 10½ min. late
through Hitchin.

Then *Solario* put up a meteoric performance. Allowing for the loss by a
slight signal check at Yaxley, her driver succeeded in making the engine
keep exactly the schedule time of the 'Silver Jubilee' – with 395 as compared
with 265 tons of train! – from Hitchin right through to Selby. By Doncaster
the 'Scarborough Flyer' had more than won back to schedule time, but
Duddington still continued to blaze away, and in the end brought his train
to a stand in York Station 5 min. early, having completed the run in 172 min.
6 sec., or 162 min. net, only 5 min. more than the 'Coronation's' 157-min.
allowance. While the 'A3', with such a load, could hardly be expected to
maintain the streamline schedule up the hill from Peterborough to Stoke,
her time of 38 min. 15 sec. for the 50·5 miles from Grantham to Doncaster
probably was a record. It included such flighty proceedings as 81½ m.p.h.
round the Grantham curve and 75 over Retford level crossing!

There were a few occasions on which, owing to minor faults developing
in 'A4' Pacifics, 'A3' engines have been commandeered at short notice to

TABLE III (C)
L.N.E.R. KINGS CROSS–YORK
Typical High Speed Runs with Gresley Pacifics

Dist.		Times	Speeds	Times	Speeds	Times	Speeds	Times	Speeds
	Engine No.	§2509		§2509		§4491		‖4473	
	,, Name	*Silver Link*		*Silver Link*		*Commonwealth of Australia*		*Solario*	
	Load tons tare	220		254		312		371	
	,, ,, full	235		270		330		395	
miles		min. sec.	m.p.h.	min. sec.	m.p.h.	min. sec.	m.p.h.	min. sec.	m.p.h.
0·00	KINGS CROSS	0 00	—	0 00	—	0 00	—	0 00	—
2·50	FINSBURY PARK	5 18	50	5 12	—	5 06	—	6 16	—
4·95	Wood Green	7 41	70½	7 44	61½	7 33	—	9 11	—
12·70	Potters Bar	14 43	66	15 11	64	14 37	67	17 37	—
17·70	HATFIELD	18 22	90	19 09	*81	18 25	86½	21 55	77
								Sig. stop	
23·50	*Woolmer Green*	22 42	76½	23 38	73	22 36	79	35 20	51½
28·55	Stevenage	26 49	80½/*68	27 45	77/73	26 28	90/*67	40 04	72
31·90	HITCHIN	29 23	—	30 21	80	28 56	88	42 38	80½
37·10	Arlesey	32 38	98/*86	33 54	90/86	32 15	94½	46 04	91
44·15	Sandy	37 17	92	38 53	82/88	37 03	90	51 02	85½
51·75	St Neots	42 19	88	44 21	80	42 15	83½	56 41	76
55·95	Offord	‡Sig. stop	—	47 39	*68	45 22	90/*70	59 51	81
58·85	HUNTINGDON	51 13	80½	50 00	76	47 40	80½	62 07	74
62·00	*Milepost 62*	53 35	80½	52 28	74	50 07	75	64 49	65½
69·35	Holme	58 36	98	57 39	93	55 07	98	70 30	83½
								Sigs.	
75·00	*Fletton Junction*	62 19	90	61 53	71	59 08	—	75 21	*38
76·35	PETERBOROUGH	64 31	*21	63 46	*23½	61 20	*20	77 23	*26
79·50	*Werrington Junction*	68 08	74	67 39	75	65 16	—	81 27	60
84·85	Tallington	71 59	92	71 33	90	69 23	83½	86 18	—
88·65	Essendine	74 32	90	74 08	86½	72 04	85	89 36	68
92·25	Little Bytham	76 58	88	76 38	86	74 37	82	92 47	—
97·10	Corby Glen	80 30	80½/82	80 17	78/80	78 21	76½/78	97 30	60
100·10	*Stoke*	82 48	76½	82 39	75	80 48	68	100 27	57½
		p.w.s.							
105·45	GRANTHAM	87 25	*20	86 55	80/*63	85 17	75	104 40	81½
		—	—	—	—	p.w.s.	*25		
109·70	Barkston S. Jct.	93 42	—	90 36	78	89 56	—	107 49	—
120·10	NEWARK	100 53	95½/*80	98 08	88/*82	97 08	90/*70	114 56	90/85
126·30	Carlton	105 50	*69/86½	103 16	*69/84	101 58	85	119 33	82
133·75	*Markham*	111 03	83½	108 46	75	107 16	76½	125 45	64
138·60	RETFORD	114 35	92/*65	112 33	83/*71	110 58	88/*67	129 40	84/*75
143·95	Ranskill	118 33	92/*70	116 37	87/*66	115 08	86½/*65	133 31	81½
149·50	*Milepost 149½*	122 47	74/83½	121 19	67/81	119 50	67	137 48	71/83½
155·95	DONCASTER	128 12	*72½	126 40	*67	125 11	*62	142 55	*67
160·20	*Shaftholme Junction*	131 23	83½	130 11	79/*69	128 42	eased	146 20	—
165·90	Balne	135 21	92	134 42	84	133 15	,,	150 51	76
173·00	*Brayton Junction*	140 09	93½	139 47	87	138 40	,,	156 11	—
174·30	SELBY	141 55	*30	141 18	*32	140 40	*28	157 53	*34
178·50	Riccall	146 07	75	145 49	72½	145 28	eased	162 31	62
183·95	Naburn	150 01	90	149 59	82½	150 01	,,	167 14	72
186·15	*Chaloner's Whin Jct.*	152 00	*52	152 03	*53	152 13	,,	169 08	—
188·15	YORK	†155 02	*20	†154 38	*27	155 36	,,	172 06	—
188·15	¶Net times (min.)	¶148	—	¶155	—	154	—	162	—

* Speed restriction.
† Passing time.
‡ At Paxton box, 53·7 miles, 44 min. 8 sec. to 45 min. 8 sec. from Kings Cross.
§ Class 'A4'.
‖ Class 'A1'.
¶ Equivalent time to dead stop.

work the streamline trains. Two such substitutions took place in one week in March, 1939; and not only did No. 2595 *Trigo* and No. 2507 *Singapore*, in the capable hands of Driver Nash and Fireman Gilbey, prove themselves equal to the task, but on both days time lost by late starts was regained. *Trigo* covered the 268·35 miles from Newcastle to Kings Cross in 229 min., or 225 min. net; *Singapore* made the even more notable time of 227½ min., or 222¼ min. net, so doing the entire run at an average speed of 72·3 m.p.h. This is probably the fastest time that has ever been achieved by rail between Tyneside and London with steam power.

A journey on one of the streamline trains was always, of course, an experience of the greatest interest to the recorder of locomotive performance. In Table III (C) I have set out the details of three such runs in the down direction. On the first, *Silver Link*, with the seven-coach load of 235 tons that was invariable until the eighth vehicle was built into the train, had made the usual energetic start, with speed rising to 90 m.p.h. at Hatfield and 98 at Arlesey, when we were brought to a dead stand for signals at Paxton, between St Neots and Offord. This was a most unusual occurrence, seeing that it was customary to keep two complete signal sections clear ahead of each of the streamliners. Here we stood for 60 sec. precisely.

Starting away again like a rocket, *Silver Link* attained 80 m.p.h. in no more than 5 miles and passed Huntingdon, 5·2 miles, in 6 min. 5 sec.; the 3 miles at 1 in 200 to milepost 62 were surmounted at a steady 80 and down the other side we touched 98 once again, so clearing Fletton Junction in 17 min. 11 sec. from the dead start at Paxton, 21·3 miles away! We were only a minute late through Peterborough – 61 min. net for the 76·35 miles from London – and despite a subsequent permanent way check, we passed Retford on time. At eleven different points on the journey speed rose to between 90 and 98 m.p.h.; and of these maxima the most notable were those attained on level track, such as 92 m.p.h. at Tallington, a recovery in 5 miles from 69 over Muskham troughs to 90 at Crow Park, the steady 90–93½ over some miles between Shaftholme Junction and Selby, and the very unusual 90 before Naburn.

Finally, we reached Darlington, 232·25 miles from Kings Cross, in 194 min. 40 sec., 3¼ min. early; I calculate that the net times were 121 min. to Doncaster, 147¾ min. to passing York at a walking pace, and 187¼ min. to Darlington – a net gain of 10¾ min. on schedule. Over the 160·3 miles from Potters Bar to Brayton Junction, Selby, our net average speed – allowing for the Paxton stop and Grantham permanent way check, but not for any of the regular speed restrictions – worked out at 81·4 m.p.h. throughout.

The second run in Table III (C) is the one made, with Sparshatt at the regulator of *Silver Link*, on the test trip described in full in Section 8. On this occasion, in August, 1936, the dynamometer car had been added to the then-normal seven-coach formation of the 'Silver Jubilee', bringing the total weight up to 270 tons.

The third run in this table was the inaugural down run of the 'Coronation', already mentioned in Section 9, with Driver Dron in charge of No. 4491

Commonwealth of Australia. Perhaps the most brilliant feature of this run was the starting time of 18 min. 25 sec. from Kings Cross to Hatfield, with a 330-ton load; all the way we were doing well, and the time of 125 min. 11 sec. past Doncaster, 3¼ min. less than schedule, then justified the driver in easing his engine perceptibly. But even so, York was reached in 155 min. 36 sec., 1½ min. early. In those days, as already mentioned, the demands of the timetable were much less exacting over the North Eastern and Scottish Areas than over the Southern Area, so that by York, going north, the hardest of the work was over. When the three-aspect signalling came into use between York and Northallerton, however, there was some slight adjustment of schedules, and matters north of York brightened up considerably. I had one northbound run with No. 2512 *Silver Fox* and the eight-car 'Silver Jubilee', 265 tons in gross weight, on which we reached 94 m.p.h. on dead level track, and covered 15·4 miles of level or slightly rising track at an average speed of 90·6 m.p.h. On a post-war test run made in 1946, the same engine, travelling south with a 207-ton train, and with Driver Leonard of York in charge, ran the level 27·0 miles from Northallerton to Skelton Bridge in 17 min. 58 sec., at an average of almost exactly 90 m.p.h. for the whole distance, touching a top speed of 93½ m.p.h. at Raskelf; cut-off was 35 per cent throughout, with regulator wide open.

If such speeds could be attained and maintained by Gresley's 'A4s' on level track, it is a matter of no surprise that maxima of over 100 m.p.h. could be reached with ease downhill. I have referred previously to the fact that *Silver Link*, on her immortal 'Silver Jubilee' trial trip, was keeping up a steady 109 m.p.h. after the descent from Stevenage had flattened out to level at Tempsford, and even went over the 'hump' at St Neots, with approach grades of 1 in 330 up, at 104½ m.p.h. O. S. Nock has recorded a run with *Commonwealth of Australia*, with 325 tons on the up 'Coronation', on which a maximum of 105 m.p.h., attained at Essendine, was continued, with fluctuations between 105 and 106, for 6¾ miles during which the gradient flattens gradually from 1 in 200 to level. In all her locomotive history, Britain has never possessed speedier steam locomotives than these.

To show the work of which the same locomotives were capable with really heavy loads, in Table III (D) I have set out the details of two runs from Grantham to Kings Cross, both with trains of 500 tons weight or over. On the first of these 'A4' Pacific No. 4466 *Herring Gull* was faced with the task of working the 510-ton 'Flying Scotsman' over the 105·45 miles to Kings Cross in 105½ min., and did so comfortably, with 3 min. to spare. While the sustained 90 m.p.h. from Little Bytham to Essendine with this load was a matter for remark, something considerably more notable was the time of 22 min. 21 sec. for the 26·95 miles from Huntingdon to Hitchin, against the rising tendency of the road – a very fast time for the down direction but an amazing time for an up train so loaded.

Yet the same feat was very nearly repeated by *Osprey* with her 500-ton load, as shown in the next column. The latter train was the 5.30 p.m. from Leeds to Kings Cross, and we had been delayed at Doncaster, in marshalling

TABLE III (D)
L.N.E.R. GRANTHAM–KINGS CROSS
Typical Heavy Load Runs with Gresley 'A4' Pacifics

	Engine No.	4466			†4494		
	„ Name	Herring Gull			†Osprey		
	Load, tons tare	478			474		
	„ „ full	510			500		
Dist.		Times	Speeds	Dist.	Times	Speeds	
miles		min. sec.	m.p.h.	miles	min. sec.	m.p.h.	
0·00	GRANTHAM	0 00	—	0·00	0 00	—	
5·35	Stoke .	10 02	40	5·35	9 16	46	
8·35	Corby Glen	13 00	—	8·35	12 11	74	
13·20	Little Bytham	17 23	90	13·20	16 05	—	
16·80	Essendine .	19 49	90	16·80	18 56	77½	
20·60	Tallington .	22 25	—	20·60	22 03	—	
25·95	Werrington Junction	26 35	*60	25·95	26 52	*60	
				29·10	30 50	—	
29·10	PETERBOROUGH	30 23	*25	0·00	0 00	—	
30·45	Fletton Junction	33 00	—	1·45	3 45	—	
36·10	Holme	38 52	71½	7·00	9 25	71½	
41·95	Abbots Ripton .	44 25	53½	12·85	14 39	57	
46·60	HUNTINGDON	48 49	76½	17·50	18 54	76½	
49·50	Offord	51 09	72½	20·40	21 17	71½	
53·70	St Neots .	54 45	68	24·60	25 03	64½	
57·95	Tempsford .	58 12	77½	28·85	28 38	75	
61·30	Sandy	60 50	76½	32·20	31 23	77½	
64·30	Biggleswade	63 14	69	35·20	33 47	70½	
68·35	Arlesey	66 41	74	39·25	37 13	75	
73·55	HITCHIN .	71 10	60	44·45	41 38	64½	
76·90	Stevenage .	74 52	51	47·80	44 59	58½	
80·40	Knebworth	78 34	—	51·30	48 19	—	
83·45	Welwyn North .	81 28	—	54·35	50 58	—	
87·75	HATFIELD .	84 53	79	58·65	54 26	79	
92·75	Potters Bar	89 10	66	63·65	59 09	58½	
96·30	New Barnet	92 14	75	67·20	62 28	eased	
100·50	Wood Green	95 47	*64	71·40	66 02	—	
102·95	FINSBURY PARK	98 17	—	73·85	69 03	—	
105·45	KINGS CROSS .	102 39	—	76·35	73 44	—	

* Speed restriction.   † No. 4500 *Sir Ronald Matthews* to Peterborough.

the load, by the obstinate refusal of two buckeye couplers to disengage, notwithstanding the combined six-cylinder effort of a 'K3' Mogul and an 'A4' Pacific to make them do so. Eventually we got away from Doncaster 18 min. late, behind 'A4' 4-6-2 No. 4500 *Sir Ronald Matthews*. Time recovery began at once. To Grantham we ran the 50·5 miles in 52 min. 12 sec., picking up 4¾ min., and that notwithstanding a permanent way slowing at Tuxford. From Grantham we ran the 29·1 miles to Peterborough, even though not exceeding 77½ m.p.h. 'down the hill', in 30 min. 50 sec., and another 3¼ min. of the arrears were wiped off.

But it was Driver Ovenden, on No. 4494 *Osprey*, which was substituted for *Sir Ronald Matthews* at Peterborough, who made the pace. For he gained no less than $11\frac{1}{4}$ min. from Peterborough to Kings Cross, and so arrived dead on time (we had overstayed our allowance at Peterborough by a minute). On this run outstanding work uphill was added to that on the level, particularly the minimum speed of $58\frac{1}{2}$ m.p.h. at Stevenage after the whole of the long climb from the Ouse valley, finishing with 5 miles at 1 in 200. So well had we done that Ovenden was able to ease his engine after Hatfield for quite a moderate run into the terminus; had we repeated the fast sprint of *Herring Gull* we might have completed the 76·35 miles from Peterborough to Kings Cross in just over 72 min., which would have been a gain on schedule of 13 min. from Peterborough alone.

It was during the first year or two of the war that the Gresley Pacifics had to handle their biggest trains, many of which were heavier than anything ever hauled before or since by unassisted locomotives on passenger service in Great Britain. Twenty-coach loads were common on trains like the 'Flying Scotsman', and it was nothing unusual, particularly in the up direction, for 21, 22, or even 23 to be taken, crammed with passengers from end to end. At the time I published details of a run with this train, timed by the Rev. G. C. Stead, in which 'A4' Pacific No. 4901, then named *Capercaillie*, hauling a twenty-two-coach load of 665 tons tare and not less than 730 tons gross, ran the 24·9 miles between Otterington and Poppleton Junction, again on the high speed Darlington–York stretch, in 19 min. 57 sec., at an average of no less than 75·0 m.p.h., reaching a top speed of $78\frac{1}{2}$ m.p.h. on the level at Raskelf. It has been calculated that the drawbar horse-power needed for this feat must have been in the region of 2,200 continuously.

By contrast with her flying exploits on the 'Silver Jubilee', on 5th April, 1940, *Silver Link* was faced with the herculean task of lifting a twenty-five-coach train out of Kings Cross – so lengthy, in fact, that the head of the train, engine included, was in Gasworks Tunnel, and a man had to be sent to the tunnel mouth to give the driver the 'right away'. A full 16 min. elapsed before this vast assemblage of 750 tons tare and 830 to 850 tons gross made its appearance at Finsbury Park, but from there the overtaxed 'A4' succeeded in running the 102·95 miles to Grantham in 123 min. To Grantham *Silver Link* had dropped 11 min., but from Grantham, with 105 min. allowed to York, 52 min. on to Darlington, and 50 min. from Darlington to Newcastle, the additional loss was 4 min. only.

It may be added that even one of the original 'A1' engines, designed by Gresley for the haulage of 600-ton trains, No. 2549 *Persimmon*, at about the same period worked a twenty-four-coach train of 759 tons tare and some 850 tons gross from Peterborough to Kings Cross in 96 min., losing 2 min. only on the 94-min. schedule then in force for the Leeds train concerned. During those war years the London & North Eastern Railway management had good cause to be grateful to Sir Nigel Gresley for his 'big engine' policy, which had provided them with a stud of locomotives of such exceptional power and reliability to meet the tremendous strain of war conditions.

A belated but emphatic tribute to the success of Gresley's 'A4' Pacific design came with the extensive locomotive exchange trials of 1948, when

engines of this type worked between Kings Cross and Leeds, Euston and
Carlisle, Paddington and Plymouth, and Waterloo and Exeter, in competition
with London Midland Region 'Duchess' Pacifics and rebuilt 'Royal Scot'
4-6-os, Western Region 'King' 4-6-os, and Southern Region 'Merchant Navy'
Pacifics. The engines used were *Mallard*, *Seagull* and *Lord Faringdon*.
Unfortunately that susceptible middle big-end gave trouble on three different
'foreign' runs, either in the preliminary or the actual test weeks, necessitating
the removal of *Mallard* and *Seagull* from their trains, which was a blot on an
otherwise splendid record.

The finest feats were those of *Seagull*, coming up from Plymouth on
5th May. Permanent way relaying brought Driver Burgess down to 16 m.p.h.
in Plympton Station, right at the foot of the formidable 1 in 41 climb to
Hemerdon box. Yet, with cut-off opened out to 50 per cent and regulator
wide open, the engine spurted to 24 m.p.h. and then gamely lifted her 350-ton
train up the terrific incline without the veriest suspicion of a slip, and without
the speed at any point falling below 18½ m.p.h. – a magnificent performance.
Later in the same journey, and now with 525 tons, *Seagull* streaked out of
Taunton to such purpose that we ran 25·5 miles from the start to Alford,
largely with grades against the engine, in 25 min. 10 sec. – a feat that I have
never equalled with a comparably loaded Great Western engine. Moreover,
the Official Report reveals that the 'A4' supremacy extended also to coal and
water consumption. Through the entire series of exchange tests, the average
'A4' coal consumption, 3·06 lb per drawbar-horsepower-hour, and water
consumption, 24·32 lb per drawbar-horsepower-hour, were the lowest of all
the engines tested, whether express passenger, mixed traffic or freight.

The nearest approach in coal consumption was the L.M.R. 'Duchess'
4-6-2, with an average of 3·12 lb. The standard Western Region 'King',
tested only on the Western and Eastern Regions, when using Yorkshire coal,
to which its blast and draught arrangements were unsuited, burned 3·57 lb of
coal and evaporated 28·58 lb of water per drawbar-horsepower-hour. Even
when, in later months, a standard 'King' was tested with Welsh coal between
Paddington and Plymouth only, with all the advantages of running over its
own main line, the consumption remained at 3·33 lb per drawbar-horsepower-
hour, and a 'King' experimentally fitted with high temperature superheat
and also burning Welsh coal, could not bring the figure below 3·10 lb. By
comparison, when the 'A4' with Yorkshire coal had the advantage of working
over E.R. metals only, the coal consumption was as low as 2·92 lb per drawbar-
horsepower-hour. So, in the 1948 exchange, Gresley succeeded with a
vengeance, even if posthumously, in reversing the results of the historic
exchange of 1925!

The 'A4' Pacifics have always been engines capable of being driven with
the regulator full open and in short cut-offs; indeed, drivers have been encouraged to handle them in this way, though with light loads full regulator
working would result in excessive speeds and in such cases a partial closing is
essential. I have before me three runs recorded on the footplate by R. I.
Nelson which demonstrate the methods of handling needed respectively with

gross loads of 325, 435 and 505 tons. With the 325-ton 'Talisman' No. 60021 *Wild Swan* worked up to 89 m.p.h. on the level between Thirsk and York on 15 per cent cut-off with three-quarters regulator. Later, the 1 in 200 to Peascliffe Tunnel was climbed at a minimum of 59 m.p.h. on 12 per cent, again with three-quarters regulator which meant 215 lb pressure in the steam-chest out of 230 lb in the boiler. Down from Stoke summit 12 per cent and then 10 per cent, with the regulator opening diminishing from three-quarters to half (200 lb down to 160 lb in the steam-chest out of the 200–210 lb in the boiler), worked the train up to 93 m.p.h. at Essendine. Even more remarkable, perhaps, was the minimum speed of 64 m.p.h. at the top of the long 1 in 200 to Stevenage on 12 per cent cut-off with three-quarters regulator. On this journey the 268·3 miles from Newcastle to Kings Cross were run in 242 min. net. Driver Blacklock was in charge.

With the twelve-coach 435-ton train the famous No. 60022 *Mallard*, Driver R. Turner of Kings Cross, accelerated to 84 m.p.h. on the very slightly easier than level track southwards to Pilmoor, with full regulator and 12 per cent cut-off, and held speed at the 84 m.p.h. level with 10 per cent cut-off. Full regulator and 15 per cent took the train up the 1 in 200 to Peascliffe tunnel at 59 m.p.h. and the further 1 in 200 to Stoke summit at 55 m.p.h., while the continued use of full regulator but no more than $7\frac{1}{2}$ per cent cut-off produced a top speed of 85 m.p.h. by Essendine. Up the long grade to Stevenage full regulator was in use all the way, with cut-off advanced gradually from 14 to 16 per cent, and the minimum speed was 61 m.p.h. This last was the more surprising in that *Mallard* on this run was inclined to prime, with the result that the boiler pressure in the later stages of the run had dropped to 175–190 lb per sq in. from the rated 250 lb.

Last of the three was No. 60034 *Lord Faringdon*, in charge of the redoubtable Driver Hailstone. From a start at Grantham in this case, it needed a cut-off increased gradually from 25 to 30 per cent to accelerate the 505-ton load up the 1 in 200 to 42 m.p.h. by Stoke summit; then 15 per cent cut-off, still with full regulator, was enough for a maximum of 84 m.p.h. at Essendine. After stopping at Peterborough, Hailstone used full regulator almost the whole way to London, varying his cut-off constantly according to the gradients. Up the 1 in 200 of Abbots Ripton bank the speed fell finally to 60 m.p.h. with a maximum of 32 per cent cut-off; and with from 25 to 33 per cent the last $2\frac{1}{2}$ miles of the 1 in 200 climb to Stevenage were mounted at a steady 61 m.p.h. Over a number of the easier stages the cut-off came down to 15 to 20 per cent, and a late start of $7\frac{3}{4}$ min. from Peterborough was converted into an arrival of 1 min. early, the time for the 76·35 miles being 76 min. 22 sec., or $74\frac{1}{4}$ min. net.

It is notable that in the locomotive exchange trials of 1948 the Eastern Region 'A4' Pacifics were the only express engines tested that were worked with full regulator openings – that is, with no throttling of the steam – which accounts for the fact of their showing the best efficiency figures of all, in terms of coal and water consumptions per drawbar-horsepower-hour. In their present form the 'A3' Pacifics can be and are handled in much the same way;

and the steam passages of both are so well designed that with full regulator the drop in pressure from boiler to steam-chest is seldom more than 5 to 10 lb per sq in.

11 – *Numbers, Names and Notes*

IN this section it is necessary to summarise a part of the information which has gone before, and to add certain items of interest, before our survey of the Gresley Pacifics can be regarded as complete. First of all, as to numbers and names. Table III (G) gives the numbers and names of the whole of the 114 6 ft 8 in. Pacifics built during the Gresley *régime*, between 1922 and 1938 inclusive, in the order in which the engines appeared. In parallel columns there are shown the original L.N.E.R. numbers, the L.N.E.R. numbers under the Thompson renumbering scheme of 1946, and the present British Railways numbers.

The names of the series, in the course of time, have become rather a mixed bag. After starting away with *Great Northern, Sir Frederick Banbury* (one of the G.N.R. directors up to the time of the grouping) and *Flying Scotsman*, Gresley began the long list of names of racehorses which at various times had won the country's classic events; of these he used seventy-four in all, interrupted by *Prince of Wales* (No. 2553), *Centenary* (No. 2555), which was named to commemorate the Railway Centenary of 1925, and *William Whitelaw* (No. 2563), named after the Chairman of the newly-formed London & North Eastern Railway. After the 'A4' class had been introduced, the gentleman last named was promoted to 'A4' rank, and No. 4462 *Great Snipe* was changed from winged to merely pedestrian status by being renamed *William Whitelaw*, while the previous two-legged *William Whitelaw* (No. 2563) became the four-legged *Tagalie*. The racehorse *motif* had some odd results at times, as, for example, when the scandalised delegates to a Methodist Conference found *Robert the Devil* at the head of their special train, whether by accident or design is not related.

The racehorse names continued throughout the 'A3' series of Pacifics, but with the introduction of the 'A4s' a change took place. The first four of these, Nos. 2509 to 2512 inclusive, received names appropriate to the 'Silver Jubilee' theme – *Silver Link, Quicksilver, Silver King* and *Silver Fox*. When 'A4' building recommenced with No. 4482, the first bird names were introduced, and would have continued without interruption but for decisions taken when the 'Coronation' and 'West Riding Limited' streamliners were introduced. Special names thus were conferred on Nos. 4488 to 4492 inclusive and 4495 and 4496 for the working of these trains. But No. 4488 originally was named *Osprey* before becoming *Union of South Africa;* while for No. 4489 the first nameplates made, but never used, were *Buzzard*, then the engine emerged and ran as *Woodcock*, and this was changed within a matter of months to *Dominion of Canada*. The *Woodcock* nameplates were transferred to No. 4493 and the *Osprey* nameplates to No. 4494. Nos. 4495 and 4496 were named *Golden Fleece* (after a week or so as *Great Snipe*), and *Golden Shuttle* respectively, and another exception to the bird series was No. 4498 *Sir Nigel Gresley*, named after the designer.

After the Second World War there arose a sudden passion to immortalise directors and officers of the pre-nationalisation railways by naming engines after them, and, as a result, many of the beautiful bird names disappeared. Those lost in this way were *Kestrel*, *Sea Eagle*, *Osprey*, *Great Snipe* and *Herring Gull* (mentioned in an earlier chapter), *Gadwall*, *Pochard*, *Garganey*, *Capercaillie* and *Peregrine*. With the most profound respect to the distinguished gentlemen concerned, one cannot help wondering if the name *Andrew K. McCosh* can have quite the same publicity appeal as *Osprey*, or if *Walter K. Whigham* is any adequate substitute for *Sea Eagle* or *Miles Beevor* for *Kestrel*, to name but three typical examples. *Kestrel*, *Osprey*, *Peregrine* and *Sea Eagle* are names that have since reappeared among the Peppercorn 'A1' Pacifics, but not the remaining bird titles.

To mark his great services to the Allied cause in the war, General Eisenhower was honoured in the naming after him of No. 4496, previously *Golden Shuttle* and now *Dwight D. Eisenhower*. It may be added that originally Nos. 4466 and 4467 were to have been *Hirondelle* and *Condor;* but eventually *Herring Gull* and *Wild Swan* were the names chosen. *Mallard*, typical genus of wild duck, proved a worthy successor indeed to the *Wild Duck* of historic exploits on the L.N.W.R. years earlier. One curious example of changed names concerns an 'A1', No. 2564, which ran at first as *Knight of the Thistle*, but apparently there was some technical error in this designation, which was amended later to *Knight of Thistle*. In Table III (G) the earlier names of engines which had their names altered subsequently are shown in brackets, with the present names following.

Throughout the 'A1' and 'A3' series, Gresley applied his engine names in curved cast brass nameplates fitted above the driving wheel splashers. With the advent of the 'A4' engines, splashers disappeared, and something new had to be devised. Straight nameplates for the smokebox sides, similar to those used already on the 'P2' 2-8-2 engines, were cast for *Silver Link*, and duly applied, but their appearance did not meet with the approval of Gresley's daughter, who acted as his 'art adviser', and they were removed. He was then content with the singularly poor substitute of painting the names, not even in Gill Sans lettering, along the middle of the streamlined casing. When No. 4482 *Golden Eagle* was turned out of Doncaster, however, the elegant straight nameplates fixed on the smokebox sides reappeared, and have since become standard, the 'Silver Jubilee' engines being altered to correspond when their colour was changed from grey to blue. The seven 'Coronation' and 'West Riding' engines, with No. 4498 *Sir Nigel Gresley*, were distinguished by receiving chromium-plated nameplates, railway initials, numbers and certain other decorations, the initials and numbers in relief, and this practice also later became standardised for engines of this class. With the renumbering in the 60,000s, however, the relief lettering disappeared.

Hitherto I have referred to the Gresley Pacifics only by their original

L.N.E.R. numbers, which, as previously mentioned, were bestowed in somewhat haphazard fashion, as blocks of numbers became available at the time of construction. The various sequences, in order of construction, were 4470 to 4481 (previously G.N.R. Nos. 1470 to 1481), 2543 to 2582, 2743 to 2752, 2595 to 2599, 2795 to 2797, 2500 to 2512, 4482 to 4498, 4462 to 4469, 4499 and 4500, and 4900 to 4903. Eventually therefore, there was one unbroken series from 2543 to 2582, another from 4462 to 4500, with Nos. 2500 to 2512, 2595 to 2599, 2743 to 2752, 2795 to 2797, and 4900 to 4903.

During the Thompson *régime* a complete renumbering of all London & North Eastern Railway locomotives on systematic lines was decided on. It had an interim phase, during which a few of the Gresley Pacifics received numbers in the 500s and 600s. Then came the final L.N.E.R. numbering, with the 'A4s' numbered consecutively from 1 to 34, and the 'A3s' from 35 to 112 – a total of 113, No. 4469, as previously mentioned, having been destroyed at York. Renumbering began in 1946, and two years later, the L.N.E.R. having now become a part of British Railways, the work had to begin all over again with 60,000 added to the L.N.E.R. numbers. A certain proportion of the Thompson renumbering was done in the same sequence as that in which the engines were built, but not all. In particular, the 'A4' Pacific serial numbering today is nothing like the building sequence, for the 'personalities' among the engine names were almost all moved up to the 'top of the form', to take the numbers 1 to 8 (except *Miles Beevor, Walter K. Whigham*, and *Lord Faringdon*, who were not commemorated in this way until after the renumbering had taken place, and so got left among the birds), and were followed by the 'Dominions' and the 'Silver Jubilee' series before the bird names began. This involved a considerable rearrangement.

A word may now be said about Pacific colours. London & North Eastern green and standard lining was carried on uninterruptedly until the appearance of *Silver Link* and her three sisters in 1935, painted in silver-grey with the side valances in a darker grey shade and the sloping smokebox front in black. At first *Silver Link* had her light grey sides carried right into the sharp angle made by the sloping front and valance at their convergence above the bufferbeam, but later this corner was cut off by carrying the black of the smokebox round the sides in a graceful curve, considerably improving the side view of the engine. This became the standard method for the remaining 'Silver Jubilee' engines.

As 'A4' building recommenced, with No. 4482, the new 'A4s' at first were painted and lined in standard green. When the 'Coronation' was about to be introduced, however, a series of experiments was tried with various shades of blue, all on No. 4488, until finally the attractive shade of Garter blue was decided on. During these experiments No. 4489 was running in workshop grey. With the blue there was combined a dark red finish for the wheels, the whole making for a most striking appearance. Later the 'Silver Jubilee' Pacifics and all the green 'A4s' were repainted in blue, and the entire class became uniform in appearance. After the depressing black interlude of the

Second World War, Garter blue was reinstated. but this was later replaced by the standard British Railways dark green, similar in colour and lining to the former Great Western Railway colours.

The Gresley Pacifics have had their share of serious casualties. Of these by far the worst, apart from the destruction by bombing of No. 4469, was the accident in which No. 2744 *Grand Parade* was involved at Castlecary, between Edinburgh and Glasgow, on 10th December, 1937. In a thick snowstorm the Pacific was working the 4.3 p.m. Edinburgh–Glasgow express when the driver overran signals at danger, and at a full 60 m.p.h. ran into the rear of the 2 p.m. from Dundee to Glasgow, which was held up at Castlecary by a signal failure, 35 passengers being killed. The rear end of the latter train was smashed up beyond recognition, and the leading vehicles of the Edinburgh express were badly damaged, which is not surprising in view of the calculation that the collision absorbed some 54,000 ft-tons of energy. The damage to *Grand Parade* herself was so extreme that the No. 2744 which emerged from Doncaster subsequently, and later carried the number 60090, was practically a new engine.

In most of the other serious main line accidents of later years on the L.N.E.R., whether collisions or derailments, the engines have been 'V2' 2-6-2s and not Pacifics. Of unusual casualties to Gresley Pacifics one was on 10th May, 1926, when No. 2565 *Merry Hampton* was deliberately derailed by strikers at Cramlington, Northumberland, during the coal dispute of, that year, when hauling the up 'Flying Scotsman', though fortunately at so low a speed that relatively little damage was done. A far more serious derailment was that of 26th October, 1947, in which *Merry Hampton*, strange to relate, was involved once again. The engine was working the southbound Sunday 'Scotsman', and the driver, carrying on the footplate an unauthorised 'passenger', ran past all warning signals of engineering work in progress south of Goswick, in Northumberland, and had eleven of his fifteen coaches off the road on the reverse curve leading into the up relief line, to which his train was being diverted; 28 lives were lost.

One extraordinary accident in which an 'A4' was concerned, though the engine itself suffered no damage whatsoever, occurred on the evening of Sunday, 4th February, 1945, when the 6 p.m. express was leaving Kings Cross for Leeds and Bradford. The load was 17 coaches of about 590 tons weight, and the engine, No. 2512 *Silver Fox*, stalled in Gasworks Tunnel. Eventually the train got on the move, but when the driver thought he was moving forwards, actually the train was moving backwards. The road had been re-set after the train had entered the tunnel, but when the Kings Cross signalman saw the tail of the train reappearing, he tried hastily to reverse the switch, to get the train back into the platform it had just left. He was a second or two too late. As a result, the points moved between the two bogies of the rear coach, and several coaches were derailed, skewing themselves across the track and demolishing a signal bridge; two passengers were killed.

12 – *The Gresley Conjugated Motion*

A WORD now is needed concerning the controversy which has always raged, and doubtless will continue to do so, over the merits or demerits of the Gresley conjugated valve-motion. Its opponents would be hard put to it to dispute that many of the most notable feats of British express locomotive performance, including the highest speed with steam on record, have been achieved by engines so fitted. Conversely, on their side of the argument, there is the fact of the heating troubles experienced with the middle big-ends of Gresley Pacifics, some on occasions which have brought these failures very prominently under notice, particularly those of *Silver Fox* and *Mallard* after the high speed tests of 1936 and 1938, and of *Mallard* and *Seagull* in the 1948 locomotive exchanges. Even the observer without technical knowledge will not fail to notice that the exhaust beats of a Gresley Pacific often are not in perfectly regular sequence, but that the engines tend to have a slightly syncopated beat, acoustically obvious when they are working hard.

The first Gresley conjugated motion, as applied in 1918 to Great Northern Railway 2-8-0 No. 461, with its vertical levers in rear of the cylinders, was a much more complicated affair than the simple 2-to-1 arrangement ahead of the cylinders that he standardized soon after. In changing from the former to the latter, it is probable that he was influenced by H. Holcroft of the then South Eastern & Chatham Railway, who nine years earlier, when in the drawing office at Swindon Works of the Great Western Railway, had devised a conjugated motion for three-cylinder engines which, under Churchward's direction, he had patented. Though Gresley never admitted any such paternity for his own gear, it is known that he consulted Holcroft in the matter, and the similarities between the two arrangements cannot escape notice.

There are two reasons why the centre valve of an engine fitted with the Gresley derived motion tends to over-run. The first is the deflection of the stay supporting the main fulcrum of the 2 to 1 lever which takes its movement from the two outside valve-motions (and possibly some slight deflection of the lever itself), and the second is wear and tear of the pin joints of the conjugated gear. As compared with the original 'K3' engines, Nos. 1000 to 1009, on which the over-running of the centre valve first became apparent, Gresley in his Pacifics had strengthened the stay referred to, and also had provided the fulcrums of both the main 2-to-1 levers and the 'equal' levers of the gear with ball and roller bearings, to minimise wear; but even these modifications did not provide a complete cure. It had been estimated that by over-running the cut-off in the middle cylinder at high speeds can rise to some 10 per cent. higher than that in the two outside cylinders.

It has never been possible to indicate an 'A4' Pacific, because with the streamlined casing there is no footplating on which to mount the indicator and the observer. In his paper to the Institution of Locomotive Engineers, to which reference has been made previously, however, B. Spencer mentioned the indicating of 'A3' Pacific No. 2751, *Humorist*, in which a comparison was made of the work done in the engine's three cylinders. At speeds up to 45 m.p.h. there was little difference; but from then on the over-running began to be perceptible. With a 540-ton train, at 57 m.p.h. the horsepowers developed by the two outside cylinders were 460 and 518 and by the middle cylinder 558; at 63 m.p.h. 394 and 472 outside and 547 inside; and at 75 m.p.h. 402 and 480 outside and as much as 585 inside. If there were such a difference at 75 m.p.h., to what point might the difference increase at 90 or 100 m.p.h.?

In the early days of the 'A4' design, L.N.E.R. locomotive maintenance in general was of so high a standard that the derived motions could be kept in first-class running order, and so gave little trouble unless some particularly extravagant demand was made on the engines. Mention has been made already of some exceptional endurance feats, over considerable distances, of 'A4' Pacifics on difficult assignments like the 'Coronation' streamliner and the non-stop 'Flying Scotsman', and these prove that the Gresley derived motion can stand up to any amount of hard work if properly maintained. But as the engines were turned into more general service, on a common-user basis, in the strenuous speed conditions of the years immediately before the Second World War, the middle big-end trouble began to increase to such an extent that something had to be done about it. Of all the Pacifics the 'A4s' were always the most susceptible, for the streamlining reduced the amount of cool air circulating between the frames; moreover, it might make it difficult for a driver to detect an overheated bearing by his sense of smell until the trouble had reached serious proportions.

The first step taken was before the war, and it was one of prevention rather than cure. Through the middle crank-pin of each Pacific, 'A1', 'A3', and 'A4' alike, a hole was drilled large enough to accommodate what is known colloquially as a 'stink bomb', or, in more dignified parlance, a detector. This is a metal cylinder containing amyl acetate vapour, and closed at one end by a glass bulb and sprinkler of the type used in automatic fire extinguishers. At a predetermined temperature (about 160°F.) this bulb bursts, and unlooses a smell of so pungent a description that it is almost certain to be noticed in the cab. These detectors have proved most valuable, making it possible to detect big-end heating even before the melting of the bearing metal, let alone the damage to or complete disintegration of the brasses which may follow a bad case of heating.

During the war things went from bad to worse. In the early days of the war the Pacifics were flogged unmercifully in handling trains of 700 to 800 tons gross weight, and sometimes even more, and with shortage of staff and materials the standard of maintenance fell steadily at the same time. For example, the grease lubrication of the 2-to-1 motion, until then invariably carried out by a fitter rather than the driver, went by default, as did various other kinds of skilled attention to their motion that the engines had been accustomed to receive. Wear in all the pins increased as a result of inadequate lubrication and of the failure to keep the derived gear clear of ash during smokebox cleaning; excessive mileage between overhauls took its toll; the quality of lubricating oil declined steadily. Thus the number of middle big-end failures went up by leaps and bounds.

After the war there was a substantial measure of recovery and at certain sheds in particular, in response to more careful attention and the allocation of individual engines to individual pairs of crews as far as possible, the Pacifics once again began to show their characteristic reliability and prowess in performance. At the ripe age of twenty-six years, for example, in 1949 'A3' Pacific No. 60106 *Flying Fox*, stationed at Grantham, ran 8,689 miles on express trains in the four weeks between mid-May and mid-June; 'A4' Pacific No. 60030 *Golden Fleece*, also from Grantham shed, completed 19,030 miles, mostly on the heavy 'Flying Scotsman' and 'Aberdonian' turns, between 14th February and 3rd May; while No. 60003 *Andrew K. McCosh* (of Kings Cross shed) ran 4,528 miles in no more than twelve consecutive days. Nevertheless the three middle big-end failures which occurred during the 1948 locomotive exchanges, with 'A4' Pacifics which had been specially tuned up for the tests, showed that a cure for the trouble had still to be found. It is undeniable, also, that though the inspection and preparation of the post-Gresley three-cylinder engines, with their three independent sets of valve-motion, may take longer than that of the Gresley engines with the 2-to-1 conjugated gear, the former have scored in the long run by lower maintenance costs.

13 – The Final Years

WHAT has just been written will help to explain some of the developments which have taken place since Sir Nigel Gresley's untimely death in 1941. As an experiment, four of the 'A4s', Nos. 60003, 60012, 60014 and 60031, had their middle cylinders lined up to 17 in. diameter, $1\frac{1}{2}$ in. less than that of the outside cylinders. While this arrangement might have helped to equalise the cylinder horsepowers at high speeds, it resulted in a very unequal effort from the three cylinders at lower speeds, as well as cutting down the tractive effort. The 18o in. diameter of the middle cylinders of these engines, however, has since been restored. But all the Pacifics built under the superintendence of Gresley's successors, as described in Chapters IV and V, were provided with three independent sets of Walschaerts motion, one for each cylinder.

Not until after 1950 was there found a solution of the middle big-end difficulties, and it came from Swindon with the appointment of K. J. Cook as Mechanical & Electrical Engineer of the Eastern and North Eastern Regions. He had been thoroughly trained in the high standards of accuracy in fitting for which Swindon is noted, and in a very short time he began to apply similar methods at Doncaster and Darlington. One of the innovations was the installation in the Doncaster erecting shop of a Zeiss optical lining-up instrument for checking the alignment of frames, cylinders and horn guides.

Gresley's fondness for ample tolerances in bearings is common knowledge, and jointly with his use of heat-treated nickel-chrome steel connecting and coupling rods, with their exceptional resonance, there came about the proverbial 'Gresley knock', which made his engines acoustically recognizable from a considerable distance away. As soon as Cook, with the help of the Zeiss equipment, tried a reduction of these tolerances, heating troubles began to develop, even when the Pacifics were no further away from the shops than their trial runs after overhaul. But then followed in succession the replacement of the bronze liners in the middle big-ends by steel ones, with improved methods of lubrication, which almost completely eliminated middle big-end heating; the fitting of manganese steel liners to horn-cheeks and axleboxes; and finally the replacement of the resonant alloy steel rods by forgings of ordinary carbon steel. Reduced tolerances now became possible without fear of heating trouble, and with a number of the engines the maximum cut-off was increased from 65 to 75 per cent to permit more rapid acceleration.

The results of these relatively simple changes were remarkable. Up to 1939 no 'A4' Pacific was allowed to run more than 80,000 miles before going into the works for heavy repairs. By 1960 the average mileage of all the engines of this type shedded at Kings Cross had reached 6,000 miles over a four-week period, while individual engines were scoring up 10,000 and even 11,000 miles – probably an all-time record for Gresley Pacifics. This was helped by transferring all heavy valve and piston examinations from Kings Cross to Doncaster, which had better facilities for the purpose. The 'A3s' also were running more reliably than ever before, and accumulating mileages up to 100,000 between general overhauls. Further, the changes mentioned in the last paragraph resulted in a quietness of running unknown with these Pacifics previously.

A further alteration of note has been the fitting of double blast-pipes and double chimneys to the whole of the 'A3s' and the 'A4s'. The surprise is that this desirable change, which even with present-day coal has permitted a reversion to the 15 per cent cut-offs and even less of pre-war days, and has reduced the average 'A3' coal consumption by over 6 per cent, was not made at a much earlier date, seeing that the cost per engine of the alteration, even at present prices, is no more than £240. But it has brought in its train the nuisance of drifting exhaust. Almost alone among British Pacifics, the Gresley 'A3s' have never carried smoke deflectors, apart from the experimental fittings already described on *Coronach* and *Humorist*, but something of the kind evidently is needed. So in 1960 deflectors of the German type, attached to the upper part of the smokebox only and extending well out in front, were fitted to No. 60049 *Galtee More;* since then other Pacifics of the same type have been equipped similarly, and this is to be standard equipment for the whole class. There is less need of such provision, of course, on the wedge-fronted 'A4s'.

In reviewing these changes, it should be remembered that none of the Pacifics have to perform duties as exacting as those they had to shoulder before the war. The fastest post-war trains have been limited to nine-coach formations, of a maximum of 315 tare tons, and have fallen considerably short in scheduled speed of the streamline services of 1935–1939. The only exception has been the summer non-stop Kings Cross–Edinburgh 'Elizabethan', on which for some time 'A4' Pacifics were working eleven-coach loads of just over 400 tare tons on a schedule allowing only 390 min. for the 392·8 miles; by 1961, the last year of steam haulage, the train had come down to ten coaches and the allowance had increased to 395 min., but even so this involved harder work than with the same train in 1939.

At the end of 1961 the whole of the Gresley Pacifics were still in service, with two exceptions – 'A4' No. 4469 *Sir Ralph Wedgwood*, which as previously mentioned was damaged beyond repair at York by an enemy bomb, and No. 4473 (British Railways No. 60104) *Solario*, broken up in 1960 after a working life of 37 years. Several others have been withdrawn since. In these austere and strictly utilitarian days, the graceful locomotive lines initiated by Gresley have been rapidly disappearing, and the engines themselves, now being replaced on so many of their former duties by diesel power, must follow suit before very long.

But the deterioration in the quality of steam locomotive work which set in on other Regions as diesel-electric units began to infiltrate on the principal express passenger services did not show itself in the least degree on the East Coast main line. The rejuvenated 'A3' Pacifics continued to put up performances almost indistinguishable from those of the 'A4s', and the post-war Peppercorn 'A1s' were not able to beat either in the matter of power output. Maximum speeds in the 90–100 m.p.h. range became almost commonplace from the middle 1950s onwards, especially over the historic racing ground from Stoke Summit towards Peterborough, and I cannot do better than conclude this chapter with a couple of outstanding 'A4' runs, one in 1959 and the other in 1961, by engines in the 22nd and 24th years of their age respectively.

The first of these fine exploits was on 23rd May, 1959, with a special train in celebration of the Jubilee of the Stephenson Locomotive Society. A train of eight coaches had been made up, with every seat occupied, weighing 271 tons empty and 295 tons gross, or almost identical in tonnage with the pre-war 'Coronation' streamliner *minus* the observation car. At its head, most appropriately, was No. 60007 *Sir Nigel Gresley*, which has always been one of the most competent of the 'A4' series. And at the regulator was Bill Hoole, one of the most renowned drivers of all time over the Great Northern main line, ably assisted by Fireman Hancox, both of Kings Cross shed. The run was to be to Doncaster and back, with a schedule of 97 min. for the 105·45 miles from Kings Cross to Grantham, after which the train was routed *via* Lincoln to Doncaster, and then 144 min. for the 155·95 miles from Doncaster back to London. A special relaxation of the overall 90 m.p.h. speed restriction had been granted by the Chief Civil Engineer for this historic occasion.

So it was that on the down journey 101 m.p.h. was reached at Three Counties, and a time of 22 min. 10 sec. was achieved over the 30·3 miles from Stevenage to Huntingdon, including a 69 m.p.h. slowing over the Offord curves. But the major excitement of this run was up the long ascent to Stoke, for Hoole had promised us a minimum of 80 m.p.h. over the summit, and

TABLE III (E) E.R. KINGS CROSS–DONCASTER
Stephenson Locomotive Society's Jubilee Runs, 23rd May, 1959
Engine: 'A4' 4-6-2 No. 60007 *Sir Nigel Gresley. Load:* 8 coaches, 271 tons tare, 295 tons gross

Dist.		Sched.	Actual	Speeds
miles		min.	min. sec.	m.p.h.
0·00	DONCASTER . .	0	0 00	—
2·75	Black Carr Junction . .	—	4 42	—
4·60	Rossington . . .	—	6 21	70
6·45	Milepost 149½ . .	—	7 55	68/71½
8·25	Bawtry	—	9 37	—
			p.w.s.	*40
12·00	Ranskill	—	13 36	†80½
17·35	RETFORD . . .	19	17 49	*65
16·45	Gamston . . .	—	20 33	70¼
22·20	Milepost 133¾ . .	—	22 00	72½
24·75	Dukeries Junction . .	—	23 54	80½/83½
28·50	Crow Park . . .	—	26 43	‡76
29·65	Carlton	—	27 38	82/*64
35·85	NEWARK . . .	35	32 42	—
			p.w.s.	*28
40·60	Claypole . . .	—	39 28	56½
44·45	Hougham . . .	—	43 18	69
46·25	Barkston S. Junction .	44	44 53	69
50·50	GRANTHAM . .	48	48 19	80½
53·85	Great Ponton . . .	—	50 58	76¼
55·85	Stoke	—	52 31	75
58·85	Corby Glen . . .	—	54 36	95
63·70	Little Bytham . . .	—	57 27	109/112
67·30	Essendine	—	59 24	104
71·10	Tallington . . .	—	61 40	95
74·05	Helpston . . .	—	63 49	—
			p.w.s.	*25
76·45	Werrington Junction .	—	67 04	—
79·60	PETERBOROUGH . .	72	71 55	*22
80·95	Fletton Junction . .	—	74 08	—
83·35	Yaxley	—	76 35	eased
86·60	Holme	—	79 29	68
88·60	Connington South . .	—	81 05	79
92·45	Abbots Ripton . . .	—	84 09	74/84
97·10	HUNTINGDON . .	90	87 49	*70
100·00	Offord	—	90 24	*65
104·20	St Neots . . .	—	93 44	80½
108·45	Tempsford . . .	—	96 30	100
111·80	Sandy	—	98 33	96/98
114·80	Biggleswade . . .	—	100 29	90
118·85	Arlesey	—	103 22	§83½
120·25	Three Counties . .	—	104 17	87
124·05	HITCHIN . . .	111	107 01	80½
127·40	Stevenage . . .	—	109 36	78/*69
130·90	Knebworth . . .	—	112 27	75
132·45	Woolmer Green . .	—	113 44	*67
135·65	Welwyn Garden City .	—	116 25	72½
138·25	HATFIELD . . .	124	118 36	70½
143·25	Potters Bar . . .	129	122 50	72½
146·80	New Barnet . . .	—	126 14	eased
151·00	Wood Green . . .	—	130 09	—
153·45	FINSBURY PARK . .	—	132 37	—
			p.w.s.	
155·95	KINGS CROSS . .	144	137 42	—

* Speed restriction.   † At milepost 140.   ‡ Speed eased.   § At Langford.

we were to see if this was possible. A 40 m.p.h. slowing had been needed at Werrington Junction because of permanent way work, but then No. 60007 was opened out to 30 per cent cut-off, with full regulator, and the sparks began to fly. By Tallington speed had risen to 79 m.p.h. on the level; up 1 in 440 and 1 in 264 to Essendine it increased to $80\frac{1}{2}$ and on the two miles of level beyond to $83\frac{1}{2}$; most of the subsequent $4\frac{1}{4}$ miles at 1 in 200 was climbed at over 80 m.p.h., and only at the end of it, at milepost $95\frac{1}{2}$, was there a momentary drop to 79; the $1\frac{1}{2}$ level miles through Corby Glen produced $83\frac{1}{2}$ m.p.h., and with a final advance in cut-off to 40 per cent the last 3 miles at 1 in 178 were carried by storm at a minimum of 81 m.p.h. This was a wonderful effort indeed, and calculating from resistance formulae commonly used must have required an equivalent drawbar horsepower rising to a maximum of 2,200.

Table III (E) sets out what happened on the up journey. The highlights came after *Sir Nigel* had maintained 69 m.p.h. up the 1 in 200 to Peascliffe tunnel, and had accelerated to an unusual 80 through Grantham station. The impetus took the train up the final 1 in 200 to Stoke at a minimum of 75 m.p.h., all on $27\frac{1}{2}$ per cent cut-off, and then followed the thrilling flight down towards Peterborough, with its top speed of 112 m.p.h. between Little Bytham and Essendine. As the drain on the boiler had reduced the pressure to 200 lb, Hoole now brought his cut-off back from the 30 per cent that he had been using down the bank; otherwise a slightly higher maximum might have been attained, though not, I think, more than 115 m.p.h. at most. But even so the 7 min. 4 sec. for the 12·25 miles from Corby to Tallington was the fastest, so far as I can trace, that has ever been recorded over this length; *Mallard*, on the occasion of her epic 126 m.p.h. maximum, was severely eased down from Essendine onwards. Our average from Corby to Tallington had been exactly 104 m.p.h.

Further excitements were to come. For after the restrained running now compulsory over Stilton Fen, south of Peterborough, to Holme, speed rose in 2 miles of level from 68 to 79 m.p.h., and the $4\frac{1}{2}$ miles of 1 in 200 past Abbots Ripon were mounted at a minimum of 74; next, after the easing through Huntingdon and over the Offord curves, followed one of the most striking feats of the day. It was the acceleration, on 35 per cent cut-off, from 65 to $80\frac{1}{2}$ m.p.h. up the rise to St Neots, and then, on the very slight descent beyond, to yet another 100 at Tempsford, with a maintained 96–100 m.p.h. for some distance afterwards on practically level track. Finally, nearly at the end of a run on which the 'A4' had been worked so hard, there was the minimum of 78 m.p.h. at Stevenage – a drop of no more than 9 m.p.h. up the whole of the gradient from Three Counties, finishing with a lengthy 1 in 200.

Although our gross time had been 137 min. 42 sec. for the 155·95 miles from Doncaster, the net was not more than 131 min., and if this be compared with the 'Coronation's' $127\frac{1}{2}$ min. schedule, pass to stop, in 1939, regard had to be paid to the 1959 restrictions to 65 m.p.h. from Yaxley to Holme, 60 m.p.h. from Hatfield to Kings Cross, and to various others which did not

TABLE III (F)
N.E. & SCOTTISH REGIONS – NEWCASTLE–EDINBURGH
Engine: 'A4' 4-6-2 No. 60004 *William Whitelaw*
Load: 8 coaches, 272 tons tare, 285 tons gross

Dist.		Sched.	Actual	Speeds
miles		min.	min. sec.	m.p.h.
0·00	NEWCASTLE . .	0	0 00	—
0·60	Manors East . . .	—	3 15	*23
2·70	Benton Bank . . .	—	6 26	55
5·00	Forest Hall . . .	—	8 49	63
7·70	Annitsford . . .	—	11 14	71
9·90	Cramlington . . .	—	13 10	65
13·90	Stannington . . .	—	16 22	82
16·60	MORPETH . . .	20½	18 47	*40
20·20	Longhirst . . .	—	22 13	76
23·25	Widdington . . .	—	24 39	70
28·55	Acklington . . .	—	29 01	76/*70
31·95	Warkworth . . .	—	31 44	79
34·85	ALNMOUTH . .	37	34 07	*60
37·50	Longhoughton . .	—	36 22	72
39·45	Little Mill . . .	—	37 58	74
43·15	Christon Bank . . .	—	40 37	86
46·15	Chathill . . .	—	42 40	90
			sigs.	*56
51·65	BELFORD . . .	52	47 06	61½
			sigs.	*38
55·00	Smeafield . . .	—	50 50	70
58·60	Beal	(†3)	53 58	85½/88
63·60	Scremerston . . .	—	57 08	76½/74
65·80	Tweedmouth . . .	—	58 56	*45
67·00	BERWICK . . .	69½	60 31	*46
67·95	Marshall Meadows . .	71	61 44	56/67
			p.w.s.	*15
72·60	Burnmouth . . .	—	67 54	45
74·25	Ayton	—	69 35	64/78½
79·20	Reston Junction . .	82	72 46	76
83·30	Grantshouse . . .	87	76 51	72½
			p.w.s.	*40
88·00	Cockburnspath . .	—	81 37	70
93·15	Oxwellmains . . .	—	85 43	79
95·35	DUNBAR . . .	97	87 28	*60
101·05	East Linton . . .	—	92 15	77/81
106·70	DREM	—	96 34	78/76
111·25	Longniddry Junction .	—	100 04	83
115·00	Prestonpans . . .	—	102 53	77
			sigs.	*8
118·35	Monktonhall Junction .	117	108 16	—
			sigs.	*11
121·45	PORTOBELLO . .	120	115 42	45
124·45	EDINBURGH . .	126	120 56	—

* Speed restriction.   † Recovery time (min).

exist in the days of the streamliners. Some 25 miles of the day's circuit had been completed at an average of 100 m.p.h., and about 55 miles at an average of 90; and it was also a record for a British steam locomotive to have reached the three-figure level of speed at three different points, all well separated, on the same day. There could have been no finer 'swan song' to celebrate Driver Hoole's retirement shortly afterwards, and at the same time to commemorate a notable locomotive society's jubilee.

Two years later Ronald I. Nelson recorded, much further to the north, the remarkable run set out in Table III (F). The train was the down afternoon 'Talisman', with its normal eight-coach load of 272 tons tare and 285 tons gross; and Driver P. B. Robertson and Fireman J. Reid, of Edinburgh Haymarket shed, took it over at Newcastle 5 min. late with their 'A4' Pacific No. 60004 *William Whitelaw*. This train is mounted on roller bearings throughout, which helps to explain the astonishingly rapid recoveries from the various slacks; but there is little doubt that the engine was being worked as hard as *Sir Nigel Gresley* on the previous run to achieve such times and speeds as these.

Up the 1 in 200 from Benton Bank to Forest Hall speed rose from 55 to 63 m.p.h.; from Morpeth to Longhirst came the first of the lightning accelerations, from 40 to 76 m.p.h. in just over 3½ miles, partly down at 1 in 208; more outstanding still was the rise from 60 to 74 m.p.h. up the 1 in 170 from Alnmouth to Little Mill, which also must have demanded an equivalent drawbar-horsepower of over 2,000. After the two signal checks speed again rose rapidly to 88 m.p.h. on the slight descent past Beal.

Another tremendous output of energy was up the long climb that succeeds the Berwick slack. A rate of 67 m.p.h. that had been attained up the 1 in 190 was cut short by a permanent way slowing, but from 76 m.p.h. attained between Ayton and Reston Junction the speed dropped by no more than 3½ m.p.h. up 6 miles at 1 in 200 to Grantshouse. Over the undulations beyond Dunbar from 76 to 83 m.p.h. was the sustained speed, and some 10 min. had been gained on schedule when the final signal checks spoiled the end of the run. Even so, the stop at Edinburgh Waverley was dead on time. While the actual time for the 124·45 miles from Newcastle was all but 121 min., the net time was not more than 109¼ min., that is, 10¾ min. less than the 'Coronation' streamliner schedule in 1939. Thus the Gresley Pacifics are continuing to win their spurs up to the very end of their history, and twenty years after their eminent designer's death. It was significant indeed that on 8th June, 1961, the day of the Duke of Kent's wedding in York Minster, the engine chosen to work from Kings Cross to York the train carrying Her Majesty the Queen and many British and foreign royalties was not a 'Deltic' diesel, nor a Type '4' 2,000 h.p. diesel, nor a Peppercorn 'A1' Pacific, but a faithful twenty-four-year-old Gresley 'A4' Pacific, No. 60028 *Walter K. Whigham*!

Sir Nigel Gresley died on 5th April, 1941, in harness, as he himself surely would have wished. He had been Locomotive Engineer of the Great Northern Railway from 1911 to 1922, and Chief Mechanical Engineer of the London &

North Eastern Railway from the formation of the latter company in 1923 until 1941, a total of 30 years. Many honours came to him during his career, including the O.B.E. for his services in the First World War, awarded in 1920; the honorary degree of Doctor of Science from Manchester University in 1936; and the dignity of Knight Bachelor in the Birthday Honours of the same year.

In no uncertain fashion he left the impress of his personality on the locomotive practice of Great Britain. Many of his designs, and his Pacifics in particular, can still hold their own with their later competitors, and will remain with us for some little time yet as a reminder both of one of the most exciting periods of British locomotive history and also of one of the most able and versatile of all British locomotive engineers. We salute his honoured memory.

TABLE III (G)
THE GRESLEY PACIFICS – NUMBERS, NAMES, CLASSES
AND BUILDING DATES

L.N.E.R. original No.	Thompson renumbering	British Railways No.	Name*	Original class	Date of building	Present class	Notes
4470	113	60113	Great Northern	AI	1922	AI/I	A
4471	102	60102	Sir Frederick Banbury . . .	,,	,,	A3	B
4472	103§	60103	Flying Scotsman	,,	1923	,,	CP
4473	104	60104	Solario	,,	,,	,,	—
4474	105	60105	Victor Wild	,,	,,	,,	D
4475	106	60106	Flying Fox	,,	,,	,,	—
4476	107	60107	Royal Lancer	,,	,,	,,	—
4477	108§	60108	Gay Crusader	,,	,,	,,	E
4478	109§	60109	Hermit	,,	,,	,,	—
4479	110	60110	Robert the Devil . . .	,,	,,	,,	—
4480	111	60111	Enterprise	,,	,,	,,	G
4481	112§	60112	St Simon	,,	,,	,,	—
2543	44	60044	Melton	,,	1924	,,	—
2544	45	60045	Lemberg	,,	,,	,,	H
2545	46	60046	Diamond Jubilee . . .	,,	,,	,,	—
2546	47	60047	Donovan	,,	,,	,,	—
2547	48	60048	Doncaster	,,	,,	,,	—
2548	49§	60049	Galtee More	,,	,,	,,	—
2549	50§	60050	Persimmon	,,	,,	,,	—
2550	51	60051	Blink Bonny	,,	,,	,,	—
2551	52§	60052	Prince Palatine . . .	,,	,,	,,	—
2552	53§	60053	Sansovino	,,	,,	,,	—
2553	54§	60054	Prince of Wales . . .	,,	,,	,,	—
2554	55	60055	Woolwinder	,,	,,	,,	—
2555	56	60056	Centenary	,,	1925	,,	—
2556	57	60057	Ormonde	,,	,,	,,	—
2557	58	60058	Blair Athol	,,	,,	,,	—
2558	59	60059	Tracery	,,	,,	,,	—
2559	60§	60060	The Tetrarch	,,	,,	,,	—
2560	61	60061	Pretty Polly	,,	,,	,,	—
2561	62	60062	Minoru	,,	,,	,,	—
2562	63§	60063	Isinglass	,,	,,	,,	—
2563	64	60064	(William Whitelaw) Tagalie . .	,,	1924	,,	K
2564	65	60065	Knight of Thistle . . .	,,	,,	,,	K
2565	66	60066	Merry Hampton . . .	,,	,,	,,	K

L.N.E.R. original No.	Thompson son renumbering	British Railways No.	Name*	Original class	Date of building	Present class	Notes
2566	67	60067	Ladas	,,	,,	,,	K
2567	68	60068	Sir Visto	,,	,,	,,	KN
2568	69 §	60069	Sceptre	,,	,,	,,	K
2569	70 §	60070	Gladiateur	,,	,,	,,	K
2570	71	60071	Tranquil	,,	,,	,,	K
2571	72	60072	Sunstar	,,	,,	,,	K
2572	73	60073	St Gatien	,,	,,	,,	K
2573	74 §	60074	Harvester	,,	,,	,,	GK
2574	75	60075	St Frusquin	,,	,,	,,	K
2575	76	60076	Galopin	,,	,,	,,	K
2576	77 §	60077	The White Knight	,,	,,	,,	KM
2577	78	60078	Night Hawk	,,	,,	,,	K
2578	79	60079	Bayardo	,,	,,	,,	GK
2579	80	60080	Dick Turpin	,,	,,	,,	K
2580	81	60081	Shotover	,,	,,	,,	GKM
2581	82	60082	Neil Gow	,,	,,	,,	K
2582	83	60083	Sir Hugo	,,	,,	,,	K
2743	89	60089	Felstead	A3	1928	,,	—
2744	90	60090	Grand Parade	,,	,,	,,	X
2745	91	60091	Captain Cuttle	,,	,,	,,	—
2746	92	60092	Fairway	,,	,,	,,	—
2747	93	60093	Coronach	,,	,,	,,	U
2748	94	60094	Colorado	,,	,,	,,	—
2749	95 §	60095	Flamingo	,,	1929	,,	—
2750	96	60096	Papyrus	,,	,,	,,	Q
2751	97	60097	Humorist	,,	,,	,,	V
2752	98 §	60098	Spion Kop	,,	,,	,,	—
2595	84	60084	Trigo	,,	1930	,,	—
2596	85	60085	Manna	,,	,,	,,	—
2597	86	60086	Gainsborough	,,	,,	,,	—
2598	87 §	60087	(Rock Sand) Blenheim	,,	,,	,,	—
2599	88	60088	Book Law	,,	,,	,,	—
2795	99	60099	Call Boy	,,	,,	,,	—
2796	100	60100	Spearmint	,,	,,	,,	—
2797	101	60101	Cicero	,,	,,	,,	—
2500	35 §	60035	Windsor Lad	,,	1934	,,	O
2501	36	60036	Colombo	,,	,,	,,	—
2502	37	60037	Hyperion	,,	,,	,,	—
2503	38	60038	Firdaussi	,,	,,	,,	—
2504	39	60039	Sandwich	,,	,,	,,	—
2505	40 §	60040	Cameronian	,,	,,	,,	—
2506	41	60041	Salmon Trout	,,	,,	,,	—
2507	42	60042	Singapore	,,	,,	,,	—
2508	43	60043	Brown Jack	,,	1935	,,	—
2509	14	60014	Silver Link	A4	,,	A4	†RW
2510	15	60015	Quicksilver	,,	,,	,,	R
2511	16	60016	Silver King	,,	,,	,,	R
2512	17	60017	Silver Fox	,,	,,	,,	R
4482	23	60023	Golden Eagle	,,	1936	,,	—
4483	24 §	60024	Kingfisher	,,	,,	,,	—
4484	25 §	60025	Falcon	,,	1937	,,	—
4485	26 §	60026	(Kestrel) Miles Beevor	,,	,,	,,	—
4486	27 §	60027	Merlin	,,	,,	,,	—
4487	28	60028	(Sea Eagle) Walter K. Whigham	,,	,,	,,	—
4488	9	60009	(Osprey) Union of South Africa	,,	,,	,,	S
4489	10	60010	(Woodcock) Dominion of Canada	,,	,,	,,	SZ
4490	11	60011	Empire of India	,,	,,	,,	S
4491	12	60012	Commonwealth of Australia	,,	,,	,,	SW

L.N.E.R. original No.	Thompson renumbering	British Railways No.	Name*	Original class	Date of building	Present class	Notes
4492	13	60013	Dominion of New Zealand	,,	,,	,,	S
4493	29	60029	Woodcock	,,	,,	,,	—
4494	3	60003	(Osprey) Andrew K. McCosh	,,	,,	,,	W
4495	30	60030	(Great Snipe) Golden Fleece .	,,	,,	,,	T
4496	8	60008	(Golden Shuttle) Dwight D. Eisenhower	,,	,,	,,	T
4497	31	60031	Golden Plover	,,	,,	,,	W
4498	7	60007	Sir Nigel Gresley . . .	,,	,,	,,	—
4462	4	60004	(Great Snipe) William Whitelaw	,,	,,	,,	—
4463	18	60018	Sparrow Hawk	,,	,,	,,	—
4464	19	60019	Bittern	,,	,,	,,	—
4465	20	60020	Guillemot	,,	,,	,,	—
4466	6§	60006	(Herring Gull) Sir Ralph Wedgwood .	,,	1938	,,	—
4467	21	60021	Wild Swan	,,	,,	,,	—
4468	22	60022	Mallard	,,	,,	,,	†‡VF
4469	—	—	(Gadwall) Sir Ralph Wedgwood .	,,	,,	,,	Y
4499	2	60002	(Pochard) Sir Murrough Wilson .	,,	,,	,,	—
4500	1	60001	(Garganey) Sir Ronald Matthews .	,,	,,	,,	—
4900	32	60032	Gannet	,,	,,	,,	—
4901	5	60005	(Capercaillie) Sir Charles Newton .	,,	,,	,,	V
4902	33	60033	Seagull	,,	,,	,,	VF
4903	34	60034	(Peregrine) Lord Faringdon .	,,	,,	,,	VF

NOTES: * Names in brackets are original names of engines subsequently renamed. † Ran 43 miles at 100 m.p.h. and touched 112½ m.p.h., 27th September, 1935. ‡ Attained 126 m.p.h., 7th July, 1938 A: Completely rebuilt in 1945 by E. Thompson with three independent sets of Walschaerts valve-motion banjo dome, double exhaust and 250-lb pressure. B: First Gresley Pacific to work a 610-ton passenger train, 3rd September, 1922. C: Exhibited at British Empire Exhibition, Wembley, 1924. D: Worked between Paddington and Plymouth, G.W.R., in the exchange tests, April–May, 1925. E: First Pacific to have completely redesigned valve-motion for short cut-off working, 1925. F: Took part in Locomotive Exchange Trials over L.M., W. and S. Regions, summer of 1948. G: Rebuilt with 220-lb boiler and 43-element superheater, 1927. H: Rebuilt as 'G' and with cylinders lined up to 18¼ in. diameter, 1927. K: Built by the North British Locomotive Company. L: Fitted temporarily with 62-element superheater, 1926. M: Fitted with A.C.F.I. feed-water heaters and feed-pumps, 1929. N: Last original 'A1' Pacific to be converted to 'A3', 1949. O: First 'A3' Pacific to be fitted with banjo dome for steam collection, 1934. P: Locomotive used on the London–Leeds high-speed test, 30th November, 1934, and first Gresley Pacific to attain 100 m.p.h. Q: Locomotive used on the London–Newcastle high-speed test, 5th March, 1935; maximum speed 108 m.p.h. R: Assigned to the 'Silver Jubilee' streamline workings and at first painted grey. S: Assigned to the 'Coronation' streamline workings. T: Assigned to the 'West Riding Limited' streamline workings. U: Used for experiments in smoke deflection in 1932. V: Fitted with smoke deflectors, double blast-pipe and double chimney. W: Middle cylinder lined up to 17 in. diameter, 1948. X: Severely damaged in Castlecary collision, 10th December, 1937; practically a new engine, 1938. Y: Damaged beyond repair by a German bomb at York, 29th April, 1942, and subsequently scrapped. Z: Carries on smokebox bell presented by the Canadian National Railways. § For a brief period about 1947, before the Thompson renumbering scheme came into force, the following Gresley Pacifics carried the temporary numbers shown in brackets: 4472 (502), 4477 (507), 4478 (508), 4481 (511), 2548 (517), 2549 (518), 2551 (520), 2552 (521), 2553 (522), 2559 (528), 2562 (531), 2568 (537), 2569 (538), 2573 (542), 2576 (545), 2749 (558), 2752 (561), 2598 (565), 2500 (570), 2505 (575), 4483 (585), 4484 (586), 4485 (587), 4486 (588) and 4466 (605), twenty-five engines in all.

TABLE III (H)
LEADING DIMENSIONS OF GRESLEY PACIFICS

Class	'A1'	'A3'	'A4'
Cylinders (3), diameter . . .	20 in.	19 in.	18½ in.
,, stroke . . .	26 in.	26 in.	26 in.
Driving wheels, diameter . .	6 ft 8 in.	6 ft 8 in.	6 ft 8 in.
Heating surface, tubes . . .	2,715 sq ft	2,477 sq ft	2,345 sq ft
,, ,, firebox . . .	215 sq ft	215 sq ft	231 sq ft
,, ,, total . . .	2,930 sq ft	2,692 sq ft	2,576 sq ft
Superheating surface . . .	525 sq ft	706 sq ft	750 sq ft
Firegrate area	41·25 sq ft	41·25 sq ft	41·25 sq ft
Working pressure, per sq in. . .	180 lb	220 lb	250 lb
Tractive effort (at 85 per cent b.p.) .	29,835 lb	32,910 lb	35,455 lb
Adhesion weight	60·00 tons	66·15 tons	66·00 tons
Total engine weight (working order) .	92·45 tons	96·25 tons	102·95 tons
Tender coal capacity . . .	9 tons	9 tons	9 tons
,, water ,, . . .	5,000 gal.	5,000 gal.	5,000 gal.
,, weight (working order) .	56·30 tons	56·30 tons	*64·95 tons
Engine and tender weight . .	148·75 tons	152·55 tons	*167·90 tons

* Corridor tender.

IV

THE THOMPSON PACIFICS,
LONDON & NORTH EASTERN RAILWAY

1 – *The Revolt from Gresley*

NEXT in the London & North Eastern line of succession in the Mechanical Department was Edward Thompson, and he duly assumed the position of Chief Mechanical Engineer on the death of Sir Nigel Gresley in 1941. In more ways than one it was not the happiest of appointments. For one thing, Thompson was 60 years of age, which is relatively late in life to assume so big a responsibility. In the second place, most of his engineering life had been spent on the North Eastern Railway or in the North Eastern Area of the L.N.E.R., and he was therefore traditionally North Eastern in outlook; he had married a daughter of Sir Vincent Raven; and from the formation of the London & North Eastern Railway in 1923, when as described in Chapter II it was Gresley rather than Raven who was chosen to direct L.N.E.R. locomotive affairs, there had been no love lost between Darlington and Doncaster.

Moreover, had it not been for the grouping, when A. C. Stamer succeeded Raven at Darlington (but, of course, as Chief Assistant Mechanical Engineer under Gresley), Thompson would have had every prospect eventually of following him as the North Eastern Railway's Chief Mechanical Engineer. Thompson had spent six years at Stratford in charge of the locomotives of the former Great Eastern Railway, and did some good work there, especially in matters like valve-setting, but still, of course, playing second fiddle. To these frustrations there may be added an aversion to Gresley and all his works that was shown unmistakably as soon as Thompson took the L.N.E.R. reins into his own hands. By now Bulleid was safely out of the way, having for four years past been pursuing his adventurous course on the Southern Railway; but others who had been closely associated with Gresley found themselves out of favour with the 'new king which knew not Joseph'. Wartime provided a convenient opportunity for transferring various of these men elsewhere, in particular the Technical Assistant (Locomotive), B. Spencer, who had had no small influence on Gresley's work.

Nevertheless certain things must be said in justification of the drastic steps which Thompson took immediately after appointment. Whereas Gresley put design before everything else, Thompson, apart from the years that he had spent in charge of carriage and wagon work, had been concerned mainly with maintenance. By 1941, shortage of labour owing to war conditions was becoming acute, and whatever could be done to ease maintenance difficulties was now of paramount importance. It was little surprise, therefore, when

Thompson decided to cut away the valances above the coupled wheels of all the 'A4' Pacifics, in order to make their motion more accessible. But he was also opposed to Gresley's use of three cylinders rather than two in all but the most powerful classes, notwithstanding the better balancing obtained with the three-cylinder arrangement (this, for example, had made possible the use of the 'Sandringham'-type 'B17' 4-6-0s on the weight-restricted Great Eastern line, despite 6½ tons more adhesion weight than the ex-G.E.R. 'B12' 4-6-0s). Above all, Thompson was opposed root and branch to the Gresley derived motion for the inside cylinders of three-cylinder engines, again not without some reason from the maintenance point of view.

The firstfruits of the new design activity at Doncaster were seen at the end of 1942 in the emergence of the first 'B1', a straightforward and handsome 4-6-0 of a type that was greatly multiplied and has proved very nearly, though perhaps not quite, the equal in capability of the Stanier Class '5' 4-6-0 design of the London Midland & Scottish Railway. Strictly it has no place in this chronicle except in so far as it introduced certain Thompson ideas which were to become standard in Pacific construction also. These were a new type of front end, with the cylinders cast separately, and this was rather curious, for the Raven practice in all his North Eastern three-cylinder designs had been to use a single casting for all the cylinders and their valve-chests.

The bogie also was of a new design, taking the weight of the front end of the main frames through spherical surfaces on to bronze slippers, with the centre-line of these slippers in a direct line with the main bogie frame. Instead of the swing links which had been standard for many years with Great Northern and London & North Eastern bogie engines, side control was exercised by helical springs, which permitted a maximum movement of 4 in. on either side of the engine centre-line.

The next happening was one which caused a great deal more comment. In 1934, to obviate the considerable amount of piloting needed over the difficult main line of the Scottish Area between Edinburgh and Aberdeen, and to permit faster starts from the principal intermediate stations (in almost every case up steep gradients) Gresley had introduced the first and only eight-coupled express passenger engines ever to run on a British railway. These magnificent machines, six in number of Class 'P2', were of the 2-8-2 type, and so far as concerns performance fully justified themselves. With their 220 lb pressure, three 21 in. by 26 in. cylinders, 6 ft 2 in. driving wheels, 43,460 lb tractive effort and, above all, 79 tons adhesion weight, they could tackle loads hitherto unheard-of over the main line concerned, even up to 600 tons.

In the middle 1930s I had a number of runs behind the 'P2s', certain of which were described in *British Locomotive Practice and Performance*. On one with No. 2002 *Earl Marischal*, before the engine left Doncaster for Scotland, we had a seventeen-coach load out of Kings Cross of 545 tons tare and 580 tons full, which the 2-8-2 lifted through Finsbury Park without a vestige of slip in no more than 5 min. 51 sec. from the start. There was no particular hurry up the 1 in 200 to Potters Bar, but the 46·4 miles from Stevenage to

Fletton Junction were run in 40 min. 39 sec., with a top speed of 79 m.p.h., and Peterborough, 76·35 miles, was reached in 79 min. 56 sec., 6 min. early; the train was the 4 p.m. down. With load reduced there to 375 tons tare and 400 tons gross *Earl Marischal* then cut every succeeding schedule time, running the 29·1 miles from Peterborough to Grantham in 31 min. 45 sec., the 14·65 miles on to Newark in 15 min. 54 sec., the 18·5 miles from Newark to Retford in 20 min. 17 sec., and the final 17·35 miles to Doncaster in 19 min. 47 sec., all start to stop and compared with booked times of 36, 17, 22 and 20 min. respectively.

On the route for which they were designed such trains as the 'Aberdonian', which at that time ran undivided as compared with the two separate trains of later years, had no terrors for the 'P2s'. My friend W. A. Willox once timed a southbound run out of Aberdeen on which No. 2001 *Cock o' the North* was saddled with a load of 511 tons tare and 550 tons gross, but soared up the long initial climb from Aberdeen with such vigour that on the steepest stretch, inclined at 1 in 102, there was no lower speed than 42 m.p.h., while up the second big climb, from Stonehaven, the 7·15 miles were covered at an average of 51·1 m.p.h., despite the fact that much of the grade is at 1 in 92–102. Speed rose to 76 m.p.h. down Marykirk bank, and the 27·75 miles from Portlethen to Craigo, the climb out of Stonehaven included, were run in 28 min. 6 sec. So Stonehaven, 16·15 miles, was passed in 21 min. 36 sec., Kinnaber Junction (where there was the usual dead slowing for the divergence), 38·0 miles, in 44 min. 10 sec., and Montrose, 40·6 miles, was reached in 50 min. 1 sec., exactly 8 min. early! The considerably lighter 'Aberdonian' of today, a train of 405 to 425 tare tons, hauled by twin diesel units with a combined horsepower of 2,730, is allowed 51 min. for the same run.

There was therefore no question as to the competence of the 2-8-2s, but it was being secured at a price. The constant curvature of this line both produced a good deal of heating of coupled axleboxes, owing to the great length of the rigid coupled wheelbase – 19 ft 6 in. – and the engines also had a tendency to spread the track on curves. Personally I have never understood how American railways, such as the Santa Fe and the Union Pacific, could build their immense 4-8-4 locomotives, more than twice the size, weight and power of the biggest British 2-8-2 or 4-6-2, and work them without trouble over steeper gradients and sharper curvature than almost anything found between Edinburgh and Aberdeen, whereas Gresley's 'P2' 2-8-2s had to be condemned on these grounds. They would have been of priceless value had they been transferred during the war years to assist with the enormous wartime trainloads between Kings Cross and Newcastle, over a main line where their long coupled wheelbase would have given no difficulty; but Thompson was determined to get rid of them as 2-8-2s, and regarded their heating trouble as ample justification for rebuilding them as Pacifics. In the rebuilds he incorporated a number of his own ideas.

The first of the six to appear in Pacific guise, in January, 1943, was No.2005 *Thane of Fife*. The leading pair of coupled wheels had been removed, and the frames ahead of what had been the second pair had been cut in order to weld

The last Pacific type to emerge from Doncaster Works – Peppercorn Class 'A1' No. 60152 Holyrood starting away from Edinburgh with an express to Carlisle by the Waverley route.

[Eric Treacy

Many changes in appearance took place during the Thompson and Peppercorn régimes. Above, the single-chimney Peppercorn 'A2', No. 60525 A. H. Peppercorn, had some grace of line. [*John Robertson*

Left, the substitution of stovepipe double chimney for the previous flared single chimney resulted in an unhappy decline in the appearance of 'A2' No. 60533 Happy Knight. *Today its chimney is rimmed.*

[*P. Ransome-Wallis*

Below, matters have improved with the 'A1' Pacifics, however, and there is dignity about No. 60156 Great Central, *one of the five named after pre-grouping companies and bearing their coats-of-arms.* [*G. Wheeler*

Above, the original appearance of Stanier's second Pacific, No. 6201
Princess Elizabeth, *with stovepipe double chimney, top-feed but no dome,
and Midland type tender.* [British Railways

No. 6201 Princess Elizabeth, *now provided with a dome but with the original
tender, at speed with the 16-coach up 'Royal Scot' south of Rugby.*
[F. R. Hebron

On the record Euston–Glasgow non-stop run of November 16, 1936: No. 6201
Princess Elizabeth, *with large standard tender, accelerating from the Preston
slack as she passes Oxheys.* [W. S. Garth

The final form of one of the 'Princesses', with dome on the rear ring of the boiler barrel and separate top-feed casing, also standard high-sided tender. No. 46204 Princess Louise is climbing Madeley bank, south of Crewe, with a summer relief express from Glasgow to Euston.

[Derek Cross

Above: at various times L.M.R. Pacifics have been loaned to the Western Region. Here No. 46210 Lady Patricia, *piloted by W.R. No.* 6834 Dummer Grange, *is descending the 1 in 50 of Rattery Bank with the up 'Cornish Riviera Express'.* [D. S. Fish

Below, at the other end of the country No. 46201 Princess Elizabeth *waits at Carlisle Citadel alongside 4-6-0 No. 45724* Warspite *to take a London express on to Glasgow.* [Eric Treacy

Above, No. 46205 Princess Victoria, *showing the motion fittings needed in 1938 for the change from independent motions for all four cylinders to a derived motion for the inside cylinders.*

[*Colin P. Walker*

The forward turbine side of turbine-driven 4-6-2 No. 6202, as originally built. [*British Railways*

The reverse turbine side of No. 6202, after the engine had been fitted with smoke deflectors. The train is the heavy 5.25 p.m. express from Liverpool to Euston. [*H. C. Casserley*

After conversion in 1952 from turbine to four-cylinder propulsion – No. 46202 Princess Anne.

[*Eric Treacy*

The rebuilt 'Turbomotive', No. 46202 Princess Anne, *leaving Crewe for Euston with the 7.50 a.m. train.* [*P. Ransome-Wallis*

No. 6220 Coronation, *first of the Stanier streamlined Pacifics, as originally built.*

No. 6232 Duchess of Montrose, *one of the first five 'Coronation' Pacifics built without streamlining, in 1938. Note the single chimney as first applied.*
[*British Railways*

No. 6233 Duchess of Sutherland, *of the same 1938 non-streamlined series, later modified with double blastpipe and chimney and streamlined cylinder ports.* [*British Railways*

No. 6235 City of Birmingham, *originally streamlined, as rebuilt without streamline casing but with smoke deflectors and also double chimney. Note the sloping smokebox top.* [*British Railways*

on an entirely new front end. New cylinders of 20 in. diameter replaced the previous 21 in. cylinders, the outside cylinders being moved backwards in order to drive what had been the third pair of coupled wheels, while the inside cylinder continued to drive what was now the leading pair. That is to say, Gresley's common crank axle for all cylinders had been replaced by divided drive. The outside Walschaerts motion now worked the outside piston-valves only, while a separate Walschaerts gear was provided for the inside valve; all three piston-valves were of 10 in. in place of 9 in. diameter, providing for a freer steam flow.

The new Thompson bogie replaced the former leading radial axle, and had to be moved sufficiently far forward to clear the outside cylinders, giving the rebuilt engine a very ungainly appearance. While the bogie thus had advanced, the length of the boiler barrel had been shortened from 19 ft to 16 ft $11\frac{3}{4}$ in., in order to permit more direct steam-pipes to the outside cylinders, and this meant a backward extension of the smokebox also, which was now of exceptional length. The double blastpipe of the original 2-8-2 was retained, and the smokebox was crowned by an ugly double stovepipe chimney, flanked by small smoke deflectors attached to the upper part of the smokebox. By these changes the evaporative heating surface was reduced from 2,714 to 2,453 sq ft and the superheating surface from 777 to 680 sq ft; although the working pressure was increased from 220 to 225 lb per sq in., the tractive effort went down from 43,460 to 40,320 lb.

But the worst loss, needless to say, was in adhesion weight; while the engine weight in working order declined from $107\frac{1}{4}$ to $101\frac{1}{2}$ tons, the weight on the coupled wheels fell from 79 to 66 tons, reducing the factor of adhesion from 4·06 to 3·67. It would have been difficult indeed to recognize the misshapen 'A2/2' Pacifics, as they now became, as rebuilds of the sleek and impressive 'P2' 2-8-2s, and owing to their slipping propensities in their new guise they became so unpopular, on their return to Scotland, that they had to be transferred eventually to Great Northern sheds. It is significant that of all the ex-L.N.E.R. Pacifics, these six engines have been the first as a class to go to the scrap-heap.

Whatever else might be alleged against these Thompson rebuilds, however, there was nothing wrong with their front end arrangement, as was demonstrated by their capacity for high speed. This is evident in the two runs, timed by Sir James Colyer-Fergusson, which are set out in Table IV (A). The trains concerned were the Newcastle portion of what later became the 'West Riding' out of Kings Cross, and the corresponding return working, each booked non-stop between Darlington and Doncaster; both runs were recorded on the same day. Because of many delays south of York, only the York–Darlington sections are tabulated. On the northbound run the 80 m.p.h. line was crossed about 12 miles out of York; against the slightly rising tendency of the road *Earl Marischal* kept just above 80 and then rose to 84 on the seven level miles past Thirsk. Over the 31·8 miles from Tollerton to Croft Spa the average speed was 79·8 m.p.h. A start-to-stop run from York to Darlington would have taken about $38\frac{1}{2}$ min.

But this was eclipsed on the southbound run the same afternoon. The start of this from Darlington was relatively leisurely, with the mile-a-minute rate barely attained up the 1 in 391 to Eryholme, but from Thirsk onwards the speed was as high as anything I have ever known with an Eastern or North Eastern Pacific, if not higher, and almost certainly the highest on record with a British 6 ft 2 in. engine on level track. The 92–92½ m.p.h. from Thirsk to Sessay was on the dead level; the 95 at Raskelf was down 1 in 740; and the 92½ past Tollerton was being maintained on the level again. Over the 20·95 miles from Otterington to Beningbrough speed averaged 92·5 m.p.h., and over the 32·75 miles from Danby Wiske to milepost 1 88·7 m.p.h. A stop at York could have been made in 37 min. or a shade over from Darlington.

TABLE IV (A)
N.E.R. YORK–DARLINGTON
Engine: Class 'A2/2' No. 60502 Earl Marischal
Load: 6 coaches, 207 tons tare, 220 tons gross

Dist.		Sched.	Actual	Speeds
miles		min.	min. sec.	m.p.h.
0·00	YORK	†0	†0 00	*20
1·00	Milepost I	—	1 54	—
5·55	Beningbrough . . .	—	6 30	70
9·75	Tollerton	—	9 54	76½
11·20	Alne	11	11 00	78½
13·35	Raskelf	—	12 36	81
16·10	Pilmoor	—	14 40	80/79
18·00	Sessay	—	16 18	80½
22·20	THIRSK	20	19 10	83½/84
26·50	Otterington . . .	—	22 18	81¼
29·95	NORTHALLERTON . .	26	24 56	76
33·75	Danby Wiske . . .	—	27 56	79½
37·20	Cowton	—	30 33	78
38·95	Eryholme	—	31 57	76½
41·55	Croft Spa	—	33 56	79
44·10	DARLINGTON . .	40½	37 13	—

Dist.		Sched.	Actual	Speeds
miles		min.	min. sec.	m.p.h.
0·00	DARLINGTON . .	0	0 00	—
2·55	Croft Spa	—	5 14	56
5·15	Eryholme	6	7 53	59½
10·35	Danby Wiske . . .	—	12 38	79
14·15	NORTHALLERTON . .	14	15 08	77
17·60	Otterington . . .	—	17 46	86
21·90	THIRSK	20	20 31	92
26·10	Sessay	—	23 16	92½
28·00	Pilmoor	—	24 31	93
30·75	Raskelf	—	26 16	95
32·90	Alne	28	27 38	94
34·35	Tollerton	—	28 35	92½
38·55	Beningbrough . . .	—	31 21	88
43·10	Milepost I . . .	—	34 46	—
44·10	YORK	†38	†36 25	*30

* Speed restriction.   † Passing time.

The next Thompson move concerned the last four of a series of Gresley 'V2' 2-6-2 engines which had been under construction at Doncaster when he took over. These he decided to build instead as Pacifics, with many features similar to those of the rebuilt 2-8-2s. They included the divided drive and staggered cylinder arrangement, with three separate sets of Walschaerts motion, the same enormously long smokebox, and the Thompson bogie. The boiler and firebox were unchanged, save for the installation, for the first time in any L.N.E.R. locomotive, of a rocking grate and a hopper ashpan. The cylinders were increased in diameter from $18\frac{1}{2}$ to 19 in., and with 5 lb added to the former 220 lb pressure gave an increase in tractive effort from 33,370 to 36,390 lb. But again the factor of adhesion was reduced, this time from 4·30 to 4·06, to some extent nullifying any advantage from the increase in maximum cut-off from 65 to 75 per cent. These four, classified as 'A2/1', are probably under-boilered, and have not distinguished themselves. These were the only Pacifics ever turned out of Doncaster Works with six-wheel tenders. They also received Scottish names – *Highland Chieftain, Duke of Rothesay, Waverley* and *Robert the Bruce*, like those of the rebuilt 'P2s', but with later Pacifics the racehorse tradition was continued.

2 – *The Rebuilding of 'Great Northern'*

NEXT there appeared, in 1945, a conversion which aroused a great deal more criticism than that of the Gresley 2-8-2s. For Thompson took Gresley's pioneer Pacific, the original *Great Northern* of 1922, and changed it into a machine of such hideous appearance as might well have made its designer turn in his grave. The rebuilding, as with that of its predecessors, included divided drive, and this involved moving the bogie forward by no less than 2 ft 8 in., increasing the engine wheelbase from 35 ft 9 in. to 38 ft 5 in. The three cylinders, each with its own valve-motion, were reduced in diameter from 20 in. to 19 in., but from the tractive point of view this reduction was more than balanced by the increase in working pressure from 180 to 250 lb (at that date *Great Northern* had not been converted to the 'A3' class, with 220 lb boiler, as had others of the original Class 'A1'), bringing the tractive effort up from 29,835 lb to 37,400 lb, or more than the 35,455 lb of an 'A4'.

Again the shortened boiler barrel was installed – 17 ft $11\frac{3}{4}$ in. instead of 18 ft $11\frac{3}{4}$ in. between tubeplates – but whereas the total heating surface came down from 2,930 sq ft to 2,576 sq ft, the superheating surface went up from 525 to 749 sq ft. Despite an increase in adhesion weight from 60 to 66 tons, and in total engine weight from $92\frac{1}{2}$ to $101\frac{1}{2}$ tons, yet once again the factor of adhesion was reduced, from 4·50 to 3·95. A rocking grate and a hopper ashpan, as with the 'A2/1' conversions, were a desirable addition from the maintenance point of view. The rebuilding included a double blastpipe and plain stovepipe double chimney, and the unsightly appearance of the whole was intensified by carrying the raised running-plate right back to the cab, and perching a tiny pair of cab side-sheets above it – a feature which later the designer was compelled to alter to a cab of more normal appearance.

The converted engine was intended to figure as the prototype of future L.N.E.R. express locomotive design, but hardly did so. Indeed, when in the following year, 1946, an engine was required to head a special train planned to test if the post-war East Coast track could stand a return to pre-war streamline speeds, it was not the converted *Great Northern* that was selected by the motive-power authorities, but the Gresley 'A4' *Silver Fox*. True to tradition, the 'A4' treated us to an average of 91·1 m.p.h. over the 23·6 miles from Otterington to Skelton Bridge, and to a speed only a shade lower in the opposite direction, with start-to-stop times of 70 min. 2 sec. over the 80·2 miles from York to Newcastle and no more than 68 min. 4 sec. from Newcastle to York (the fastest time I have ever known). The latter was followed, on the up journey, by a top speed of 102 m.p.h. on the descent from Stoke towards Peterborough, and all this on through locomotive workings between Kings Cross and Edinburgh.

Had the rebuilt No. 4470 been in use it might have been a very different story. Indeed, I have never heard of any performance worthy of record by the converted engine, and it cannot escape note that no similar rebuilding of any other Gresley Pacific was attempted. One of the unhappiest features of this conversion was that it should have been applied to this particular engine, and that what represented so complete a departure from the principles established by systematic and logical development at Doncaster should have to continue to carry the honoured name *Great Northern*.

3 – *The Thompson 'A2s' and their Work*

IN 1946 there appeared Thompson Pacific No. 500 in the new system of numbering that had now been adopted, the 2,000th engine to be turned out of Doncaster Works. It was a 6 ft 2 in. Pacific, based generally on the converted 'P2' design, even to the inclusion of a firegrate with 50 sq ft of area, and sharing certain of the weaknesses of the latter. Externally the principal change in appearance resulted from the fitting of full-size smoke deflectors, this being the first London & North Eastern locomotive class to be so dealt with; also the banjo dome had disappeared in favour of a diminutive dome cover of ordinary shape. Building of these engines continued to a total of fifteen, Nos. 500 and 511 to 524 inclusive, but as Thompson reached the age limit for retirement in 1946, most of them were turned out under his successor. It may be remarked that whereas it was nearly at the end of his distinguished career that Sir Nigel Gresley's name, and under instruction from the L.N.E.R. directors, appeared on one of his locomotives, the very first entirely new Pacific designed by Edward Thompson, No. 500, later No. 60500, carried the latter's name.

These last Thompson Pacifics received the classification 'A2/3', and have been the best of the 4-6-2s turned out during his superintendence. Even

Haymarket shed in Scotland overcame its aversion to post-Gresley developments by making good use of them, and of this Table IV (B) gives ample evidence. Haymarket's 'A2/3' 4-6-2 No. 60519 *Honeyway* was turned out to work no less distinguished an express than the afternoon 'Talisman' up to Newcastle, and an excellent job was made of the run; E. Ros Birkett's record of the trip unfortunately did not include any speeds. But an average of 68·2 m.p.h. was maintained from Prestonpans to Longniddry, 73·8 from

TABLE IV (B)
SCOTS AND N.E. REGIONS: EDINBURGH–NEWCASTLE
Engine: Class 'A2/3' 4-6-2 No. 60519 *Honeyway*
Load: 9 coaches, 313 tons tare, 325 tons gross

Dist.		Sched.	Actual	Speeds
miles		min.	min. sec.	m.p.h.
0·00	EDINBURGH . . .	0	0 00	—
3·00	Portobello . . .	5	5 40	†
6·10	*Monktonhall Junction* .	9	9 25	†
9·45	Prestonpans . .	—	12 35	—
13·20	Longniddry Junction .	—	15 53	—
17·75	DREM	20	19 35	—
20·75	East Fortune . .	—	21 55	—
23·40	East Linton . . .	—	24 09	—
29·10	DUNBAR . . .	30	29 04	—
33·75	*Innerwick* . . .	—	33 37	—
36·45	*Cockburnspath* . .	—	36 04	—
41·15	Grantshouse . .	44	41 54	—
46·25	Reston Junction . .	50	46 37	—
51·85	Burnmouth . . .	—	51 06	—
56·50	*Marshall Meadows* .	59	54 48	†
57·45	BERWICK . . .	60½	55 50	†
58·65	Tweedmouth . . .	—	57 28	—
63·60	*Goswick*	—	62 08	—
			sigs.	†
65·85	Beal	—	64 20	—
72·80	Belford	74½	71 22	—
75·20	*Lucker*	—	73 32	†
78·30	Chathill	—	76 21	—
81·30	*Christon Bank* . .	—	78 21	—
85·00	*Little Mill*	—	82 11	—
86·95	Longhoughton . .	—	83 54	—
89·60	ALNMOUTH . .	89½	85 58	†
92·50	*Warkworth* . . .	—	88 35	—
95·90	Acklington . . .	—	91 45	—
98·85	*Chevington* . . .	—	94 25	—
101·20	Widdrington . . .	—	96 33	—
105·90	Pegswood . . .	—	100 33	—
107·85	MORPETH . . .	106	102 27	*
110·55	*Stannington* . . .	—	105 58	—
112·95	*Plessey*	—	108 15	—
116·75	*Annitsford*	(‡3)	111 47	—
119 45	*Forest Hall* . . .	—	114 13	—
122·80	Heaton	—	117 45	*
124·45	NEWCASTLE . . .	128	121 37	—

* Speed restriction, severe. † Speed restriction, slight or moderate.
‡ Recovery time (min.)

there to Drem, 77·1 on to East Fortune and 70·0 thence to East Linton; even better was the 48·3 m.p.h. average up the 1 in 96 from Cockburnspath to Grantshouse. So the unusual time of 55 min. 50 sec. – 4¾ min. inside schedule – was made from the Edinburgh start to Berwick. There were no other features of note, save the 57·9 m.p.h. average from Christon Bank up to Little Mill, largely at 1 in 150. But *Honeyway* ran into Newcastle 6½ min. early, in 121 min. 37 sec. for the 124·45 miles from Edinburgh, or 120 min. net – exactly equal to the pre-war 'Coronation' schedule, and with the same load.

Table IV (C) sets out the most astonishing run that I have ever known in the northbound direction between York and Darlington, for which the infelicitously named 'A2/3' No. 60524 *Herringbone*, stationed at York, was responsible; the times leave those of *Earl Marischal* in Table IV (A) well behind. Beyond Thirsk speed reached 90 m.p.h. on the dead level, and, moreover, with an eleven-coach train of 380 gross tons. Between mileposts 2

TABLE IV (C)
N.E.R. YORK–DARLINGTON
Engine: Class 'A2/3' No. 60524 *Herringbone*
Load: 11 coaches, 359 tons tare, 380 tons gross

Dist.		Actual	Speeds
miles		min. sec.	m.p.h.
0·00	YORK	0 00	—
2·00	*Milepost 2* . . .	4 24	—
5·55	*Beningbrough* . .	7 45	75
9·75	*Tollerton*	10 55	80¼
11·20	*Alne*	12 00	85
16·10	*Pilmoor*	15 25	86
18·00	*Sessay*	16 55	87
22·20	THIRSK	19 25	89/90
26·50	*Otterington* . .	22 35	88
29·95	NORTHALLERTON . .	25 00	87
33·75	*Danby Wiske* . . .	27 35	87
38·95	*Eryholme*	31 15	82
43·00	*Milepost 43* . . .	34 13	—
44·10	DARLINGTON . .	36 29	—

and 43, 41 miles were reeled off at an average of 82·5 m.p.h., and between Tollerton and Danby Wiske, 24 miles at 86·4 m.p.h. It would not be possible to find a more striking illustration than this of the galloping propensities of Thompson's Pacifics, and in this case against the gradually rising tendency of the road. I am indebted to Major R. A. Colville for this log.

And what of the economic effect of the changes in design made by Thompson? One of his earliest activities on assuming office had been, quite characteristically, to prepare for the L.N.E.R. directors a list of all the failures of Gresley engines that he could trace, and in particular of failures attributable to the latter's derived valve-motion. It was hardly surprising, therefore, that in January, 1945, the Chief General Manager, in his turn, required from Thompson some information as to what improvements had been effected under his direction up to that time. Relative coal consumption figured in this enquiry, and led to some trials, which were conducted by the then Locomotive Running Superintendent of the Western Section, Southern Area, G. A. Musgrave.

The engines tested were No. 3697 *Duke of Rothesay*, an 'A2/1' of the adapted 'V2' type (later No. 60508); No. 2003 *Lord President* (later No. 60503), one of the rebuilt 2-8-2s – both have since been scrapped – and 'A4' Gresley Pacific No. 2512 *Silver Fox* (now No. 60017). Post-war passenger services were still limited in number, and though their timings were easy, the loads were very heavy. The trains chosen were the 10.30 a.m. from Kings Cross to Leeds and the 7.50 a.m. back; and the 9.40 a.m. from Kings Cross to Grantham and the 3.17 p.m. back; two freight trains also figured in the tests. The results were hardly flattering to Thompson. The average consumption of No. 2003 was 70·8 lb of coal to the mile, and of No. 3697 69·0 lb, whereas the 'A4' did the same work on 52·3 lb to the mile. A second passenger test, without the 'A4', brought the 'A2/2' consumption down to 62·8 lb, and the 'A2/1' down to 60·2 lb, but both were still well above the 'A4' figure. On the freight workings the 'A2/2' burned 68·7 lb and the 'A2/1' 63·8 lb to the mile.

An endeavour was made to excuse the high consumption of the Thompson engines by the fact that their boilers were working at 225 lb pressure only as compared with the 'A4's' 250 lb. The 6 ft 2 in. engines were regarded as better at starting than the 'A4', both because of smaller driving wheels and also because their maximum cut-off had been lengthened to 75 per cent, but the 'A4' gave the higher power output at speed. The independent valve-gears of the Thompson engines were claimed as a great improvement on Gresley's 2-to-1 operation of his centre valve-gear from the outside motions, but there was little in the trials to support the contention. Praise was also given to the steam-operated reversing gear of the 'A2/1' Pacific, though the locomotive inspector's comment was that when steam reversing had been tried previously it had given trouble in maintenance, and that time alone would prove whether No. 3697's equipment would be more reliable.

As these tests had been conducted in bad winter weather, it was decided to have another series in the following spring and early summer, using the same locomotives. This time, doubtless because the engine-crews by now had become more accustomed to handling the Thompson engines, the results were a good deal closer. On the passenger workings No. 2003 burned an average of 46·1 lb to the mile, or 0·084 lb per train ton-mile; No. 3697's figures were 43·3 lb and 0·079 lb respectively; but No. 2512 continued to lead with 40·5 lb per mile and 0·075 lb per train ton-mile. On the freight workings the 'A4' still beat the 'A2/2' by a small margin – 45·2 against 45·4 lb to the mile or 0·072 against 0·076 lb per train ton-mile – but now the 'A2/1' made the best showing, 41·4 lb per mile or 0·066 lb per ton-mile. However, this was no discredit to the 'A4', which had been designed for high-speed passenger service, whereas the 'A2/1' had been converted from a type intended primarily for fast freight work. Moreover, No. 3697 had the advantage over No. 2512 of a rocking grate and a hopper ashpan.

The report contained the rather naïve statement that 'it was considered by the locomotive inspector that the "A2/2" and "A2/1" classes worked the freight trains easier than the "A4" class engine'! The report also commented on the fact that with the Thompson engines the enginemen had to exercise care in manipulating their regulators when starting away from stops 'to prevent excessive slipping'. The word 'excessive' was significant.

Later in the same year, 1945, there followed a test of Thompson's rebuilt Gresley Pacific, No. 4470 *Great Northern*, against 'A4' Pacific No. 4466 *Sir Ralph Wedgwood* (now Nos. 60113 and 60006 respectively) – in the latter case an amusing choice, as though in an endeavour to convince the Chief General Manager that even though a Gresley Pacific bore his name, it would not necessarily have any superiority over the Chief Mechanical Engineer's latest handiwork! And in this case, at least so far as concerns coal consumption, Thompson was right. These trials took place in November, 1945, and since the tests earlier in the same year the passenger trains concerned had been considerably accelerated, though the loads were not quite so heavy; as a result the consumptions per mile were less than previously with the 'A4', but greater per train ton-mile. Actually the results were as nearly as possible a dead heat. No. 4466 averaged 0·086 lb of coal per train ton-mile and 39·9 lb per mile, as compared with No. 4470's 0·085 lb and 39·8 lb respectively.

The rebuilt *Great Northern*, like the 'A2/1' Pacific in the earlier tests, had the advantage of a drop gate and hopper ashpan. The Musgrave report on these tests commented on the difficulties experienced with No. 4470 due to drifting exhaust; also that hand reversing gear had been fitted in place of the steam reversing gear on the 'A2/1' Pacifics, which had now been removed – an interesting confirmation of the locomotive inspector's doubts of No. 3697's steam reverse in the previous tests. The inspector also commented on No. 4470's tendency to slip unless handled very carefully. As to relative maintenance costs, No. 4470 had not been in service long enough, in its rebuilt condition, to permit any reliable comparison with No. 4466.

So ended Thompson's brief reign. Some of his innovations had been valuable, especially from the servicing and maintenance point of view. These included the rocking grate and hopper ashpan, and with little doubt also the three independent sets of valve-motion in place of the Gresley derived gear for the inside cylinder piston-valve. Steaming was assisted by the provision of 10-in. in place of 9-in. piston-valves – one of the reasons for the free running of these engines at high speed despite driving wheels of no more than 6 ft 2 in. diameter. Changes of a less helpful description were the reduction in adhesion factors, divided drive with shorter connecting-rods, and the considerably lengthened wheelbase necessitated by the moving backwards of the outside cylinders. As remarked at the beginning of this chapter, Thompson's tenure of office could hardly be described as the happiest period of London & North Eastern locomotive history, and as already mentioned also, some of his Pacifics have had the shortest life of all those built for that company.

TABLE IV (D)
LEADING DIMENSIONS OF THOMPSON PACIFICS

Class	*'A1/1'	†'A2/1'	‡'A2/2'	'A2/3'
Cylinders (3), diameter . .	19 in.	19 in.	20 in.	19 in.
,, stroke . .	26 in.	26 in.	26 in.	26 in.
Driving wheels, diameter .	6 ft 8 in.	6 ft 2 in.	6 ft 2 in.	6 ft 2 in.
Wheelbase, coupled . .	14 ft 6 in.	13 ft 0 in.	13 ft 0 in.	13 ft 0 in.
,, total . . .	38 ft 5 in.	36 ft 8 in.	36 ft 11 in.	36 ft 11 in.
Heating surface, tubes and flues	2,345 sq ft	2,216 sq ft	2,216 sq ft	2,216 sq ft
,, ,, firebox .	231 sq ft	215 sq ft	237 sq ft	245 sq ft
,, ,, total . .	2,576 sq ft	2,431 sq ft	2,453 sq ft	2,461 sq ft
Superheating surface . .	749 sq ft	680 sq ft	680 sq ft	680 sq ft
Firegrate area . . .	41·25 sq ft	41·25 sq ft	50·0 sq ft	50·0 sq ft
Working pressure, per sq in. .	250 lb	225 lb	225 lb	250 lb
Tractive effort (85 per cent) .	37,400 lb	36,385 lb	40,320 lb	40,430 lb
Adhesion weight . . .	66 tons	66 tons	66 tons	66 tons
Engine weight (working order)	101½ tons	98 tons	101½ tons	101½ tons
Engine and tender weight .	159½ tons	§150 tons	161¾ tons	161¾ tons
Length over buffers . .	73 ft 2 in.	69 ft 5 in.	72 ft 8½ in.	72 ft 11 in.

* Rebuilt Gresley Pacific type. † Adaptation of 'V2' 2-6-2- type.
‡ Rebuilt Gresley 'P2' 2-8-2 type. § With 6-wheel tender; all others 8-wheel tenders.

TABLE IV (E)
NAMES, NUMBERS AND BUILDING DATES OF THOMPSON PACIFICS

B.R. No.	Name	Present class	Date of building	Notes
60500	Edward Thompson . .	A2/3	1946	—
60501	Cock o' the North . .	A2/2	*1944	A
60502	Earl Marischal . . .	,,	* ,,	,,
60503	Lord President . . .	,,	* ,,	,,
60504	Mons Meg	,,	* ,,	,,
60505	Thane of Fife . . .	,,	*1943	,,
60506	Wolf of Badenoch . .	,,	*1944	,,
60507	Highland Chieftain . .	A2/1	,,	B
60508	Duke of Rothesay . .	,,	,,	,,
60509	Waverley	,,	,,	,,
60510	Robert the Bruce . .	,,	1945	,,
60511	Airborne	A2/3	1946	,,
60512	Steady Aim . . .	,,	,,	,,
60513	Dante	,,	,,	,,
60514	Chamossaire . . .	,,	,,	,,
60515	Sun Stream . . .	,,	,,	,,
60516	Hycilla	,,	,,	,,
60517	Ocean Swell . . .	,,	,,	,,
60518	Tehran	,,	,,	,,
60519	Honeyway	,,	1947	,,
60520	Owen Tudor . . .	,,	,,	,,
60521	Watling Street . . .	,,	,,	,,
60522	Straight Deal . . .	,,	,,	,,
60523	Sun Castle . . .	,,	,,	,,
60524	Herringbone . . .	,,	,,	,,

* Date of rebuilding.
A: Rebuilt Gresley Class 'P2' 2-8-2 type original numbers 2001 to 2006 inclusive.
B: Adapted Gresley 'V2' 2-6-2 type, original numbers 3696 to 3699 inclusive.

V

THE PEPPERCORN PACIFICS, LONDON & NORTH EASTERN RAILWAY

1 – *The Standard 'A2' Class*

THE part played by Arthur H. Peppercorn in developing London & North Eastern Pacifics was but brief, seeing that his term as Chief Mechanical Engineer lasted only from the summer of 1946 until the end of the second year of nationalization in 1949; and he died in 1952 at the relatively early age of 62. All his railway life had been spent on the Great Northern Railway or the Southern Area of the L.N.E.R., and from 1941 he had occupied the dual position of Mechanical Engineer, Doncaster, and Assistant Chief Mechanical Engineer to Thompson. On his appointment to succeed the latter in 1946, it soon became clear that some Great Northern traditions at least had returned with him; several of the executives formerly associated with Gresley who had been transferred to other work, notably the Chief Technical Assistant, B. Spencer, also resumed their former positions. As a result, while the Pacifics built under Peppercorn's superintendence retained certain useful features which had been introduced by Thompson, in various other respects they showed a reversion to Gresley standards.

The intended series of thirty Thompson 6 ft 2 in. Pacifics was brought to an end, after no more than fifteen had been built, with No. 524 *Herringbone* (what a name to fasten on an unhappy locomotive!); and the remaining fifteen, redesigned by Peppercorn, were different in many respects. Divided drive, with three independent sets of valve-gear, was retained, but the outside cylinders were moved back to the normal position central with the bogie. Although in appearance No. 525 still fell short of a Gresley Pacific, a fair proportion of the Doncaster grace of line had reappeared. Once again the banjo dome was in evidence, and a flared chimney, though rather curiously this was a reversion, with the exception of one later engine, to a single chimney above a single blastpipe. Full-size smoke deflectors had now become a standard feature. The altered position of the cylinders made possible a compact machine once again, with a wheelbase of 34 ft 4 in. instead of the 36 ft 11 in. of the Thompson 'A2/3' series, and longer connecting-rods. The boilers of the two types were identical, yet in view of the shortening of the engine and despite a reduction in boiler weight by the use of 3 per cent nickel alloy plates, it was surprising that the Peppercorn version weighed only half a ton less than that of Thompson – 101 as compared with 101½ tons.

The V-fronted cab, which Thompson had abandoned, returned, and also was widened, allowing the vacuum ejector to be lowered and much improving the look-out ahead. Rocking grate, hopper-type ashpan and self-cleaning smokebox were useful details of equipment, also a turbo-generator and electric lighting. As mentioned in the last paragraph, one of the series (to whose numbers 60,000 had now been added under the British Railways renumbering scheme), No. 60539 *Bronzino*, was built with double blastpipe and chimney; later Nos. 60526, 60529, 60532, 60533 and 60538 received similar equipment. Fifteen of these engines were built, in place of the balance of 'A2/3' Pacifics that had been ordered, with numbers running from 60525 to 60539 inclusive. As with their immediate predecessors, there was the same haste to commemorate the designer, by naming the first engine of the class after him; so No. 60525 started its career as No. 525 *A. H. Peppercorn*.

It is pleasant to be able to record that Scottish engine-sheds, Haymarket (Edinburgh) and Ferryhill (Aberdeen) in particular, which as previously mentioned had been strongly pro-Gresley and anti-Thompson, and had packed both the rebuilt 'P2' 2-8-2s and the rebuilt No. 4470 back across the Border as soon after their receipt as possible, took quite kindly to the Peppercorn 'A2s', and in the succeeding years these engines have done some very good work over the difficult road between Edinburgh and Aberdeen. This is illustrated by the performance which appears in Table V (A), when the engine was No. 60527 *Sun Chariot*, one of the best of the bunch, with Driver Quinn of Tay Bridge shed, Dundee, at the regulator. The run was timed by R. I. Nelson, a frequent traveller over this route, who regards it as one of the best that he has recorded with this type of engine.

The start out of Aberdeen is a gruelling climb, rising at 1 in 96 from the platform end to Ferryhill, and then, after some easier grades, continuously at 1 in 118–154–116–102 (past Cove Bay)–164–153 for 5 miles to the summit at milepost 234. To maintain 47–46 m.p.h. up the steepest part of this climb was first-class work with a 400-ton train, and helped to a gain of all but 4 min. to Stonehaven. Out of Stonehaven is another steep climb, on which *Sun Chariot* attained 36 m.p.h. up 1 in 85–92, accelerated to 47 m.p.h. up an easier mile, and completed 1¼ miles up at 1 in 102 at a minimum of 44½ m.p.h.; notwithstanding very easy running down most of the subsequent descent, a further 3½ min. was gained to Montrose.

From here the locomotive faces the steepest of all the climbs in the southbound direction, at first of 1½ miles at 1 in 88 to Usan, and then mostly at 1 in 111 to the summit at milepost 26¾; on the first stretch *Sun Chariot* attained 28½ m.p.h., on the 1 in 111 31 m.p.h., and by the summit 39 m.p.h. The timing of 20 min. for the 13·65 miles from Montrose to Arbroath is a sharp one, and the Pacific did no better than just to keep it. Even out of Arbroath there is a short 1 in 115 up before the lengthy level past Carnoustie is reached; on the latter the 4-6-2 maintained 69–71 m.p.h., and would have gained 1¾ min. to Dundee but for a concluding signal check. Total gains to engine on this excellent run were about 9¼ min. net.

It may be added that one of the Peppercorn 'A2' Pacifics – No. 60526 *Sugar Palm* – is the only 6 ft 2 in. engine of London & North Eastern or Eastern Region origin which has ever been authentically recorded as having

TABLE V (A)
SCOTTISH REGION: ABERDEEN–DUNDEE
Engine: Class 'A2' 4-6-2 No. 60527 *Sun Chariot*
Load: 11 coaches, 381 tons tare, 400 tons gross

Dist.		Sched.	Actual	Speeds
miles		min.	min. sec.	m.p.h.
0·00	ABERDEEN . . .	0	0 00	—
0·65	Ferryhill Junction . .	—	3 01	16½
4·80	Cove Bay	9	9 32	47/46¼
7·10	Milepost 234 . . .	—	12 17	53
10·40	Newtonhill . . .	—	15 19	64/63
11·55	Muchalls	—	16 22	68
13·40	Milepost 227½ . . .	—	18 18	59/69½
16·15	STONEHAVEN . .	25	21 07	—
1·00	Milepost 223¾ . . .	—	3 31	31
2·55	Dunnottar	—	5 55	41/47
5·50	Carmont	—	9 36	44½
7·15	Drumlithie . . .	—	11 26	56
11·10	Fordoun	—	14 56	68
14·40	LAURENCEKIRK . .	19	17 57	64
15·50	Milepost 209¼ . . .	—	19 04	63
17·60	Marykirk	—	20 45	72½
19·75	Craigo	—	22 26	78½
21·85	Kinnaber Junction . .	29	25 24	*15/53½
24·75	MONTROSE . . .	33	29 27	—
2·05	Usan	—	6 11	28½
4·00	Milepost 26¾ . . .	—	9 28	39½
7·45	Inverkeilor . . .	13	13 02	71/63
8·75	Cauldcots	—	14 13	67/58
10·65	Letham Grange . . .	—	16 00	63½/61
13·10	St Vigeans Junction . .	19	18 42	—
			p.w.s.	*15
13·65	ARBROATH . . .	20	20 26	—
1·40	Elliott Junction . . .	—	3 32	18½
4·35	Easthaven . . .	—	6 27	64½
6·15	Carnoustie . . .	—	8 03	69
7·75	Barry Links . . .	—	9 23	71
10·70	Monifieth . . .	—	11 54	70
13·05	BROUGHTY FERRY .	—	13 57	69
			sigs.	*10
16·30	Camperdown Junction . .	—	18 59	*15
17·05	DUNDEE	22	21 25	—

* Speed restriction.

reached the three-figure level in speed. This was in 1961 with the up 'West Riding', which reached 101 m.p.h. at Essendine. Not surprisingly, this was one of the series with double blastpipe and chimney.

2 – *The 'A1' Class*

THE name of Peppercorn will be most permanently associated with the final series of Pacifics, the present Class 'A1'. It has been asserted that these were the development for new construction of the Thompson Class 'A1/1' rebuild of No. 4470, now No. 60113, but a more accurate description would be that they were the 6 ft 8 in. version, intended for fast passenger service, of the 6 ft 2 in. Peppercorn 'A2' series. Many parts of the two were interchangeable, including the boiler, with its firegrate of 50 sq ft area. In this respect the new 'A1' differed from all the Gresley 6 ft 8 in. Pacifics, which had 41·25 sq ft firegrate area only; in the 'A1s', also, the length of barrel between tubeplates, 17 ft, was shorter than the 19 ft of an 'A3' or the 18 ft of an 'A4'. These facts may help to explain why the 'A1' Pacifics have always had the reputation – confirmed by the tests about to be described – of being heavier on coal than the 'A4s'. Nos. 60153 to 60157 inclusive were fitted with roller bearings throughout.

The tests just mentioned took place in 1949, and were made in order that the performance of the 'A1' and 'A2' Pacifics might be compared with that of the Gresley 'A4s' in the historic exchange trials of the previous year between locomotives of the various Regions of British Railways. The Peppercorn engines selected were No. 60114 *W. P. Allen* of the 'A1' type, and No. 60539 *Bronzino* of type 'A2'; whereas the latter was the only 'A2' which started its career with a double blastpipe and chimney, the former at first had been built at Doncaster with a single blastpipe only, though in common with all the 'A1s' it acquired a double blastpipe later. These tests were conducted with the Darlington dynamometer car, and were altogether more thorough and scientific than the rough-and-ready tests of Thompson's Pacifics described in Chapter IV.

'Normal power' trials took place with 485–500-ton trains between Kings Cross and Leeds, and 'high power' tests with 600–615-ton loads between Kings Cross and Grantham. No. 60114 had run 47,000 miles since the last heavy repair, and No. 60539 about 40,000 miles. The same enginemen were used throughout, accompanied by the same locomotive inspector, to ensure uniform handling methods, and the report commented appreciatively on how skilful this control had been by Driver Moore and his mate. The former was commended for handling his regulator in such a way as to prevent practically any slipping when starting, and the latter for providing sufficient steam to meet every power demand, with clean exhaust and little black smoke, while at the same time avoiding any appreciable blowing-off when the engines were standing or running under easy steam.

Comparing the 'normal power' tests with those of the 'A4s' in 1948, No. 60114 burned an average of 1·7 per cent more coal and No. 60539 3·6 per cent more; water consumptions were 4·4 and 3·3 per cent higher respectively. The coal burned in the 1949 tests, however, had a lower calorific value than that used by the 'A4s' in 1948, and allowing for this difference, the excess of the 'A1' and 'A2' consumptions came down to 1·3 and 1·8 per cent. In the 'high-power' tests the 'A2' beat the 'A1' by 1 per cent in coal and 1·5 per cent in water consumption; the boiler efficiencies were 5·0 and 1·5 per cent lower in the 'high-power' than in the 'low-power' trials.

For an increase in output from 600 to 900 drawbar h.p., water consumption proportionately to output came down by 9·0 per cent with the 'A1' and 9·8 per cent with the 'A2'. Among high drawbar h.p. figures, No. 60114, cutting off at 40 per cent, reached 2,108 at 61·2 m.p.h. and 2,052 at 55·4 m.p.h.; No. 60539 attained 2,138 on 45 per cent cut-off at 63·2 m.p.h., and 2,054 on 35 per cent cut-off at 64·3 m.p.h. To maintain point-to-point times it was generally necessary to work the 'A1' Pacific in a longer cut-off than the 'A2'.

The report contained some interesting observations on firebox design. It was evident that the 50 sq ft firegrate area of the Peppercorn Pacifics was less economical than the 41·3 sq ft of the Gresley engines, even with the most competent firing, when working at medium output. When working at high power, however, the coal consumption on the larger grate would rise by some 20 per cent only, whereas on the smaller grate it might be expected to rise by at least 30 per cent, and this might indicate an advantage in allocating 'A1' and 'A2' Pacifics to the harder duties.

It was remarked that the Peppercorn Pacifics had 14 sq ft more firebox heating surface than the Gresley 'A4s', the effect of which, with a thin fire and low burning rate, would be to cause a higher rate of evaporation round the firebox in comparison with that round the tubes; this would result in an increased rate of temperature fall between the combustion chamber and the smokebox. As the 'A4' also had 70 sq ft more superheating surface than the 'A1' or 'A2', in the conditions just mentioned there was the probability with the latter of wet steam being carried over into a restricted steam space. The general impression that the Peppercorn 'A1' Pacifics burn more coal than the Gresley 'A4s' would seem to be confirmed by this report, though the difference was relatively slight; the comparison would have been more convincing had an 'A4' been tested in exactly the same conditions as the 'A1' and the 'A2'.

3 – Some 'A1' Performances

WE come now to the performance of the Peppercorn 'A1' Pacifics in day-to-day service. There has never been any doubt as to their capacity for high-speed work, and of this Tables V (B) and V (C) provide ample proof. Table V (B) gives the details of a couple of runs on the very fast down morning 'West Riding', which at the time they were made was allowed 96½ min. for the

106·7 miles from Hitchin to Retford, start to stop. This train has always been worked by engine-crews from Copley Hill shed, Leeds, who have given a consistently good account of themselves and their engines. At this period a disincentive to timekeeping South of Retford was a 10-min. 'recovery time' between Retford and Doncaster, but on the first of the two runs, which I timed, Driver Brown and Fireman Owen had a punctual start from Hitchin, and most unusually were nearly 5 min. early into Retford. On the second run, recorded by W. Alan Parker, the Hitchin start was 4 min. late, and Driver Wallis, despite out-of-course delays, brought his train into Retford dead on time.

On both runs the ten-coach load exceeded by 25 tare tons the maximum of 315 tare tons for which this schedule is laid down. On my run No. 60117 *Bois Roussel*, with 355 gross tons, for once had an absolutely clear road, and was not over-exerted on the rising grades; at the top of the long 1 in 200 before

TABLE V (B)

Engine, 'A1' 4-6-2 No. Load, tons tare/gross				†60117 340/355		‡60123 345/360	
Dist.			Sched.	Actual	Speeds	Actual	Speeds
miles			min.	min. sec.	m.p.h.	min. sec.	m.p.h.
0·00	HITCHIN . . .		0	0 00	—	0 00	—
5·20	Arlesey		—	6 09	74	6 09	75
9·25	Biggleswade . . .		—	9 18	85/86½	9 11	86/88
12·25	Sandy		—	11 27	83½/86¼	11 14	86/88
15·60	Tempsford . . .		—	13 50	85	13 35	86
19·85	St Neots . . .		—	16 55	79/85	16 36	83/88
24·05	Offord		—	20 02	*70	19 35	*78
26·95	HUNTINGDON . .		23	22 26	71¼	21 49	78
30·10	Milepost 62 . . .		—	25 17	61	24 27	67
37·45	Holme		—	30 46	88	29 54	90
40·70	Yaxley		—	33 12	79	32 12	81
43·10	Fletton Junction . .		—	35 03	71	34 01	73
						sigs.	*9
44·45	PETERBOROUGH . .		38½	36 40	*22	37 23	*22
47·60	Werrington Junction .		43	41 16	59	41 50	60½
50·00	Helpston . . .		—	43 30	67	44 04	67
52·95	Tallington . . .		—	45 58	69	46 41	70
56·75	Essendine . . .		50½	49 27	70½	49 56	71
60·35	Little Bytham . . .		—	52 22	66/60	53 00	68½/65
65·20	Corby Glen . . .		—	57 06	61	57 24	67½
68·20	Stoke		—	60 08	57/74	60 14	62
73·55	GRANTHAM . .		66	64 44	*67	64 38	80/76
77·80	Barkston S. Junction .		69½	68 21	77½	67 51	82
83·45	Claypole . . .		—	72 17	85	71 44	91
						sigs.	*62
88·20	NEWARK . . .		78½	75 28	90/*75	75 37	70/*64
94·40	Carlton		—	80 21	76½	81 03	76
99·30	Dukeries Junction . .		—	84 25	65	85 10	65
101·85	Milepost 133¾ . .		—	86 48	61½	87 28	67½
103·60	Garnston . . .		—	88 23	70½	89 00	77
106·70	RETFORD . . .		96½	91 45	—	92 31	—

* Speed restriction.   † *Bois Roussel.*   ‡ *H. A. Ivatt.*

Corby Glen the minimum speed was 60 m.p.h., and at Stoke summit 57 m.p.h. But on the second run No. 60123 *H. A. Ivatt*, after a brilliant start to Fletton Junction – 43·1 miles in 34 min. 1 sec. – was badly delayed by signals through Peterborough, and was then opened out with such vigour as to achieve minima of 65 m.p.h. before Corby and 62 m.p.h. at Stoke, by which point the time of the previous run was being overhauled. Less caution was shown by *H. A. Ivatt*'s driver through Grantham, and speed had reached 91 m.p.h. by Claypole when there came a second signal check. The times of the two runs from Hitchin to Retford were 91 min. 45 sec. and 92 min. 31 sec. respectively, but the net time on *H. A. Ivatt*'s run was about 87½ min., 9 min. less than that scheduled, despite the slight overload.

One of the finest performances of an 'A1' that I have ever known took place in November, 1958, when No. 60140 *Balmoral* was substituted at a moment's notice for a Type '4' 2,000-h.p. diesel that had failed at York on the up afternoon 'Talisman'. It was fortunate indeed that so experienced an observer as R. I. Nelson was on the train, and so was able to make a detailed record of the engine's work, in the capable hands of Driver R. Turner of Kings Cross and his mate. This followed a start 26 min. after the booked passing time of the express at York. The nine-coach load of 308 tons tare and 325 tons gross almost exactly equalled that of the pre-war 'Coronation' streamliner, when the latter was running with its observation car attached, and in Table V (C) I have shown the latter's schedule alongside that of the 'Talisman' for comparison purposes. The running of the 'Talisman' was assisted by the fact that this set of coaches is carried on roller bearings throughout.

Apart from the sections over which signal or permanent way delays were experienced, it will be seen that *Balmoral* was more than keeping the 'Coronation' point-to-point times. Some of the hillclimbing was of notable quality, as, for example, the minimum speed of 68 m.p.h. up the 1 in 200 climbs both to Peascliffe Tunnel and to Stoke, and in particular the minimum of 73 m.p.h. at the crest of the long climb, finally at 1 in 200, to Stevenage. High speeds were attained wherever possible, culminating in a maximum of a shade over 100 m.p.h. past Essendine. By Finsbury Park, despite all the delays, just over 5 min. remained to effect a punctual arrival, and it was a sad reward to Driver Turner, after such a magnificent effort, to be stopped by signal at Holloway. Thus it was 2½ min. behind schedule time when the 'Talisman' came to a stand at Kings Cross. Careful estimation gives a net start-to-stop time of 158 min. for the 188·15 miles from York, or 4 min. less than the 162 min. 'Coronation' pass-to-stop allowance, and with lower speeds inwards from Hatfield than those run habitually by the streamline trains in 1939.

The 100½ m.p.h. at Essendine on this run is a reminder of other three-figure maxima that have been noted by correspondents with 'A1' Pacifics. *Balmoral* took 2 min. 10 sec. over the 3·60 miles from Little Bytham to Essendine, average speed 99·7 m.p.h. A time of 2 min. 9 sec. has been recorded by H. J. J. Griffith when travelling behind No. 60125 *Scottish Union*, average 100·5 m.p.h. and maximum 102; this was with a load of 267 tons tare and

TABLE V (C)   E.R. YORK–KINGS CROSS
Engine: Class 'A1' 4-6-2 No. 60140 Balmoral
Load: 9 coaches, 308 tons tare, 325 tons gross

Dist.		Schedule		Actual	Speeds
miles		min.	min.	min. sec.	m.p.h.
0·00	YORK	‡0	‡0	§0 00	—
2·00	Chaloners Whin Junction .	—	—	4 17	45
9·65	Riccall	—	—	11 10	77
13·85	SELBY . . .	14	14½	14 52	*40
18·40	Templehirst . . .	—	—	19 17	73
22·25	Balne	—	(†4)	22 20	77½/85
27·95	Shaftholme Junction . .	—	31	26 30	82
32·20	DONCASTER . . .	30½	36	30 03	*56
36·80	Rossington . . .	—	—	34 20	69½
38·65	Milepost 149½ . . .	—	—	35 55	66
				sigs.	*20
40·45	Bawtry	—	—	38 46	
				sigs.	*45
44·20	Ranskill	—	—	42 53	61/73½
49·55	RETFORD . . .	45½	52	47 28	*65/69
54·40	Milepost 133¾ . . .	—	—	51 48	66
61·85	Carlton	—	—	57 08	92½/*77
68·05	NEWARK . . .	61½	68	61 35	79/80½
72·80	Claypole	—	(†4)	65 11	79
78·45	Barkston S. Junction . .	—	81	69 34	74/68
82·70	GRANTHAM . . .	73½	85	73 07	70½/72
88·05	Stoke	—	90	77 41	68
91·05	Corby Glen . . .	—	—	80 01	85½
95·90	Little Bytham . . .	—	—	83 10	99
99·50	Essendine . . .	—	98	85 20	100½
103·30	Tallington . . .	—	(†2)	87 42	95
108·65	Werrington Junction . .	—	106	91 30	*70
				sigs.	*10
111·80	PETERBOROUGH . .	97	111	95 45	
113·15	Fletton Junction . . .	—	—	98 12	48½
115·55	Yaxley	—	—	100 34	69
118·80	Holme	—	—	103 08	78
120·80	Connington S. . . .	—	—	104 37	81
124·65	Abbots Ripton . . .	—	—	107 38	71
				p.w.s.	*20
129·30	HUNTINGDON . .	113	128	113 50	68½
132·20	Offord	—	—	116 17	74/77
136·40	St Neots	—	—	119 34	76
140·65	Tempsford . . .	—	—	122 40	86½
				p.w.s.	*30
144·00	Sandy	—	139	126 21	47
147·00	Biggleswade . . .	—	—	129 10	74
151·05	Arlesey	—	—	132 25	80½/83
156·25	HITCHIN . . .	134	149	136 13	77
159·60	Stevenage . . .	—	(†2)	138 52	73/80
163·10	Knebworth . . .	—	158	141 37	78
164·65	Woolmer Green . . .	—	(†2)	142 46	79
167·85	Welwyn Garden City .	—	—	145 03	90
170·45	HATFIELD . . .	145½	166	146 51	*75
173·70	Brookmans Park . .	—	(†1)	149 25	74
175·45	Potters Bar . . .	—	172	150 53	72½
179·00	New Barnet . . .	—	(†4)	153 54	69
				p.w.s.	*25
183·20	Wood Green . . .	—	—	159 15	64
185·65	FINSBURY PARK . .	—	186	161 49	—
			(†2)	sig. stop	*0
188·15	KINGS CROSS . .	162	193	169 12	—

* Speed restriction. † Recovery time (min.). ‡ Passing time. § From dead start.
I: 'Coronation' schedule, 1939. II: Schedule to which this run was made, 1958.

285 tons gross. No. 60114 *W. P. Allen*, with 336 tons tare and 365 tons gross, covered the same stretch in 2 min. 11 sec. (98·9 m.p.h.) with a top speed of exactly 100 m.p.h., as logged by K. R. Phillips. So the 'A1s' yield little, if anything, to the 'A4s' when it comes to high-speed achievement.

Like the Gresley 'A4' Pacifics, the Peppercorn 'A1s' can be run with full regulator, but probably are not so driven to quite the same extent, except for their hardest work. On a run recorded by R. I. Nelson on the footplate of No. 60123 *H. A. Ivatt*, the down 'Queen of Scots' Pullman was made up to the unusually heavy load of eleven cars, with a gross weight of 450 tons. Even so, Driver Cartwright of Copley Hill used no more than three-quarters regulator – 210–220 lb per sq in. in the steam-chest out of 220–240 lb in the boiler – to get up the initial 1 in 200 to Potters Bar, with cut-off advancing from 15 to 20 per cent and speed falling gradually from 54 to 46 m.p.h. Not until after passing Peterborough was the regulator opened to full for any considerable distance; with between 16 and 18 per cent cut-off speed rose to 72½ m.p.h. beyond Tallington, and to 74 on the short level after Essendine with 20 per cent; up the 4½ miles at 1 in 200 to milepost 95½, now in 23 per cent, the minimum was 64½ m.p.h., and with a final cut-off increase to 25 per cent up the 3 miles at 1 in 178 to Stoke summit the lowest speed was 64½ m.p.h., and this with a trailing load of 450 tons.

Beyond Doncaster again full regulator was in use for most of the distance to Ardsley summit; on 22 per cent cut-off 2 miles at 1 in 150 to Hemsworth were surmounted with a drop in speed from 63½ to 60 m.p.h., and 61 was the minimum up the continuation of the same grade to milepost 169½. Finally, up 2¾ miles at 1 in 100 from milepost 175, after slowing through Wakefield speed increased to 37½ m.p.h. by Lofthouse and further to 43 m.p.h. on the last 1 in 122 to Ardsley, this on a cut-off of 25 per cent. When the regulator was fully open, the drop in pressure from boiler to steam-chest was no more than 5 lb per sq in. There were two signal stops, three other signal checks and four permanent way checks on this run, but overall time was improved on by 2 min., and the net time was not more than 176½ min. for the 185·7 miles as compared with the 195 min. schedule then operative. This was an admirable example of the competence of a Peppercorn 'A1', which at no point was being extended to achieve such times and speeds.

The names conferred on the 'A1' Pacifics have been another very mixed bag. Among personalities other than *W. P. Allen* of the Railway Executive Committee (No. 60114), there came a selection of past locomotive engineers of the constituent companies of the L.N.E.R. – *Archibald Sturrock* (No. 60118), *Patrick Stirling* (No. 60119) and *H. A. Ivatt* (No. 60123) of the Great Northern, and *Sir Vincent Raven* (No. 60126), *Wilson Worsdell* (No. 60127) and *Edward Fletcher* (No. 60142) of the North Eastern. One cannot help thinking that if three each from these two railways could be commemorated in this way, it might have been possible similarly to remember the distinguished work of James Holden on the Great Eastern Railway and John G. Robinson on the Great Central Railway, both of whose engines outlasted many of their contemporaries on the other constituent lines.

Next came railway commemorations. Unhappily *Great Northern* was the name still carried by Thompson's ungainly rebuild of No. 60113; *North Eastern* went to No. 60147, *Great Central* to No. 60156, *Great Eastern* to No. 60157, and *North British* to No. 60161, in each case with the embellishment of the coat-of-arms of the former company. One or two of the fine bird titles which had been displaced from 'A4' Pacifics by the less euphonious names of L.N.E.R. directors now reappeared, such as *Kestrel* (No. 60130), *Osprey* (No. 60131), *Sea Eagle* (No. 60139), and *Peregrine* (No. 60146); new bird names were *Kittiwake* (No. 60120) and *Curlew* (No. 60122). But the twice abandoned *Great Snipe* was not seen again, nor *Herring Gull*, *Gadwall*, *Pochard*, *Garganey* and *Capercaillie*. As to the remainder of the names, these were either a further selection of racehorses, or were taken from the Scott novels, some of the latter having been carried previously by North British Atlantics or 4-4-0s, while the others were innovations. Sir Walter Scott himself gave the name to No. 60143. By and large, 'A1' Pacific naming has been a very haphazard process.

In all, forty-nine Peppercorn 6 ft 8 in. Pacifics were built, and their construction was more speedy than that of any previous L.N.E.R. Pacific series; indeed, between the appearance of No. 60114 *W. P. Allen* in August 1948 and that of Nos. 60160–60162 in December 1949 the interval was no more than sixteen months. With the Thompson rebuild, No. 60113, the total number of 'A1' Pacifics is thus fifty engines. Before the first scrappings began, the lines in England and Scotland which formed a part of the former London & North Eastern Railway possessed a total of 202 Pacific locomotives, classified as follows:

TABLE V(D)
SUMMARY OF L.N.E.R. PACIFICS

Class	Number built	Driving wheel dia.	Notes on types and rebuildings	
			Number	Type
A1	49	6 ft 8 in.	49	Peppercorn type
A1(1)	1	,, ,,	1	Former 'A3' type rebuilt by Thompson
A2	15	6 ft 2 in.	15	Peppercorn type
A2/1	4	,, ,,	4	'V2' 2-6-2 type adapted by Thompson
A2/2	6	,, ,,	6	Former 'P2' 2-8-2 type rebuilt by Thompson
A2/3	15	,, ,,	15	Thompson type
A3	*78	6 ft 8 in.	*51	Built as original 'A1' type and rebuilt by Gresley
,,	,,	,, ,,	27	Gresley type
A4	†34	,, ,,	†34	Gresley type

* Fifty-two of original 'A1' type built and converted to 'A3', but one rebuilt further by Thompson into present 'A1' class.
† Thirty-five built, but one destroyed in air raid at York.

In his 1961 presidential address to the Institution of Locomotive Engineers, J. F. Harrison revealed that in their first twelve years of service the five roller-bearing 'A1' Pacifics, Nos. 60153 to 60157, had run 4,800,000 miles between them; one, indeed, had completed a million miles, which meant an average of 228 miles for every day since it had left Doncaster Works – a proud record indeed. By 1961 these five engines were averaging 120,000 miles between major overhauls, or 50 per cent more than the general Pacific average; such a figure not merely provides the justification for the cost of roller bearing equipment, but creates surprise as to why no further engines of either this or the other Pacific classes were similarly fitted. The entire series of forty-nine Peppercorn Pacifics had averaged just over 200 miles a day for between twelve and thirteen years from the date of their construction – a record shared by no other British locomotive type.

The operating authorities of the London & North Eastern Railway and its successors had every reason to be grateful to Gresley, Thompson and Peppercorn for having provided them with such ample power for their main line workings, both passenger and freight. Taking into account also the 184 Gresley 'V2' 2-6-2 engines, the eastern side of England today is still better equipped in this respect than any other part of the country.

TABLE V (E)
LEADING DIMENSIONS OF PEPPERCORN PACIFICS

Class	'A1'	'A2'
Cylinders (3), diameter . .	19 in.	19 in.
,, stroke . .	26 in.	26 in.
Driving wheels, diameter .	6 ft 8 in.	6 ft 2 in.
Wheelbase, rigid . . .	14 ft 6 in.	13 ft 0 in.
,, total . . .	36 ft 3 in.	34 ft 4 in.
Heating surface, tubes and flues	2,216 sq ft	2,216 sq ft
,, ,, firebox . .	245 sq ft	245 sq ft
,, ,, total . .	2,461 sq ft	2,461 sq ft
Superheating surface . .	680 sq ft	680 sq ft
Firegrate area . . .	50 sq ft	50 sq ft
Working pressure, per sq in. .	250 lb	250 lb
Tractive effort (85 per cent) .	37,400 lb	40,430 lb
Adhesion weight . . .	66 tons	66 tons
Engine weight (working order)	104 tons	101 tons
Engine and tender weight .	164½ tons	160¼ tons
Length over buffers . .	73 ft 0 in.	71 ft 0½ in.

TABLE V (F)
NAMES, NUMBERS AND BUILDING DATES OF
PEPPERCORN PACIFICS

Number	Name	Class	Built
60114	W. P. Allen . . .	A1	1948
60115	Meg Merrilies . . .	,,	,,
60116	Hal o' the Wynd . .	,,	,,
60117	Bois Roussel . . .	,,	,,
60118	Archibald Sturrock . .	,,	,,
60119	Patrick Stirling . . .	,,	,,
60120	Kittiwake	,,	,,
60121	Silurian	,,	,,
60122	Curlew	,,	,,
60123	H. A. Ivatt . . .	,,	1949
60124	Kenilworth . . .	,,	,,
60125	Scottish Union . .	,,	,,
60126	Sir Vincent Raven . .	,,	,,
60127	Wilson Worsdell . .	,,	,,
60128	Bongrace	,,	,,
60129	Guy Mannering . . .	,,	,,
60130	Kestrel	,,	1948
60131	Osprey	,,	,,
60132	Marmion	,,	,,
60133	Pommern	,,	,,
60134	Foxhunter	,,	,,
60135	Madge Wildfire . . .	,,	,,
60136	Alcazar	,,	,,
60137	Redgauntlet . . .	,,	,,
60138	Boswell	,,	,,
60139	Sea Eagle	,,	,,
60140	Balmoral	,,	,,
60141	Abbotsford . . .	,,	,,
60142	Edward Fletcher . . .	,,	1949
60143	Sir Walter Scott . . .	,,	,,
60144	King's Courier . . .	,,	,,
60145	Saint Mungo . . .	,,	,,
60146	Peregrine	,,	,,
60147	North Eastern . . .	,,	,,
60148	Aboyeur	,,	,,
60149	Amadis	,,	,,
60150	Willbrook	,,	,,
60151	Midlothian	,,	,,
60152	Holyrood	,,	,,
*60153	Flamboyant . . .	,,	,,
*60154	Bon Accord . . .	,,	,,
*60155	Borderer	,,	,,
*60156	Great Central . . .	,,	,,
*60157	Great Eastern . . .	,,	,,
60158	Aberdonian . . .	,,	,,
60159	Bonnie Dundee . . .	,,	,,
60160	Auld Reekie . . .	,,	,,
60161	North British . . .	,,	,,
60162	Saint Johnstoun . .	,,	,,
60525	A. H. Peppercorn . .	A2	1947
†60526	Sugar Palm . . .	,,	1948
60527	Sun Chariot . . .	,,	,,
60528	Tudor Minstrel . . .	,,	,,
†60529	Pearl Diver . . .	,,	,,
60530	Sayajirao	,,	,,

paper noted the unhappy fact that the engine had overheated that part of her anatomy known as the 'hot box'!

The second Pacific, No. 6201 *Princess Elizabeth,* joined *The Princess Royal* in 1933, but it was not until 1935 that the next ten locomotives of the series made their appearance. The dimensions of No. 6203 *Princess Margaret Rose* made it clear that the lesson of inadequate superheat in the first two engines had been learned and that the deficiency had been rectified. For the super-heater was doubled; and thirty-two elements instead of sixteen increased the superheating surface from 370 to 623 sq ft. By adapting the forward part of the firebox to form a combustion chamber, the designer increased the firebox heating surface from 190 to 217 sq ft – another valuable gain – while reducing the length between tubeplates from 20 ft 9 in. to 19 ft 3 in. The heating surface from tubes and flues decreased from 2,523 sq ft to 2,097 sq ft. By a later modification of these boilers the total went up again to 2,299 sq ft.

Not a few troubles were experienced with the 'Princesses' after they entered service. Principles of design which had been traditional at Swindon for long past, but which depended on the use of Welsh coal and the scientific handling methods in which Great Western drivers and fireman had been trained, were not automatically to achieve the same success on the L.M.S.R., whose engine-crews were to learn that their new and imposing 4-6-2s needed a good deal of 'nursing' if they were to give of their best.

There were mechanical difficulties also. It had been an error to position the outside cylinders over the trailing wheels of the bogie; there was a tendency for these cylinders to work loose, and eventually strips of metal had to be welded to the main frames in order to secure the flanges of the cylinder castings more firmly, though even then not with complete success. Again, there were fractures of the rear truck frames, which were experienced similarly with the 'Duchesses' and led to the last two of the latter being equipped with cast steel truck frames.

Another Swindon speciality, the regulator working in the superheater header (in the absence of a steam dome) was found to be troublesome, and not a few header fractures occurred. For the same reason the regulator proved to be stiff in action, so that slipping by these engines, with their relatively low ratio of adhesion, was not easy to control. In the end all the 'Princesses' were provided with steam domes, to which the regulators were transferred. All these points weighed heavily with Stanier when the designs for the 'Coronation' class were in preparation.

In due course Nos. 6200 and 6201 were rebuilt in conformity with Nos. 6203 to 6212 inclusive, and the superheating surface was increased further to 653 sq ft, but the boiler modification mentioned above cut this to 598 sq ft. The high-sided tender, with curved upper plates conforming in profile with the cab roof, and accommodating 9 tons of coal and 4,000 gallons of water, had become standard by the time that Nos. 6203 to 6212 had been built, and Nos. 6200 and 6201 were equipped similarly. In 1938 No. 6205 *Princess Victoria* had her two inside sets of Walschaerts valve-motion removed and rocking-levers fitted, to enable the outside valve-motions to work the valves of the inside cylinders – a reversal of the G.W.R. practice of operating the valves of the outside cylinders of four-cylinder engines by the inside motions. After this change No. 6205 acquired a reputation for rough riding, but the original arrangement persisted until the engine was withdrawn in 1962.

2 – *Glasgow to Euston in 5¾ hours*

THE purpose behind the Stanier Pacific design was to provide locomotives capable of making the run between Euston, London, and Glasgow Central, 401½ miles apart, without change, though, of course, with change of crew intermediately, either at Crewe or Carlisle. It was also intended that the engines should be able to handle 500-ton trains over both Shap and Beattock summits without help, the former 915 ft and the latter 1,014 ft above sea-level. With pre-war quality of coal and locomotive maintenance, loads of this magnitude could be dealt with singlehanded, notwithstanding the 4 miles at 1 in 75 which form the south ascent to Shap summit, and the 10 miles at between 1 in 69 and 1 in 88 up to Beattock summit. During the Second World War, however, there came a reversion to the banking of all northbound trains from Beattock up to Beattock summit, with time definitely allowed in the schedules for the purpose.

With little doubt the most notable round trip ever undertaken by an engine of the original 'Princess Royal' series was that of No. 6201 *Princess Elizabeth* on 16th and 17th November, 1936. The purpose of the test was to obtain data on which to base the schedule of the 'Coronation Scot' streamline service, planned for introduction in the following summer. On 16th November, therefore, No. 6201, in charge of Driver T. J. Clarke and Fireman C. Fleet, of Crewe, worked a seven-coach test train without a stop over the 401½ miles from Euston to Glasgow, and on the following day the feat was repeated in the opposite direction with eight coaches. The most remarkable feature of the test, however, was that the schedule was no more than 6 hours, and, even more startling, that this was cut to 5 hours 53 min. 38 sec. going north, and to 5 hours 44 min. 15 sec. coming south. The latter time entailed an average speed of 70 m.p.h. for the entire distance, Beattock and Shap summits included.

Some of the times and speeds achieved on this run might have seemed almost incredible but for the careful record that was made public after the run, as set out in Table VI (A). Many miles in both directions were covered at 80 to 90 m.p.h.; the top speed going north was 95½ m.p.h. at Sear's Crossing, between Cheddington and Leighton, and coming south 95 m.p.h. approaching Crewe, in the latter case on the dead level. The 31·3 miles from Carnforth up to Shap summit were reeled off at an average of 70·5 m.p.h., with a minimum of 57 m.p.h. up the final 4 miles at 1 in 75; from Carlisle to Beattock summit, 49·6 miles, including the climb from just above sea-level to 1,014 ft above the sea, the astounding time of 41 min. 42 sec. was achieved –

TABLE VI (A)
L.M.S.R. EUSTON–GLASGOW CENTRAL
Non-Stop Test Runs
Engine: 4-6-2 No. 6201 *Princess Elizabeth*
DOWN: 16th November, 1936   UP: 17th November, 1936
Load: 7 coaches, 225 tons tare,   *Load:* 8 coaches, 255 tons tare,
230 tons gross   260 tons gross

Dist.	Sched.	Times		Dist.	Sched.	Times
miles	min.	min. sec.		miles	min.	min. sec.
0·00	0	0 00	EUSTON	401·35	360	344 15
5·40	8	7 24	WILLESDEN JUNCTION .	395·95	352	335 45
		p.w.s.				p.w.s.
17·45	18	18 55	WATFORD JUNCTION .	383·90	342	325 38
31·65	30	29 55	Tring	369·70	331	315 30
46·65	41	40 32	BLETCHLEY . . .	354·70	318	304 27
59·90	51	50 53	Roade	341·45	308	294 33
69·70	—	62 46	Weedon	331·65	—	287 08
82·55	70	68 33	RUGBY*	318·80	289	276 05
97·10	82	81 08	NUNEATON . . .	304·25	277	264 33
110·00	95	92 53	TAMWORTH . . .	291·35	264	252 58
116·25	100	97 38	Lichfield	285·10	259	248 37
124·30	106	103 36	Rugeley	277·05	253	242 25
133·55	114	111 52	STAFFORD* . . .	267·80	245	233 46
147·65	127	123 47	Whitmore . . .	253·70	233	222 53
158·00	136	132 52	CREWE*	243·35	223	213 17
174·30	149	146 00	*Weaver Junction* . .	227·05	209	200 37
182·15	156	153 30	WARRINGTON . .	219·20	202	193 34
193·90	168	164 55	WIGAN . . .	207·45	190	182 42
197·15	171½	168 30	*Standish Junction* .	204·20	186½	179 58
203·55	177	173 36	*Euxton Junction* . .	197·80	—	174 42
209·00	183	179 15	PRESTON* . . .	192·35	175	168 55
218·50	191½	188 05	Garstang . . .	182·85	167	161 00
230·00	200	196 35	LANCASTER . .	171·35	158	152 07
236·25	205	201 28	CARNFORTH . .	165·10	153	147 12
243·55	—	206 45	Milnthorpe . . .	157·80	—	141 45
249·10	215	211 38	OXENHOLME . .	152·25	143	137 18
256·15	—	218 04	Grayrigg . . .	145·20	—	131 22
262·10	227	223 06	Tebay . . .	139·25	132	126 15
267·55	233	228 12	*Shap Summit* . .	133·80	127	121 50
281·25	245	240 05	PENRITH . . .	120·10	114	109 15
294·30	—	250 00	Wreay . . .	107·05	—	99 12
299·10	260	255 24	CARLISLE* . . .	102·25	97	93 20
307·70	268	263 27	Gretna Junction . .	93·65	90	86 10
315·70	—	270 38	Kirtlebridge . .	85·65	—	79 55
324·75	282	277 40	LOCKERBIE . .	76·60	77	72 49
338·70	293	287 35	Beattock . . .	62·65	66	62 29
348·70	306	297 06	*Beattock Summit* .	52·65	57	54 20
351·60	—	299 26	Elvanfoot . . .	49·75	—	51 57
362·20	—	309 25	Lamington† . .	39·15	—	43 17
365·90	—	313 15	SYMINGTON . .	35·45	—	40 35
372·60	328	319 30	CARSTAIRS* . .	28·75	33	34 30
377·55	—	324 44	*Craigenhill Summit* .	23·80	—	30 16
383·10	338	329 38	LAW JUNCTION* . .	18·25	22	24 30
		p.w.s.				p.w.s.
388·50	344	336 34	MOTHERWELL* . .	12·85	16	16 50
		p.w.s.				p.w.s.
394·75	—	344 03	Newton	6·60	—	9 05
		p.w.s.				p.w.s.
401·35	360	353 38	GLASGOW CENTRAL .	0·00	0	0 00

* Speed restriction.   † Severe slack, down journey only.

71·4 m.p.h. – and up the 10 miles of Beattock bank proper speed hovered continuously round the 56 to 57 m.p.h. mark. Up Shap the cut-off ranged from 25 to 32 per cent, and up Beattock from 30 to 37½ per cent.

Maximum indicated h.p. ranged between 2,413 and 2,448, and the biggest drawbar h.p. was 1,350. Coal consumption on the northbound journey was 46·8 lb per mile, but coming south, notwithstanding the heavier train, higher speed, and some very bad weather, the consumption was brought down to 44·8 lb per mile, a tribute to the admirable management of the engine by the crew. By now, of course, *Princess Elizabeth* had the benefit of the thirty-two-element superheater, and also of a dome for the collection of steam, in place of the earlier perforated pipe arrangement.

One of the finest runs that I ever noted personally behind an engine of this class was on the down 'Royal Scot' in the early part of 1937, when that master of his craft, Laurie A. Earl, was in charge, with Fireman Abey, of No. 6206 *Princess Marie Louise*. We had a big train of sixteen vehicles, 492 tons tare and 515 tons with passengers and luggage. I had been incautious enough to show my face in the vicinity of the footplate shortly before starting from Euston, and this was the result. In Table VI (B) the times and speeds between Euston and Rugby are set out in detail. We were delayed in the earlier stage of the run, though even so it was obvious that the engine had no

TABLE VI (B)
L.M.S.R. EUSTON–RUGBY
Engine: 4-6-2 No. 6206 *Princess Marie Louise*
Load: 16 coaches, 492 tons tare, 515 tons gross

Dist.		Sched.	Actual	Speeds
miles		min.	min. sec.	m.p.h.
0·00	EUSTON	0	0 00	—
5·40	WILLESDEN JUNCTION .	10	10 37	—
8·05	Wembley	—	13 22	59
11·40	Harrow	—	16 54	55
17·45	WATFORD JUNCTION .	23	23 10	62½
20·95	Kings Langley . .	—	26 35	61
24·50	Hemel Hempstead . .	—	30 05	60
			p.w.s.	*15
27·95	Berkhamsted . . .	—	36 15	—
31·65	Tring	38	41 59	—
36·10	Cheddington . . .	—	45 49	79
40·20	Leighton	—	48 50	85/80½
46·65	BLETCHLEY . . .	51	53 33	83½/79
52·40	Wolverton . . .	—	57 46	85
54·75	Castlethorpe . . .	—	59 31	—·
59·90	Roade	63	63 33	72½
62·85	Blisworth	66	65 55	76½
69·70	Weedon	—	71 12	79
75·30	Welton	—	75 36	70½
80·30	*Hillmorton* . . .	—	79 45	75
82·55	RUGBY	87	83 14	—

* Speed restriction.

difficulty in maintaining a mile a minute up the long stretches of 1 in 335 before Tring.

The running then became spectacular indeed. After two maxima of 85 m.p.h. down the 1 in 333 before Bletchley, we swept up a similar grade to Roade at a minimum of 72½ m.p.h.; and a top speed of 79 m.p.h. on but little easier than level track to Weedon was followed by a minimum of 70½ m.p.h. at Kilsby Tunnel. From Tring to Hillmorton, just before slowing down to the Rugby stop, a distance of 48·6 miles was covered at an average speed of 77·2 m.p.h. – and this with a 515-ton train! The net time over the 82·6 miles from Euston to Rugby was 79 min.; and though the running on to Crewe was a little less spectacular, a net non-stop time of 150 min. from Euston to Crewe would have been a matter of little difficulty.

TABLE VI (C)
L.M.S.R. LANCASTER–PENRITH
Engine: 4-6-2 No. 6209 *Princess Beatrice*
Load: 14 coaches, 448 tons tare, 470 tons gross

Dist.		Sched.	Actual	Speeds
miles		min.	min. sec.	m.p.h.
0·00	LANCASTER . . .	0	0 00	—
3·10	Hest Bank . . .	—	4 50	—
6·25	CARNFORTH . . .	8	7 39	70½
10·75	*Burton* . . .	—	11 53	60
13·55	Milnthorpe . . .	—	14 17	70½
15·45	*Hincaster Junction* . .	—	16 04	59
19·10	OXENHOLME . . .	21	19 50	53½
22·60	*Hay Fell*	—	24 04	45½
26·15	*Grayrigg*	—	29 02	40½
32·10	TEBAY	36	34 48	71½
35·10	*Scout Green* . . .	—	38 18	39½
37·55	*Shap Summit* . . .	45	43 10	27
39·70	Shap	—	45 51	—
47·00	*Clifton* . . .	—	52 17	76½
51·25	PENRITH	59	56 24	—

It may be added that Earl, as usual, was keeping the regulator of *Princess Marie Louise* wide open for most of the way up to Tring, with 30 per cent cut-off up Camden bank, 25 per cent from Camden to Willesden, 20 per cent as far as the Berkhamsted check, and 30 per cent in recovering from there up to Tring. From Tring onwards, the opening varied between 20 per cent downhill and on the level, and 25 per cent on the 1 in 330 climbs to Roade and to Kilsby Tunnel.

One of the hardest tasks ever imposed on 'Princess Royal' Pacifics was during the years immediately preceding the introduction of the 'Coronation Scot', when the down 'Midday Scot', heavily loaded by the inclusion of through portions from Liverpool and Manchester, was booked to cover the 51·25 miles from Lancaster over Shap summit to Penrith in 59 min. start to stop, and this with a load which might rise to fifteen and even sixteen coaches.

The best run that I timed during that period is set out in Table VI (C), when No. 6209 *Princess Beatrice*, with a fourteen-coach train of 448 tons tare and 470 tons gross, made the run in 56 min. 24 sec. It will be noted that the minimum speed up the $2\frac{1}{2}$ miles at 1 in 134 beyond Carnforth was 60 m.p.h.; that the long climb of 12·6 miles from Milnthorpe to Grayrigg was completed in 14 min. 45 sec., with a minimum of $40\frac{1}{2}$ m.p.h. on the final 2 miles at 1 in 106; and that the 5·6 miles from Tebay to Shap summit, mostly at 1 in 75, were run in 8 min. 22 sec.

As to the improvement in efficiency of the 'Princess Royal' Pacifics resulting from their equipment with thirty-two-element superheaters, a run in 1935 with the 5.25 p.m. from Liverpool to Euston by No. 6200 *The Princess Royal* gives ample proof. With a fifteen-coach train of 453 tons tare and 475 tons gross the 152·6 miles from Crewe to Willesden Junction were run in 129 min. 33 sec. start to stop. Apart from the usual speed restrictions at Stafford and Rugby, the only other slack was over the pitfall at Polesworth. Highlights of the performance were the drop only from 60 to $57\frac{3}{4}$ m.p.h. up the 1 in 177 of Madeley bank, and the time of 12 min. 33 sec. for the 15·0 miles from Bletchley up to Tring, with an absolute minimum of 67 m.p.h.; maximum speeds were $80\frac{1}{2}$ m.p.h. at Standon Bridge, 80 beyond Rugeley, $85\frac{1}{2}$ at Hademore, 82 at Brinklow, $85\frac{1}{2}$ at Weedon, 82 at Castlethorpe, $86\frac{1}{2}$ at Kings Langley and $85\frac{1}{2}$ at Wembley; the 67·25 miles from Welton to Wembley took no more than 52 min. 17 sec., for an average of 77·2 m.p.h.

Three days later No. 6200 made a test run with a 461-ton special train, which included the dynamometer car, from Crewe to Glasgow and back. Minimum speeds going north were 43 m.p.h. at Grayrigg and 35 at Shap summit, while the 10 miles at 1 in 88–69 from Beattock up to Beattock summit were completed without the speed falling below 30 m.p.h. Coming south, a very fast run was made over the 66·9 miles from Symington to Carlisle in 59 min. 41 sec.; after that 45 m.p.h. was attained up the 1 in 132 from Carlisle to Wreay, and on the long 1 in 125 up to Shap the lowest rate was 49 m.p.h. Yet all this was done on a coal consumption of 52·6 lb per mile, which worked out at an average of 2·88 lb per drawbar-h.p.-hr, *The Princess Royal* thus tying with the high efficiency figure attained by the Great Western Railway's 4-6-0 *Caldicot Castle* nine years earlier. The first withdrawals of 'Princess Royal' Pacifics for scrapping took place in 1961, after a history of the class that had been by no means without distinction.

3 – The 'Turbomotive'

IN 1935, simultaneously with the second series of Stanier Pacifics of the 'Princess Royal' type, Nos. 6203 to 6212, the vacant place, No. 6202, was filled by a locomotive which differed radically in design from its immediate neighbours. Boiler, wheels and wheel spacings were almost identical with those of the other Pacifics; it was the mode of propulsion which had been changed. Instead of cylinders and reciprocating motion, No. 6202 was propelled by turbines; one, the larger, on the left-hand side of the engine, providing for forward motion, and the other and smaller turbine, on the right-hand side, for reverse. No. 6202 never had any official name; but the title 'Turbomotive' later became fastened on to the engine as a nickname rather more expressive than euphonious.

At various periods of locomotive history the idea of turbine propulsion has appealed to locomotive engineers. With turbine drive, the torque or turning motion applied to the driving axle is absolutely smooth and even. There is no hammer-blow, as with cylinders and reciprocating motion; the tendency of the driving wheels to slip when the power is applied, due to fluctuation in the torque, is avoided; and for these reasons it is possible to use a greater proportion of the locomotive's weight for adhesion, and to obtain a higher starting tractive effort. When built, No. 6202 carried axle-loads up to 24 tons, as compared with a maximum of 22½ tons on any British cylinder-propelled locomotive up to that date, although the adhesion weight was slightly reduced later.

The steady drawbar pull of a turbine-driven locomotive should help to reduce the cost of maintenance of all the mechanical parts and of the locomotive as a whole. As compared with the many individually lubricated parts of a locomotive driven by ordinary reciprocating motion, the gearing of a turbine locomotive can be completely enclosed in an oil-bath, which also should be an advantage from the maintenance point of view. As to thermal efficiency, the maximum possible advantages of turbine propulsion cannot be realized without condensing, and this is what No. 6202 lacked. The addition of a condensing plant is a bulky and weighty complication which has probably done more than any other factor to impede the development of turbine propulsion on locomotives. But without a condenser it is questionable whether the other advantages enumerated can ever balance the much higher constructional cost of a turbine-driven locomotive.

Two previous experiments had been made in Great Britain with turbo-condensing locomotives, both on the L.M.S.R. or its predecessors. In 1922 a locomotive of this type, built by Armstrong, Whitworth & Co. to the Ramsay patents, was tried on the late Lancashire & Yorkshire Railway, and in 1928 this was followed by the remarkable locomotive built by Beyer, Peacock & Co. to the Swedish Ljungström design, which made a number of journeys on the Midland Division.

I well remember one run which I had behind her on the then 12.20 p.m. from Manchester Central to St Pancras, on which we made the fastest climb from Cheadle Heath up the steep incline to Peak Forest that I had ever known up to that time – 17·5 miles in 27 min. 40 sec. with 260 tons – but experience showed that the locomotive needed a good deal of modification, and the builders were not prepared to carry on indefinitely with such expensive experiments unless they had some ultimate assurance of railway backing in so doing. So this promising locomotive disappeared from view, and nothing more was heard of her.

The proposal to experiment once again with turbine propulsion was based

Above, at speed near Standish on its northbound run – the streamlined 'Coronation Scot', headed by 4-6-2 No. 6224 Princess Alexandra.

[*Eric Treacy*

Below, on the Baltimore & Ohio Railroad, U.S.A., No. 6220 Coronation *(actually No. 6229 temporarily renumbered and renamed) with some of the new stock specially built for the 'Coronation Scot' service, but never so used.*

[*W. R. Osborne*

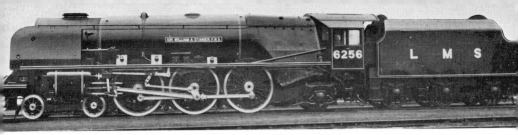

Above, last but one of a distinguished line: No. 6256 Sir William A. Stanier, F.R.S., *modified by H. G. Ivatt with roller bearings to all wheels, altered rear-end framing, and other changes.* [British Railways

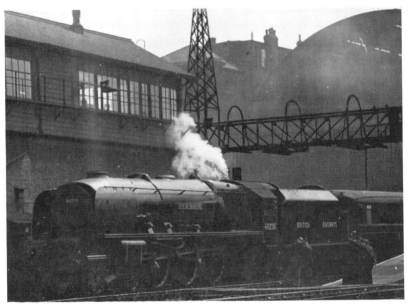

Stanier Pacifics have made various excursions over the lines of other Regions. No. 42636 City of Bradford *at Kings Cross, E.R., with a Leeds express in the 1948 locomotive exchange.* [R. E. Vincent

The same engine heading the 'Atlantic Coast Express', S.R., through Vauxhall, with a tender from a Ministry of Supply 2-8-0 to provide additional water capacity. [P. Ransome-Wallis

A stiff test for a 'Duchess' – No. 46257 City of Salford *climbing to Dainton summit with the down 'Cornish Riviera Express' of the Western Region.*

[W. S. Fish

On temporary loan to replace W.R. 'King' 4-6-0s under repair: No. 46237 City of Bristol *at Snow Hill station, Birmingham, heading a Birkenhead– Paddington express.* [B. Sackville

Dropping down from Shap Summit with the morning Glasgow–Birmingham express. The photographer has caught No. 46242 City of Glasgow *at the precise moment when the tender coal-pusher is in use, shown by the exhaust above the tender.* [*Derek Cross*

The vital importance of smoke deflectors – a striking shot of No. 46246 City of Manchester *near Crawford in the Scottish Lowlands with the up 'Royal Scot' on a frosty morning.* [*W. J. V. Anderson*

At speed in the Clyde Valley near Lamington – No. 46230 Duchess of Buccleuch with the morning express from Glasgow and Edinburgh to Birmingham.

[*W. J. V. Anderson*

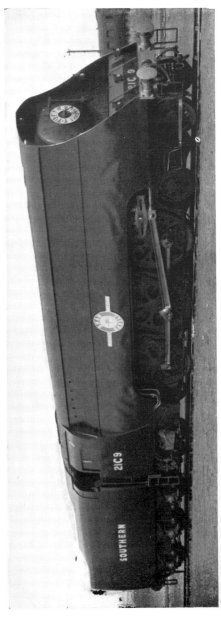

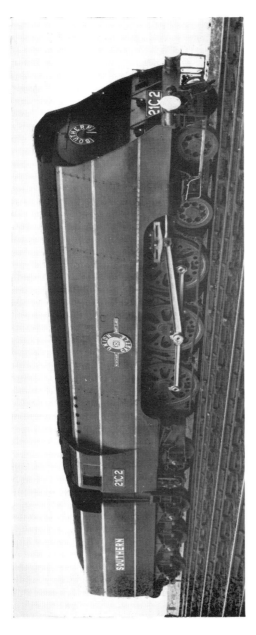

Right, No. 21C2 Union Castle, one of the Bulleid 'Merchant Navy' Pacifics as first built, showing the inverted horseshoe 'Southern' nameplate on smokebox door.
[British Railways

Left, in wartime black livery: No. 21C9 Shaw Savill. Due to drivers' superstitions of bad luck, the word 'Southern' on the smokebox door is now a complete circle.
[British Railways

Left, No. 21C17, of the second 'Merchant Navy' series, with modified front end, cab and tender.

[British Railways

Right, after the introduction of the first light Pacifics, No. 21C8 Orient Line with lengthened smoke deflectors and further modification of cab.

[L. Elsey

Above, early front end modifications of the 'Merchant Navy' Pacifics: left, as originally built, with horseshoe 'Southern' nameplate and number immediately below smokebox door, and right, with circular 'Southern' nameplate, number immediately above buffer-beam, headlamps above number, and enlarged aperture in upper casing showing chimney. [British Railways

Below, after the first major smoke deflection modification: No. 21C5 Canadian Pacific *heading the up 'Atlantic Coast Express' near Honiton, showing inverted trough above smokebox.* [W. N. Lockett

on the success of a non-condensing turbine locomotive of the Ljungström type which had been introduced in 1932 on the Grangesburg–Oxelösund Railway of Sweden. Stanier, with a representative of the Metropolitan-Vickers Company, which was interested in the project, visited Sweden to see the Ljungström locomotive at work, and their conclusions were so favourable that the decision was made to build No. 6202 as a turbine-driven locomotive, and without a condenser. The contract for the turbine equipment was placed with Metropolitan-Vickers.

On taking the road, No. 6202, unlike most experimental locomotives, proved to have the simplest and cleanest outline of all the Pacifics other than the streamliners. A long casing ran down the left side of the engine, above the running-plate, to a larger casing abreast of the smokebox, above and below the running-plate, which housed the forward turbine. On the right side, a similar but smaller casing at the leading end housed the reverse turbine; from there back to the cab an ordinary footplating, with splashers for the coupled wheels, was provided.

From the first No. 6202 had a double chimney; and though the original boiler, like that of *The Princess Royal*, possessed no steam-dome, this was soon changed to a domed boiler with thirty-two-element superheater affording 653 sq ft heating surface. Later this was exchanged for a forty-element super-heater with 577 sq ft only; but the final boiler fitted had a forty-element superheater with triple-flow elements and 825 sq ft superheating surface. The softness of the blast gave such trouble with drifting steam – and, equally, with smoke sucked back into the cab, which made the 'Turbomotive' one of the dirtiest of all L.M.S.R. engines to drive – that smoke-deflectors had to be fitted at an early date, and No. 6202 was thus the first L.M.S.R. Pacific to carry them.

The layout of the 'Turbomotive' was interesting. The sixteen-stage forward turbine nominally developed 2,600 h.p. at 62 m.p.h., and transmitted its power through a treble-reduction gear, with a ratio of 34·4-to-1, to the leading coupled axle. At a speed of 90 m.p.h., the turbine was running at a speed of 13,500 r.p.m. The forward turbine was always in gear, whether the engine was running forwards or backwards; the reverse turbine normally was idle, and could be brought into action only if the engine was stationary. This was done by means of a dog-clutch. As previously mentioned, the reverse turbine was smaller than the forward turbine; it was for slow-speed use only, either in shunting or moving the engine light, and worked through the forward gearing with an additional gear, or quadruple-reduction gearing in all.

The vitally important business of lubrication was assured by enclosing all the transmission shafts and gears in a suspended case, supplied with lubricant by a closed force-feed oiling circuit. Two of the pumps were steam-driven and were at work continuously, even when the engine was standing; they forced the oil through at a pressure of about 7 lb per sq in. The third pump was of a reversible gear type, worked off the motion, and so came into operation directly the locomotive started; at 60 m.p.h. this boosted the oil pressure up to 16 lb per sq in. These pumps were submerged in the sump. The oil was strained before use, and cooled after use.

The method of driving the 'Turbomotive' differed entirely, of course, from the handling of an ordinary reciprocating steam locomotive. The regulator acted as a stop-valve and nothing more; it was kept fully open during the run. In the place in the cab occupied normally by the reversing wheel there was the control box. Steam was allowed to pass to the turbines by means of the control handle; if this was turned in a clockwise direction, steam was admitted successively to six valves, the driver using as many valves as necessary according to the power demand – starting, uphill, level, downhill, and so on. For reversing, there was a safety handle to ensure that no attempt was made to reverse with the forward turbine still in action; when this was locked, turning the control wheel counter-clockwise admitted steam to three valves in succession supplying the reverse turbine.

In January, 1946, a most illuminating paper on the design and performance of No. 6202 was read by R. C. Bond, at that time the newly-appointed Mechanical Engineer of L.M.S.R. Locomotive Works, before the Institution of Locomotive Engineers. It was no secret that the locomotive, while it had done excellent work on fast and heavy express trains – generally the 8.30 a.m. from Euston to Liverpool and the 5.25 p.m. back – had spent more than half its life in the shops, as a result of failures of various kinds. In the first ten years there were thirteen casualties, six due to failure of the reverse turbine, four to oil leakages, two to serious failures of the forward turbine, and one, the most troublesome of all, to a failure originating in the flexible drive between the slow-speed gear wheel and the leading coupled axle.

A particularly disconcerting failure was a breakage of the main forward turbine spindle when the engine was travelling at over 60 m.p.h. near Leighton Buzzard, though fortunately without causing an accident. Several of the failures resulted in a complete locking of the wheels, making the engine immovable until the leading coupled wheels could be jacked up clear of the rails. The persistence with which Sir William Stanier and his staff pursued their research with this engine, despite all such discouragements, was praiseworthy indeed; R. C. Bond's paper seemed to suggest that the 'Turbomotive' was to be regarded as an encouraging, but not a conclusive, experiment.

My liveliest recollection of the 'Turbo' is that of travelling up one evening from Crewe, during the late war, with a railway chief engineer who later became a member of the Railway Executive; we had spent the day at a Midland steelworks, and it had been one of most uncomfortably high wind, which by now was beginning to blow itself out. From Crewe we were to take the combined Liverpool and Manchester 'diner', an exceedingly heavy train, and my heart sank when I saw No. 6202 rolling up the platform at the head of the Liverpool portion. 'I'm afraid we're going to lose time', I remarked to my companion, thereby presenting him with a joke against myself which he used for a long time afterwards.

For actually No. 6202 proceeded to gain 11½ min. from Crewe to Watford, and that despite two signal checks and a train made up to seventeen vehicles, of 560 tons tare and fully 610 tons gross weight! True, the 168-min. wartime schedule then in force for the 140·55 miles was easy enough; but we cut it to 156 min. 29 sec., or 153 min. net, ran 96 miles of the journey at an average of just over 60 m.p.h., and all without exceeding 66 m.p.h. at any point. A particularly good effort was to cover the 15·0 miles from Bletchley up to Tring at an average of 56·8 m.p.h. One of the most fervent admirers of the 'Turbomotive' was always Driver L. A. Earl, to whose exploits reference has been made already.

Indeed, there is little doubt that in capable hands No. 6202, despite the comparative inflexibility of working imposed by there being only six hand-controlled valves and therefore, in effect, six ranges only in power output, could put up better performances than the 'Princess Royal' Pacifics. This was proved by an exhaustive series of tests between Euston, Carlisle and Glasgow in 1936, in which the 'Turbomotive' was tried with its three different boiler variations against engines of the former type. In general, No. 6202 made the better times and speeds on a lower coal consumption. On two runs with the 'Royal Scot' from Euston to Glasgow, No. 6202 with her first boiler showed a coal consumption of 2·86 and 3·14 lb per drawbar-h.p.-hr; on one with the second boiler the figure was 2·91 lb; while with the third boiler and its 832 sq ft of superheating surface the consumption was brought down to 2·81 and 2·74 lb on two runs. The nearest to this by a 'Princess Royal' Pacific was 2·86 lb with No. 6210; 3·04 and 3·10 lb were the consumptions with No. 6212.

Yet in the end, after No. 6202 had run some 440,000 miles and had been in store for some time pending a decision as to her future, it was realized that considerable expense would be involved in renewing the main turbine, and that in the circumstances it would be more economical to rebuild the engine as a standard four-cylinder Pacific; it was in this form that she emerged from Crewe Works early in 1952 as No. 46202 *Princess Anne*. In appearance the converted engine resembled one of the original 'Princess Royal' series rather than a 'Duchess' Pacific, because her boiler was pitched with its centre-line 9 ft 1 in. above rail level as compared with the 9 ft 6 in. of a 'Duchess', and also because her cylinders were set well back from the bogie centre-line. But the rebuild copied a 'Duchess' in being fitted with the same outside steam-pipes leading to the massive casing above the valve-chests. Alas, the career of *Princess Anne* in her new form was one of unhappy brevity. For on 8th October, 1952, she was one of the three engines involved in the terrible double collision at Harrow Wealdstone, and was so badly damaged that scrapping was inevitable. So ended a notable British locomotive experiment.

4 – 'Coronation', the 'Duchesses' and the 'Cities'

THE 'Coronation Scot' service was duly inaugurated between the two cities on 5th July, 1937. The train itself proved not to be streamlined, but was made up of standard stock refurnished on rather more elaborate lines than the ordinary main line vehicles, and painted blue with horizontal white lines. It was also somewhat disappointing that after the brilliant times made by *Princess Elizabeth* in the previous November nothing more ambitious than a $6\frac{1}{2}$-hour schedule in each direction, including one stop only – at Carlisle – had been decided on, notwithstanding the increased speed capacity of the new streamline Pacifics to run the train.

These five locomotives, Nos. 6220 to 6224 inclusive, were the next development of the Stanier Pacific design, and incorporated a number of modifications, some of which were very significant. The first and most obvious, of course, was the fully streamlined casing, of which the form was decided after experiments had been carried out in the wind tunnel of the L.M.S.R. Research Station at Derby. A brilliant shade of blue was adopted for the engine, diversified by the horizontal white lines mentioned in the last paragraph, which started in a 'V' shape above the coupling at the leading end, and swept round both sides of the engine as horizontal lines past cab and tender to continue along the length of the train. The streamlined casing was cut away at the centre to expose most of the coupled wheels, the whole effect being very striking.

The changes in the boiler were considerable. From 9 ft 1 in. above rail level the centre-line went up to 9 ft 6 in., and while the diameter of the barrel at the front end decreased fractionally from 5 ft 9 in. to 5 ft $8\frac{1}{2}$ in., the taper towards the firebox was increased, so that the maximum diameter became 6 ft $5\frac{1}{2}$ in. instead of 6 ft 3 in. The increased barrel diameter at the rear end, coupled with 3 in. added to the driving wheel diameter, made it necessary to lift the front corners of the firebox to the extreme limit permitted by the loading gauge. The firebox itself was enlarged, now providing a firegrate area of 50 as compared with 45 sq ft, and a firebox heating surface of 230 instead of 217 sq ft.

The total evaporative heating surface thus became 2,807 sq ft as compared with the 2,516 sq ft of the 'Princesses' after they had received their enlarged superheaters. The most complete breakaway from Swindon practice was seen in the forty-element superheater, which with its heating surface of 856 sq ft was bigger than that of any other British locomotive type, even though at a later stage reduced to 830 sq ft. The one respect in which the superheater might have been improved would have been by the use of flue tubes of larger diameter than $5\frac{1}{8}$ in.; had the $5\frac{1}{2}$-in. diameter flues of a modern 'Britannia' boiler been installed, there need not have been the limitation to 600–620°F. maximum steam temperature customary with the 'Duchesses'.

In view of the high sustained speeds for which these engines had been designed, the driving wheel diameter was increased from 6 ft 6 in. to 6 ft 9 in.; and to give approximately the same tractive effort as before, $\frac{1}{4}$ in. was added to the diameter of the cylinders, making $16\frac{1}{2}$ in. To allow of freer steaming, the piston-valve diameter was enlarged from 8 in. to 9 in.; at the same time the four sets of valve-motion were cut down to two, with the inside valves worked by rocking shafts from the outside motions. Maximum valve-travel was very slightly reduced, and became $7\frac{1}{32}$ in. instead of $7\frac{1}{4}$ in. At first these locomotives were provided with single blast-pipes and chimneys; the doubling was to come later, after successful experiments with the non-streamlined *Duchess of Abercorn*.

A considerable novelty for Great Britain was embodied in the tender, in the shape of a steam-operated coal-pusher, in which a steam cylinder was used to push the coal forwards towards the fireman, so lightening his work, especially on such long and arduous duties as the 299-mile run between Euston and Carlisle. By a rearrangement of the interior of the tender, the coal capacity was increased from 9 to 10 tons; in view of the frequency of water troughs on the principal L.M.S.R. main line, eleven sets in all between Euston and Glasgow, the 4,000 gallons water capacity was still regarded as adequate, and was not increased. The tender side-sheets were prolonged backwards, in order to increase the streamline effect, and were provided with large holes on each side through which to push the hose when water was being taken from water-columns. These changes made very little difference in tender weight, no more than from $55\frac{3}{4}$ to $56\frac{1}{4}$ tons in running order. The combined weight of engine and tender together was increased from 159 to $164\frac{1}{2}$ tons; the length overall diminished slightly from 74 ft $4\frac{1}{4}$ in. to 73 ft $9\frac{3}{4}$ in.

In the following year, 1938, there emerged from Crewe Works, first a series of five streamline Pacifics, Nos. 6225 to 6229 inclusive, and then five more, Nos. 6230 to 6234, which had precisely the same proportions as the streamliners, but from which the streamline casing was omitted. As the building of streamlined engines was resumed in 1939, it might have been thought that the new 'Duchesses' were a temporary expedient only; actually they foreshadowed the complete disappearance of streamlining from L.M.S.R. locomotives after a relatively short interval.

By many connoisseurs of locomotive outline, the non-streamlined 'Duchess' and 'City' Pacifics have always been highly regarded. No express passenger locomotives in Great Britain have had a more stately and impressive appearance than these massive machines. Better balance of line might have been obtained with a longer tender, had that been possible; the bulbous casing above the cylinders at the front end, to conceal the streamlined ports, did not assist the appearance, neither did the extensive and varied collection of fittings distributed along the running-plate above the wheels – a 'marine store', as one writer has amusingly described it – but these were minor blemishes. Moreover, 'handsome is as handsome does' is the maxim that really matters, and when it comes to performance, which is dealt with in the next chapter, the 'Duchesses' have given no uncertain exhibition of their capabilities.

Much their best work was done after the experimental fitting, in 1934, of a double blastpipe and double chimney to No. 6234 *Duchess of Abercorn*. This was not of the Kylchap type, as used on the L.N.E.R., which embodied a series of petticoats, one below the other, between the base of the chimney and the blast orifices. The L.M.S.R. arrangement was merely that the blast-pipe branched into two, and that two chimneys, contained in one elongated casing, were fitted above. The chief advantage, as is generally known, is that of doubling the surface area of the exhaust cone, so improving the draught, especially when the engine is being worked at short cut-offs with a relatively soft blast. In addition, the increased area of the doubled blast orifice helps in the rapid release to the chimney of the spent steam, so tending to reduce back pressure and to make the engines very free-steaming machines at high speed. A test which was made in 1939 with *Duchess of Abercorn*, hauling a 600-ton train over both Shap and Beattock summits, produced power outputs, both indicated and drawbar h.p., that had never been equalled previously by any other type of locomotive in Great Britain, and were a triumphant vindication of the design. What is not generally known, however, is that a fortnight before the 600-ton test over Shap and Beattock, No. 6234 was tested in her original condition over the same course with a train of the same weight, and failed both to keep up her full steam pressure and also to keep time. In the intervening two weeks the change was made from single blastpipe and chimney to double, with the results that are now historic; the details of these runs are given in Section 6 of this chapter. From then on, all the last series of Pacifics, from No. 6220 onwards, were fitted with double blastpipes and chimneys as they came into Crewe for general overhaul or repairs.

By direction of Lord Stamp, President of the Executive of the L.M.S.R., the building of streamliners was resumed with No. 6235 in 1939, and this continued during the Second World War until No. 6248. The President's view was that, apart from any benefit that might result at high speed through reduction in air resistance, there was a certain appeal to the public in the streamline exterior, which was therefore a publicity asset.

But with No. 6249, which came out early in 1944, it was seen that the fitting of streamlined casings had been abandoned, after twenty-four of the engines – Nos. 6220 to 6229 and 6235 to 6248 inclusive – had been provided with them. This change of policy was destined to be followed by one even more drastic. Lord Stamp was now dead, having lost his life by enemy action; Stanier, who had been loaned to the Ministry of Production as Scientific Adviser in 1942, and had received the well-deserved honour of knighthood in the New Year Honours of 1943, had retired from the service of the L.M.S.R. early in 1944. So the Chief Mechanical Engineer's Department decided to put practical maintenance considerations before publicity; the second change was a decision to do away with streamlining altogether.

It was no longer possible to keep the engines in their condition of pre-war cleanliness externally, or to paint them in the spectacular fashion of the first streamliners, and from the publicity point of view a coal-begrimed streamline casing is worse than none at all. As to the reduction in atmospheric resistance that the casing makes possible, this becomes of measurable value only at speeds of, say, 80 m.p.h. and upwards, and as the maximum speed limit for the time being was down to 75 m.p.h., no economic value was to be derived from the streamlining. Further than this, the presence of the casing made the boilers and various other parts of the engine less accessible for inspection and repair, and so increased maintenance costs.

The first of the streamliners to be 'defrocked' was No. 6235 *City of Birmingham*, which emerged in this condition from Crewe Works about the middle of 1946. As compared with the non-streamlined 'Duchesses' and

'Cities', there were some noticeable changes in appearance. Of these the most startling was that of the smokebox front. In the streamlined engines, the top of the smokebox had been inclined downwards in front in order to conform to the rounded shape of the casing at the front end. In the de-streamlining, the original smokebox was retained, sloping sharply downwards from the chimney in the forward direction, with a most ugly effect. But in later re-boilerings all these engines were fitted with smokeboxes of the normal type. The practice also was begun in the later engines of having no curved plating from the main running plate, ahead of the cylinders, down to the buffer-beam, another feature which did not enhance the beauty of the engines.

Large smoke-deflector plates were added on both sides of the smokebox, though these were not the first so to be mounted on Stanier Pacifics. Apart from the turbine-driven No. 6202, No. 6232 and 6252 of the non-streamlined series were so equipped in the previous year, in order to deal with the nuisance of drifting exhaust, and eventually all the non-streamlined or de-streamlined Pacifics were provided with deflectors. After the conversion of No. 6235, de-streamlining went on steadily, and was completed by 1949.

One further development remains to be chronicled. It was the completion at the end of 1947, just before the L.M.S.R. became merged in British Railways, of Pacific No. 6256, named, most appropriately, after the famous designer of the series, *Sir William A. Stanier, F.R.S.* Certain important changes had been made by Sir William's successor, H. G. Ivatt. Roller bearings were fitted throughout; Timken tapered roller bearings were used for all axleboxes other than those housing the crank axle, which were of the Skefko type. A new type of superheater element was fitted which increased the superheating surface to the unprecedented figure, for a British locomotive, of 979 sq ft.

The rear end of the engine was redesigned; in place of the two subsidiary frame-plates spliced on the main frames to assist in carrying the firebox end of the boiler, the main frames terminated ahead of the firebox, from which a kind of bar frame, riveted to the main frames, extended backwards under the firebox to the hind buffer beam. Rocking grate, self-emptying ashpans and self-cleaning smokebox were all provided, in accordance with what became the standard practice of the London Midland Region. In the cab a novel feature was that the percentage markings of the reversing gear were shown on a revolving drum, instead of the usual needle moving along a horizontal indicator. The latter became a standard fitting on British Railways loco-motives.

No. 6256 and her sister engine No. 6257 *City of Salford* brought the total of Stanier Pacifics to fifty-one – twelve of the original 'Princess Royal' class, thirty-eight of what has usually been termed the 'Duchess' class, and the turbine-driven No. 6202, later converted to another 'Princess Royal'. The blank in the numbering between 6213 and 6219 inclusive was never filled. To all these numbers 40,000 was added as part of the national renumbering scheme. By 1961 the massive invasion of Type '4' diesels had caused the majority of the 'Princess Royal' Pacifics to go into store, as a prelude to breaking up, and the 'Duchesses' for the most part had been demoted to main line duties of a secondary description.

5 – The 'Coronation Scot' on Trial

NOT many weeks after the emergence of *Coronation* from Crewe Works, the new streamliner was made to give a full-dress demonstration of her powers. On 5th July, 1937, the 'Coronation Scot' train was due to begin a daily 6½-hour service between Euston and Glasgow. Six days previously, on 29th June, a trip in the new train was arranged for the benefit of the Press. One of the two kitchen cars was cut out of the nine-car train, leaving eight coaches with a tare weight of 263 tons, and a gross weight of 275 tons behind the tender. As with the non-stop Euston–Glasgow runs made by *Princess Elizabeth* in the previous November, Driver T. J. Clarke of Crewe was at the regulator, and he was ably assisted by Fireman J. Lewis.

It was an open secret that something out of the ordinary in the realm of speed was to be attempted on this journey. For nearly two years, since the 'Silver Jubilee' made its startling *début* on 27th September, 1935, the L.N.E.R. had monopolized the speed limelight in Great Britain, and the L.M.S.R. felt that this could no longer be tolerated. In the spring of 1935 the L.N.E.R. had raised the speed 'ceiling' on rails to 108 m.p.h., in the autumn to 112½ m.p.h., and a year later to 113 m.p.h.; and this last was the figure to be beaten.

Now the L.M.S.R. had no nice long stretch of well-aligned track with a continuous 1 in 200 down gradient, like that of the L.N.E.R. southwards from Stoke summit, on which to make its speed records; the only possible location seemed to be the descent from Whitmore summit towards Crewe. This begins gently at 1 in 348 for 1¾ miles, steepens to 1 in 177 for 3¼ miles, and then flattens out to 1 in 269 for 2¾ miles, by which time the train is within a mile and a quarter of Crewe station. Too uncomfortably near, indeed, for a record speed, as events were to prove.

The special had been scheduled to run to the 'Coronation Scot' point-to-point timings, and nothing out of the ordinary was to be attempted till after Stafford. Nevertheless we made a fairly exciting start to Tring, passing Willesden at 68 m.p.h., accelerating to 82 m.p.h. up the 1 in 339 to Carpender's Park and to 86½ at Watford, after which we maintained 80½ m.p.h. steadily up the ensuing 1 in 335 to Tring. It was certainly good going to clear Willesden in 7 min. 53 sec., Watford in 17 min. 2 sec., and Tring, 31·65 miles, in 27 min. 45 sec. from Euston. But speed was not allowed to exceed 87½ m.p.h. at any point; so we went on steadily – 38 min. 57 sec. to Bletchley, 46·65 miles; 66 min. 28 sec. to Rugby, 82·55 miles; 89 min. 24 sec. to Tamworth, 110·0 miles; and 109 min. 56 sec. to Stafford, 133·55 miles, where we were 5 min. ahead of time. Stafford was passed very slowly, at 30 m.p.h., and we were well past Norton Bridge before *Coronation* was really opened out. Over the summit at Whitmore we went at 85 m.p.h., and then things really began to happen.

The next few minutes are best recounted by R. A. Riddles, at that time Personal Assistant to Mr Stanier; he was riding on the footplate, and described his experiences vividly in a Presidential Address to the Junior Institution of Engineers. 'We had decided not to pick up water at Whitmore', he said, 'and so to avoid reducing speed. The exhaust was humming with a continuous roar like that of an aeroplane engine. The white mileposts flashed past and the speedometer needle shot up through the "90s" into the "100s" to 100, 111, 112, 113, 114 miles an hour, but beyond this – no!

'Basford Hall sidings 1½ miles away now; spectators from Crewe coming into view along the lineside; and the train still hurtling on at 114 m.p.h.! On went the brakes, off the regulator; but on we sailed, with flames streaming from the tortured brake-blocks. The signals for Platform No. 3 at Crewe, entered by a reverse curve with a 20 m.p.h. speed restriction, came into sight. We were still doing 60 to 70 m.p.h. when we spotted the platform signal. The crockery in the dining car crashed. Down we came to 52 m.p.h. through the curve, with the engine riding like the great lady she is. There wasn't a thing we could do but hold on and let her take it. And take it she did; past a sea of pallid faces on the platform we ground to a dead stand, safe and sound and still on the rails.'

In company with D. S. M. Barrie and S. P. W. Corbett, who were similarly engaged, I was timing in the train, and as it had been on all the previous L.N.E.R. record runs, the excitement of these moments was intense. From milepost 148, half a mile north of Whitmore, the speeds we jointly agreed over successive half-miles were 86·5, 88·2, 90·9, 93·6, 94·5, 96·8, 98·9, 102·3, 103·4, 105·9, 107·1, 108·4, 109·8, 111·1, 112·5, 112·5 m.p.h. – these last two between posts 155 and 156. It was agreed also that this could be interpreted as a peak of 113 m.p.h., exactly equal to the L.N.E.R. record, and as the official 114 m.p.h. was taken off the engine speed indicator, which could hardly be regarded as a dead accurate method of recording, to this day it is by no means certain that the L.N.E.R. figure had been beaten. It must be admitted, however, that speed was still rising steadily on the 1 in 269, to the point when steam was shut off, and given a little more space *Coronation* could probably have got above the 115 m.p.h. level.

But the quotation from R. A. Riddles does not quite complete the story of that last hectic couple of minutes. My own commentary in *The Railway Magazine* read thus: 'We were now within 2·1 miles of the centre of Crewe Station. Brakes were applied, and with vigour, but at first they seemed to make little or no impression on the flying wheels; for we hurtled from post 156 to post 157 in 34·4 seconds – a shade under 105 m.p.h. Just over a mile still to go! Now, as Crewe *habitués* realize, the entry to Platform 3 is no mere single crossover – it consists of a crossover leftwards from fast to slow, followed by a second double crossover to the left, and then by a right-handed crossover into the platform. Therefore we had to negotiate, in succession, three reverse curves in the crossovers themselves, and six entry and exit curves, hitting the first – according to my figures – at 57 m.p.h.! By now, of course, speed was falling rapidly, but the sight of the approaching train tearing in and out of this sinuous length of track, as seen from the station platforms, must have been hair-raising; no wonder there were some pallid faces! 'The condition of the track itself must have been superlative to sustain such terrific thrusts as those to which it was subjected with no worse damage than one or two fractured chairs, and to pass the weighty locomotive through without overturning. It is amazing indeed to examine the figures once again, and to realize that what might have been regarded as an optimistic booking of 8 min. for the 10·5 miles from passing Whitmore to the dead stand in Crewe station was actually cut to *six minutes fifty-eight seconds!*

One postscript only is needed to this story. It was provided by Vice-President Sir Ernest Lemon, who was in charge of the party, as he addressed

TABLE VI (D)
L.M.S.R. EUSTON–CREWE
Trial Trip of the 'Coronation Scot', 29th June, 1937
Engine: 4-6-2 No. 6220 *Coronation*
Load: 8 coaches, 263 tons tare, 270 tons gross

DOWN JOURNEY					UP JOURNEY			
Dist.	Sched.	Actual	Speeds		Dist.	Sched.	Actual	Speeds
miles	min.	min. sec.	m.p.h.		miles	min.	min. sec.	m.p.h.
0·00	0	0 00	—	EUSTON	158·00	135	119 00	—
1·00	—	2 33	†32	Milepost I	157·00	—	116 57	—
3·15	—	5 29	54	Kilburn	154·85	—	114 33	*79
5·40	8	7 53	68	WILLESDEN JUNCTION	152·60	127	112 50	*85
8·05	—	10 05	76	Wembley	149·95	—	111 05	95
11·40	—	12 27	79	Harrow	146·60	—	109 00	96
13·30	—	14 04	82	Hatch End	144·70	—	107 45	85
17·45	18	17 02	86½	WATFORD JUNCTION	140·55	117½	104 53	*84
20·95	—	19 40	82	Kings Langley	137·05	—	102 30	99
24·50	—	22 20	80½	Hemel Hempstead	133·50	—	100 16	93
27·95	—	24 55	80½	Berkhamsted	130·05	—	97 59	90/*85
31·65	30	27 45	80½	TRING	126·35	107	95 23	86½
36·10	—	30 55	87½	Cheddington	121·90	—	92 21	89/87
40·20	—	33 56	*75	Leighton	117·80	—	89 32	93/*85
46·65	41	38 57	82	BLETCHLEY	111·35	93	85 10	89
52·40	—	43 08	86/*77½	Wolverton	105·60	88½	81 08	*83
54·75	—	44 57	79	Castlethorpe	103·25	—	79 36	100
59·90	51	48 56	76½	Roade	98·10	84	76 22	88½
62·85	53½	51 09	86	BLISWORTH	95·15	82	74 24	92
69·70	—	56 20	*77	Weedon	88·30	—	69 41	92/*79
75·30	—	60 38	82/78	Welton	82·70	—	65 46	86
80·30	—	64 23	85	Hillmorton	77·70	—	61 51	67½
82·55	70	66 28	*39	RUGBY	75·45	66	59 27	*40
83·20	—	67 35	*38	Rugby No. 7	74·80	—	58 25	88½/*40
88·10	—	72 20	79	Brinklow	69·90	—	54 42	*85
91·40	—	74 47	82	Shilton	66·60	—	52 29	93½
93·50	—	76 27	79	Bulkington	64·50	—	50 58	86
97·10	82	79 05	83	NUNEATON	60·90	54	48 29	90
102·30	—	83 08	*72	Atherstone	55·70	—	44 41	83/*71
106·50	—	86 33	75	Polesworth	51·50	—	41 27	*78
110·00	94	89 24	77/*73	TAMWORTH	48·00	42	38 55	90
116·25	99	94 25	76½/72	LICHFIELD	41·75	37	34 44	92
121·00	—	98 10	80½	Armitage	37·00	—	31 02	88
124·30	106	100 46	*71	Rugeley	33·70	31	29 18	90
127·15	—	103 20	*60	Colwich	30·85	—	27 05	80/*71
129·55	—	105 29	70½	Milford	28·45	—	25 13	75
133·55	115	109 56	*30	STAFFORD	24·45	23	20 58	*30
136·85	—	113 43	58½	Great Bridgeford	21·15	—	18 25	82
138·85	120	115 45	60	Norton Bridge	19·15	18	16 51	*74
143·40	—	119 44	75½	Standon Bridge	14·60	—	13 32	90
147·65	127	122 48	85	Whitmore	10·35	11	10 42	§80½
150·05	—	124 27	94½	Madeley	7·95	—	8 44	74
153·25	—	126 25	108	Betley Road	4·75	—	6 06	71½
157·00	—	128 27	‡114	Milepost 157	1·00	—	2 23	—
158·00	135	129 46	—	CREWE	0·00	0	0 00	—

* Speed reduced for curves.   † At top of Camden Bank.   ‡ At Milepost 156.   § At top of Madeley Bank.

the guests at the Press lunch. Commenting on the sudden and violent embraces of standing members of the party, to an *obbligato* of crashing crockery, that had preceded the hectic entry to Crewe, he remarked, 'Of course, gentlemen, you will realize that we shan't need to do this kind of thing on every trip of the "Coronation Scot"; we were coming in a little faster than we shall have to do in the ordinary course.' 'A little faster' – well, well! It would hardly be wise to make such an experiment a second time!!

Nothing daunted, however, the operating authorities had arranged a return trip to Euston in 135 min. from Crewe, and had given Driver Clarke a free hand in the matter of time. The run that he actually made was one of the fastest ever recorded in Great Britain. Schedule was cut by 16 min.; we covered the 158·0 miles to Euston in precisely 119 min., at an average of 79·7 m.p.h. throughout. From Betley Road to Kilburn we reeled off 150·1 miles, including both Stafford and Rugby slowings, at 83·2 m.p.h.; and the 72·15 miles from Welton to Kilburn were run at an average of no less than 88·9 m.p.h.

We just reached 100 m.p.h. again at Castlethorpe, north of Wolverton, and all but did so a third time at Kings Langley, where the speed was 99 m.p.h. There were speeds of 93 to 95 m.p.h. at other points. Rugby proved to be exactly the midway point in time; the 75·45 miles from Crewe to Rugby took 59 min. 27 sec., and the 82·55 miles on to Euston 59 min. 33 sec. The time of 10 min. 13 sec. for the 15·6 miles from Bletchley to Tring was a magnificent uphill effort, even though the gradient be no steeper than 1 in 333. The times and speeds of this stirring trip appear in Table VI (D); it was one of the great occasions of British locomotive history.

Somewhat surprisingly, the times of the up run were almost precisely repeated twenty years later by No. 46244 *King George VI* when working tthe up 'Caledonian'; the eight-coach load had the same tare, 264 tons, but passengers and luggage made the gross load up to 280 tons. No record remains as to why this feat of speed was planned, but every preparation had been made to keep the road clear, and it is a great misfortune that the London Midland authorities did not include in these preliminaries any invitation to a competent observer to travel with the train it order to time the run in detail. In consequence, we have only the bare times to the nearest minute at stations where working timetables show passing times. The day was 5th September, 1957.

No. 46244 left Carlisle on time, in charge of Driver W. Starvis and Fireman J. Tumilty of Camden depot. No exceptional effort was made to Crewe, but despite delays reckoned to have cost in all 8 min., at Penrith, Hest Bank and Norton Crossing, Crewe was passed 12 min. early, in 135 min., or 127 min. net, for the 141 miles from Carlisle. From Crewe to Euston the 158 miles were then covered in 118 min. – 1 min. less than *Coronation*'s time in 1937 – but the difference is accounted for by the fact that the latter was starting from rest; southwards from Whitmore the times of the two runs were practically a dead heat. This being so, it is probable that *King George VI* also reached the 100 m.p.h. mark, especially at Kings Langley, for the time of the later run from Tring to Watford was a shade faster than that of *Coronation*. So the

so also was the time of 16 min. 30 sec. for the 10 miles of the bank proper, all at 1 in 69 to 1 in 88 up. Here the cut-off was advanced finally to 40 per cent. On the long 1 in 200 climbs before Lockerbie, surmounted on 20 to 25 per cent cut-off, speed did not fall below 57 m.p.h., and the average from Gretna to Lockerbie was 59·3 m.p.h.; then came a rapid spurt to 80 at Nethercleugh, reduced to 60 up the 1 in 202 to Beattock Station, and finally to a shade under 30 m.p.h. at Beattock summit.

For some unexplained reason, the descent past Elvanfoot to Lamington was not taken as fast as the schedule had allowed, and with the allowance for taking water at Symington more than doubled, the train had dropped 3¾ min. from Carlisle on passing Carstairs. But a fast run down the Clyde valley into Glasgow recovered almost all the arrears; actually the engine had gained about 10 min. in all in running between Crewe and Glasgow.

No more than 2 hours had been assigned for turning *Duchess of Abercorn* round at Glasgow, and no special preparations had been made for servicing or attention to the fire; the main purpose was to test the reaction of the locomotive to a round of 487 miles in normal service conditions as to time and gradients, but in extreme limit conditions as to load. It is therefore remarkable indeed that the finest effort made by the engine in all the hard slogging of that memorable day was in returning south from Glasgow in charge of Driver N. McLean and Fireman A. Smith of Polmadie. The actual time they made from Glasgow Central to Carlisle – 106 min. 30 sec. – with a tare load of 604 tons, exceeded by 1½ min. only the schedule allowance of the nine-coach 'Coronation Scot' of 297 tons weight.

Load duly considered, some of the times in Table VI (F) were simply astounding. The steepest climbing of the southbound journey is from Motherwell to Law Junction, where the flattest of the inclination is 1 in 137, and most of it is round about 1 in 102; here *Duchess of Abercorn* averaged 46·7 m.p.h. From Symington up the Clyde Valley the average speed throughout to Beattock summit was 63·4 m.p.h.; actual speeds were 43 m.p.h. on the 1 in 99 before Law Junction, between 47 and 44 m.p.h. on to Craigenhill summit, a reduction to 25 through Carstairs, 57 at Thankerton, 50 through Symington, 65 at Lamington, a steady 62 up to Abington, 65 at Crawford, 63 before and 68 through Elvanfoot, and then, *mirabile dictu*, a *minimum* of 62 up the final 1 in 99 to Beattock summit. Who would have dreamed of a single-headed train of twenty coaches swarming up to the lonely summit cabin at more than a mile a minute? On to Carlisle no time was wasted, as is clear by the average of 77·3 m.p.h. from Beattock to Gretna; so the Polmadie crew brought their train triumphantly into Carlisle Citadel 9½ min. ahead of time.

At Carlisle, Driver Garrett and Fireman Farrington took over again, and there was some further first-class running. Out of Carlisle the line climbs at 1 in 131 to Wreay, on which speed rose to 42 m.p.h.; with the easier climbing through Southwaite and Calthwaite came an acceleration to 54 m.p.h., followed by 69 to 73 m.p.h. on to Penrith, where the curve compelled a reduction to 53 m.p.h. From Penrith to Shap summit, with more than 8 miles of climbing at 1 in 125 or thereabouts, speed never fell below 38 m.p.h. and

TABLE VI (F)
L.M.S.R. GLASGOW–CREWE
600-Ton Test Run
Engine: 4-6-2 No. 6234 Duchess of Abercorn
Load: 20 coaches, 604 tons tare, 610 tons gross

Dist.		Sched.	Actual
miles		min.	min. sec.
0·00	GLASGOW CENTRAL .	0	0 00
12·85	MOTHERWELL† . .	19	19 45
18·25	LAW JUNCTION† .	29	26 40
28·75	CARSTAIRS* . . .	43	39 30
35·45	Symington . . .	51	48 15
39·15	Lamington . . .	—	52 08
44·55	Abington	—	57 13
47·10	Crawford	—	59 36
49·75	Elvanfoot . . .	—	62 03
52·65	*Beattock Summit* . .	69	64 40
62·65	Beattock	79	73 35
76·60	LOCKERBIE . . .	91	84 25
93·65	Gretna	106	97 45
102·25	CARLISLE . . .	116	106 30
4·80	Wreay	—	8 59
7·30	Southwaite . . .	—	11 52
10·70	Calthwaite . . .	—	15 11
12·95	Plumpton	19	17 45
17·85	PENRITH† . . .	24	21 50
31·55	*Shap Summit* . . .	43	40 15
37·00	Tebay	48	44 40
42·95	Grayrigg	—	50 23
50·00	Oxenholme . . .	60	56 30
62·85	CARNFORTH . .	71	67 00
69·10	LANCASTER† . .	76	72 20
80·60	Garstang	87	84 00
90·10	PRESTON* . . .	97	93 35
99·40	Coppull	—	105 53
105·20	WIGAN† . . .	116	113 05
116·95	WARRINGTON† . .	128	126 10
124·80	*Weaver Junction†* . .	136	134 25
141·00	CREWE	153	153 05

* Speed restriction, severe.
† Speed restriction, moderate or slight.

averaged 44·4 m.p.h. So the exacting 31·4 miles from Carlisle up to the top of Shap were run in 40 min. 15 sec. from the dead start, or 2¾ min. less than the time allowed. After that there was nothing of note to chronicle, and time was kept exactly from Carlisle to Crewe.

Table VI (G) is a historic document, for the details of the upgrade work done on this day's round, which it sets out, reveal some outstanding records for British steam locomotive power. These include drawbar horsepowers ranging up to the record figure of 2,511, and indicated horsepowers (arrived at by calculation from the drawbar figures) up to no less than 3,333. Drawbar horsepowers ranging from 1,800 to 2,000 were maintained over considerable distances. Firing must have been a strenuous job, for the engine was burning

TABLE VI (G)

L.M.S.R. 600-TON TEST RUNS, CREWE-GLASGOW AND BACK – DETAILS OF UPHILL WORK

	CREWE-GLASGOW						GLASGOW-CREWE					
Direction of run	CREWE-GLASGOW						GLASGOW-CREWE					
Location of climb	Carnforth–Shap Summit			Gretna–Beattock Summit			Motherwell–Beattock Summit			Carlisle–Shap Summit		
Section of climb	Carnforth to Oxenholme	Oxenholme to Tebay	Tebay to Shap Summit	Gretna to Lockerbie	Lockerbie to Beattock	Beattock to Summit	Motherwell to Law Junction	Carstairs to Symington	Symington to Summit	Carlisle to Plumpton	Plumpton to Penrith	Penrith to Shap Summit
Length of ascent, miles	12·96	13·08	5·69	17·27	13·96	10·13	5·42	6·74	17·28	13·03	4·77	13·68
Average drawbar h.p.	1,870	1,668	1,830	1,598	1,609	1,724	1,923	1,520	1,860	1,822	2,000	1,560
Maximum drawbar h.p.	2,120	1,934	2,065	1,733	1,823	2,081	1,998	1,638	2,282	2,511	2,394	2,331
Maximum i.h.p. (calculated)	3,209	2,806	2,963	2,236	2,556	2,761	2,583	2,138	3,333	3,248	3,241	3,021
Average speed of ascent, m.p.h.	68·0	53·0	47·9	59·3	72·5	36·8	46·7	46·1	63·4	43·9	71·4	44·4
Cut-off range, per cent of stroke	20 25	25 25	25 35	20 25	20 25	30 40	20 30	20 25	30 35	30 35	20 30	30 40
Boiler pressure, lb per sq in.	250	245	240	250	245	245	250	245	245	245	230	245

an average of 68·7 lb of coal to the mile, or 75·7 lb per sq ft of grate per hour; water was disappearing at an average of 53·1 gallons to the mile, so that *Duchess of Abercorn* was evaporating 7·74 lb of water per lb of coal. In relation to the tremendous power output, a coal consumption of 3·12 lb per drawbar-h.p.-hr was certainly not excessive.

The results of these Crewe–Glasgow trials were fully confirmed when No. 46225 *Duchess of Gloucester* was tested sixteen years later on the stationary testing plant at Rugby. Here it was proved that the boiler could deliver 40,000 lb of steam per hour to the cylinders continuously, representing a drawbar h.p. of 2,250; by comparison, for short bursts on the steepest climbs in the 1939 trials the drawbar h.p. rose to 2,510 – a higher figure than has been attained by any other Pacific locomotive type in Great Britain. But the rate of firing involved in the latter power output would be beyond the powers of any fireman working manually for more than a short period of time.

In the Rugby tests No. 46225, when delivering steam to the cylinders at the rate of 20,000 lb per hour, was burning 2·0 lb of coal per drawbar-h.p.-hr at 30 m.p.h., 2·21 lb at 50 m.p.h. and 2·98 lb at 70 m.p.h. With the steam rate boosted to 30,000 lb per hour the corresponding figures were 2·20 lb at 30 m.p.h., 2·17 lb at 50 m.p.h. and 2·43 lb at 70 m.p.h. At the latter rate of steam production, 37 per cent cut-off at 30 m.p.h. produced an indicated h.p. of 1,894 and a drawbar h.p. of 1,734; 26½ per cent at 50 m.p.h. gave 2,068 indicated h.p. and 1,764 drawbar h.p.; while with 22 per cent at 70 m.p.h. the indicated h.p. rose to 2,100 and the drawbar h.p. to 1,570. The rate of firing in the latter case was 3,820 lb of coal per hour.

Another test was one made with No. 6220 *Coronation* on the 6½-hour 'Coronation Scot' between Euston and Glasgow, made up to 331 tare tons, or 345 tons gross, by the addition of the dynamometer car. The coal consumption on the 401½-mile run totalled about 7 tons, which worked out at 39·2 lb per mile and 3·03 lb per drawbar-h.p.-hr; the average drawbar h.p. over the entire length of the run was 825. All these figures show a high degree of competence on the part of the 'Duchess' Pacifics of which Sir William Stanier, the designer, may well be proud.

It was understood at the time that the purpose of the 1939 trial was to explore the possibility of reducing independent train workings by combining trains as far as possible, especially north of Crewe, but no attempt was ever made subsequently to reproduce or even to approach the exploits of *Duchess of Abercorn* in ordinary service. Since *Coronation* attained 114 m.p.h. on the down Press trip of the 'Coronation Scot', and 100 m.p.h. on the return journey, for example, there has been no further authenticated example of a 'Duchess' reaching the three-figure level in speed (except possibly on the 1957 'Caledonian' run with No. 46244 described at the end of Section 5).

In day-to-day running the 'Duchess' Pacifics are frequently worked with full regulator, as I saw for myself when riding on No. 46242 *City of Glasgow* from Crewe to Carlisle with Driver Byers and Fireman Thom at the head of the 'Midday Scot', shortly after the Second World War. The timing was very easy – 183 min. for the 141·0 miles – but the load was heavy; we had behind us sixteen bogies weighing 515 tons tare and 550 tons gross. While 10 per cent cut-off and half regulator were sufficient to maintain 69 m.p.h. down the easy grades past Hartford and Acton Bridge, and from 15 down to 10 per cent took us along the level from Garstang to the approach to Lancaster at a speed rising from 64 to 66 m.p.h., at Carnforth the regulator went over to full for the long climb to Shap summit. Passing Milnthorpe at 61½ m.p.h. on 17 per cent cut-off, Driver Byers increased to 20 per cent at Hincaster Junction, 22 at Oxenholme and 25 at Lambrigg Crossing; up the 1 in 173 to Hincaster speed fell to 51 m.p.h., up the 1 in 193–111 to Oxenholme to 43 m.p.h., and up the subsequent 1 in 124–131 to 35 m.p.h. at Lambrigg Crossing.

Then, unfortunately, we got signals on at Mosedale Hall, and again while climbing from Tebay to Shap summit; in recovering from the latter check 40 per cent cut-off was used.

The boiler pressure throughout was well maintained; indeed, at one stage when mounting Grayrigg bank the engine was blowing off for a short distance. There were many delays on this run, but time was kept exactly; the net time of 166 min. represented a gain of 17 min. on schedule. The impression throughout was one of the locomotive's easy competence; and the clean pages of my notebook and writing as legible as if I had been in a coach testify both to the admirably draught-proof design of the cab and to the perfectly smooth riding of this big machine.

Some drivers, however, prefer longer cut-offs and never to open their regulators to full. On a journey with the 'Red Rose' from Liverpool to Euston, recorded by R. I. Nelson on No. 46250 *City of Lichfield* with a thirteen-coach train of 404 tons tare and 430 tons gross, nothing more than half the main regulator was used at any point by Driver Stevenson, but south of Crewe the cut-off was never below 22 per cent. On the easy grades past Standon Bridge and Norton Bridge three-eighths of the main valve and 22 per cent cut-off produced a maximum speed of no less than 92 m.p.h.; one-quarter of the main valve and 30 per cent gave an acceleration from 43 to 59 m.p.h. up the 1 in 370 to Kilsby Tunnel, and with the same positions the 15·0 miles from Bletchley up to Tring were run in 12 min. 21 sec., with a minimum of 68 m.p.h. up the long 1 in 330.

This was another run with many checks, including a dead stand at Blisworth due to a signal failure; but the 158·0 miles from Crewe to Euston were run in 2 min. 41 sec. less than the scheduled 165 min., and the net time was no more than 140¼ min. Steaming was so free that the engine was blowing off at a number of points on the journey, but my correspondent, who is a very experienced recorder of locomotive performance, remarked that coal consumption appeared to be on the heavy side.

In the locomotive exchange trials of 1948 a 'Duchess' Pacific participated, in the heavyweight class, in competition with an L.N.E.R. Gresley 'A4' Pacific, a Bulleid Pacific of the Southern Railway, a Great Western 'King' 4-6-0 and a rebuilt L.M.S.R. 'Royal Scot' 4-6-0; but on the whole the performance of the Stanier Pacific was disappointing. The engine selected was No. 46236 *City of Bradford*, and her driver was evidently obsessed with the urge to keep his coal consumption to the lowest possible limit; as a result the performance of the engine throughout was well below her capabilities. The regulator was seldom more than half open, and much of the work was done on the first valve only, with 15 per cent cut-off. Only once was an equivalent drawbar h.p. up to 2,400 recorded, when climbing Seaton bank of the S.R., but this was transitory, and the figure was well down on the upper part of the climb. No. 46236 did, however, make two of the best ascents of the formidable gradients to Dainton and Rattery summits of the W.R., exerting a maximum equivalent drawbar h.p. of 1,865 on the former and 1,817 on the latter. The one occasion on which the engine's regulator was opened to full, with 50 per cent cut-off, was in climbing the 1 in 42 of the W.R. Hemerdon bank.

It was a different story, however, when in 1956 No. 46237 *City of Bristol* was loaned to the Western Region for trials against one of the 'King' class 4-6-0s which had been modified with thirty-two-element superheater, double blastpipe and double chimney. In large measure, as we have seen already, Stanier's Pacifics were derivatives in design from the 'Kings', and now both types had advanced a long way from their designers' original low superheat ideas, with a corresponding improvement in their performance. In the 1948 locomotive exchange the work of the 'King' had been as mediocre as that of the L.M.R. 'Duchess', but these 1956 Paddington–Plymouth runs were in another category altogether. With the L.M.R. 'City', also, it was of particular interest that the Western Region provided its own crews to man the 'foreigner'; on the down run Driver Harris and Fireman Tobin of Old Oak were in charge. It was my privilege to ride in the dynamometer car in each direction with both locomotives, and thus to witness at first hand what was practically a dead heat between the 4-6-0 and the 4-6-2.

On the down journey, with a fourteen-coach train of 461 tons tare and 485 tons gross to Westbury, *City of Bristol* was slightly slowed for permanent way repairs at Maidenhead, after having reached 76 m.p.h. on the level at Slough, and then followed a 17 m.p.h. permanent way slack through Reading West; but with speed mostly above 60 m.p.h. up the rising grades of the Kennet valley, the 'Limited' went over Savernake summit at 55 m.p.h., in 72 min. 20 sec. for the 70·1 miles from Paddington. Maximum speeds of 83 m.p.h. near Lavington and 82 at Curry Rivel Junction (130·8 miles in 122 min. 21 sec. from the start) were separated by an unusually high 64 m.p.h. over Brewham summit. Despite a 20 m.p.h. permanent way check at Athelney, Taunton, 142·75 miles, was passed in 134 min. 42 sec.; minimum speed up the 1 in 86–80 to Whiteball tunnel was 47 m.p.h.; Exeter, 173·5 miles, was cleared in 162 min. 20 sec.; and with more than the usual caution round the Dawlish curves, Newton Abbot, 193·7 miles, was reached in 187 min. 16 sec., 2¾ min. early, or 181¾ min. net.

From Newton westwards the run was robbed of further interest by the provision of an assisting locomotive, and the same on the return journey; but from Newton up to Paddington, with Driver Emery and Fireman Harris of Laira and a twelve-coach train of 393 tons tare and 420 tons gross, some first-class running was done by the 'City'. Exceptional features were the minimum speed of 52 m.p.h. up the climb to Brewham, with its approach grades of 1 in 98 to 1 in 81; the rapid acceleration from 75 m.p.h. at Heywood Road Junction to 80 in the ensuing 6 miles of level; and the sustained 80 m.p.h. on the level from Slough to West Drayton. Eventually Paddington was reached at 4.30 p.m., 10 min. early, in 193 min. 45 sec. (183 min. net) from Newton Abbot, schedule for the 193·7 miles being 202 min.; 157½ min. net from Exeter, 173·5 miles; and 126½ min. from Taunton, 142·75 miles. At various locations on both up and down journeys drawbar horsepowers up to 1,400 and even 1,500 were recorded, though far short of *Duchess of Abercorn's* 2,510 drawbar h.p. in the Crewe–Glasgow tests of 1939.

7 – 'Coronation' across the Atlantic

IN 1939 one of the Stanier Pacifics went across the Atlantic, with a train of new L.M.S.R. stock, to represent British railways at the New York World's Fair in 1939. Although the engine bore the name and number 6220 *Coronation*, actually it was No. 6229 *Duchess of Hamilton* which made the trip, carrying the former's number and nameplates. Seven coaches of brand-new stock built for the 'Coronation Scot', and in part articulated, together with a standard 12-wheel sleeper, accompanied the engine. The locomotive was in its fully streamlined condition, equipped with the bell and electric headlight required by American law for running over the railways of the U.S.A. Fitting the automatic control equipment now in general use on the principal American main lines was not thought worth the trouble and expense involved, however, and for this reason little high-speed running could be attempted on the other side of the Atlantic.

Shipment took place in January, 1939, from Southampton, to which point *Coronation* made her way over the Southern Railway. On arrival at Baltimore, the locomotive and train were deposited on Baltimore & Ohio metals, and began an extensive tour which took them also over the Pennsylvania, Louisville & Nashville, Alton, New York Central System (including the Michigan Central, 'Big Four' and Boston & Albany), and New York, New Haven & Hartford railroads. In this way cities as far apart as Baltimore, Washington, Philadelphia, Pittsburgh, Cincinnati, Louisville, Indianapolis, Chicago, Detroit, Cleveland, Buffalo, Albany, Boston, Hartford, and many others, were visited, on a round trip of 3,121 miles, which lasted from 21st March to 14th April, before the train reached New York to take its place in the exhibition.

R. A. Riddles was in charge of the train, and in the Presidential Address to the Junior Institution of Engineers, to which I have referred previously, he gave a diverting account of some of his experiences of the trip. 'Unloading took place in temperatures which varied from 74 degrees one day to 26 degrees the next', he said. 'Ice formed on everything. It was intensely cold, and the first major problem arose when the driver contracted pneumonia and was laid up for a month. I decided I would do the firing and let the fireman do the driving.

'Our first day out with a trial run to Washington for Press purposes started at 6 a.m. and finished at 10.30 p.m. Unfortunately, British and American locomotives are designed to burn widely different types of coal, and that provided at Baltimore by our standards was little more than slack. We had to refill the tender at Washington, and I compute that on that day we burnt 11 or 12 tons of coal – or dirt! I admit to having done a little driving in lieu of firing.

'Touring under these conditions, even minor mechanical troubles were each a major headache. Our first trouble was a broken spring-bolt. This was made of manganese molybdenum steel, and there was nothing like it available locally, so we chose a valve spindle forging of similar tensile strength, and turned it down to make a bolt. At Harrisburg our brick arch, of a new design, began to come adrift, and as we had the Allegheny Mountains ahead of us' – with a rise of 1,055 ft in 10·8 miles from Altoona to the 2,193-ft altitude of Gallitzin Tunnel, and a grade steepening from 1 in 58 to 1 in 40, the speaker might have added, for such is the profile of the Pennsylvania main line at this point – 'we had to put in one of the two spare arches which we carried.

'The work was so badly done that a third arch was necessary; St Louis looked to be a big centre where labour should be available, so I ordered the third arch to be ready there – but what a hope! A boilermaker and his coloured mate turned up to meet us and offered themselves as the only ones available to do the job. Meanwhile, three of the front rows of bricks of the arch already fitted were found on our arrival at St Louis to have fallen into the firebox, forming a fused mass. Although by this time it was 1 a.m., and we had to be away by 9 p.m. the next day, I had to insist on breaking up the fallen arch and getting it out through the drop-grate – no easy task with bricks which were white-hot and too large individually to be dropped through the small opening without being broken down.

'With the job done by 4.30 a.m., I got to the hotel, where from my appearance I should have been refused admission but for the magic name "Coronation Scot". I had a bath and some sleep; up at 8 a.m. for another bath, and off to the train to get hold of the Mayor and to open the exhibition. To allow the engine to cool down we waited until 2 p.m. before getting busy, but there was still a pressure of some 50 lb of steam in the boiler. Only the boilermaker would go into the firebox, and there were only the boilermaker, our own mechanic and myself to see the whole business through. In we went, and suffice it so say that 3 hours of heaving lumps of firebrick, some weighing 25 lb and others up to 80 lb (the whole arch weighs 17 cwt), inside an engine firebox with 50 lb pressure of steam all round you, is an experience not readily to be forgotten! However, the job was finished by 5 p.m., and an hour or so later the fire was in again and all was going well. Another bath, a rump steak and a bottle of champagne, and bed.

'By 9 p.m. I was driving the train away to Springfield, some 120 miles distant, where we arrived at 11.35 p.m. for another bath and bed after what might fairly be termed a busy day, but not without further incident. Anxious to get to our destination, running at 70 to 75 miles an hour, at a place called Plainview, up went a red flare, an American method of indicating an emergency sighted by running crews. On went the brake – regulator shut – and the train came to a stand some 200 to 300 yards from a motor-car that had missed its way and straddled the track. I drew the train up to the obstruction, and getting down on the track met a very white-faced gentleman who told us he couldn't move. We got him back in his seat, and with our endeavours, together with his engine, in a smell of burning rubber as the tyres scraped on the ends of the rails, he shot forward into the night, and we went on, perhaps a little more soberly.'

While *Coronation* was in New York the Second World War broke out. In view of the risk that would have been entailed in trying to bring the engine overseas, as well as the shortage of shipping space, it was decided for the time being to leave her over in the United States. The train was moved to Jefferson-ville, Indiana, where it was used during the war as living quarters for the U.S. Army Quartermaster Corps; the engine went to Baltimore. By 1943, however, the risk of returning the locomotive was faced, and *Coronation* returned, this time to Cardiff, from which she travelled by way of the G.W.R., Hereford and Shrewsbury, to Crewe.

Nameplates and numbers were exchanged again with those of *Duchess of Hamilton*, and No. 6220 became the real *Coronation* once more. Headlight and bell were removed, and there is nothing now visible on No. 6229 *Duchess of Hamilton* to recall her exciting Transatlantic experiences.

8 – Names, Locations and Casualties

THE naming of the Stanier Pacifics has not followed any very consistent plan. At the time of the Press trip with *The Princess Royal*, first of the series, a witticism that went the rounds was that the new engine was a daughter of *King George V* of the G.W.R. and of the *Royal Scot* of the L.M.S.R., of which Queen Mary was then the Colonel-in-Chief. Lady members of the Royal Family provided names for No. 6201 and Nos. 6203 to 6212, including *Lady Patricia* (of Connaught) and *Queen Maud* (of Norway); No. 6212 *Duchess of Kent* was the first of the series to receive the name of a duchess. No official name was ever bestowed on turbine-driven Pacific No. 6202 until after rebuilding in 1952, when she became *Princess Anne*.

It was not until the 'Coronation' series came out, beginning with No. 6220 *Coronation*, that British queens came in for attention, with No. 6221 *Queen Elizabeth* (whose husband had not become King George VI when the first series of Pacifics was built), and No. 6222 *Queen Mary* (succeeding the 'George the Fifth' 4-4-0 that had carried the same name in earlier years). But it was several years later before the name of *King George VI* appeared on Pacific No. 6244. Meantime, after two more 'Princesses', Nos. 6223 and 6224, there came a series of ten 'Duchesses', Nos. 6225 to 6234. Then followed the lengthy

'City' series, which continued until the last of the Pacifics, interrupted only by No. 6244 just mentioned, and by No. 6256 *Sir William A. Stanier, F.R.S.* Most of the 'City' Pacifics were taken to the towns bearing their names for official naming ceremonies, even though in some cases this involved running the engines over considerable lengths of line from which such heavy locomotives normally are barred. No. 6251 *City of Nottingham* behaved herself in a rather unladylike fashion after the celebrations at Nottingham, by straying from the track at the Lincoln end of the station, and holding up the train service for quite a considerable time before she could be rerailed.

The sheds at which the Stanier Pacifics have been stabled have been chiefly Camden, for the London end of the main line; Crewe North; Edge Hill, Liverpool; and Polmadie, Glasgow. The round journey of 387 miles from Euston to Liverpool and back was made regularly by these engines; even longer, of course, was the continuous 401½ miles of the Euston–Glasgow Central journey. For some years the latter was made without change of engine on a number of services daily, but with change of enginemen at Crewe or Carlisle. One of the night sleeping-car trains in each direction ran by the Glasgow & South Western route, via Dumfries and Kilmarnock, and this lengthened the journey to 414½ miles. In later years the through workings were broken down, and change of engine *en route* was reverted to, usually at Carlisle, until the 'Caledonian' was introduced in 1957. Pacifics then resumed through working between Euston and Glasgow, and also on the 'Royal Scot' and 'Midday Scot' when these trains went on to similar 'XL Limit' timings with strictly limited loads.

Through nine months in each year, when the rival East Coast 393-mile run of the 'Elizabethan' between Kings Cross and Edinburgh was not in operation, these were the longest through locomotive workings in Great Britain. Over the same nine months 'Duchess' Pacifics were making the longest regular steam-operated non-stop runs in the world, comprising Euston–Kingmoor (Carlisle), 301 miles; Euston–Carlisle Citadel, 299 miles; and Carlisle No. 12 Signalbox–Euston, 297¾ miles. The stops at Kingmoor and Carlisle No. 12 were for change of engine crew and train examination, by trains which did not require to call at Carlisle for passenger purposes. The through Euston–Glasgow workings have now been taken over by diesel power.

In addition to the two routes between Carlisle and Glasgow – via Carstairs and Dumfries respectively – the Pacifics worked regularly between Crewe and Perth. At various times the engines working on the night 'sleepers' into and out of Perth have filled out their diagrams by making trips from Perth to Aberdeen and back, or from Perth to Glasgow (Buchanan Street) and back. From time to time, also, they have been seen in Princes Street, Edinburgh.

For some time before the Second World War Pacifics of the original 'Princess Royal' series were stationed at Longsight, Manchester, for working the up 'Mancunian' and the down 'Lancastrian', in both cases via Crewe; engines of this type are barred from the Stoke-on-Trent route for reasons of weight. Also for a short time during the war Pacifics of the same class were used on the heavy day 'Irish Mails' through between Euston and Holyhead. After the war Pacifics were seen again in London Road, Manchester, and also in Chester, working from Crewe; and a common 'running-in' turn for Pacifics, either new or after repair, was from Crewe to Shrewsbury and back. Not until the modern diesel invasion have L.M.S.R. Pacifics been set to perform such undignified tasks as the haulage of freight trains, which has frequently fallen to the lot of L.N.E.R. Pacifics, even the streamliners, in the war years and since.

The Stanier Pacifics have had their share of casualties in running. On 10th September, 1940, it became necessary to entrust streamlined Pacific No. 6224 *Princess Alexandra* to a 'passed fireman' and a 'passed cleaner', who joined the engine 3 min. before starting time on the 10 a.m. from Glasgow Central to Euston. Unused to so large an engine, they were unfortunate enough to uncover the crown of the firebox on the climb to Craigenhill, with the result that between Cleghorn and Carstairs the boiler blew up. The fireman succumbed as a result of scalding, but astonishingly little harm was done to the train. By a most amazing coincidence, on the night of 5th March, 1948, No. 6224 suffered exactly the same casualty again when working the 9.25 p.m. from Glasgow Central to Euston, and at Lamington, no more than 12 miles from the scene of the previous burst. On this second occasion the engine was in charge of an experienced crew and the driver lost his life. On 15th May, 1944, No. 6225 *Duchess of Gloucester* was travelling northwards at speed with the 'Services Sleeper' (8.40 p.m. Euston–Glasgow) south of Gretna when the engine was derailed without warning at Mossband Box, on a stretch of track that was not in good running order; three passengers were killed.

On 21st July, 1945, No. 6231 *Duchess of Atholl* was involved in a serious smash at Ecclefechan, when working the 1 p.m. express from Glasgow to Euston, through the driver running past signals at danger, and on into a freight train which was being shunted. Both enginemen lost their lives; but although the damage to the train was considerable, there was no loss of life among the passengers. In 1947 two of the Pacifics were in trouble. No. 6235 *City of Birmingham*, bringing south the 10 a.m. from Glasgow to Euston on 18th May, was in collision with a light engine near Lambrigg Box, on Grayrigg bank. The express should have been slowing to stop, for the up line was being repaired, and the train was required to reverse on to the down line; but the driver ran past all warning signals. That no worse results were suffered in this collision is surprising, as it occurred on the high Docker Viaduct.

One of the worst accidents was that which befell No. 6244 *King George VI*, when hauling the 8.30 a.m. express from Euston to Liverpool on 21st July, 1947, at Grendon, between Atherstone and Polesworth. Here again the track appears to have been in less than first-class running order, due in part, no doubt, to the terrible weather in the earlier months of the year, and the engine left the track when travelling at a fairly high speed. Five passengers lost their lives. Damage to the engine itself, however, was negligible, and it was soon on the rails again; it was a streamliner when the accident occurred, but reappeared from Crewe in the de-streamlined condition.

Another very serious Pacific casualty occurred at midnight on 16th April, 1948; No. 6251 *City of Nottingham*, hauling the southbound 'West Coast Postal', was involved in the disastrous collision near Winsford with the 5.40 p.m. from Glasgow to Euston, which had been stopped after the communication cord had been pulled by a young soldier, who in this selfish way aimed at expediting his journey home to Winsford. The crash was due to a signalman's error in admitting the 'Postal' into the section already occupied by the standing passenger train.

The tragic end of the rebuilt turbine-driven Pacific, No. 46202 *Princess Anne*, in the disastrous Wealdstone collision of 8th October, 1952, has been referred to in Section 3. The Pacific on the up Perth express, which was the cause of the accident, was No. 46242 *City of Glasgow*, but this engine, though seriously damaged, was repaired and returned to service.

A near disaster also occurred with No. 46236 *City of Bradford* during the locomotive exchange trials of 1948, when working the 7.50 a.m. over Great Northern metals from Leeds Central to Kings Cross. At the approach to Peterborough her driver, who was somewhat hard of hearing, failed to catch the pilotman's warning to reduce speed, and began to do so all too late, with the result that the facing-points at the entry curve to the station were taken at a speed nearer 60 than 50 m.p.h., instead of the prescribed 20 m.p.h. As with the entry to Crewe of *Coronation* on the 'Coronation Scot' Press trip, described in Section 5 of this chapter, the margin between safety and disaster was very small indeed, and it says a great deal for permanent-way maintenance at both places and for Stanier's chassis design that nothing worse happened than a severe shaking-up for the passengers.

In view of the number of Pacifics in service, and the extensive mileage they have run, however, it must be admitted that the number of casualties has been extremely small, and it is doubtful if any of those which have happened, even the derailments, could be attributed to the locomotives themselves.

The Stanier Pacifics have had an exceedingly fine record, with no superiors in performance in Great Britain, and possibly, indeed, no equals when maximum output has been called for. It is fitting indeed that the first L.M.S.R. locomotive ever to bear the name of a chief mechanical engineer should be No. 6256 *Sir William A. Stanier, F.R.S.*, also the first locomotive engineer since Stephenson to receive the honour of election to the Royal Society, and the distinguished designer of a distinguished class.

TABLE VI (H)
THE STANiER PACIFICS – BUILDING DATES

Date of building	No.	Name	Type
1933	6200	The Princess Royal . . .	Original non-streamlined series
,,	6201	Princess Elizabeth . . .	,, ,,
1935	6202	(Unnamed)†	Turbine-driven, non-streamlined
,,	6203	Princess Margaret Rose . .	Original non-streamlined series
,,	6204	Princess Louise . . .	,, ,,
,,	6205	Princess Victoria . . .	,, ,,
,,	6206	Princess Marie Louise . .	,, ,,
,,	6207	Princess Arthur of Connaught .	,, ,,
,,	6208	Princess Helena Victoria . .	,, ,,
,,	6209	Princess Beatrice . . .	,, ,,
,,	6210	Lady Patricia	,, ,,
,,	6211	Queen Maud	,, ,,
,,	6212	Duchess of Kent . . .	,, ,,
1937	6220	Coronation	Streamlined, later de-streamlined
,,	6221	Queen Elizabeth . . .	,, ,,
,,	6222	Queen Mary	,, ,,
,,	6223	Princess Alice	,, ,,
,,	6224	Princess Alexandra . . .	,, ,,
1938	6225	Duchess of Gloucester . .	,, ,,
,,	6226	Duchess of Norfolk . . .	,, ,,
,,	6227	Duchess of Devonshire . .	,, ,,
,,	6228	Duchess of Rutland . . .	,, ,,
,,	6229	Duchess of Hamilton . .	,, ,,
,,	6230	Duchess of Buccleuch . .	Non-streamlined series
,,	6231	Duchess of Atholl . . .	,, ,,
,,	6232	Duchess of Montrose . .	,, ,,
,,	6233	Duchess of Sutherland . .	,, ,,
,,	6234	Duchess of Abercorn . .	,, ,,
1939	6235	City of Birmingham . . .	Streamlined, later de-streamlined
,,	6236	City of Bradford . . .	,, ,,
,,	6237	City of Bristol . . .	,, ,,
,,	6238	City of Carlisle . . .	,, ,,
,,	6239	City of Chester . . .	,, ,,
1940	6240	City of Coventry . . .	,, ,,
,,	6241	City of Edinburgh . . .	,, ,,
,,	6242	City of Glasgow . . .	,, ,,
,,	6243	City of Lancaster . . .	,, ,,
,,	6244	King George VI . . .	,, ,,
1943	6245	City of London . . .	,, ,,
,,	6246	City of Manchester . . .	,, ,,
,,	6247	City of Liverpool . . .	,, ,,
,,	6248	City of Leeds	,, ,,
1944	6249	City of Sheffield . . .	*Non-streamlined series
,,	6250	City of Lichfield . . .	,, ,,
,,	6251	City of Nottingham . . .	,, ,,
,,	6252	City of Leicester . . .	,, ,,
1946	6253	City of St Albans . . .	,, ,,
,,	6254	City of Stoke-on-Trent . .	,, ,,
,,	6255	City of Hereford . . .	,, ,,
1947	6256	Sir William A. Stanier, F.R.S. .	,, ,,
1948	6257	City of Salford . . .	,, ,,

* Built after retirement of Sir William Stanier.
† Rebuilt in 1952 as four-cylinder 4-6-2. No. 46202 *Princess Anne;* scrapped in 1953 after Wealdstone collision.
Note: From 1948 40,000 was added to all the foregoing numbers.

TABLE VI (J)
THE STANIER PACIFICS – LEADING DIMENSIONS

Type†	No. 6200 as built	Nos. 6200–1 and 6203–12 as modified	Streamlined series	Nos. 6220–6257 as modified
Cylinders (4), diameter . .	16¼ in.	16¼ in.	16½ in.	16½ in.
,, stroke . .	28 in.	28 in.	28 in.	28 in.
Driving wheels, diameter .	6 ft 6 in.	6 ft 6 in.	6 ft 9 in.	6 ft 9 in.
Bogie ,, ,, .	3 ft 0 in.	3 ft 0 in.	3 ft 0 in.	3 ft 0 in.
Trailing ,, ,, .	3 ft 9 in.	3 ft 9 in.	3 ft 9 in.	3 ft 9 in.
Wheelbase, coupled . .	15 ft 3 in.	15 ft 3 in.	14 ft 6 in.	14 ft 6 in.
,, total engine .	37 ft 9 in.	37 ft 9 in.	37 ft 0 in.	37 ft 0 in.
Heating surface, firebox .	190 sq ft	217 sq ft	230 sq ft	230 sq ft
,, ,, tubes and flues	2,523 sq ft	2,299 sq ft	2,577 sq ft	2,577 sq ft
,, ,, total . .	2,713 sq ft	2,516 sq ft	2,807 sq ft	2,807 sq ft
Superheating surface . .	370 sq ft	598 sq ft	856 sq ft	*830 sq ft
Firegrate area . . .	45 sq ft	45 sq ft	50 sq ft	50 sq ft
Working pressure, per sq in. .	250 lb	250 lb	250 lb	250 lb
Adhesion weight . . .	67·5 tons	67·5 tons	67·1 tons	67·1 tons
Weight of engine in working order	104·5 tons	104·5 tons	108·1 tons	106·4 tons
Water capacity of tender .	4,000 gal.	4,000 gal.	4,000 gal.	4,000 gal.
Coal capacity of tender .	9 tons	10 tons	10 tons	10 tons
Weight of engine and tender .	158·6 tons	160·1 tons	164·5 tons	163·2 tons
Maximum height above rail .	13 ft 2 in.	13 ft 2 in.	13 ft 2⅝ in.	13 ft 2 in.
Maximum width . . .	9 ft 0 in.	9 ft 0 in.	8 ft 10⅝ in.	9 ft 0 in.
Engine and tender, length overall	74 ft 4¼ in.	74 ft 4¼ in.	73 ft 9¾ in.	73 ft 10¼ in.
Tractive effort (at 85 per cent, b.p.)	40,300 lb	40,300 lb	40,000 lb	40,000 lb

* Nos. 6256–6257, 979 sq ft superheating surface.
† British Railways numbers all with 40,000 added.
Note: No. 6202 (turbine driven) had boiler generally uniform with Nos. 6200–1. Weight of No. 6202 in working order, 110·6 tons; adhesion weight, 69 tons.

VII

THE BULLEID PACIFICS, SOUTHERN RAILWAY

1 – *A Revolutionary Design*

WE come now to one of the last, and certainly the most controversial, of all the British Pacific designs – the Bulleid Pacifics of the Southern Railway. Before his appointment in 1937 as Chief Mechanical Engineer of the S.R., O. V. S. Bulleid had been Personal Assistant to Sir Nigel Gresley, Chief Mechanical Engineer of the London & North Eastern Railway, and had spent most of his life at Doncaster. Unlike Edward Thompson, whose antipathy to Gresley and all his works has been described in Chapter IV, Bulleid had no such aversion; but although certain features of Gresley design appeared in Bulleid's new locomotives, it soon became clear that the pupil had no intention of slavishly copying the master. Quite on the contrary, Bulleid proved to be one of the most original thinkers, if not indeed the most venturesome, of all British locomotive designers in history.

While such enterprise makes for progress, it can also prove expensive. Bulleid was never a man to conduct lengthy experiments with features that break away from tradition, and thus to prove by a period of trial whether such features will make for increased efficiency and reliability or not. His first Pacific design was packed with novelties, some completely untried in locomotive work, but despite the severe handicaps imposed by war – the year was 1941 – ten of these engines were put in hand at once, and others soon followed. Some of the innovations have proved valuable; in particular, Bulleid's all-welded Pacific boiler has few equals for steaming, and certainly no superior, among the other Pacific boilers in the country. It was a different matter, however, with his chain-driven valve-motion and its oil-bath, applied in all to 140 locomotives, and the first detail to call for removal when rebuilding took place under the auspices of British Railways. But I am anticipating.

As will be seen in Chapter IX, Bulleid was not the first Southern Railway C.M.E. to design a Pacific locomotive for that company. By 1930 the working of the Continental boat expresses to and from Dover and Folkestone was becoming an increasing problem, because these heavy trains had to be sandwiched in between the dense electric services before they got clear of London, and in addition had to be worked over severe gradients to the summit at Knockholt; also the Southern operating authorities were keen on acceleration. The Maunsell 'Lord Nelson' 4-6-0s were barely adequate, as Bulleid personally observed when, soon after his appointment, he made a number of footplate trips on which 'Lord Nelsons' were worked 'all out' on his instructions. It was Maunsell himself who prepared the first Pacific design in 1933, but difficulties with the Chief Civil Engineer over weight, and finally ill-health, resulted in the task of producing a suitable 4-6-2 being left to Maunsell's successor. Not until 1941 did the first Bulleid Pacific, No. 21C1 *Merchant Navy*, appear from Eastleigh Works.

It is often forgotten that the primary purpose in designing a Pacific for the Southern Railway, as just mentioned, was the working of boat trains over the Eastern Section. Because of the need for high tractive effort and, with it, adequate adhesion, eight-coupled wheels were seriously considered. Doubtless with the L.N.E.R. Gresley 'Cock o' the North' class in mind, Bulleid thought first of a 2-8-2, but the use of a leading pony truck seemed inadvisable, in view of the sharp curves into and out of Victoria and Dover Marine, and of the difficulties experienced with the Gresley 'P2' 2-8-2s north of the Border. For the same reason, together with the desire to keep engine and tender within the limits of existing 70-ft turntables, the idea of a 4-8-2 also had to be dismissed. The Pacific wheel arrangement was the only logical alternative.

By the time the first of these engines took the rails, war had brought the Continental passenger traffic to an end, and the first batch therefore was drafted to the Western Section. Subsequently Bulleid Pacifics displaced 'Lord Nelsons' from the Continental trains until the former in their turn were supplanted by diesel and electric locomotives. But the Pacifics were designed under Eastern Section weight and clearance restrictions, the latter in particular being severe. Their maximum height above rail could not exceed 13 ft 1 in., and the height of the cab cornice above rail had to be kept down to 10 ft 11 in.; the maximum permissible in width was 9 ft over the cab and 8 ft 10 in. over the cylinders. No other British Pacific design has been subject to such drastic restrictions.

Many of Bulleid's boldest developments in this design were directed towards reduction of weight, and were a complete breakaway from British locomotive tradition up to that time. Electric welding had made such advances in its technique and reliability that the designer decided to make use of it to the utmost degree. Throughout engine and tender welding replaced riveting wherever possible, and the boldest decision of all was to fit the first British all-welded boiler, thereby saving in the weight both of the large number of rivets normally used and of the metal in lap joints. Although the first two 'Merchant Navy' Pacifics incorporated a number of weighty steel castings, to strengthen the frames, the weight of these engines was found on completion to exceed the calculated weight, and in the later engines it was found practicable to replace some of these, and also certain heavy steel forgings, by lighter parts fabricated from welded steel plate.

There was no superstructure of the kind normally used in locomotive practice, with running-plate, splashers, and so on. Instead, the boiler was concealed under a thin casing of steel plate, conforming at the rear end to the shape of the wide Belpaire firebox, and extending forwards to terminate in two wings intended to function as smoke deflectors. This casing was carried on bearers or ribs of channel section, attached to the main frames. The smokebox was of the same shape as the casing, and its top, of thin steel plate, supported an equally light steel plate chimney. There would probably have been further savings of weight had it been possible to use light alloys for various parts, but this was wartime, and such alloys were unobtainable.

In view of the weight of the first two Pacifics having proved excessive, further weight reductions became necessary. In addition to the use of fabricated parts instead of steel castings and forgings, as already mentioned, the frame structure was lightened by using thinner plates; steel was removed by cutting holes in the plates wherever this could be done without loss of strength; thinner plates also were used for the cab and other parts of the external plating of the engines.

Bulleid had decided on a working pressure as high as 280 lb per sq in., and this, with its associated high temperatures, ruled out the use of copper for the firebox. Plenty of experience was available as to steel fireboxes, and welded steel had the great advantage that the troublesome lap joints needed with copper could be eliminated. In ordinary maintenance, also, defective parts of a steel firebox could be cut out, and new portions welded in. The substitution of welded steel plate, $\frac{3}{8}$-in. thick, for copper resulted in a saving of $1\frac{1}{2}$ tons in weight for each firebox alone.

The first ten boilers were made by the North British Locomotive Company, and were completely successful; X-ray examination of all the welds provided the necessary safeguard. An unusual feature of the tapered boiler was that the taper was on the underside of the barrel rather than, as is general, on top; the idea was to provide maximum steam space along the whole length of the barrel rather than at the firebox end only. This arrangement had the advantage of providing better clearance for the inside cylinder, with its valve-chest above, and also helped in stimulating the flow of water downwards from the clack-boxes towards the firebox. In the first ten Pacifics the front end of the barrel was tapered, and the rear end was parallel, but in the later engines this order was reversed.

In the firebox design Bulleid broke boldly away from British tradition by installing two of the Nicholson thermic syphons so widely in use in other countries; the only other British locomotive that has ever been so fitted was Gresley's 'Bantam Cock' 2-6-2 of the same year, 1941. These syphons, the modern development of the Drummond water-tubes of former London & South Western days, are arranged longitudinally in the firebox rather than transversely; they begin as tubes leading out of the lower part of the firebox tubeplate, and then spread out as narrow water-spaces until they extend to almost the whole length of the inner firebox at the point where they reach the crown. This passage from the lower part of the boiler to the firebox crown both assists in circulation and at the same time provides additional and valuable heating surface in the hottest part of the fire.

The thermic syphons might have been expected to help in establishing the reputation of the Bulleid boiler for rapid steaming, but the tests at Rugby, described later, failed to confirm this expectation. The syphons, however, certainly did add strength to the firebox structure and provide substantial support for the crown sheet and the brickwork of the arches. The safety-valves, three in number, were removed from their usual position to the front ring of the barrel; it was not thought wise to have them above or near the firebox, where turbulence might cause water as well as steam to pass through them at times of blowing off. The same effect can be produced in their present position, however, when water surges forward in the boiler as brakes are applied, so not much was gained by this alteration.

2 – *The Valve-Motion and other Novelties*

By far the most revolutionary departure from traditional practice was, of course, the chain-driven valve-motion. Bulleid, like Gresley, was not in favour of divided drive and of the increased frame length and short connecting rod that are unavoidable if the inside cylinder drives on the leading coupled axle. Equally, he did not favour the use of the Gresley derived motion for his inside cylinder, because of the disadvantages that have been dealt with in Chapter III. An ordinary Walschaerts motion could not be accommodated between the frames of a locomotive whose middle cylinder drove the second coupled axle because the leading coupled axle would be in the way of certain of its parts. This difficulty had been got over in the Southern three-cylinder 2-6-0s and the former 'River' 2-6-4 tanks by a modification of the Walschaerts gear, using twin eccentrics and a very short combination lever, but such a solution did not commend itself for the new design; neither did the use of poppet-valves.

The designer therefore decided to evolve an entirely new type of valve-motion. The idea in his mind was that economies might be effected both in maintenance, and also in the time needed for oiling in preparing an engine at the start of its working day, if the motion could be enclosed in an oil-bath. Modern boilers are of such large diameter as severely to cramp the space available to accommodate the motion, so making parts of it very difficult of access for oiling and inspection, and waste of time can occur in this way. The original plan was to derive the motion direct from the driving axle, but when this was found to be impracticable, Bulleid decided to use a separate three-throw crankshaft for the purpose, as this would permit the desired enclosure of all three sets of valve-motion within an oil-tight casing. It was first intended to drive this crankshaft by means of gears and a propeller shaft, as with a rotary cam poppet-valve motion, but owing to war conditions the needed gears also were unobtainable.

So the chain-drive was decided on. The crankshaft working the expansion links was driven by two chains, one horizontal from the crank axle to an intermediate sprocket wheel, and the other vertical down to the crankshaft, which was located at the bottom of the oil-bath sump. This arrangement allowed for the up-and-down movement of the crank-axle on its springs without affecting the working of the valve-motions. The crankshaft, revolving at the same speed as the crank-axle, and with each crank phased with its own big-end, imparted the motion to the three piston-valves. In view of th confined space into which three sets of valve-motion had to be fitted, the maximum throw of the expansion links was arranged to be three-eighths only of the maximum valve-travel, the difference being taken up by a proportionately unequal length of the rocker arms.

It thus became possible to enclose the inside cross-head and slide-bars, the inside connecting-rod with its big and little ends, the crank axle and all three sets of valve-motion in an oil-bath with a sump holding 40 gallons of lubricating oil. From the sump two gear-pumps, driven off the three-throw crankshaft, sprayed oil continuously through perforated pipes, at a pressure of from 15 to 20 lb per sq in., over the moving parts not actually immersed in the oil. The sprocket on which the two chains worked was designed to be adjustable in position, so that any stretching of the chains might be taken up if necessary. A steam-operated reversing gear was provided, but despite considerable subsequent modification to permit the driver to make smaller adjustments of cut-off, and to eliminate the 'creeping' of the gear away from the position in which it had been set, this, like the chain-driven motion itself, was not one of the successful features of the Pacific design.

To help in obtaining the high tractive effort required, Bulleid decided on a driving-wheel diameter of 6 ft 2 in. only. Such is the freedom of exhaust with modern valve-setting and front-end design that high speeds are attainable with driving wheels of smaller diameter than that thought essential for express passenger work in days gone by, and he had had experience with Gresley's 'Green Arrow' 2-6-2 mixed traffic engines, which had shown themselves able to run freely at speeds up to 90 m.p.h. So, as this reduced size would help him in conforming to the restriction of height within which he had to work, it was on 6 ft 2 in. that Bulleid settled for his Pacifics. To avoid unduly high piston speeds when the engines were running fast, however, he decided to limit his piston stroke to 24 in.; the dimensions of the three cylinders therefore were made 18 in. by 24 in.

The two outside cylinders were very slightly inclined, at 1 in 40, but to enable the piston rod of the inside cylinder to clear the leading coupled axle, so that all three cylinders might drive on the middle axle, it was necessary to incline the inside cylinder as steeply as 1 in 7¾. Great pains were taken in the design to provide the steam with as smooth a flow as possible. Thus to keep the steam passages from piston-valves to cylinders as straight as possible outside admission valves were fitted, with rocker arms to provide the necessary movement. Various other fittings at the front end showed a good deal of ingenuity, though at the same time adding to the complication of these revolutionary locomotives. The Lemaître multiple-jet exhaust arrangement, with five blast jets arranged in a circle, which had proved so successful with the 'Lord Nelson' 4-6-0s, was adopted in the Pacifics also.

A further departure from tradition was in the design of the wheels. In the United States considerable use was being made with cast steel wheel centres of the Boxpok type, instead of spoked wheels, and, in conjunction with the Sheffield steel firm of Firth Brown, Bulleid evolved a similar type of wheel

Above, light Pacific No. 21C162 with the side deflectors curved inwards, at the head of down Dover express passing Knockholt.
[Eric Treacy

Right, No. 21C11 General Steam Navigation with modified side deflector and rounded casing to outside cylinders.
[M. W. Earley

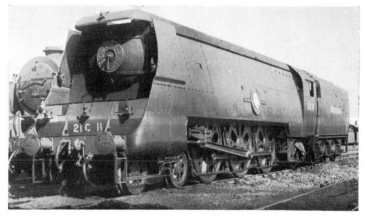

Below, the first modification after wind tunnel experiments, at Southampton University, as carried out on No. 21C10 Blue Star.
[British Railways

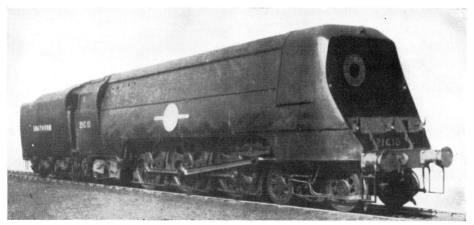

Above, 'West Country' Pacific, No. 21C101 Exeter, as originally built, with nameplate and the city's coat-of-arms. [*British Railways*

Left, No. 34019 Bideford, with lengthened smoke-deflectors, fitted temporarily for oil-burning. The top of the oil tank can be seen on the tender.
[*F. F. Moss*

Below 'Battle of Britain' No. 21C157 starting out of Broadstairs with the short-lived 'Thanet Belle' Pullman. Note the final front end arrangement and the modified cab. [*J. C. Flemons*

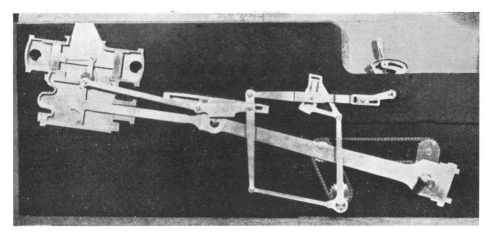

Some of the unusual design features of Bulleid Pacifics. Below, left, the trailing truck arrangement, later adopted as standard in the British Railways Pacific designs. Above, a model showing the arrangement of the Bulleid-Walschaerts chain-driven valve-motion for one cylinder.

Above, one of the Bulleid-Firth-Brown 'Boxpok' driving wheels, with cast steel centres.

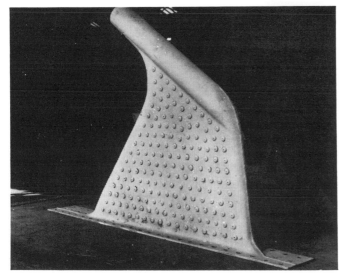

Left, Nicholson thermic syphon. It is seen in an inverted position, with the connection to the firebox crown below, and to the front tubeplate above.

[All, British Railways

Above, on 'foreign' metals – 'Battle of Britain' Pacific No. 34059 Sir Archibald Sinclair, *on loan to the Great Eastern Line, leaving Norwich Thorpe for Liverpool Street with the 'Norfolkman' in May, 1949.*

Below, furthest North – 'West Country' Pacific No. 34004 Yeovil *about to leave Perth and climb over the 1,484 ft altitude of Druimuachdar with the 4 p.m. train for Inverness in the 1948 exchange trials.* [F. Moss

Another memento of the 1948 locomotive exchanges – 'Merchant Navy' 4-6-2 No. 35019 French Line C.G.T. heading the 1.30 p.m. Western Region express from Paddington to Plymouth through Sonning Cutting in May, 1948.

[*M. W. Earley*

Past and present. Above, 'Merchant Navy' 4-6-2 No. 35009 Shaw Savill, before rebuilding, approaching Clapham Junction with the 1 p.m. from Waterloo to the West of England.   [R. E. Vincent

Below, after rebuilding – No. 35012 United States Lines accelerating out of Waterloo with the same express.   [Brian E. Morrison

Carrying the 'Golden Arrow' emblems 'Battle of Britain' 4-6-2 No. 34086 **219** *Squadron climbing Kemsing bank with this express when diverted via Maidstone because of Sunday work in progress on the Tonbridge main line.* [*Derek Cross*

At a curious stage in the smoke deflection experiments – 'West Country' 4-6-2 No. 34035 Shaftesbury with an all-round cowling over the smokebox, at speed between Paddock Wood and Marden with the 3.10 p.m. from Charing Cross. [*Derek Cross*

Unusually at work on the Eastern Division – rebuilt 'Merchant Navy' Pacific No. 35015 Rotterdam Lloyd *at speed near Ashford with the down 'Golden Arrow'.* [*P. Ransome-Wallis*

With 6,000-gallon tender – rebuilt 'Merchant Navy' 4-6-2 No. 35012 United States Lines *getting into speed past Berrylands with the 10.30 a.m. down Bournemouth 2 hour train.* [*Derek Harman*

centre, the 'B.F.B.', for his Pacifics. The rims of spoked wheels do not offer a completely uniform support for the tyres, as they can withstand less compressive stress between the spokes than at the points where the spokes join the rim; the solid castings, however, offer equal resistance round the whole of the circumference. The tyres of such wheels, therefore, have less tendency to work loose than with spoked wheels. The 'B.F.B.' (Bulleid-Firth-Brown) wheel centres have been lightened by a series of cavities (leaving a series of eight ribs somewhat resembling eight half-spokes of large size) and also by a number of holes; in this way the weight of these wheels is about 10 per cent less than that of ordinary spoked wheels.

Clasp brakes were fitted, but in order that the pressure might be exerted through the centre of each coupled wheel, the brake-blocks had to be arranged diagonally, with the brake-block of one wheel above that of its neighbour, owing to limited space. There was no room available on the engine for a vacuum cylinder, so a steam cylinder was used to operate the engine brakes (thereby also making possible some economy in weight), but the tender brakes were vacuum-operated.

While the leading bogie was in general similar to that of a 'Lord Nelson' 4-6-0, the trailing truck was of a novel design. It employed the three-point suspension principle, with the weight of the rear end of the locomotive transmitted through sliding pads, and spring side control. This arrangement has helped to make the Bulleid Pacifics some of the smoothest-riding locomotives in the country, as I can testify from personal experience, and it is not surprising that the British Railways standard Pacifics of later years, in which, it was claimed, all the best features of British locomotive design were incorporated, were equipped with trailing trucks of almost identical design.

Yet another unusual feature of the Bulleid Pacifics was the absence of any reciprocating balance. It is essential with any locomotive fully to balance the rotating parts, but the opinion of locomotive engineers is divided as to what proportion of the reciprocating parts should be balanced. Too much reciprocating balance tends to increase 'hammer-blow' on the rails; too little may lead to severe lateral oscillation, particularly in a two-cylinder engine. But Bulleid was venturesome enough to dispense altogether with reciprocating balance with his Pacifics, and with the help of three-cylinder propulsion the result has been successful. This feature has helped to contribute to the steadiness of running already mentioned, and high-speed tests have demonstrated that, with the elimination of reciprocating balance, there is a complete elimination of hammer-blow.

An unusual measure of comfort was provided in the cab. Protection from the elements was ensured by fitting a small cab on the front of the tender also, with windows on both sides giving the driver a look-out backwards when running in reverse. Only in summer weather have these cabs proved so shut in as to be uncomfortably hot. A small steam-driven generator set provided electric lighting, used in the cab after dark or in tunnels to illuminate the reversing gear, cut-off indicator, water gauges and injectors;

this also provided current for the headlamps, and for lamps inside the boiler casing to light up the motion during oiling or inspection.

The fireman's work was simplified by the provision, for the first time on a British locomotive, of a power-operated firedoor. By means of a small steam cylinder, worked by a pedal on the cab floor, the fireman, pivoting on the foot depressing the pedal, could swing round with his shovel from the tender opening to the firedoor without having first opened the latter, or having depended on his driver to do so for him, or, worse, having to leave it open for the whole time during a spell of firing. Another assistance was given to the fireman by fitting both injectors on his side of the engine, so that he could look after both without having to disturb the driver.

The first Pacific tenders accommodated 5,000 gallons of water, but later on, in order to avoid the necessity for taking water on the Bournemouth run, ten of the engines were provided with 6,000-gallon tenders—the biggest water capacity of any tenders in Britain, and six-wheel tenders at that. In this connection it must be remembered that the Southern Railway was the only one of the four main line railways that never laid down any water-troughs, though the former London & South Western Railway got as near to doing so as to fit some of its tenders with water scoops.

For the numbering of his Pacifics Bulleid adopted a curious modification of the Continental system of prefixing the actual number of the engine with its wheel notation. For in the latter he placed the 'C' for three coupled axles last, and prefixed it by '2' for the two bogie axles and '1' for the trailing truck. The first 4-6-2, *Channel Packet*, thus became No. 21C1, followed by 21C2, 21C3, and so on. This plan was never popular, and after nationalization was replaced by a normal series of numbers. In the naming, some consideration was given at first to commemorating Allied victories in the war, but as at that date these had hardly been numerous or impressive, the idea was abandoned; actually, a model of one of the engines, on which various types of nameplate and figures were tried, carried the name *The Plate*, in honour of the sinking of the *Graf Spee* – an odd name for a locomotive, and very soon abandoned!

Finally, in view of the lengthy maritime associations of the Southern Railway and its predecessors, the titles of shipping lines using Southampton were decided on, with the nameplates bearing the house flag of the company as well as the name. Both right-handed and left-handed plaques had to be cast for each engine, so that the flag might be seen flying the right way! As is often the case with a series of names, some of them read rather curiously, such as *Blue Funnel* and the cryptic *French Line C.G.T.* The Southern Railway came under a certain amount of criticism at that time for allowing the building of locomotives of such a type as this at a critical stage of the war (not to mention the lavish series of naming ceremonies with which each started its career), when the far greater need was for heavy freight engines, let alone tanks for the 17th Army.

The first Pacifics carried on the smokebox door a cast plate, with the word 'Southern' in the form of an inverted horseshoe. Such is superstition, however, that some drivers regarded this emblem as likely to bring bad luck, and their objection was taken by the management seriously enough to result in the substitution of a casting completely circular in shape. Eventually, with the introduction of the British Railways standard practice of exhibiting loco-motive numbers on the smokebox doors, all the 'Southern' smokebox plates disappeared.

The year 1941 saw the emergence from Eastleigh of the first five 'Merchant Navy' Pacifics, and the first ten were completed by August of the following year. A gap then ensued until December, 1944, and the next ten appeared between then and June, 1945. After an interval of more than three years, No. 35021 took the rails in September, 1948, and the last of the thirty engines, No. 35030, was completed in April, 1949, sixteen months after the Southern Railway had become the Southern Region of British Railways.

3 – The Lightweight Pacifics

WE come now to the smaller Pacifics of the 'West Country' and the 'Battle of Britain' classes, nicknamed the 'Lightweights', the first of which was turned out of Eastleigh Works in the summer of 1945. There were various sections of the Southern Railway with lighter track and underline bridgework of less strength than the standards prevailing on the principal main lines, from which the heavier engines were prohibited. Some of these might be used from time to time, however, as diversionary routes for important main line traffic, as, for example, the original L.S.W.R. main line from Brockenhurst to Wimborne and Weymouth via Ringwood. There were also all the lines west of Exeter, over which nothing heavier than one of the 2-6-0s was permitted to run, not to mention various other routes that might be expected to require enhanced power before very long. But it has been a matter of criticism as to whether these demands were sufficient to call for the building of no fewer than 110 of the light Pacifics, many of which have spent, and still do spend, much of their time hauling trains of two to four coaches on the North Devon lines, or similar duties elsewhere which could be handled with complete competence by much smaller and less expensive locomotives.

The 'Merchant Navy' and 'West Country' Pacifics were unique in their precise similarity of appearance despite their differing power; apart from the clue given by number and name, it has always needed an expert eye to dis-tinguish between the two. The boiler barrel of the 'West Country' was only 1½ in. shorter than that of the 'Merchant Navy', but its diameter at the front end was 5 ft 6 in. as compared with 5 ft 9¾ in. The firebox of the former also was shorter, reducing the distance between the rear driving axle and that of the trailing truck from 10 ft to 9 ft. The distance between the driving and rear coupled axles was brought down from 7 ft 6 in. to 7 ft 3 in., so that the engine wheelbase came down from 36 ft 9 in. to 35 ft 6 in. The piston stroke remained 24 in., but the cylinder diameter was reduced from 18 in. to 16⅝ in. The very high working pressure of 280 lb per sq in. was, however, retained.

In order to ensure maximum route availability, lightening of weight was carried to even more extreme lengths than it had been with the bigger Pacifics. As compared with the 'Merchant Navy' 21 tons on each coupled axle, the maximum 'West Country' axle-load was kept down to 18¾ tons; the latter locomotives weighed 86 tons in working order without tender, as compared with the 94¾ tons of the former. A smaller tender also was provided, accommodating 4,500 gallons of water and 5 tons of coal and weighing just over 42½ tons in running order, compared with the 47¾ tons of the 'Merchant Navy' tender, which had a tank capacity of 5,000 gallons. With Nos. 34071 to 34090, however, the tender water capacity was enlarged to 5,500 gallons and the weight loaded to 47¼ tons, to enable these engines to make longer runs without taking water. Eventually the number of 5,500-gallon tenders was increased to forty-six.

Among other routes over which the light Pacifics were designed to work, though they never actually did so, was that between Tonbridge and Hastings, with its tight clearances. For this reason the cab width had to be restricted to 8 ft 6 in., as compared with the 9 ft of the larger engines. This had the effect of narrowing the cab windows, from which the look-out was distinctly poor. The matter was made worse by the position of the brake ejector, which as in the 'Merchant Navy' Pacifics was located directly in front of the window on the driver's side, blocking an even larger proportion of the view through the narrower window. But after the first seventy light Pacifics had been built, the remainder were all provided with cabs 9 ft wide.

In all, 110 of the light Pacifics were built, and from the appearance of the first, No. 21C101 (later No. 34001) in November, 1945, building went on with little interruption until the emergence of No. 34110 *66 Squadron* in January, 1951. Up to No. 21C148 (now No. 34048 *Crediton*) West Country names were given, all without exception of places west of Salisbury. From this point onwards it was decided to change to names associated with the war, and in particular with the Battle of Britain, which had been fought so largely in the skies above Kent; for this reason the next series has always been known as the 'Battle of Britain' class, though practically identical with the 'West Country' engines. From No. 21C149 onwards there came *Anti-Aircraft Command* and *Royal Observer Corps*; then notable figures in the persons of *Winston Churchill* (No. 34051 has never yet received the accolade, like its famous namesake!), *Lord Dowding, Sir Keith Park* and *Lord Beaverbrook*; followed by a mixture of people, air stations, aeroplanes and individual squadrons. The last-mentioned, all of which had operated in the south-east of England, gallant indeed though they were, have hardly provided very distinctive names for locomotives – simply the word *Squadron* preceded by a number.

Well before the last light Pacific had been built, the war had ended and nationalization had taken place, and with it renumbering, with the 'West Country' numbers running from 34001 to 34048, and the 'Battle of Britain' series from 34049 to 34090; the last of these received the compendious title *Sir Eustace Missenden, Southern Railway* to commemorate the last General

Manager of the Southern Railway, who had been in charge of its affairs throughout the war period. From No. 34091 to No. 34108 West Country names were reverted to, but the last two, No. 34109 *Sir Trafford Leigh-Mallory* and No. 34110 *66 Squadron*, form part of the Battle of Britain series.

Apart from being the first Pacifics to travel over many Southern Region lines, the 'West Country' 4-6-2s have broken fresh ground in various other directions. In the exchange trials of 1948, described in Section 6, engines of this type were the first Pacifics ever permitted to work passenger trains over the Midland Division of the London Region between St Pancras and Manchester, or over the Highland main line of the Scottish Region, which took one of them as far from its native heath as Inverness. A year later No. 34059 *Sir Archibald Sinclair* was loaned to the Great Eastern Line of the Eastern Region, and was the first Pacific ever to run between Liverpool Street and Norwich. The three routes named all resembled one another in being subject to severe weight and clearance restrictions, to which a 'West Country' Pacific was able to conform.

On their own line the Bulleid Pacifics have been far more than equal to every demand made on them, from the performance point of view, but at a cost in fuel, lubrication and maintenance which resulted ultimately in the rebuilding of all the 'Merchant Navy' and sixty of the 'West Country' Pacifics into their present form, as described in Section 8 of this chapter.

4 – *Teething Troubles*

WITH so many previously untried features incorporated in the Bulleid Pacifics, a varied and prolonged period of teething trouble was to be expected; and so it proved. As mentioned earlier, the cessation of Continental passenger traffic during the war caused the transfer of the 'Merchant Navy' Pacifics to the West of England main line, but breakdowns in their earliest years were so numerous that for a long time their services had to be confined to freight working. Bit by bit many of their defects were mastered, though even then it could hardly be claimed that these engines were as reliable as some of their conventional contemporaries. Such is the price that has to be paid for advance; and these venturesome designs certainly added a great deal to locomotive knowledge and also embodied new features that have since proved valuable.

The first serious difficulty was not mechanical; it was that of drifting exhaust, blanketing the front of the cab and interfering with the drivers' already limited vision. No previous British engine had had its chimney top flush with the boiler casing, with no part of it whatever projecting, but the designer had hoped that the provision of a channel for air from the front of the locomotive round and up behind the chimney would carry the exhaust high enough to clear the cab. It did not, however, and a considerable enlargement of the opening in the upper casing round the chimney gave no better results.

The wind tunnel at Southampton University was then called to assist in the investigation, a model of the engine, on a scale of one inch to the foot, being used for the purpose, and imitation smoke being produced by using vaporized paraffin. These tests showed that conditions might be improved if separate wind deflectors were fitted, proud of the two front ends of the casing, and if these were curved slightly inwards at the front edges. This arrangement was tried on No. 21C10 *Blue Star*, but while it certainly helped, it had the disadvantage of further restricting the driver's look-out ahead.

Part of the last change also was a bending downwards of the outer edge of the upper casing, and the next step was to develop this into an independent cowling, looking rather like an inverted dish, across the top of the smokebox front, with air spaces on both sides of it. This was a considerable advance, and was applied to the first twenty engines, but was not as yet a complete cure, especially in damp and misty conditions, when condensed steam tends to beat down and cling to the flat top and sides of a locomotive with such a completely smooth profile. The independent side screens or smoke deflectors were next considerably lengthened in a backwards direction, and this brought to completion all that could be done at the front end. Some attention also was devoted to the rear end of the engine, by changing the front of the cab to a V-shape, but this was mainly to increase the width of the front windows, and to make them readily accessible to the crew for cleaning, through the nearest side windows.

It may be wondered why, in all these experiments, Bulleid never tried a wedge front, like that of one of the L.N.E.R. 'A4' Pacifics, or a rounded nose, like an L.M.S.R. 'Coronation' Pacific, but the answer is that the 'Merchant Navy' design saved weight, as compared with these alternatives, and also gave unhindered access to the smokebox door. It should also be emphasized that the designer never regarded these Pacifics as being streamlined, but merely as 'air-smoothed'.

To many it was little source of surprise that the chain-driven valve-motion and the oil-bath gave trouble. The bath itself proved far from oil-tight; difficulty was found in preventing leakage where the driving axle passed through the frames, as well as through joints in the bath structure, and cracks in the metal, caused by vibration and flexing of the frames on curves, were not uncommon. Not only did these leaks cause an excessive consumption of lubricating oil, but the oil that escaped distributed itself in various directions, with unexpected results. It got on to the rails of the track, helping to account for the unenviable notoriety acquired by these engines for slipping. The leaks also led to the soaking of adjacent parts of the boiler and firebox lagging with oil, causing fires which at times were very troublesome. A casualty of another kind was that water at times found its way into the oil-bath because of condensation or leakage from boiler fittings; consequently a fitter had to check every engine before it began its day's work, and to drain any water by a cock fitted at the bottom of the bath.

Against these disadvantages, however, there was the major advantage that the designer had in mind, and that was in copious lubrication. In contrast to the three-cylinder Gresley Pacifics of the L.N.E.R., it has been rare for a Bulleid Pacific to be taken out of service because of a defective inside cylinder big-end. On the other hand, no defects inside the oil-bath could be detected during daily examination, and when anything did go wrong extensive damage could take place, such as puncturing of the oil-bath and, on occasion, a minor explosion.

The chains proved reliable enough, but unsuitable for operating valve-gear with any degree of precision. The longer chain had no fewer than 118 links, and though there has been no stretching of the links themselves, in the course of time the wear of pins and holes, and also of the teeth of the intermediate sprocket wheel, have had the same effect. At a general overhaul the length of the longer chain was found to have increased, in some of the engines, by as much as 6 in., with the result that there has been a considerable sag, and wear of another kind has been caused by rubbing against other parts of the motion. The sprocket wheel can be moved to take up some of this slack, or a link or two can be removed from the chain, but with the complete enclosure of the motion this is no easy task to carry out in a running shed. No means was ever devised to correct the chain tension automatically. Enclosure of the motion obviously created no small difficulty for driver and fitters, for minor irregularities of working that might have been corrected in a few minutes with any ordinary valve-motion have caused an engine to be taken out of service because the nature of the defect was both invisible and inaccessible; even when an oil-bath has been drained and opened, there has been little space for a mechanic to work inside it.

The drastic cutting down of weight, in order to conform to track restrictions, has also brought its penalties. Among them has been the breakage of main frames; to investigate this trouble two of the 'West Country' Pacifics, No. 34005 *Barnstaple* and 34039 *Boscastle*, for a time were fitted with shelters at the front end, so that movements of the frames during running, and in particular flexure, might be watched, to try to ascertain if the frames were not sufficiently braced.

Slipping trouble concentrated attention on sanding, the arrangements for which were not ideal. Ladders were needed to reach the filling holes for the sandboxes, which were located in the upper part of the boiler casing. The escape of oil from the oil-bath has tended to clog the sand pipes; and the sanding gear fitted to the leading coupled wheels eventually had to be removed because sand was finding its way on to the slidebars – a trouble which was not cured by providing the slidebars with covers. In the course of cleaning the smokeboxes after the day's work, particles of ash could find their way into the mechanical lubricators, because the latter were located immediately below the smokebox front, and this also was the reverse of helpful. Many other modifications had to be made in these designs as the result of experience; few, if any, other British locomotive classes, indeed, have undergone so extensive a series of changes, and over so long a period after their first taking the rails, but this could hardly be unexpected in view of the many hitherto untried features in their design.

5 – *The All-Welded Boilers*

THE great asset of the Bulleid Pacifics has been their boilers. A team of expert welders was assembled at Eastleigh Works, and worked out by lengthy trial and error – with 'blood and sweat' if not actual 'tears' in the boiler shop, as revealed in a paper presented in 1958 to the Institution of Locomotive Engineers by M. G. Burrows and A. L. Wallace on Southern Region experience with steel fireboxes – the 'make and break' technique which eventually became standard practice. The method is to bring the boiler plates together with their edges forming an angle of 70 degrees, and then, with a gap of about $\frac{1}{8}$-in. at the root of the 'V', to move an 8-gauge electrode in a semi-circular arc from one side of the 'V' to the other; after breaking the arc the process is then repeated in the opposite direction, forming a bridge of metal. The bridge is gradually built upwards at the rate of about sixty strikes to the minute until the root run is complete. After removal of the slag a straight run is then taken along the length of the 'V', and a third run, this time down hand with a No. 6 electrode, completes the process. Eventually a welding school was established at Eastleigh, for the training of welders from other motive power depots, in order that it might not be necessary to send all locomotives needing boiler repairs to Eastleigh for the purpose.

Many troubles had to be overcome before the welded boilers settled down to give reliable service. In the earliest days staff carrying out repairs inside the fireboxes from time to time were alarmed by loud reports; these had been caused by the sudden development of cracks. Some of the most vulnerable points have been the attachment of the thermic syphons to the firebox crown and the welding of their lower ends into the tubeplate; other cracks have developed from the stay-holes and also in the backplate below the firehole door. It was soon found that excessive contraction was the cause, due to cold water having been used to wash out a hot boiler; for this reason it is now an instruction that each Pacific must be allowed to stand for at least twelve hours after the end of its day's duty, and that all hot ash must be removed from the combustion chamber at the rear end of the barrel, before washing out begins.

A second trouble which had to be mastered was corrosion. It first showed itself by leaking stays; but a more serious discovery was that a side wrapper plate of the firebox of one of the first ten 'Merchant Navy' Pacifics, which to that date had run 169,000 miles, was beginning to bulge. Investigation showed that corrosion had taken place to such an extent as to reduce the thickness of the steel from $\frac{3}{8}$ in. to $\frac{1}{4}$ in. The firebox was then taken out, and corrosion was found all round the interior, especially at the back end of the crownplate and around and between the syphons, though it was reassuring that none of the welded seams had been attacked. There was nothing wrong with the steel; the trouble lay with the feed water.

The French National Railways at that time were achieving considerable success in cutting down the cost of boiler maintenance and increasing the periods between washings out with their 'T.I.A.' (Trâitement Intégrale Armand) treatment of feed water, and Bulleid decided to give it a trial. The success was immediate. The principle of the T.I.A. treatment is an automatic dosage of the feed water with a chemical compound stored in a container in the tender, while the engine is running, in order to prevent hard scale from being deposited on the various heating surfaces.

More recently, the T.I.A. system has been superseded by the Southern Region's own method of feed-water treatment. Each Pacific tender is fitted with a perforated tube, which is charged with chemical briquettes composed mainly of soda and tannin; these dissolve gradually as feed water is added. The tannin forms a protective barrier on the boiler-plates; the soda causes the scale-forming matter to separate as a sludge in the boiler, from which it is blown out over a pit by way of a blow-down cock, or, if necessary, while the engine is running. Blowing-down is performed once every 150 to 200 miles or less. As a result, instead of every 10 to 14 days, boilers now need to be washed out every 56 days only; more important still, the boilers remain scale-free and require remarkably little in the way of repairs. In view of the substantial benefits conferred by this form of water treatment, it is surprising that no other Region has given it any more than experimental use.

The paper by M. G. Burrows and A. L. Wallace, previously referred to, gave some interesting figures concerning the life of Southern Pacific all-welded boilers. Up to the time when the paper was presented, in 1958, the first 'Merchant Navy' boilers had run an average mileage of 229,000 each only, but the next boilers, after the 'T.I.A.' treatment had begun, had averaged 560,000 miles each, with from one to three lifts apiece, during their life, for examination and repair, and an average life before the first lift was required increased from 176,000 to 257,000 miles. The average mileage of 'West Country' boilers from entry into service to the first lift had gone up from 97,000 to 245,000 miles.

In 1948 Bulleid fitted 'Merchant Navy' Pacific No. 35005 *Canadian Pacific* with an automatic stoker of the American Berkeley type. For many years past it had been a legal requirement in North America that any steam locomotive with a firegrate of more than 50 sq ft in area must be automatically fired, and though the 48·6 sq ft of the Bulleid Pacific firegrate fell a little short of this figure, he was well aware – as was proved later in the tests on the Rugby plant – that the steaming capacity of his boiler was so great as to be beyond the capacity of a single fireman if it was exploited to the full.

The tender was equipped with a coal pusher, and with conveyor screws which crushed and delivered the fuel to a distributor plate located inside the firehole door. The screws were driven by a small steam engine fitted in the tender, and the quantity of fuel fired was governed by the speed of this engine. From the distributor the finely divided coal was discharged into the firebox by a set of steam jets, and the flow of steam to each nozzle could be regulated in such a way as to ensure even distribution over the grate. The fire-hole door was provided with peep-holes, through which it was possible at any time to see the condition of the fire. Actually the mechanical stoker did not obstruct the firehole door, and manual firing could be resorted to if necessary.

Unfortunately this 'iron fireman' could not deal with large-size Yorkshire or Welsh coal, for lumps bigger than a 6-in. cube tended to jam the conveyor screws. As had been the experience in the U.S.A., this type of firing worked well enough with small and dusty coal, but at a heavy consumption rate. Pulverized coal could pass out of the chimney almost unburnt, some finding its way unpleasantly through carriage windows, while the improvement in steaming was negligible. This explains why no other engines of the class were dealt with similarly.

Another experiment in firing was when 'West Country' Pacifics Nos. 21C119 *Bideford* and 21C136 *Westward Ho !* were equipped in 1946 to burn oil fuel. The Government had decreed that owing to coal shortage oil-firing was to be adopted on an extensive scale – to a total, indeed, of 1,217 locomotives – and this was the first application on the Southern Railway. But it was an ill-thought-out decision, and within a year, after a considerable amount of money had been spent in fitting locomotives and in depot equipment – by the Great Western Railway in particular – it was rescinded. Fortunately the Southern had not gone very far, and the two Pacifics mentioned were the only ones so fitted.

To sum up the experience with the Bulleid Pacifics, though some of their features have proved troublesome, in the various ways described, others have had exceptional success. In the boilers there has been an almost complete elimination of leaky tubeplates, and eroded or wasted joints in the fireboxes. Broken spokes or loose tyres of coupled wheels have been unknown, as also overheated big-ends of inside connecting-rods or overheating of axleboxes. In these and other respects the 'Merchant Navy' and 'West Country' engines have helped to make British locomotive history.

Few of them have been involved in any serious mishaps, but one major exception has been 'Battle of Britain' Pacific No. 34066 *Spitfire*. On 4th December, 1957, this unrebuilt 4-6-2, at the head of the 4.56 p.m. from Cannon Street to Ramsgate, collided in dense fog beyond St Johns with the rear of the 5.18 p.m. from Charing Cross to Hayes, and brought down on to the wreckage the overline bridge carrying the Nunhead–Lewisham loop line, with the loss of no fewer than ninety lives. Apart from this disaster, one of the worst in British history, the Bulleid Pacifics have had a remarkably clean record.

6 – *The* 1948 *Locomotive Exchanges*

THE first tests of note to which the Bulleid Pacifics were subjected were those of the locomotive exchange trials in 1948, the first year of nationalization. 'Merchant Navy' Pacifics, in the 'heavyweight' class, were pitted against L.M.S.R. 'Duchess' and L.N.E.R. 'A4' Pacifics, and G.W.R. 'King' and L.M.S.R. 'Royal Scot' 4-6-0s; while 'West Country' Pacifics had as their rivals L.M.S.R. Class '5', L.N.E.R. 'B1' and G.W.R. 'Hall' 4-6-0s. In the lighter class the 'West Countries' had a considerable advantage in power, of course, over the other three competitors.

One record made by a Bulleid Pacific during these trials that remains unchallenged in Great Britain is that Driver Swain and Fireman Hooker of Nine Elms worked No. 34004 *Yeovil* through over the 568½ miles between Euston and Inverness, piloting L.M.S.R. locomotives on passenger expresses between Euston and Perth as a preliminary to the trials proper over the Highland main line. Incidentally, the Southern enginemen were not without unofficial warnings as to what they might expect up in the north. On the way to Carlisle lay Shap, a miniature Matterhorn, likely to stall any engine with a dirty fire. Druimuachdar summit would almost certainly be under snow; and the Highland men usually opened their sand valves somewhere about Stanley Junction and kept them open until they were clear of Slochd summit (whereas the sand supply of a Bulleid Pacific would last about 15 min. with the valves fully open!).

The 'Merchant Navy' engines selected were No. 35017 *Belgian Marine*, 35019 *French Line C.G.T.* and 35020 *Bibby Line*, though in the event the last-named was not needed and did not participate; No. 35018 *British India Line* was used on the home tests between Waterloo and Exeter. The chosen 'West Country' Pacifics were Nos. 34004 *Yeovil*, 34005 *Barnstaple* and 34006 *Bude*. In order that they might be able to pick up water on the 'foreign' lines, all six engines were fitted with standard L.M.R. tenders, and No. 34004 in addition had to be equipped with tablet-catching apparatus for working over the single-track sections of the Highland main line. At the time when the tests were made the Southern enginemen were accustomed to a more strict standard of timekeeping than that which was common elsewhere in the country, and from the time and speed point of view put up better performances than many of the rival engine-crews, some of whom were handicapped by a determination to keep coal consumption down to the lowest possible limits.

The most notable 'Merchant Navy' feat that I timed personally was on one of the southbound runs of *Belgian Marine* from Carlisle, with a load of 503 tons tare and 525 tons gross. Driver Swain and Fireman Hooker were in charge. Signal checks made the train late away from Penrith. In 2 miles, partly level and partly at 1 in 193 up, speed rose to 46 m.p.h.; then, on the 7 miles at 1 in 125 up past Clifton and Thrimby Grange the rate settled down to an unvarying 41 m.p.h., increased to 46 on the subsequent 1¼ miles at 1 in 142 and to 51 on the level half-mile through Shap station; the minimum on the final 1¼ miles at 1 in 106–150 to the summit was 46 m.p.h. From Penrith to Shap summit, 13·7 miles, the time of 20 min. 31 sec. cut the schedule by 6½ min. The official report showed that this performance required an actual drawbar-h.p. output of 1,540 on the 1 in 125 and 1,629 on the final 1 in 106, or equivalent drawbar-h.p. figures (referred to level track) of 1,860 and 1,920 respectively; the climb was made on a cut-off of 33 per cent, with the regulator as nearly full open as to give a pressure of 215 to 225 lb in the steam-chest out of a boiler pressure maintained at just over 250 lb. These figures had been almost exactly duplicated by *Belgian Marine* two days earlier.

A near-casualty of this test week occurred when *Belgian Marine* was working the 505-ton 'Royal Scot' up to Shap from the opposite side. Just north of

Tebay station the train was brought to a dead stand by adverse signals. Fortunately the 4-6-2 was still on the 1 in 134 up-grade that precedes the 4 miles at 1 in 75, but even so Driver Swain had to exercise the utmost caution, in getting restarted in very bad weather conditions, to prevent his engine from slipping. For $2\frac{1}{4}$ min. he had to back his engine, with extreme care, before he got the driving wheels in the right position for a start. But this was more than atoned for two days later, when, owing to a permanent way slack before Tebay, *Belgian Marine*, loaded to 530 gross tons, hit the foot of the 1 in 75 at $57\frac{1}{2}$ m.p.h. only. After about 2 miles of the grade, when speed had fallen to $26\frac{1}{2}$ m.p.h., Driver Swain opened out to 43 per cent cut-off with full regulator, with the result that the drawbar pull rose from 6·18 to 8·6 tons and the equivalent drawbar h.p. from 1,710 to 1,835. Moreover, notwithstanding this tremendous effort, the boiler pressure rose slightly – from 260 to 263 lb per sq in. – and the admirable design of the steam passages was seen in the fact that the steam-chest pressure on this final stage of the climb increased to 255 lb, only 8 lb less than that in the boiler.

No other engine tried over this route came anywhere near these Southern Pacific figures on the climbs to Shap. Also among good 'Merchant Navy' climbs was that of *French Line C.G.T.* with 505 tons from Taunton start to Whiteball summit, 10·85 miles, in 17 min. 18 sec., with a minimum of 30 m.p.h. on the final 3 miles at 1 in 90–80–127. Similarly *Belgian Marine* did well, on the way up from Leeds to Kings Cross, to clear Stoke summit, 5.35 miles from the Grantham start, in 9 min. 37 sec. with a 535-ton train, attaining $47\frac{1}{2}$ m.p.h. up the continuous 1 in 200; this produced an equivalent drawbar h.p. rising to 1,659, yet was done on a cut-off of no more than 25 per cent, with a pressure of 200 lb per sq in. in the steam chests.

But it was the 'West Country' Pacifics that carried off the major honours in the 1948 exchange. On the Great Central main line of the Eastern Region *Bude* was the only one of the four competitors that succeeded in keeping time with the test loads, and, indeed, in bettering the test schedules; on a run that I timed with the 10 a.m. from Marylebone to Manchester there was a total net gain of 14 min. It must be conceded, however, that this was a Class '6' 4-6-2 competing against Class '5' 4-6-0s.

With a load of 360 tons tare and 380 tons gross, Driver Swain accelerated up 6 miles at 1 in 105 from 27 m.p.h. through Rickmansworth to 45 m.p.h. by Amersham; later, the 31·2 miles from Aylesbury to Woodford Halse, mainly against the engine, were run in 31 min. 24 sec. start to stop, with minima of 59 m.p.h. up the long 1 in 176 to Finmere, and 64 up the corresponding grade to Helmdon. Even more noteworthy was the acceleration from a 20-m.p.h. permanent way slowing past Hucknall to precisely 50 m.p.h. up the continuous 1 in 132 climb to Annesley. On this climb the cut-off was 30 per cent and the regulator wide enough open to give 225 lb pressure in the steam-chests out of the 245 lb in the boiler, and this brought the equivalent drawbar h.p. up to 1,960; the corresponding figures for the climb to Amersham were 25 per cent; 235 lb and 270 lb per sq in.; and 1,639 h.p. respectively.

In the reverse direction the same engine developed the highest equivalent drawbar h.p. of all the locomotives ('heavyweights' included) in these exchange trials. This was in climbing out of Leicester with a train of 375 tons tare and 395 tons gross, which was taken up the 7 miles at 1 in 176 from Whetstone at a speed that settled down to a steady 58–57 m.p.h., with the engine cutting off at 27 per cent, and working at all but full regulator; there was 240 lb pressure in the steam-chests out of the 260 lb in the boiler. The actual drawbar h.p. so developed rose to 1,667, which meant an equivalent drawbar h.p., referred to level track, of 2,010 – the only occasion on which 2,000 h.p. was exceeded during the trials. Two days earlier I timed *Bude*, similarly loaded, to make a most vigorous start southwards out of Aylesbury. Less than half a mile from the platform end there begins the 1 in 117 climb to Dutchlands summit, uninterrupted for $5\frac{1}{2}$ miles save for brief easings through Stoke Mandeville and Wendover stations. Once again with 27 per cent cut-off and wide-open regulator, *Bude* worked up to $47\frac{1}{2}$ m.p.h. before Wendover, accelerated to 50 through the station, settled down to 48 on the 1 in 117, and attained 51 on the easier final mile; the drawbar h.p. involved was 1,416 actual and 1,777 equivalent.

Some of the proceedings in Scotland with *Yeovil* were amusing. The 'West Country' 4-6-2 showed herself capable of gaining a quarter of an hour or so on any of the timings; on one of the northbound test trips the total net gain was $20\frac{1}{2}$ min. The diverting part of this run was that after the banker – Pickersgill 4-4-0 No. 14501 – had come on to the rear of the 380-ton train to assist up to Dalnaspidal, Swain started with such vigour as to 'wind' his supposed helper, and the stop at Struan had to be prolonged while the latter recovered its breath! Then the tremendous climb of 11 miles, almost all at 1 in 70, was attacked so determinedly that with speed varying between $34\frac{1}{2}$ and 42 m.p.h. the $11 \cdot 3$ miles from Struan up to Dalnaspidal were completed in 19 min. 23 sec. instead of the 31 min. allowed! With 25 per cent cut-off and full regulator, *Yeovil* was putting out an average drawbar-h.p. – actual, not equivalent – of 1,115 for 10 miles continuously. Coming south on the following day, the engine averaged 1,377 h.p. at the drawbar for 5 miles, on 35 per cent cut-off, up the 1 in 80 to Druimuachdar, with an equivalent maximum of 1,950. The attained speed on the 1 in 80 was 37 m.p.h., increased to 46 on the final 1 in 100. Up the long 1 in 60 southwards out of Inverness the Southern 4-6-2 was able to keep up 25 to 27 m.p.h. with a 275-ton train, and to gain $6\frac{3}{4}$ min. in the first $10 \cdot 8$ miles to Daviot.

It must be emphasized, however, that although some of the Southern Pacific horsepower figures were the highest achieved in the 1948 exchanges by any of the contestants, on other test occasions certain of the locomotives, notably the L.M.S.R. 'Duchesses' and the L.N.E.R. 'A4s', have recorded considerably higher figures when on test, as has been mentioned in earlier chapters. Moreover, the enlivening performances of the 'Merchant Navy' and 'West Country' Pacifics were secured at a cost of high coal consumption. The official report revealed that in average coal consumption relatively to power output – lb of coal per drawbar-h.p.-hr – the 'West Country' Pacifics were at the bottom of the list of all the engines tested, their figure being 4·11 lb; the 'Merchant Navy' engines did better, with 3·60 lb, but were still far below the two leading competitors, the L.N.E.R. 'A4s' with 3·06 lb and the L.M.S.R. 'Duchesses' with 3·12 lb.

In water consumption relatively to output the Southern position was even worse, the 'West Country' 4-6-2s again being bottom, with 31·68 lb of water per drawbar-h.p.-hr, and the 'Merchant Navy' 4-6-2s next with 30·43 lb; at the top of the list again were the L.N.E.R. 'A4s', with 24·32 lb only. But when it came to the evaporation rate – that is, the steaming capacity of the boiler as expressed in lb of water evaporated per lb of coal burned – the position was completely reversed, with the 'Merchant Navy' Pacifics second only to the L.M.S.R. 'Duchesses' – 8·45 as compared with 8·67 lb; in this comparison the L.N.E.R. 'A4s' took seventh place, with 7·92 lb, whereas the 'West Country' Pacifics were fifth, with 7·94 lb. The moral of these results is that what the Bulleid Pacifics gained by their high boiler efficiency they more than lost by their lower efficiency at the front end.

Further adverse influences on their overall thermal efficiency were the throttling of the steam due to small regulator openings (coupled with the fact that they were never linked up to less than 25 per cent cut-off), and the almost imperceptible but frequent slipping that took place, even at speed, which entailed loss of power. When running from Paddington to Plymouth, *French Line C.G.T.* slipped so badly on the 1 in 50 of Rattery bank that sanding had to continue for 2¼ miles right off; directly sand was applied the drawbar pull rose from 6·53 to 7·44 tons. The official report notes that although both the 'Merchant Navy' and 'West Country' Pacifics steamed freely, there was a tendency for both types to throw out dirty exhaust, indicating that the fuel was not being completely consumed – another pointer to a front-end design which left a good deal to be desired.

7 – Under Test at Rugby

BUT a much more accurate appraisal of the Bulleid design came with the testing of No. 35022 *Holland-Amerika Line* on the Rugby plant five years later, the subject of Bulletin No. 10 in the Performance and Efficiency Test series of the British Transport Commission. The first plant tests were over an equivalent mileage of 10,300, and were accompanied by the usual road tests with the dynamometer car, which covered an actual total of 3,840 miles. The engine was then fitted with a boiler having no thermic syphons in the firebox, and underwent a further 2,820 miles of testing on the plant and 1,140 miles on the road. No. 35022 had run 1,115 miles after general overhaul before the tests began.

In the steaming tests the first discovery was that the cut-off figure shown on the footplate indicator had no consistent relation with the actual cut-off. One day on 10 per cent cut-off the engine showed a bigger drawbar pull at 15 to 20 m.p.h. than it had exerted just previously with 15 per cent, whereas on the following day the pull at 15 per cent was doubled, and at 20 per cent was more than half as much again. Short cut-offs tended to lengthen without the driver having made any alteration in his cut-off setting, and at high speeds, with short cut-off settings, there were times when the power output of the engine rose to figures which theoretically were impossibly high for the nominal cut-off in use, showing that the actual cut-off must have been greater than that indicated on the cut-off scale. The steam reversing gear also tended to creep, and special measures had to be taken to keep it fixed at the test position which had been selected. At times the pull on the drawbar increased as the speed rose – an almost unprecedented phenomenon – and in general the speed of the engine varied uncontrollably over a wide range.

Needless to say, there was no question about the ability of the Bulleid boiler to steam. With Blidworth coal a steaming rate of 33,300 lb per hr was attained, with Bedwas Welsh coal 37,000 lb per hr, and with South Kirkby (although the Yorkshire product had a calorific value of 13,994 B.T.U. per lb as compared with the Bedwas 14,526 B.T.U. per lb) 39,000 lb per hr. Indeed, for 20 min. with South Kirkby the steaming rate rose to 42,000 lb per hr, and there was no indication that the limit had been reached. But it was impossible to attempt any higher output, because of the chronic slipping of the engine at high power outputs, due to oil from the oil-bath getting on to the rollers of the plant; from time to time the test had to be stopped and the rollers wiped clean before it could proceed. Worse still, some buckling of the engine side-rods took place as the result of severe slipping. But for this handicap, some record boiler outputs might have been attained.

At such steaming rates as those mentioned, the firing rate went up to more than 3,000 lb of coal an hour, and two firemen were needed to keep the firebox supplied. Firing on this scale was excessive; proof that the 'Merchant Navy' Pacific was too heavy on coal is forthcoming in the fact that the lowest steam consumption recorded was 15·9 lb per i.h.p.-hr, whereas other locomotives of comparable dimensions that had been tested at Rugby gave figures of between 13·2 and 13·8 lb. Attempts were made to improve the efficiency by varying the blastpipe arrangement, but the limited space available between the top of the inside valve-chest and the top of the chimney made an ideal arrangement impossible, and the 4-6-2 did not steam as well with any of the variations as it did with its normal multiple-jet blastpipe and large-diameter chimney. Since 1951 another engine of the class, No. 35019 *French Line C.G.T.*, had been running experimentally with a single blastpipe and chimney of normal diameter, and had done reasonably well; however, this was mainly because the Southern timetables seldom required one of the Pacifics to be in any way 'extended'.

Tests were also made, as previously mentioned, with a 'Merchant Navy' Pacific fitted with a boiler having no thermic syphons in the firebox. As these syphons help to support the brick arch, a different type of arch had to be installed, and the engine so equipped proved considerably more difficult to fire than one with the standard equipment. No improvement was obtained in combustion, and there was no reduction in the emission of smoke; the only advantage obtained was an increase in the inlet steam temperature of between 40 and 60°F.

The official report thus confirmed the experience of the Operating Department with this unusual design. It was that the Bulleid boiler had an unlimited capacity to make steam, but at an extravagant cost in coal consumption; that the valve-motion was so erratic in action that tests on successive days, though carried out in identical conditions, could give widely varying results; that various other departures from conventional practice, some of them expensive both to instal and to maintain, did not justify their cost; and that the oil-bath in particular caused so much trouble, both in waste of the lubricant itself and also in loss of power by the slipping that it caused, as far to outweigh any benefit derived from the complete enclosure of the motion. The stage thus was set for the complete rebuilding of all the 'Merchant Navy' Pacifics, and the majority of the 'West Country' type, that has taken place under the auspices of British Railways.

8 – *The Rebuilding*

FOR some time discussions had taken place between officers of the Chief Mechanical and Electrical Engineer's and the Motive Power Departments as to how the obvious defects of the original Pacific design might best be overcome. At first glance it seemed that little could be done short of scrapping and starting afresh, but unless undue expense were involved in reconstruction, it seemed a pity to lose those features of the engines which had been unquestionably successful. With great ingenuity the Chief Technical Assistant at Brighton Works, R. G. Jarvis, and his staff, under the direction of H. H. Swift, who had succeeded Bulleid, succeeded in producing plans for major modifications which could be carried out for an expenditure less than half the current cost of a new locomotive. These plans met with the approval of the Motive Power people, and also of the British Railways Central Staff, and preparations to implement them were begun in 1955.

In February, 1956, the first completely rebuilt Bulleid Pacific, No. 35018 *British India Line*, emerged from Eastleigh Works; for reasons of accountancy these engines and those subsequently dealt with have been known as 'modified Pacifics', but actually a thoroughgoing reconstruction has taken place. Its aim, needless to say, has been to reduce operating and maintenance costs, and for this reason the principal detail to be abandoned has been the chain-driven valve-motion; but those features of the design which have proved valuable, and in particular the all-welded boiler, have been retained. The redesign has been a brilliant piece of work and the rebuilding has fully justified itself.

The outside cylinders remained, but No. 35018 had a new cast steel inside cylinder fitted, with cast iron liner; the steam-chest, arranged for inside admission and also with cast iron liner, was offset to the right. To avoid undue expense, the outside cylinders were retained, and this meant the retention also of their piston-valves with outside admission, with special measures to change the actuation of the valves of the outside cylinders, previously driven indirectly by a rocking-shaft. To replace the original valve-motion, three sets of Walschaerts motion were fitted. This necessitated a certain amount of redesigning, to permit the attachment of the return cranks to the driving crank-pins and the crosshead arms to the crossheads; previously the latter were one-piece forgings with the piston-rods, but in the rebuilding were fabricated separately, with the usual cone-and-cotter fastening. The inside valve-motion is now driven by an eccentric mounted on the right-hand crank web of the driving axle, various other detail changes having been needed to transmit the motion. As a result of the rebuilding, the outside piston-valves have a maximum travel of $6\frac{3}{4}$ in., and the inside of $6\frac{5}{16}$ in.

Part of the uncertain working with the former valve-motion, and particularly the tendency for the cut-off to lengthen gradually without any alteration having been made in the setting, was found to be due to the steam reverser, and this was therefore removed and ordinary screw reversing substituted, with a type of transmission that had been introduced first on the L.M.S.R. The reversing handle is 'face on' to the driver, and, as in British Railways standard locomotives, the cut-off indicator is of the clearly-read drum type. Whereas with multi-cylinder locomotives having independent sets of valve-gear it is usually necessary to provide an auxiliary reversing shaft for the inside motion, in these rebuilds it has been found possible to use a single shaft for all three gears, lifting of the radius rods being achieved by an ingenious arrangement whereby a slide-block works in a slot in the radius rod, the former attached directly to the reversing-shaft arm.

Each Pacific has been fitted with a new smokebox, of the orthodox cylindrical type and about 12 in. longer than its predecessor; it rests on a saddle which is formed partly by the upper portion of the new inside cylinder casting and partly by a new fabricated saddle stretcher. By bolting the latter to the front of the cylinder casting as well as to the frames, additional rigidity is given to the front end of the locomotive. While the multiple-jet blastpipe was retained, with its five $2\frac{5}{8}$-in. diameter nozzles giving a total blast area of 27 sq in., important alterations were made to the draughting. The height of the chimney choke above the blastpipe orifices was reduced by 7 in. to 2 ft $7\frac{3}{8}$ in., and the diameter at the choke by $1\frac{1}{2}$ in. to 1 ft. $11\frac{1}{2}$ in., with a corresponding increase by 7 in. in the height from the choke to the chimney top, now 2 ft 2 in. The chimney diameter of 2 ft 5 in. was left unaltered, but the original stovepipe was replaced by a flared cast iron chimney. Smoke deflectors were fitted on both sides of the smokebox, and the original air-smoothed boiler casing was removed, footplates being added along both sides of the locomotive to assist in servicing and maintenance.

A new superheater header was provided, with new and direct steam passages to the cylinders, and the superheating surface was reduced from 822 to 612 sq ft. To assist both in combustion and in servicing, each rebuilt Pacific has been equipped with a rocking grate of the standard British Railways type, together with a new ashpan having butterfly doors for self-emptying. One feature of the original ashpan that has been retained, however, is its three-part division into a central section between the frames and two outer sections. Each section has two damper doors, and of the total of six, three face forwards and three backwards; they are operated by screw control on the footplate in two groups, forward and backward respectively. The Ajax type of firehole door was retained, but pedal-operated opening by steam power, which firemen were not using to the extent that the designer had anticipated, was removed. As to other cab fittings, while in general there has been little alteration, the abandonment of the steam reversing has made it necessary to provide a reversing screw handle and gearbox, and in consequence to move the driver's seat a little further back. The driver's look-out ahead has been greatly improved by the removal of the air-smoothed boiler casing.

The curious sanding arrangements on the original engines have been altered. For forward running each engine formerly had sanders ahead of each coupled wheel, but owing to sand getting into the motion, the leading sanders had been removed. For backward running sanders had been provided at the front of the tender, sanding the rails between engine and tender. In the rebuilt engines the leading sanders have been restored, and the sanders ahead of the rear pair of coupled wheels have been turned round to sand behind the driving wheels when running in reverse, which has made it possible to dispense with the sanders on the tender. Various alterations also were made to the lubrication. One happy result of the rebuilding has been purely aesthetic; it has produced a series of Pacifics which are qualified to rank in appearance as some of the most imposing in the country. As with the original engines, it is still difficult at a glance to distinguish the rebuilt 'Merchant Navy' from the rebuilt 'West Country' engines; the different types of nameplate provide the most obvious clue.

For purposes of comparison with the 1953 tests of 'Merchant Navy' Pacific No. 35022 *Holland-Amerika Line* in its original condition, a series of tests, both at the Rugby plant and on the road, were carried out in the summer of 1956 with the rebuilt No. 35020 *Bibby Line*. Two controlled road tests were made on the 3 p.m. from Waterloo to Exeter, and two back with the 12.30 p.m. 'Atlantic Coast Express' from Exeter to Waterloo. The tare weights going down were 500 and 466 tons to Templecombe and 394 tons from there, and coming up they were 400 and 436 tons to Salisbury and 472 tons on to Waterloo. Nothing very spectacular in the speed realm was attempted, save on the down run of 28th June, when a late start from Templecombe provided the excuse for a time of 43 min. start-to-stop over the 47·4 miles from Templecombe to Sidmouth Junction, or 8 min. less than the 51 min. scheduled, including 19 min. only for the 25·25 miles from Yeovil Junction to Seaton Junction, average 79·7 m.p.h.

On this run, with 415 gross tons, there was a drop only from 80 to 67 m.p.h. up the 3 miles at 1 in 80 from Crewkerne to Hewish summit; speed was then allowed to rise as high as 95 m.p.h. past Axminster. Seaton Junction was passed at 84 m.p.h., after 1½ miles up at 1 in 100, and up the subsequent

1 in 80 speeds were 74 m.p.h. at milepost 149 – end of the first mile at this inclination – 67 at milepost 150, and 48½ at milepost 152, half a mile short of the tunnel entrance, but no figure was shown in the report for the minimum on emergence from the tunnel. The maximum equivalent drawbar horse-power recorded on this climb was 1,691.

Welsh coal of Bedwas Grade 2 quality was used in the tests of No. 35020, but no attempt was made to reach the extremely high steam outputs of the Rugby tests on No. 35022, when a maximum of 37,000 lb of steam per hour was attained. With No. 35020 the maximum was 32,000 lb, at a firing rate of 4,780 lb of coal per hour. In the road tests, the average coal consumptions were 3·29–3·33 lb per traction-h.p.-hr from Waterloo to Salisbury and 3·60–3·70 lb thence to Exeter; coming up the figures were 3·80–3·94 lb from Exeter to Salisbury and 3·21–3·54 lb on to Waterloo. Comments in the report on the working of the engine during the tests include an appreciation of the free steaming, and also the fact that out of hundreds of samples taken of smokebox gas, practically all were free from carbon monoxide, indicating complete combustion. An unofficial comment was that No. 35020 gave one of the most completely predictable performances of all the locomotives that have been tested to date under the auspices of British Railways. By the improved front end, cylinder efficiency has gone up by about 18 per cent.

As to maintenance, in their original form the Bulleid Pacifics needed a complete valve and piston examination after 36,000 miles of running, but since the rebuilding the figure has gone up to 44,000 miles and even more; and whereas in the past half a truck-load of motion parts had to go back to Eastleigh for reconditioning at times of overhaul, today all the work needed can be done at the depot to which the locomotive is attached, save for an almost negligible proportion of parts that may require attention at Eastleigh. The only changes that have taken place since the rebuilding have been the substitution of coupled wheel axleboxes of steel, with let-in brasses and manganese liners, for the original bronze axleboxes, with the advantage of reduced wear.

Rebuilding of the 'Merchant Navy' Pacifics went on steadily from completion of the work on No. 35018 *British India Line* in February, 1956, until the last two, Nos. 35006 *Peninsular & Oriental S.N. Co.* and 35028 *Clan Line*, emerged from Eastleigh Works in their rebuilt form in October, 1959. The pioneer engine, *Channel Packet*, had the longest life in the original condition, one of 18½ years. Meantime the advantages of the rebuilding were so obvious that the decision had been reached to modify the 'West Country' Pacifics in similar fashion, and No. 34005 *Barnstaple* was the first to appear in the new guise, in June, 1957. Exactly four years later the sixtieth light Pacific rebuild, No. 34098 *Templecombe*, was turned into traffic. Some of the last 'West Country engines thus rebuilt had a life of no more than ten years in their former condition.

At this late stage in British steam locomotive history, it is unlikely that any further rebuilding will take place, and the remaining fifty Bulleid light Pacifics eventually will go to the scrapheap in the form in which they were built.

Meantime the Southern Region, with its thirty modified 'Merchant Navy' and sixty modified 'West Country' and 'Battle of Britain' Pacifics, can now claim to possess the most modern express passenger power in the country, likely still to have before it many years of useful service over the West of England and Southampton and Bournemouth main lines.

9 – *On the Footplate*

WHATEVER may have been the problems presented by the Bulleid Pacifics to those responsible for their maintenance, from the first there has been no doubt as to the attitude towards them of their drivers and firemen. Never before had the comfort of Southern engine-crews been studied to the extent that it had been on these engines. From personal experience I can testify that they are about the smoothest riding and quietest in action of the many steam locomotives of which I have had footplate experience. Very complete protection also was provided from the weather, though it must be added that the shape of the cab and tender front has encouraged the sucking of coal dust from the tender into the cab, with the result that these Pacifics have not been among Britain's cleanest engines on which to ride. But rebuilding has brought about an improvement in this respect.

Firing has always been a relatively simple matter. 'Opening out' a Bulleid Pacific by way of a longer cut-off or a wider open regulator, with a corresponding sharpening of the blast, produces an immediate response from the fire, as I have noted with surprise even when we have been climbing so formidable an incline as the 1 in 80 of Seaton bank, with the boiler pressure *rising* rather than falling in the process! No matter how these engines are fired, they seem to be able to steam; and from their drivers' point of view this has meant an ability more than to cope with all the varied conditions of day-to-day running, and with relative ease to make up lost time, even on the faster schedules.

It was a new experience for Southern Railway drivers to have all their controls grouped round them so as to be within reach without their having to rise from their seats, and with their cut-off indicator and gauges in full view from the same position; the only defect in the cab layout, as already mentioned, was the partial blockage of the very limited view through the driver's front window by the vacuum ejector, let alone its frequent obscuration, in the early days, by drifting steam. Also, because of the propensity of these engines to slip, drivers have had to handle their regulators with the most extreme care when starting, especially on rising gradients.

I well remember seeing an unrebuilt 'Merchant Navy' 4-6-2 trying to get a down express started on the curve and rising gradient at Andover Junction, and taking little short of 5 min. to get on the move; and Driver Swain's difficulty in getting away from a signal stop at Tebay on the way to Shap summit, in the 1948 locomotive exchange trials, has been described already in Section 6. But this slipping trouble also has been reduced by rebuilding to a fraction of what it was formerly.

Riding on the footplate of a Bulleid Pacific in its original condition was in many ways a curious experience, as the handling of the engine differed so radically from anything to which the observer was normally accustomed. The 280 lb per sq in. working pressure was little more than a reserve for contingencies, as in my experience it was rare to see the regulator of one of these engines opened to full. If ever this did happen, the steam-chest pressure would creep up to within 10 lb or even 5 lb of the boiler pressure, witnessing to the excellent design of the steam passages. But a large proportion of the work of these engines was done with no more than 100 to 150 lb per sq in. in the steam-chests, which helps to explain why they have been so heavy on coal; at times, for example, one could record high speed on easy gradients with no more than 50 lb showing on the steam-chest pressure gauge. It also explains why the working pressure was reduced to 250 lb per sq in. even before the rebuilding, when the lower figure became standard.

On a footplate run that I made with Driver Swain and Fireman Fordrey of Nine Elms in 1948 with No. 21C14 *Nederland Line*, for example, hauling a load of ten Pullmans weighing 420 tons gross, with 20 per cent cut-off and no more than 130 lb in the steam-chest, speed swept up to 75 m.p.h. in the Weybridge dip, and with 15 per cent only the train was carried over the miniature summit at milepost 31 at 66 m.p.h. Further on, with 20 per cent and 150 lb, a maximum of 77½ m.p.h. was reached beyond Hook; in these extraordinarily easy working conditions the 35.75 miles from Surbiton to Basingstoke had been covered at an average of 68·4 m.p.h.

On a journey that I made at much the same period on the 'Golden Arrow' from Victoria to Dover, on the footplate of No. 21C135 *Shaftesbury*, the 'West Country' Pacific was worked harder than the 'Merchant Navy' in the run just quoted. Driver Rickwood and Fireman Chessun, of Stewart's Lane shed, had behind them a load of 368 tons tare and 390 tons gross. Speed had to be reduced to 5 m.p.h. for a bridge reconstruction at Herne Hill, but there was plenty of steam for 40 to 45 per cent cut-off in recovering up the 1 in 100 to Sydenham Hill, with regulator wide enough open to give 200 to 230 lb per sq in. in the steam-chests out of the boiler pressure of 260 to 270 lb. Beyond Tonbridge Rickwood moved his regulator to full open, and speed on the level rose quickly to 77½ m.p.h. at Headcorn; and with the regulator then brought back to give 185 to 190 lb in the steam-chests out of the 230 to 240 lb in the boiler, speed was held at between 75 and 79 m.p.h. on to Ashford. The train was now 2¾ min. ahead of time, and the regulator therefore was moved even further back; but no more than 115 to 120 lb steam-chest pressure was sufficient to maintain 60 m.p.h. up the 1 in 275 to Westenhanger.

Much more recently I rode with Driver Chant and Fireman Stevenson on the rebuilt 'Merchant Navy' Pacific No. 35020 *Bibby Line* at the head of one of the Bournemouth two-hour trains, loaded to 400 tons tare and 420 tons gross, and though wider regulator openings were used than on most of the runs I have had with these engines in their unrebuilt condition, the maximum steam-chest pressure was never allowed to rise to more than 200 lb out of the 230 to 250 lb in the boiler, and most of the harder work was done with between 150 and 185 lb in the steam-chests. Apart from starting, the cut-offs used by Driver Chant were not less than 25 nor more than 30 per cent. After the speed had risen to 74 m.p.h. beyond Weybridge, and then had gradually fallen to 68 on the rising grades past Woking, the regulator opening was gradually increased, and with a steady rise in the steam-chest pressure from 140 to 185 lb speed also accelerated until the milepost 31 summit was carried at just over 70 m.p.h. Recovering from a 15-m.p.h. permanent way check at Farnborough, 170 lb pressure in the steam-chests and 25 per cent cut-off were sufficient to produce an acceleration to 75 m.p.h. on the level on passing Hook; down the falling gradients past Winchester 81 m.p.h. was reached with 120 lb steam-chest pressure only.

10 – *Day-to-day Performance*

THE tables that follow set out some of the most outstanding performances that have been recorded with Bulleid Pacifics, when for various reasons, chiefly the recovery of lost time, they have been driven really hard. In Table VII (A), rebuilt 'Merchant Navy' Pacific No. 35017 *Belgian Marine*, in the capable hands of Driver C. Letchford and Fireman Stanford of Nine Elms, was at the head of a twelve-coach load of 425 gross tons on one of the Bournemouth two-hour workings. After an early permanent way slowing the engine was opened out to such effect that from Hampton Court Junction to Shawford the speed at no point fell below 70 m.p.h. save for a momentary drop to 68 up the 6 miles at 1 in 249 past Worting Junction.

Much of the first 56 miles out of Waterloo is 'against the collar'; at the other summit point, milepost 31, the minimum speed was 71 m.p.h., while on the level between there and milepost 43, 82 m.p.h. was reached; down the long descent from Roundwood 90 m.p.h. had been attained when the first of a series of signal checks was experienced. In all, an average of 75·8 m.p.h. was kept up over the whole of the 57·65 miles from Surbiton to Shawford with this substantial train, and the 79·25 miles from Waterloo to Southampton Central were completed in 79 min. 12 sec., or 71 min. net. This run was recorded by G. F. Bloxam.

The second run in Table VII (A) was made by No. 21C2 *Union Castle* when new, on an experimental non-stop run to Bournemouth with a sixteen-coach train of 520 tons gross. The engine must have been worked pretty hard to reach a speed of 77 m.p.h. at Walton and again in the Weybridge dip; and the acceleration with 520 tons from the 28 m.p.h. signal check at Woking to 54 m.p.h. up the rising grades to milepost 31 also was worthy of note. Speed restrictions, such as that at Worting Junction (which with the new long switches has since been substantially raised, though not yet to the 75 m.p.h. of the previous run!) were scrupulously observed, and there was restraint also on downhill speeds, but even so Southampton Central was passed in 79 min.

TABLE VII (A)
S.R. WATERLOO–SOUTHAMPTON

Engine: Class 'MN' 4-6-2 No. Load: Coaches/tons tare/tons gross		35017‡ 12/398/425		21C2§ 16/517/520	
Dist.		Times	Speeds	Times	Speeds
miles		min. sec.	m.p.h.	min. sec.	m.p.h.
0·00	WATERLOO . . .	0 00	—	0 00	—
1·30	Vauxhall	3 28	33/50	3 45	38
3·90	CLAPHAM JUNCTION .	6 52	*48	7 30	*42
		p.w.s.	*23		
5·55	Earlsfield . . .	9 10	—	9 44	56
7·20	Wimbledon . . .	12 15	39	11 44	60
12·05	SURBITON . . .	17 26	62	16 21	66
17·10	Walton . . .	21 39	75	20 29	77
19·10	Weybridge . . .	23 22	74/77	22 09	72
21·65	West Byfleet . . .	25 22	75	24 11	77
				sigs.	*28
24·30	WOKING . . .	27 32	74	27 00	—
28·00	Brookwood . . .	30 31	73	31 29	48
31·00	*Milepost 31* . . .	33 01	71	35 00	54
33·25	Farnborough . . .	34 53	75	37 16	64
36·50	Fleet	37 25	80	40 18	68
39·85	Winchfield . . .	39 58	80/76	43 00	69
42·20	Hook	41 46	82	45 00	75
47·80	BASINGSTOKE . .	46 03	78	49 31	64
50·30	*Worting Junction* . .	48 00	75/68	52 03	*46
58·10	Micheldever . . .	54 37	78	60 00	76
66·60	WINCHESTER . . .	60 43	86	66 45	74
69·70	Shawford . . .	62 51	90	69 31	70
		sigs.	*10		
73·55	EASTLEIGH . . .	67 28	—	72 30	70
		sigs.	*33		
75·80	Swaythling . . .	71 30	—	74 33	68
		sigs.			
77·25	St Denys	73 55	—	75 44	65
78·20	*Northam Junction* . .	75 53	—	77 15	*13
79·25	SOUTHAMPTON CENT.	79 12	—	†79 31	*24
79·25	Net times (min.) . .	71	—	¶77	—

* Speed restriction   † Passing time.   ‡ *Belgian Marine* (rebuilt).
§ *Union Castle* (unrebuilt).   ¶ Equivalent net time to stop.

31 sec., and despite a second signal check, at Totton, the Bournemouth stop, 108·5 miles from Waterloo, was made in 112 min. 46 sec., or 109 min. net. Before the war the non-stop 'Bournemouth Limited' was allowed 116 min., with a tare load limited to 365 tons. The most remarkable feature of this run by *Union Castle* is that it was completed with a tender accommodating no more than 5,000 gallons of water, and no means of replenishing *en route*.

On the journey from Southampton to Waterloo, the subject of Table VII (B), the toughest test of steaming is, of course, the unbroken climb from Eastleigh to Roundwood, so superbly engineered by the builders of the London & Southampton Railway, but permitting no breathing space for locomotives up 16½ miles continuously at 1 in 252. Yet, as these records show, sustained speeds of well over 60 m.p.h. can be maintained by 'Merchant Navy' Pacifics with loads of over 400 tons, and not far short of the mile-a-minute rate with trains of more than 500 tons.

On the first run in Table VII (B), rebuilt 'Merchant Navy' 4-6-2 No. 35027 *Port Line*, with a twelve-coach train of 430 gross tons, was in charge of Driver Sprague and Fireman Barnes of Bournemouth shed, again on a Bournemouth two-hour train. Up the long incline from Eastleigh there was, as will be seen, a gradual increase in speed from 64 to 69 m.p.h. by Winchester,

TABLE VII (B)
S.R. SOUTHAMPTON–WATERLOO

Engine: Class 'MN' 4-6-2 No. Load: Coaches/tons tare/tons gross		35027‡ 12/399/430		35014§ 12/490/515†		35002¶ 13/517/555†	
Dist.		Times	Speeds	Times	Speeds	Times	Speeds
miles		m. s.	m.p.h.	m. s.	m.p.h.	m. s.	m.p.h.
0·00	SOUTHAMPTON CENT.	0 00	—	0 00	—	0 00	—
1·05	Northam Junction .	4 05	—	3 37	—	3 40	*20
3·45	Swaythling . . .	7 27	53	7 02	—	7 38	43½
5·70	EASTLEIGH . . .	9 44	64	9 42	53½	10 30	52½
9·55	Shawford . . .	13 13	68	13 47	56	14 40	55½
12·65	WINCHESTER . .	15 55	69	17 10	56	18 09	53
17·45	Wallers Ash East .	20 13	68	22 15	57½	23 32	54
21·15	Micheldever . .	23 28	67	26 00	58	27 26	56½
23·00	Roundwood . . .	25 13	65	27 58	57	29 27	56½
26·70	Wootton . . .	28 33	69	31 33	68	33 00	71½
28·95	Worting Junction .	30 55	*57	33 33	*60	34 57	*65
		sigs.	*45				
31·45	BASINGSTOKE . .	33 59	—	35 55	67	37 09	75
37·05	Hook	38 41	82	40 20	79/76½	41 36	77½/75
39·40	Winchfield . . .	40 22	84	42 12	80½	43 28	80½
42·75	Fleet	42 50	80/83	44 42	79	45 57	80½
46·00	Farnborough . .	45 20	71	47 17	75	48 30	78
48·25	Milepost 31 . .	47 13	75	49 07	75	50 14	76½
51·25	Brookwood . . .	49 26	85	51 30	82	52 33	81
		sigs.	*35				
54·95	WOKING . . .	53 14	64	54 24	*69	55 09	85
57·60	West Byfleet . .	55 36	78	56 41	75	57 01	86½/88
60·15	Weybridge . . .	57 29	83	58 47	72½	58 48	80½
62·15	Walton	58 59	83	60 30	74	60 18	82
65·90	Hampton Court Junction .	61 48	79	63 32	74	63 10	79
67·20	SURBITON . . .	62 52	68	64 36	71	64 11	77
69·50	New Malden . .	64 59	*58	66 38	68	66 10	*68
72·05	Wimbledon . . .	67 40	57/59	69 11	68	68 25	67
						sig. stop	
75·35	CLAPHAM JUNCTION	71 20	*42/55	72 18	*40	76 27	—
		sigs.				sig. stops	
79·25	WATERLOO . .	78 32	—	79 08	—	95 32	—
79·25	Net times (min.) . .	75	—	79	—	78½	—

* Speed restriction.   † Pullman stock.   ‡ *Port Line* (rebuilt).
§ *Nederland Line* (unrebuilt).   ¶ *Union Castle* (rebuilt).

followed by an equally gradual drop to 65 at Roundwood, which would mean a continuous drawbar h.p. output, referred to level track, of at least 1,700 for more than 15 min. of running. Signal checks were experienced at Basingstoke, Woking and Vauxhall, but intermediately speeds of 75 to 85 m.p.h. were maintained for most of the distance, and Waterloo was reached in 78 min. 32 sec., or 74 min. net. This run was timed by S. C. Nash.

The second log was on the up 'Bournemouth Belle' Pullman with the maximum twelve-car load, headed by No. 35014 *Nederland Line* in its unrebuilt condition. With 515 gross tons of train, speed was maintained unbrokenly at 56 to 58 m.p.h. up the long incline, and though the speeds east of Basingstoke were not as high as on the preceding run, with a completely clear road Waterloo was reached in 79 min. 8 sec., or 8 min. less than the Pullman's 87-min. allowance.

The third run, which I timed personally, was on the Friday before an August Bank Holiday; one of the Pullman brakes was off for repairs, and its place had been taken by a second-class Pullman and an ordinary bogie brake, making up a tare load of 517 tons, the maximum ever likely to be seen on Southern metals. Moreover, every seat in the train had been booked, so that some passengers from Southampton had to be turned away; the gross load was in the region of 555 tons. Nothing daunted, Driver Hill and Fireman King of Bournemouth achieved a magnificent performance with the rebuilt No. 35002 *Union Castle*.

Up to Roundwood speed was slightly lower than that of *Nederland Line*, but even so crept steadily up from 53 m.p.h. at Winchester to 56½ m.p.h. at Roundwood; from Worting onwards, however, there was considerably faster travel, with an average of 76·5 m.p.h. over the 45·35 miles from Wootton box to Wimbledon, and a top speed of 88 m.p.h. at Byfleet Junction. Unhappily, Waterloo was so congested with pre-Bank Holiday traffic that the run concluded with a series of signal checks and stops; but a passage of Wimbledon, 72·05 miles, in 68 min. 25 sec. from the Southampton start would have made a Waterloo arrival easily possible in 78½ min., or 8½ min. less than the 87-min. schedule.

It may be added that many performances by the smaller 'West Country' Pacifics fall but little short in merit of those just described. For example, rebuilt No. 34039 *Boscastle*, with a twelve-coach load of 425 tons gross, maintained between 58 and 62 m.p.h. from Eastleigh up to Roundwood, and passed Worting in 32 min. 32 sec. and Brookwood in 50 min. 32 sec.; an up Portsmouth electric crossing ahead into the slow platform at Woking brought the speed down from 84 m.p.h. to a dead stand costing 4¾ min., but despite this Waterloo was reached in 81 min. 35 sec., or just under 77 min. net. The engine crew responsible for this fine feat were Driver A. E. Purchase and Fireman F. Prior of Bournemouth; it was recorded by John G. Webber.

Table VII (C) sets out performances of 'Merchant Navy' Pacifics with trains of varying weights from Waterloo to Salisbury. On the first run No. 35017 *Belgian Marine* was at the head of the 7 p.m. from Waterloo, and Driver Cambray, of Salisbury, had a moderate ten-coach load of 355 gross tons. In the middle of peak-hour traffic, his train was delayed by signals as far as Woking, but some very fast running followed, with an average speed of 81·4 m.p.h. over the 49·35 miles from Farnborough to Tunnel Junction at Salisbury, and of 85·3 m.p.h. for 27 miles from Overton to Tunnel Junction. Between the maximum speeds of 95 m.p.h. at Andover and 94 m.p.h. down the bank beyond Porton, the climb to Grateley – 1¾ miles at 1 in 264 and 2¾ miles at 1 in 165 – was carried by storm at a minimum of 75 m.p.h. So Salisbury, 83·7 miles, was reached in 81 min. 20 sec. (3¾ min. early), and in a net time of 74¼ min. The recorder was the Rev. J. E. T. Phillips.

TABLE VII (C)
S.R. WATERLOO–SALISBURY

Engine, Class 'MN' 4-6-2 No. / *Load: Coaches/tons tare/tons gross*		35005† 10/332/355		35017‡ 12/393/425		35016§ 13/428/465	
Dist.		*Times*	*Speeds*	*Times*	*Speeds*	*Times*	*Speeds*
miles		m. s.	m.p.h.	m. s.	m.p.h.	m. s.	m.p.h.
0·00	WATERLOO	0 00	—	0 00	—	0 00	—
		sigs.	—				
1·30	Vauxhall	4 52	—	3 31	37/50	3 45	34/50
3·90	CLAPHAM JUNCTION	9 00	*42	6 59	*43	7 23	*41
7·20	Wimbledon	13 08	59	11 07	54/58½	11 36	56
				p.w.s.	*7		
9·75	New Malden	15 35	62	14 25	—	14 05	64
12·05	SURBITON	17 38	72	19 48	50	16 05	72
13·35	*Hampton Court Junction*	18 42	75	21 15	60	17 10	74
		sigs.	*30				
17·10	Walton	24 33	—	24 48	68	20 23	66½
		sigs.	—				
19·10	Weybridge	27 52	—	26 35	66/75	22 18	62/66½
21·65	West Byfleet	30 43	61	28 42	72	24 41	63½
		sigs.	*48			sigs.	*46
24·30	WOKING	33 40	—	30 56	71	27 28	—
28·00	Brookwood	37 43	58	34 05	68	31 55	55
31·00	*Milepost 31*	40 42	62	36 43	67	35 05	57½
33·25	Farnborough	42 41	72	38 37	72	37 06	71½
36·50	Fleet	45 20	81	41 21	79	39 43	78/81½
39·85	Winchfield	47 50	77	43 57	75	42 15	79½
42·20	Hook	49 37	78/83	45 49	77/82	44 03	80/83
47·80	BASINGSTOKE	53 47	78	50 05	74	48 34	66
50·30	*Worting Junction*	55 50	69	52 11	68	50 56	61½
52·40	Oakley	57 36	74	54 00	71	52 54	66
55·60	Overton	60 07	80	56 36	78	55 42	74
59·20	Whitchurch	62 41	88	59 20	84	58 35	77
61·10	Hurstbourne	64 00	90/85	60 38	88/84	60 05	78½/70½
66·35	ANDOVER JUNCTION	67 27	95	64 10	97	64 18	80
72·75	Grateley	72 03	75	68 46	69	69 45	63½
75·60	*Allington*	74 16	82	71 11	70	72 13	69
78·25	Porton	76 03	90/94	73 15	83/90	74 28	76/77
						sigs.	*20
82·60	*Tunnel Junction*	79 05	*	76 28	*50	79 00	—
83·70	SALISBURY	81 20	—	78 55	—	81 40	—
83·70	Net times (min.)	74¼	—	74½	—	78	—

* Speed restriction.
† *Canadian Pacific* (unrebuilt).
‡ *Belgian Marine* (rebuilt).
§ *Elders Fyffes* (rebuilt).

The two remaining runs were of the 'Atlantic Coast Express', during the currency of its 83-min. schedule, since reduced to 80 min. Rebuilt 4-6-2 No. 35017 *Belgian Marine*, with Driver Saunders of Salisbury, had to tackle the normal load of this train, twelve coaches of 393 tons tare and 425 tons gross. At this time the rebuilding was in progress of the underline bridge at New Malden, involving a very severe slack. Recovering well from this, the engine surmounted the rise to milepost 31 at 67 m.p.h., reached 82 on but little easier than level track beyond Hook, and carried the 1 in 249 past Worting at a minimum of 68 m.p.h. An extremely rapid finish produced 97 m.p.h. at Andover, 69 minimum at Grateley and 90 below Porton for a total time of 78 min. 55 sec. from Waterloo. The net time may be put at 74½ min. For this log I am indebted to J. C. Natzio.

The last run of the three, timed by John G. Webber, was one on which rebuilt No. 35016, again with Driver Cambray in charge, had to tackle a thirteen-coach load of 465 tons gross. After a leisurely recovery from a signal check at Woking, some notable work was done with this load from Farnborough to Hook, speed rising eventually to 83 m.p.h. before the 5-mile 1 in 249 ascent from milepost 46 to Battledown, which brought it down to 61½ m.p.h. From here the finish was unspectacular, and before the Salisbury stop there was a signal check, but the arrival was 1¼ min. early, in a total time of 81 min. 40 sec. and a net of 78½ min. The present 80-min. schedule leaves little to spare with this train.

West of Salisbury the Southern Region possesses the most steeply graded main line in Great Britain over which, owing to its admirable alignment, almost unrestricted speed is possible. This switchback includes some lengthy gradients, culminating in the 7-mile climb to Honiton summit (milepost 153½), 4½ miles of which right off are inclined at 1 in 80. Express trains which make intermediate stops have some difficult starts, as, for example, westbound from Templecombe up 1 in 100, or eastbound from Sherborne at the same grade, soon steepening to 1 in 80; the faster-timed non-stopping trains, such as the 'Atlantic Coast Express', depend to a considerable extent on the impetus from high speed downhill to carry them up the succeeding ascents.

There is a nominal limit of 85 m.p.h. throughout, of which the drivers on the first and third runs tabulated took a liberal view; but the first run in Table VII (D) was of great interest in showing that a 'Merchant Navy' Pacific, notwithstanding driving wheels of no more than 6 ft 2 in. diameter, can reach the three-figure level of speed. All three runs were timed by the Rev. J. E. T. Phillips, who is an experienced recorder closely acquainted with this line, and each was an astonishing performance.

On the run with the 100-m.p.h. maximum speed, No. 35012 *United States Lines* made an unusually slow start to Wilton with a ten-coach train, but then recovered well, accelerating up gradually rising grades to 75 m.p.h. at Tisbury, and not falling below 69 up the 2 miles at 1 in 145 to Semley. A maximum of 90 m.p.h. at Gillingham was followed by the long-continued and severe slowing for the Buckhorn Weston tunnel reconstruction. From this there was a lightning acceleration to reach 80 m.p.h. at Abbey Ford, and 2½ miles at

TABLE VII (G)
THE BULLEID PACIFICS – LEADING DIMENSIONS

Type	'Merchant Navy'		'West Country'	
	As built	As rebuilt	As built	As rebuilt
Cylinders (3), diameter . .	18 in.	18 in.	16¾ in.	16¾ in.
,, stroke . .	24 in.	24 in.	24 in.	24 in.
Wheels, driving, diameter	6 ft 2 in.	6 ft 2 in.	6 ft 2 in.	6 ft 2 in.
,, bogie, ,, .	3 ft 1 in.	3 ft 1 in.	3 ft 1 in.	3 ft 1 in.
,, trailing, ,, .	3 ft 7 in.	3 ft 7 in.	3 ft 1 in.	3 ft 1 in.
Wheelbase, coupled .	15 ft 0 in.	15 ft 0 in.	14 ft 9 in.	14 ft 9 in.
,, total engine .	36 ft 9 in.	36 ft 9 in.	35 ft 6 in.	35 ft 6 in.
Heating surface, tubes and flues	2,176 sq ft	2,176 sq ft	1,869 sq ft	1,869 sq ft
,, ,, firebox and syphons .	275 sq ft	275 sq ft	253 sq ft	253 sq ft
,, ,, total . .	2,451 sq ft	2,451 sq ft	2,122 sq ft	2,122 sq ft
Superheating surface . .	822 sq ft	612 sq ft	545 sq ft	488 sq ft
Firegrate area . . .	48·5 sq ft	48·5 sq ft	38·25 sq ft	38·25 sq ft
Boiler pressure, per sq in. .	280 lb	250 lb	280 lb	250 lb
Tractive effort (85 per cent b.p.)	37,500 lb	33,495 lb	31,000 lb	27,720 lb
Adhesion weight . . .	63·00 tons	64·90 tons	56·25 tons	58·30 tons
Total engine weight (working order	94·75 tons	97·90 tons	86·00 tons	90·05 tons

TENDERS

No.	1	2	3	4
Water capacity . . .	6,000 gal.	5,500 gal.	5,000 gal.	4,500 gal.
Coal ,, . . .	5 tons	5 tons	5 tons	5 tons
Weight full	53·30 tons	47·25 tons	*49·35 tons	42·60 tons

* First ten built, 47·80 tons.
Note: No. 1 type was built for Nos. 35021–35030; No. 2 for Nos. 34071–34090; No. 3 for Nos. 35001–35020; and No. 4 for Nos. 34001–34070 and 34091–34110. Various changes have since taken place in the allocation of these tenders.

A striking impression of one of the rebuilt 'West Country' Pacifics in its rebuilt form – No. 34031 Torrington *with the typical combined coat-of-arms and nameplate now carried by these engines.*

[*B. A. Haresnape*

At full speed through Winchester with a down Bournemouth express of post-war Bulleid stock, rebuilt 'West Country' 4-6-2 No. 34053 Sir Keith Park.

[*Bryan H. Kimber*

No. 70000 Britannia, *first of the standard Class 7 Pacific type of British Railways, and the first locomotive of any type to be built to a British Railways design.* [*British Railways*

Waiting at Carlisle Citadel to take over an express from Euston to Perth – 'Britannia' *Pacific No.* 70050 Firth of Clyde, *one of the series built for Scottish Region use.* [*Eric Treacy*

Above, with their 6 ft 2 in. driving wheels, the 'Britannia' Pacifics rank as in the 'mixed traffic' category. No. 70011 Hotspur is here seen on a Class F fast freight train on the Great Eastern Line. [P. M. Alexander

Left, with feed-water heating equipment: No. 70043 Lord Kitchener after arrival at Euston with the 'Mancunian', London Midland Region. [H. Gordon Tidey

Below, approaching Colchester with a down 'Clacton Interval' express, Great Eastern Line – No. 70030 William Wordsworth. [K. L. Cook

Above, Canton, Cardiff, is the only Western Region depot that has handled 'Britannia' Pacifics with success. No. 70025 Western Star *passing Wapley Common at speed with the down 'Capitals Limited' express.* [G. F. Heiron

Below, No. 70028 Royal Star *at the head of an up South Wales express in Sonning cutting. After the Milton accident the handrails have been removed from the side of the smoke deflectors to give better visibility.* [C. J. Blay

The use of 'Britannias' on the Western Lines of the Southern Region was but brief. No. 70009 Alfred the Great *heads the 'Bournemouth Belle' Pullman past Battledown flyover on the down journey.* [E. D. Bruton

'Britannias' *stationed at Stewarts Lane depot, Southern Region, did some good work with the 'Golden Arrow' Pullman. No. 70014* Iron Duke *is approaching Tonbridge on the down journey.* [R. A. Panting

No. *72009* Clan Stewart, *one of the ten standard Class 6 Pacifics of British Railways.*

Class 6 Pacific No. 72007 Clan Mackintosh *climbing Beattock Bank with the 9.50 a.m. from Euston to Perth. That so light a load should need a 'banker' is evidence of the poor steaming of these 4-6-2s.*

[*W. J. V. Anderson*

No. 71000 Duke of Gloucester, *the only Class 8 Pacific built under the auspices of British Railways. It differs from a 'Britannia' in having three cylinders, a double chimney and poppet-valve motion.*

[*British Railways*

Under test on the Western Region – No. 71000 Duke of Gloucester, *with indicating shelter, running into Westbury with an 18-coach train.*

[*G. Wheeler*

Climbing the 1 in 75 to Shap Summit – No. 71000 Duke of Gloucester with a special relief train, made up of Eastern Region stock, from Birmingham to Glasgow.

[Derek Cross

VIII

THE STANDARD PACIFICS, BRITISH RAILWAYS

1 – *The Principles of Design*

THE fusion of the railways of Britain into a single nationalized system, at the beginning of 1948, found the various Regions in general well supplied with express passenger power, but certain sections, the Great Eastern main lines of the Eastern Region for one, were in need, if their services were to be accelerated, of something more powerful than they possessed at that time. In the interests of economy, standardization of new types for the whole country obviously was desirable, with dimensions and weight so planned as to give each new type the widest possible range of action. At first ten new types were proposed, seven tender engines and three tanks, and of these two were to have the Pacific wheel arrangement; a third and larger Pacific was added later, and also a 2-8-2 freight type, for which eventually a 2-10-0 was substituted.

The principles underlying the new designs were set out in a paper read before the Institution of Locomotive Engineers in 1951 by E. S. Cox, at that time Executive Officer (Design) to the Railway Executive Committee. On the basis of Ivatt's renowned *dictum* that the measure of a locomotive's success is its 'capacity to boil water', each type must achieve the utmost in steam production permitted by its weight and dimensions. Simplicity must be an aim, with the least possible number of working parts, and all readily visible and accessible. Bearing performance should be on the highest possible level, by the use of roller bearings where these were financially justified, and otherwise by fitting manganese steel liners to generously proportioned plain bearings.

Shed preparation should be simplified by increased use of mechanical lubricators and grease lubrication, and shed disposal by means of self-cleaning smokeboxes, rocking grates, and self-emptying ashpans. The highest practicable adhesion factors, sensitive regulator control and efficient sanding gear should provide the maximum protection against slipping. Finally, within these requirements, large firegrate areas to promote low rates of combustion, high degree superheat and long-lap valve-motions should play their parts in promoting a high overall thermal efficiency in performance.

Now it might have been expected that as the member of the Railway Executive responsible for mechanical engineering, R. A. Riddles, and the officers for locomotive design, E. S. Cox, and for building and maintenance, R. C. Bond, had all been drawn from the former London Midland & Scottish Railway, the new designs would lean towards the existing L.M.S.R. locomotive

195

practice, which they certainly did. Moreover, so far as the Pacifics were concerned, designing at Derby Works and building at Crewe Works might have made the bias in the L.M.S.R. direction even more pronounced. But the declared intention of the locomotive exchange trials between the Regions in 1948, the first year of nationalization, had been to compare the performances of various types, both express and passenger, mixed traffic and freight, in every possible variety of service, and from these comparisons to obtain some guide as to the best constructional details from each Region to incorporate in the new designs.

Even if to a limited extent only, this happened. To the new Pacific designs the Southern Railway contributed the trailing truck, the frames central with welded horns, the three-compartment ashpan, the engine and tender draw-gear and the tyre fastening. Among London & North Eastern contributions were the three-bar slidebars and crosshead, the piston-rod packing, the little-end lubrication and other details; incidentally, this type of piston-rod packing was first developed by J. A. Hookham on the former North Stafford-shire Railway. From Great Western practice there were taken the mechanical lubrication, cylinder relief valves, smokebox door, brick arch, fusible plug and various minor fittings. London Midland & Scottish practice certainly predominated, including complete bogies, engine spring suspension, con-necting-rod big-ends, firedoors, ashpan hoppers and doors, rocking-grates, water pick-up gear, and a number of other details, some of which, however, had previously been Swindon practice introduced to the L.M.S.R. by Sir William Stanier.

Each of the main locomotive works – Derby, Doncaster, Swindon and Brighton – was made responsible for the design of one or more of the standard types (Derby, as already mentioned, for the Pacifics), but it was laid down as a principle that all the new engines should have the closest possible 'family' resemblance, and that as far as possible standard fittings settled by the Locomotive Standards Committee should be common to all. Each works was entrusted with the design of specific parts for new classes – Derby with bogies, trucks, wheels, tyres, axles and spring gear; Doncaster with coupling and connecting-rods, valve-gears and cylinder details; Swindon with boiler and smokebox details and steam fittings; and Brighton with brake gear and sanding gear. While certain of the smaller standard designs were based on existing locomotive classes, the Pacifics in the main were new designs through-out.

What all this meant to the design staffs was the subject of this comment by E. S. Cox in his paper: 'Those who are experienced in design will realize, of course, that such arrangements would not just happen as a result of even the most carefully worded instructions, and not only was a high and continuous degree of collaboration called for from all concerned, but more than that, an exceptional measure of goodwill was needed and was forthcoming from design staffs, many if not most of whom were required to work in an idiom quite foreign to their previous experience.'

So it was that when the first of the new 4-6-2s, No. 70000 *Britannia*, left

Crewe Works at the beginning of 1951, it was not merely seen externally to be quite an original production, but also was found to embody quite a number of novel features. The 'Britannia' design, in power class '7', was intended for the same class of work as that performed by Eastern and North Eastern Region Class 'V2' 2-6-2s, London Midland Region 4-6-0 'Royal Scots', Western Region 4-6-0 'Castles', and Southern Region 'West Country' Pacifics. The lighter 'Clan' Pacific design, in power class '6', was to be the equal in power of the L.M.S.R. 'Jubilee' 4-6-0s, and was intended to be suitable for service over various Scottish lines, to which the first ten of this type were to be allocated, and in England on such main lines as those of the Great Central section of the Eastern Region.

The heavy Pacific, No. 71000 of Class '8', did not emerge from Crewe until 1954, by which time the shadow of diesel traction, then sweeping over the United States, was beginning to fall here also. Consequently No. 71000 was the sole example of this class ever built; of the 'Clan' Pacifics, the least successful of the British Railways standard designs, ten only took the rails; but the 'Britannia' Pacifics were built eventually to a total of fifty-five engines, and have done some very fine work.

2 – The 'Britannias', Class '7'

THE first surprise in the design of the new 'Britannia' Pacific was to find that propulsion was to be by two cylinders and not three or four, seeing that with the multi-cylinder arrangement hammer-blow on the track at high speeds can be largely eliminated. In 1928 the Bridge Stress Committee, after a series of tests that had shown up some two-cylinder express locomotive types very badly in this respect, had made a recommendation that at a driving-wheel speed of five revolutions per second the axle hammer-blow should not exceed one-quarter of the static load, with a maximum of 5 tons, and that the entire engine hammer-blow should not be in excess of $12\frac{1}{2}$ tons.

Now whereas with three-cylinder and four-cylinder engines it had become generally agreed that reciprocating balance could be dispensed with, two-cylinder engines required it to the extent of at least 40 per cent of the weight of the reciprocating parts. However, with the use of lighter motion parts, it was found possible with the 'Britannia' design, if two cylinders were used, to limit the hammer-blow per wheel to 2·12 tons, per axle to 2·55 tons, per rail to 5·50 tons and for the whole engine to 6·60 tons, or roughly half the maxima regarded as permissible in the Bridge Stress Committee's report.

The gains achieved by two-cylinder as against multi-cylinder propulsion were simplicity and accessibility of motion parts; the elimination of a cranked axle and a split inside big-end, the former expensive in first cost and maintenance and the latter a source of trouble at high speeds unless an exceptionally high standard of maintenance is possible; and also better steaming with four exhausts per revolution than with six, which E. S. Cox claimed to have been proved by experience. He also maintained that although theoretically three-cylinder and four-cylinder engines should be better starters than those with two cylinders only, this was not observable in practice. Lastly there was the purely financial consideration that to have provided the 'Britannias' with three cylinders instead of two would have put the first cost up by £1,000 per engine, while at the same time adding 3½ tons to the weight, increasing the preparation time for each day's work by at least one-third, and increasing repair costs in proportion to the number of additional parts required.

A second cause for surprise was that the new Pacific, although a double blastpipe and chimney had been intended originally, appeared without these. The explanation of this decision given by E. S. Cox in his paper was that a series of tests on both the Rugby and Swindon testing plants had shown that special blastpipe arrangements designed to produce a higher vacuum in the smokebox for a given back pressure at maximum power output give inferior performance at low outputs, and are not therefore so versatile as the normal single blastpipe through the whole output range.

In view of the varied types of service for which the 'Britannias' were intended, and for which they were classed specifically as 'mixed traffic' engines, it was realized that most of their work would be done at relatively moderate outputs of power; hence the decision to retain the single blastpipe and chimney. These were so admirably proportioned that, as has been proved both by the Rugby and the road tests of the completed engines, and by some of their outstanding performances in day-to-day service, as set out in Section 4 of this chapter, there has been no limitation of 'Britannia' power output in consequence.

Considerable attention was devoted to the matter of free steaming. To obtain a higher degree of superheat, the flue tubes were increased in diameter to 5½ in., the biggest diameter ever tried in Great Britain. In this way the free gas area from firebox to smokebox was increased to 6·79 sq ft, a figure exceeded only by the 6·89 sq ft of the much larger London Midland 'Duchess' Pacifics. In the percentage of free gas area to grate area, however, the 'Britannia's' 16·2 per cent was a long way ahead of the 13·8 per cent of the 'Duchess'; only the L.M.R. rebuilt 'Royal Scot' 4-6-os and the Class '5' 4-6-os show higher percentages, 16·3 and 16·6 respectively.

For 20 in. by 28 in. cylinders, 11 in. diameter piston-valves and ports 2¼ in. wide provided for a high cylinder output; and steam flow was assisted to the maximum by large diameter steam passages and by designing the steam chests in such a way that their volume between the valve-heads was as large as half the swept volume of the pistons in the cylinders. Provision was made for a maximum cut-off in fore gear of 77½ per cent, to help in starting, and as a result the valve travel in full gear was nearly 7¾ in., with a steam lap of 1 $\frac{11}{16}$ in. and a lead of ¼ in. A high maximum cut-off is of little value in starting if an engine is prone to slipping, as in that event it cannot exert its full piston effort. To control the tendency to slip, the adhesion factor was kept in the 'Britannias' to a minimum of 4·23; and to give further assistance each pair of coupled wheels was provided with sanders in the forward direction, while the sandboxes themselves were fitted with steam coils, so that they might be able to deliver dry sand in all conditions. Unfortunately this desirable result was not attained, and the steam coils were removed later.

The decision to use driving wheels of 6 ft 2 in. diameter accorded with the conception of the 'Britannias' as engines of the 'mixed traffic' type. Nevertheless the performances of the L.N.E.R. 'V2' 2-6-2s, the L.M.S.R. Class '5' 4-6-0s, and, above all, of the S.R. Bulleid Pacifics, had shown that with modern front-end design, and in particular the freedom of exhaust with long-lap, long-travel valves, speeds up to 90 m.p.h. and even over could be readily attained with coupled wheels of 6 ft to 6 ft 2 in. diameter, so that the new 4-6-2s were well suited to high-speed passenger working.

To avoid, if possible, the trouble with frame fractures that had been experienced with not a few modern locomotive types, the Bulleid practice of placing the frames centrally over the horns – made possible by the fact that the firebox was carried above the frames and not between them – was followed, and with this the central mounting also of the hanger brackets. It is interesting in this connection to recall that originally bar frames were proposed, which would have been a radical departure from normal British practice; but the idea was abandoned as the various building plants of British Railways were not equipped to handle and machine lengthy box castings of this description, and because their use would increase both weight and cost.

Very careful attention was paid to springing and lubrication; in regard to the latter, Swindon practice, which had been developed to a high pitch of efficiency, was largely followed, with mechanical lubricators feeding through steam atomisers. Soft grease lubrication, serviced by shed staffs with power-operated grease-pumps, was provided for various motion parts not requiring to be lubricated with oil. Roller-bearing axleboxes were provided throughout, and manganese steel liners to the faces of both hornblocks and adjacent axlebox surfaces of all coupled axleboxes, to assist in increasing to the maximum the periods between complete overhauls. To simplify shed work, all the 'Britannias' were fitted with rocking grates, self-emptying ashpans and self-cleaning smokeboxes.

It is safe to say that in no previous British locomotive design had the ease of handling by enginemen and their comfort on the footplate been studied with the thoroughness that was applied to the new standard designs, and which first appeared in No. 70000 *Britannia*. In the previous year a full-size 'mock-up' had been prepared of the cab layout, and had been inspected by motive-power superintendents, running-shed foremen, union representatives and a number of drivers. Their opinions were invited, and certain modifications resulted, but in the main the original mock-up was faithfully copied in the new engines. The principal object was to bring all the controls within easy reach of the driver in his seated position, to enable him to operate them without taking his eyes off the road ahead, and at the same time to group all the fittings under the control of the fireman conveniently on his side of the cab.

A new type of reversing gear control had been evolved, with the operating wheel arranged longitudinally instead of transversely – and thus much easier to manipulate from the driver's position – and with an easily-read barrel-type cut-off indicator. A novelty adding greatly to the fireman's comfort was the extension of the cab floor right back to the tender front, giving him a firm floor on which to work and doing away with the customary fall-plate from the tender front. Most of the steam-pipes and valves were kept outside the cab, so helping to keep down the temperature of the latter and also improving the accessibility of this piping to maintenance staffs; the cab roof extended back to the tender front, giving very complete protection from the weather, and a sliding roof provided for cooler travel in summer.

An admirable look-out in the forward direction was provided, with angled windows to avoid glare; both they and the side windows could be opened to permit cleaning from the inside of the cab. A partition was provided on the tender front, extending upwards to the cab roof level, and with windows on both sides to give a good lookout when running backwards. The comfort of the crew was studied even to the extent of providing them with a cupboard for food lined with stainless steel, and with double doors to exclude dirt. The cab itself was mounted on the boiler instead of on the main frame, in order to eliminate movements between the one and the other, and to enable the cab front and the floorboards to fit snugly up to the boiler.

Thus the aims set out at the beginning of Section 1 of this chapter had been largely achieved. But it would be idle to deny that the accessibility of working parts to shed staffs, for speedy inspection, maintenance and repair, had been at the expense of appearance. At a time when a country like France had been striving in a measure to improve the lines of its steam locomotives, as evidenced in the big 4-6-4s built for the Northern Region, we had gone in the opposite direction. *Britannia* was an impressive-looking machine, but hardly beautiful; the very high running-plate, well above the coupled wheels, finishing at the middle of the cab front, and the numerous pipes and parts distributed over her exterior, as well as a distinctly ugly tender, together embodied a new decline in British locomotive lines. However, 'handsome is as handsome does'; and on this basis of assessment the 'Britannias' have certainly proved a credit to the design staffs concerned.

Building of 'Britannia' class Pacifics continued from the emergence of No. 70000 *Britannia* in January 1951; twenty-five were completed in that year, twenty more in 1953, and the final 10, concluding with No. 70054 *Dornoch Firth*, in 1954, making fifty-five in all. The names of these engines are about the most extraordinarily mixed bag of any individual locomotive class in Great Britain. The first, *Britannia*, was intended both to have a typically British flavour and also to commemorate the Festival of Britain. Next came No. 70001 *Lord Hurcomb*, in honour of the first Chairman of the British Transport Commission. Following him were five British *litterateurs*, from *John Bunyan* at one extreme to *Geoffrey Chaucer* at the other; these were Nos. 70002 to 70006 inclusive. From No. 70007 to 70014 came famous names of early British history; then, as Nos. 70015 to 70029 were destined for the Western Region, past Great Western Railway names were revived, including six 'Stars'.

After this, poets and writers came into the picture once again, from No. 70030 to No. 70035, and then some more historical British characters, from *Boadicea* to *Clive of India* and *Sir John Moore*; this took the numbers to 70040. Up to No. 70048 the military of later years now had a look in, with *Lord Roberts*, *Lord Kitchener* and *Earl Haig*, together with the Scouts – *Lord Rowallan* – and, in odd association, *Anzac* and *The Territorial Army 1908– 1958*. Bringing up the rear of this singularly assorted procession came Nos. 70049 to 70054. named after Scottish waterways from *Solway Firth* to *Dornoch Firth*. The last-named were intended for Scottish service, but like the others with Regional names are being dispersed in various directions.

Perhaps the most distinguished of all the 'Britannias' has been No. 70004 *William Shakespeare*, one of the only two of the class ever stationed for any length of time in the Southern Region. Attached to Stewarts Lane shed, it was the engine allocated to the 'Golden Arrow', and the superb condition in which it was maintained during this period of service was both a striking advertisement to our Continental visitors of the best in British locomotive practice, and also a tribute to the keenness and ability of the Stewarts Lane shed staff at that time.

3 – The 'Britannias' on Test

AMPLE proof of the success of the first standard design of British Railways was provided when the Locomotive Testing Committee set about the official testing of 'Britannias'. At intervals between April, 1951, and February, 1953, these tests were conducted on the Rugby plant and also over the mountainous Midland main line between Skipton and Carlisle. The first 4-6-2 tested was No. 70005 *John Milton*, after it had been in traffic for no more than 560 miles subsequent to its emergence from Crewe Works; it ran the equivalent of 6,890 miles at Rugby and about 5,000 miles in the road tests. The second locomotive subjected to test, in this case on the Rugby plant only, was the pioneer of the second series built, No. 70025 *Western Star*, which embodied certain minor modifications as the result of experience; in this case the equivalent of 6,350 miles was run.

The maximum steaming capacity of the boiler not merely proved to be something far in excess of any normal demands made by British timetables, even with Class '8' Pacifics, but also well beyond the ability of any single fireman to fire manually. At one stage on the road tests, No. 70005 was producing steam at the extraordinary rate of 37,560 lb per hour, and the ability of the engine was such that, as compared with the scheduled maximum of 420 tare tons for Class '7' engines working trains between Carlisle and Skipton on 'limited load' timings, the test loads were made up to the equivalent of nearly twice this figure – 850 tons – by the addition of two mobile testing units with their dynamic braking. The duration of each test on the road varied from 60 to 75 min., of which from 50 to 55 min. was at the higher rates of output and 45 min. at the maximum rate. On the Rugby testing plant the durations were from 90 to 140 min., including 70 min. at maximum output. In the latter case steam was being supplied to the cylinders at an average rate of 31,610 lb per hour, which also required the services of two firemen.

Details were given in the report of part of one southbound run from Carlisle, with the equivalent 850-ton train (the actual weight was 420 tons plus the mobile testing units). No. 70005 ran the 22·85 miles from Lazonby up to Crosby Garrett in 29 min. 15 sec., mostly at 40 to 45 per cent cut-off with full regulator, but at one point lengthened to 59 per cent; this proved a little too much for adhesion, however, and the engine began to slip. Later, however, the long 1 in 100–162 up from Ormside was surmounted on 50 to 55 per cent cut-off without any slipping, and drawbar horsepowers up to 2,200 and even 2,300 were measured – remarkable figures for an engine rated at no more than the Class '7' power category. At the moment of slipping the drawbar pull had just reached 10 tons; incidentally, the engine showed a greater tendency to slip at high power outputs on the testing-plant than on the road.

Coal was being fired at an average rate of 5,600 lb (2½ tons) per hour, and water was being used at 36,150 lb (3,615 gal.) per hour. The lowest speed on the 1 in 100 was 35 m.p.h.; but the report gives no details as to the behaviour of the engine on the 9 miles of almost continuous 1 in 100 from Smardale Viaduct past Kirkby Stephen to Ais Gill summit. On another run, with an actual train weight of 468 tons and an equivalent tonnage of 540, No. 70005 cut the time from Lazonby to Crosby Garrett to 28 min. 10 sec., but in much easier conditions of working, at 24 to 27 per cent cut-off for most of the climb, and 26 to 31 from Ormside to Crosby Garrett; at the foot of this steep stretch speed was 64 m.p.h., and it had fallen to 40 m.p.h. at the end of the 4½ miles. The firing rate on this run was 3,360 lb (1½ tons) per hour, but with Blidworth coal of 12,600 B.T.Us. as compared with the South Kirkby coal of 14,000 B.T.Us. used on the previous test. The water consumption on this second test averaged 22,400 lb per hour.

Throughout the tests the Davies & Metcalfe Class 'K' 11-mm. exhaust steam injector with which the 'Britannias' are fitted was able to feed up to 2,200 gallons of water per hour to the boiler, and as compared with the Western Region Type 11X live steam injector could effect an economy in coal consumption ranging from 6½ per cent to 9 per cent when working to capacity. The live steam injector, however, would deliver water up to the limit of the boiler's steaming capacity. On the whole, the designing staff had every reason to be satisfied with the results of these tests, which would appear to have been so far above normal Class '7' standards as to justify the promotion of the new Pacifics to Class '8'.

4 – Defects and their Correction

THREE years after the paper by E. S. Cox on the standard locomotive designs, presented to the Institution of Locomotive Engineers in 1951 and referred to in Section 1 of this chapter, he read a second paper to the Institution in March 1954, entitled 'Experiences with British Railways Standard Locomotives'. Of this the most interesting part was that dealing with mechanical performance, with its revelation of the teething troubles that had been experienced, and which by then for the most part had been overcome. 'In common with development work generally', he remarked, 'features which were adopted in fear and trembling have never given a moment's anxiety, and others thought from past experience to be as reliable as a rock have proved to be shifting sands indeed.'

The first trouble was the breakage of cast iron piston-heads, several cases occurring in quick succession on No. 70000 *Britannia*. The source of the trouble was located in the dome, where the level of the steam intake was no more than $11\frac{3}{4}$ in. above the water level at the top of the gauge-glass. Surges of the water in the boiler when starting and stopping, as well as over-filling of the boilers, was resulting in water being carried down to the cylinders in excessive amounts. By relatively simple alterations to the dome, the height of the intake was raised from the $11\frac{3}{4}$ in. just mentioned to $16\frac{1}{2}$ in.; also the interim precaution of substituting cast steel piston-heads for those of cast iron, with a slightly increased clearance between head and cylinder bore, was made standard. The new type of piston-head was one first introduced on the L.N.E.R. by Gresley, the light forged steel head being welded on to the piston-rod.

The next casualty was more serious. In July, 1951, No. 70014 *Iron Duke* had to be taken out of service because all the coupled wheels had shifted on their axles, and within a short time six other 'Britannias' had failed in the same way, with the additional complication of bent rods. All twenty-five engines of the class then in service had to be withdrawn until the cause of the failure had been diagnosed and a remedy had been applied. It was evidently related to the roller bearings, and light was shed on the investigation by the fact that between 1947 and 1950 there had been similar failures, seven in number, with roller-bearing-equipped London Midland & Scottish Class '5' 4-6-0s. In the latter case, as the failures had taken place at widely separated intervals over this period of four years, and no similar trouble had been experienced with the other twenty-five 4-6-0s similarly fitted, no special steps of a curative nature had been taken. It was of particular interest that all the Class '5' failures, as with the 'Britannias', had been on engines which had run low mileages only after construction.

Various factors were regarded as having contributed to these failures. One was that during assembly the roller bearing must pass over the wheel seat, which had therefore to be of smaller diameter than the journal (the opposite of the practice with plain bearings), so that the gripping surface at the wheel seat was reduced. A second was that the relatively soft plain bearing, with its essential clearances, offered a slight cushioning effect when impact forces were applied, whereas the roller bearing was relatively unyielding. A third was that alterations had been made in the traditional design of the keys helping to secure the wheels to the axles, and that as compared with the precise but laborious former methods of hand-fitting the keys, short cuts were being taken in workshop methods which were not of advantage to the keying.

A fourth factor was that, as the quartering of crank-pin holes and the balancing of wheel sets could not be carried out after the roller bearings were in position on the axles, with the workshop equipment then in use, it had become the practice to press the wheels with a light load on to a dummy axle for this work to be done, then to press them off and re-press on to the axle proper, which might result in a slightly easier fit on the latter than desirable. Finally, to compensate for the increased weight of the roller bearings, it had become the practice to save weight by boring a $4\frac{1}{2}$-in. diameter hole through the length of each axle, which contributed further to the marginal condition between adequate tightness of wheels on axles and the reverse. Some of the 'Britannias' had run 50,000 miles without trouble, including No. 70005 *John Milton*, which had undergone the strenuous tests described in Section 3 of this chapter; but for safety's sake all twenty-five of the class then in service underwent the same remedial measures, and though there have been similar failures since, they have been comparatively rare.

Experience with the wheels suggested some weakness in the coupling-rod design, and the original fluted rods, with flanges $2\frac{1}{4}$ in. wide and webs $\frac{3}{8}$ in. thick, varying in depth from $4\frac{1}{4}$ in. to 5 in., were replaced by rods of rectangular section, $1\frac{5}{8}$ in. thick and from $4\frac{1}{2}$ in. to $5\frac{1}{2}$ in. deep. No change was made from the use of plain carbon steel of up to 40 tons per sq in. tensile quality, and again no further trouble was experienced.

The next matter to be tackled was the pronounced fore-and-aft motion imparted by the 'Britannias' (and by all the other new standard types also) to their trains. This was an old problem. As the paper pointed out, 4-6-0 engines of 75 tons weight or so had worked satisfactorily in the past with some 30 to 50 per cent reciprocating balance, whereas in other exceptional cases 70 to 85 per cent had been needed, with a most undesirable increase in hammer-blow at speed, in order to reduce the discomfort of passengers in the leading coaches of a train. The trouble was traced to the amount of initial compression in the tender drawbar spring; this was then altered to ensure that in coupling up the drawhook would be pulled off its stop, against the compression of the buffers (even when engine and train were at rest), and the trouble disappeared.

Cracks in frame-plates which appeared on a number of the engines at the point of attachment of the spring hanger brackets were cured by a redesign of the latter. Three roller bearings on different 'Britannias' collapsed through water having got in and caused corrosion, and in other cases the leaking out of lubricant caused some trouble, but with co-operation from the makers these difficulties were surmounted. Troubles with front-end lubrication were mostly connected with shortage of oil, due to the mechanical lubricators having been set in such a way as to provide insufficient flow, or to the rate of delivery not having corresponded with the setting, or for other reasons.

The 'Britannias' on the Great Eastern Line had a good record for valve wear and for clean valves, but this was not the case on the Western Region, whose 'Britannias' suffered from carbonization, with consequent difficulty in withdrawing the valves. In the latter case, handling by drivers was at fault; they were not allowing a little steam through the cylinders when coasting, with the result that hot gases were being drawn down the blastpipe into the steam-chest. To control this matter by automatic means entirely would have been difficult; only the education of drivers in proper methods of handling when coasting could achieve what was needed.

An early complaint by engine-crews with the 'Britannias' was the draughtiness of the cabs. To some extent this was cured temporarily by the provision of canvas screens, but later and more effectively by rubber fairings between engine and tender. The driver's position at first was uncomfortably hot, but this was remedied by better lagging of certain steam-pipes and other expedients. Objection was also made to fixed front windows, which could not be cleaned from the inside of the cab, and these were replaced by hinged windows. While the riding of the 'Britannias' was excellent laterally, in the vertical plane they proved at first to be very hard-riding, with tiring effects on the feet, particularly of the firemen; some improvement has been effected since, however, in their riding qualities.

One of the most interesting points about this paper by E. S. Cox was the commentary at its conclusion, with the support of diagrams and tables in the paper, which showed that whether with two or more cylinders, larger or smaller driving wheels, wide or narrow grates, and even through considerable variations in back pressure, the boiler efficiencies and relative performances of the best British, French, German and American steam-locomotive types were so closely alike that the ultimate in design on traditional lines might well appear to have been reached.

5 – The 'Britannias' in Service

BRITISH driving conservatism being what it is, the 'Britannia' Pacifics had a mixed reception when first they took the road. But in one part of the country there was no doubt whatever as to the warmth with which they were welcomed; it was the area to which thirteen of the first fifteen were drafted – the Great Eastern Line of the Eastern Region. On most lines, when more powerful locomotives take the road, the advance is seldom more than from one power class to the next above it. But on the Great Eastern the sudden leap from the Class '4P' of the 'B12' 4-6-0s and the Class '5P' of the 'B1' and 'B17' 4-6-0s to the Class '7MT' of the 4-6-2s was an almost unbelievable advance, and the G.E. men took to their new mounts with enthusiasm.

With the engines came the new timetables, embodying radical accelerations and requiring higher speeds than ever before on G.E. metals, and the excellence to which the track had been brought not only made such speeds possible in comfort, but introduced engine-crews to the exhilaration of fast running of a kind that they had probably never even dreamed of previously. Indeed, in the first year or two of 'Britannia' running, the Great Eastern boasted some of the fastest scheduled runs in the country, and, at this period of post-war recovery, a higher average speed between Liverpool Street and Norwich than over such speedways as those of the London Midland Region from Euston to Birmingham or the Western Region from Paddington to Bristol. And before very long the first Great Eastern mile-a-minute schedules on record were beginning to appear in the timetables, with allowances of 44 min. only for the hilly 46·25 miles from Ipswich to Norwich and 45 min. in the reverse direction.

An article by 'Balmore' in the 1958 *Trains Annual* gave an interesting survey of the early Great Eastern experience with the 'Britannias'. For some time previously Great Eastern drivers had been encouraged to work their engines with full regulator whenever possible, and thus to make maximum use of the expansive properties of the steam; and this practice was soon found to pay with the new Pacifics. Some of the 4-6-2s, indeed, could run even the fastest trains over the easier sections of the Norwich main line at from 10 to 12 per cent cut-off. It was only when not steaming well that the 'Britannias' proved difficult to handle; with wet, small coal and the tube ends becoming furred over, enginemen at times have been in considerable difficulties when the pressure has dropped below 180 lb, even the blower having little effect in such conditions. But this has been the exception rather than the rule.

Maintenance at both Stratford and Norwich sheds was kept at a high level, and although most of the engines were rostered to make the double journey between Liverpool Street and Norwich twice in the day, as far as possible the manning of each 'Britannia' was kept to not more than three crews, whose pride in their charges was helpful both to maintenance and to performance. With mileages up to 460 and more a day, the engines have run up to 10,000 miles a month, and have averaged at least 7,000 miles; the target mileage between complete overhauls has been 140,000 miles and one 'Britannia' Pacific at least has reached 146,000 miles. In the ten years from May, 1951, No. 70006 *Robert Burns*, stationed at Norwich, covered a total of 737,916 miles on Great Eastern metals, and six others of the class all exceeded 700,000 miles in the same period. The longest daily turn during the later 'Britannia' years on the Great Eastern Line has been one from Parkeston Quay to Sheffield and back with the 'North Country Continental', preceded and followed by fast freight workings between Parkeston Quay and Good-mayes Yard; this has totalled 505 miles in the 24 hours, excluding light running. 'Britannia' availability on the Great Eastern has been in the region of 85 per cent.

In normal running conditions a saucer-shaped fire, thin over most of the firegrate but higher at the sides and especially under the door and at the back corners, has proved the best method of firing unless anything over 30 per cent cut-off has been in use. The 'Britannia' firedoor is fitted with a hinged flap, which restricts the air passing into the firebox through the firehole; skilful firemen have learned when necessary to fire over this flap, and have found this ability of no small help when using poor coal or when for any reason one of the engines has not been steaming well. Also the cab is kept cleaner when the flap is in position.

With careful handling, the 'Britannias' are not prone to slip on starting. At a certain period in 1954, however, No. 70039 *Sir Christopher Wren* developed some very curious slipping propensities on the Great Eastern Line. On a dry rail the engine would normally keep its feet, but in wet weather it would suddenly develop a violent slip at a speed of round about 55 m.p.h., when the cut-off was fixed at 20 to 25 per cent and the steam-chest pressure was anything from 80 to 200 lb per sq in. At times the slipping was so violent as to compel the use of the brakes to bring it under control. After the most careful checking of valves, regulator and weight distribution, nothing amiss was discovered; and it was surmised that the trouble might be due to a temporary sticking of the axleboxes in their guides, which relieved the normal loads on the coupled wheels and so reduced the adhesion. No. 70039 was therefore returned to Doncaster Works, where this diagnosis was confirmed; a little more clearance was therefore provided in the axlebox horns, and no further slipping of this kind was experienced. At a later date similar trouble was experienced with No. 70005 *John Milton* and No. 70036 *Boadicea*, in each case after general overhaul at Doncaster Works, and the same attention had to be given at Doncaster to put matters right.

The 'Britannias' have had their share of mishaps, and of these the worst was that which befell No. 70026 *Polar Star* when working a Western Region excursion train from Treherbert to Paddington one Sunday in November 1955. At Milton box, between Steventon and Didcot, the train was to be diverted from the main to the slow road because of permanent way relaying; the driver, however, had failed to observe this in his weekly working notice, and what with the left-hand drive to which he was not accustomed, bad weather and poor visibility as compared with a 'Castle' 4-6-0, and distraction through having a fireman unused to the route and in difficulty with a re-fractory injector, he failed to act on the warning note and partial brake application of the early warning apparatus. As a result he had the whole of his train off the road on the Milton cross-over at 50 m.p.h., with the loss of eleven lives. The engine went down the bank and over on to its side in an adjacent field; getting it back on the line was no easy task, but eventually it was rerailed and taken to Swindon, where it was found to have sustained comparatively little damage.

In January, 1960, a remarkable mishap befell No. 70052 *Firth of Tay* when working the 9.5 p.m. from Glasgow St Enoch to St Pancras. On a night of blizzard, when the train was climbing to Ais Gill summit, between Carlisle and Leeds, the driver became aware that the engine was knocking badly, and stopped his train at Garsdale to discover if he could what was wrong. In the darkness, however, he could not see anything amiss, and decided to proceed at reduced speed. What actually had happened was that the engine had shed both right-hand bottom slidebars. Down the hill from Blea Moor the speed was not limited as much as it should have been, and eventually the piston-rod, which was sustaining severe vertical bending stresses, broke, as

TABLE VIII (A)
E.R. NORWICH–LIVERPOOL STREET
Engine: Class '7' 4-6-2 No. 70039 *Sir Christopher Wren*
Load: 9 coaches, 308 tons tare, 330 tons gross

Dist.		Times	Speeds
miles		min. sec.	m.p.h.
0·00	NORWICH . . .	0 00	—
2·05	*Trowse Upper Junction* .	5 34	30½
5·20	Swainsthorpe . .	9 06	64¼
8·25	Flordon . . .	11 44	81
10·80	Forncett . . .	13 45	75
14·35	Tivetshall . . .	16 22	83½
19·95	Diss . . .	20 16	90
23·55	Mellis . . .	22 52	77½/82
		sigs.	*40
28·35	Finningham . .	26 53	—
		sigs.	*10
34·30	STOWMARKET . .	31 00	—
		sigs.	*45
37·85	Needham . . .	39 54	—
43·80	Bramford . . .	45 34	71½
		p.w.s.	*5
46·25	IPSWICH . . .	50 44	*35
50·05	*Milepost 65* . .	55 43	52
51·80	Bentley . . .	57 28	75/82
55·55	MANNINGTREE . .	60 23	*75
59·00	Ardleigh . . .	63 21	65
61·00	*Parsons Heath* . .	65 01	76½
63·35	COLCHESTER . .	67 08	*34
66·05	*Stanway* . .	70 38	56½
68·35	Marks Tey . .	72 46	69/77½
		p.w.s.	*25
72·70	Kelvedon . . .	76 34	—
76·40	WITHAM . . .	81 31	67½
79·10	Hatfield Peverel .	83 56	66
82·85	*New Hall* . .	86 54	79
85·25	CHELMSFORD . .	89 11	*52
91·40	Ingatestone . .	94 49	71½/77½
94·85	SHENFIELD . .	97 32	—
95·80	*Milepost 19¼* . .	98 19	71½
100·10	Harold Wood . .	101 24	88/*70
102·70	Romford . . .	103 29	—
105·05	Chadwell Heath .	105 19	80½
107·70	Ilford . . .	107 25	—
111·05	STRATFORD . .	110 26	*50
		sigs.	*10
113·80	*Bethnal Green East Junction* .	115 33	—
		sigs.	*10
115·05	LIVERPOOL STREET .	119 22	—
115·05	Net time (min.) . .	105	—

The 1 in 84 climb from Trowse to the Upper Junction was the only stretch taken at over 40 per cent cut-off – actually 45 – and the speed at the top of the incline was 30½ m.p.h. The impetus from 81 m.p.h. in the sharp dip at Flordon was sufficient to carry the train up the rising grades to Tivetshall at a minimum of 75 m.p.h., and with 90 m.p.h. through Diss, 'even time' from Norwich, despite the sharply curved and steeply rising start, was reached in just over 21 miles. But the preceding 4.45 p.m. from Norwich, which stopped at Diss and Stowmarket, was headed by a 'B1' 4-6-0 and was running badly, and this resulted in a string of signal checks being suffered by the special, and 5 m.p.h. for an underline bridge reconstruction at Bramford caused further delay. After the offending train had been passed at Ipswich, however, a fine effort was made to recover the lost time.

The hill-climbing on 40 per cent cut-off was remarkable; note the acceleration to 52 m.p.h. up 2 miles averaging 1 in 125 to milepost 65; a drop only from 75 to 65 m.p.h. up 2½ miles at 1 in 134 from Manningtree; a fall only from 67½ to 66 m.p.h. up 2 miles at 1 in 178 from Witham; and above all the acceleration up the almost continuous rise from Chelmsford to 77½ m.p.h. beyond Ingatestone, and the carrying of the final 1¾ miles at 1 in 135 to Ingrave summit at no less than 71½ m.p.h. – the highest minimum I have ever known at this point. With some high speed down Brentwood bank and beyond, the lateness of 4¾ min. through Ipswich had been converted to 2¾ min. early by Stratford, and despite two bad signal checks, Liverpool

TABLE VIII (B)
E.R. IPSWICH–NORWICH
Engine: Class '7' 4-6-2 No. 70035 *Rudyard Kipling*
Load: 9 coaches, 310 tons tare, 325 tons gross

Dist.		Sched.	Actual	Speeds
miles		min.	min. sec.	m.p.h.
0·00	IPSWICH	0	0 00	—
0·80	East Suffolk Junction . .	—	2 09	—
2·45	Bramford	—	3 51	63½
4·85	Claydon	—	6 02	68
8·40	Needham	—	8 57	75½
11·95	STOWMARKET . .	—	11 39	82
14·25	Haughley . . .	14½	13 25	74½
16·70	Milepost 85½ . . .	—	15 35	70½
17·90	Finningham . . .	—	16 29	77
22·70	Mellis	—	19 58	87½
26·30	Diss	—	22 21	94
28·80	Burston . . .	—	24 02	86½
31·90	Tivetshall	29	26 12	81
35·45	Forncett . . .	—	28 50	83½
38·00	Flordon	—	30 38	89/92
41·05	Swainsthorpe . .	—	32 46	86½
43·20	Milepost 112 . . .	—	34 25	81
44·20	Trowse Upper Junction .	—	35 19	*37
45·35	Trowse	—	37 03	—
46·25	NORWICH . . .	44	39 07	—

* Speed restriction.

TABLE VIII (C)
L.M.R. ST PANCRAS–LEICESTER

Engine: Class '7' 4-6-2 No. Engine: Name Load: Coaches/tons tare/tons gross		70032 Tennyson 9/297/320		70021 Morning Star 9/302/320	
Dist.		Sched.	Actual	Speeds	Actual	Speeds
miles		min.	min. sec.	m.p.h.	min. sec.	m.p.h.
0·00	ST PANCRAS . . .	0	0 00	—	0 00	—
1·55	Kentish Town . . .	4	sig. stop 6 42	*0 30	4 09	36½
3·90	West Hampstead . .	—	p.w.s. 11 32	*27 32½/55	7 40	43
6·95	HENDON . . .	10½	p.w.s. 15 36	*50 52½	10 53	67/70
9·35	Mill Hill	—	18 26	51½	13 01	63
12·40	Elstree	—	21 51	52½	16 01	59
15·20	Radlett	—	24 22	75/76½	18 24	80/82
19·85	ST ALBANS . . .	23	28 12	65	22 01	69
21·25	Sandridge . . .	—	29 30	63½	23 14	68
24·60	Harpenden . . .	—	32 23	73½	26 04	75
27·25	Chiltern Green . . .	—	34 27	80/76½	28 13	77/73
30·25	LUTON	33	36 42	81½	30 36	75½
32·75	Leagrave . . .	—	38 38	78½	32 42	71
37·25	Harlington . . .	—	41 42	94	36 14	81½
40·20	Flitwick	—	43 32	99	38 26	78
41·75	Ampthill	—	44 30	94	39 37	79½
45·00	Milepost 45 . . .	—	46 41	87½/92	42 03	84/81
49·95	Bedford North Junction .	49	50 08	77	45 35	83
53·00	Oakley	52	52 37	72/75	sig. stop 51 46	*0 —
56·70	Sharnbrook . . .	—	55 33	70	56 27	56
59·75	Milepost 59¾ . . .	58½	58 32	57½	59 45	53
62·70	Irchester	—	60 51	83½	62 22	73½
65·05	WELLINGBOROUGH .	63½	62 40	*62	sigs. 65 41	*10 15
68·25	Finedon	—	65 32	68½/71½	70 16	62/69
72·00	KETTERING . . .	70	68 48	66	sigs. 73 46	*57 64½
74·60	Glendon South Junction .	—	71 16	57½/60	76 07	61/68
78·50	Desborough North . .	—	75 31	51½/70	79 48	61/74
82·95	MARKET HARBOROUGH	82	79 35	*61/73½	84 01	*45
86·35	East Langton . . .	—	82 33	72	87 15	73
89·75	Kibworth North . .	—	85 38	61½	90 08	66
91·55	Great Glen . . .	—	87 18	75	91 38	81
95·40	Wigston Magna . .	—	90 31	*49/55	94 36	*40/58
99·10	LEICESTER . . .	99	sigs. 95 40	—	99 44	—
99·10	Net times (min.) . .	99	89½	—	90½	—

* Speed restriction.

Street was reached just over 2 min. early. Without any allowance for some over-scrupulous observance of the service slacks at Colchester and Chelmsford, the net time for the 115·05 miles from Norwich to London was 105 min., 17 min. inside schedule.

The run in Table VIII (B) was very likely the fastest that has ever been made on Great Eastern metals. No. 70035 *Rudyard Kipling*, again with a nine-coach train of 310 tons tare and 325 tons gross, was late away from Ipswich on one of the 44-min. bookings to Norwich. On the second of the level stretches on the gradual rise up the Gipping Valley the 4-6-2 reached the unusual maximum of 82 m.p.h. at Stowmarket, and this was sufficient to carry the express up Haughley bank – 2 miles at 1 in 131 – at a minimum of just over 70 m.p.h. Then 26½ miles of the undulating stretch that follows, between milepost 85½ (Finningham summit) and milepost 112 were reeled off at an average of 84·4 m.p.h., with a full mile past Diss at 94 m.p.h., so that milepost 112, 43·2 miles from the start, was passed in 34 min. 25 sec. Notwithstanding nearly 4 min. spent over the last sinuous 2 miles, the stop was effected at Norwich Thorpe in 39 min. 7 sec., a time over this 46·25 miles that will probably stand as a record for a long time to come. The driver was Newson of Norwich and the recorder J. H. Turner.

Early recipients of 'Britannia' Pacifics on the London Midland Region were Kentish Town and Trafford Park sheds of the Midland Division. Both had had some Class '7' experience with 'Royal Scot' 4-6-0s, but the 4-6-2s, though in the same power class, were easier to handle and with their free-steaming boilers offered more margin on the fast Midland timings, so that they soon became popular with a number of the engine crews. Table VIII (C) sets out two striking examples of 'Britannia' performance on mile-a-minute schedules between St Pancras and Leicester.

On the first run, recorded by N. E. Rimes, Driver W. P. Richards and Fireman E. Simpkins, with No. 70032 *Tennyson* and a nine-coach train of 320 tons, lost over 5 min. in the early stages as the result of signal and permanent-way delays, but then followed a performance of so startling a character that between St Albans and Leicester over 8½ min. was gained on schedule. After climbing the 4 miles at 1 in 176 to Sandridge at a minimum of 65 m.p.h., some very high-speed running began, culminating in a top speed of 99 m.p.h. at the foot of 5½ miles down at 1 in 202 to Flitwick; the average was all but 90 m.p.h. for 17·2 miles from Leagrave to Bedford, and 93 m.p.h. over the 7·75 miles from Harlington to milepost 45. The 3¾-mile climb to Sharnbrook summit, finishing with 3¼ miles at 1 in 119, was breasted at 57½ m.p.h., and with the train now on time there was a slight easing, though the running was still very fast. Eventually Leicester, 99·1 miles, was reached in 95 min. 40 sec., but the net time of 89½ min. was 9½ min. less than the 99 min. allowed.

The second run in this table, though the highest speed attained did not exceed 84 m.p.h., had a net time only 1 min. slower than the first. R. I. Nelson, who recorded it, was travelling on the footplate of No. 70021 *Morning Star* with Driver F. Stokes and Fireman Gerrard of Trafford Park; the load again was nine coaches, or 320 tons gross. Full regulator was used for all the harder uphill work, but with considerably shorter cut-offs than those on the Great Eastern Norwich–Liverpool Street run in Table VIII (A). Also there was a good deal more variation in the boiler pressure, which had fallen from 250 lb per sq in. at the St Pancras start to 180 lb at Luton, after the hard uphill start, though recovering to 240 lb on the easy downhill run to Bedford. From here onwards pressure kept continuously between 225 and 240 lb, with about 10 lb less in the steam-chest whenever the regulator was fully open.

Immediately after the start a cut-off of 25 to 28 per cent was used to get the train up to West Hampstead; then with 17 per cent the drop in speed up 1 in 176 was from 70 to 59 m.p.h. between Hendon and Mill Hill, and 82 to 69 m.p.h. between Radlett and Sandridge – roughly 5 miles in each case. The speed between Sandridge and Leagrave was maintained in the main with 15 per cent cut-off and half regulator; down from Leagrave one-quarter of the main valve open, with 15 per cent, sufficed for 78 to 84 m.p.h. speeds. Bedford had been passed 2 min. early (the St Pancras start was 1½ min. late) when there came the dead stand for signals at Oakley, just before the steep climb to Sharnbrook summit, and from here onwards the engine was driven a good deal harder.

Up to Sharnbrook, with full regulator, cut-off was advanced gradually from 18 to 34 per cent, the last position being sufficient to maintain a speed of 53 m.p.h. up 1 in 119. A bad signal check was experienced through Wellingborough and another slight one before Kettering, where cut-off was advanced to 25 per cent; this made possible the maintenance of a minimum of 61 m.p.h. both up the 1 in 118 to Glendon South Junction and the 1 in 130 (average) to Desborough North, from 64½ m.p.h. through Kettering and 68 at Glendon respectively. Similarly the minimum of 66 m.p.h. at Kibworth North, up 1 in 130–136 from East Langton, required from 22 to 27 per cent cut-off. Relatively to the inclinations, these speeds were roughly proportionate to those achieved by *Sir Christopher Wren* on the Great Eastern run in Table VIII (A). So *Morning Star* completed the run from St Pancras to Leicester, all checks included, in 99 min. 44 sec.; the net time did not exceed 90½ min. The times of the first of these runs from Harpenden to Kettering, added to those of the second from St Pancras to Harpenden and Kettering to Leicester, make a total of 88½ min.

Among various L.M.R. Western Division sheds to which 'Britannia' Pacifics have been drafted, the one which has probably made the best showing with them is Longsight, Manchester. Table VIII (D) sets out a fine run with the down 'Comet', on its mile-a-minute schedule from Euston to Stoke-on-Trent before the beginning of electrification work laid its heavy hand on Western Division main line schedules. The engine was No. 70031 *Byron*, with nearly the full Class '7' load on an 'XL Limit' timing – twelve bogies, 379 tons tare and 400 tons gross; the log, compiled by W. O. Knight, did not include the names of the crew.

Throughout, the performance was one of easy competence. Up the first 1 in 330 stretch, to Carpenders Park, speed kept steadily at 58–59 m.p.h., and

TABLE VIII (D)
L.M.R. EUSTON–MANCHESTER (VIA STOKE)
Engine: Class '7' 4-6-2 No. 70031 *Byron*
Load: 12 coaches, 379 tons tare, 400 tons gross

Dist.		Sched.	Actual	Speeds
miles		min.	min. sec.	m.p.h.
0·00	EUSTON	0	0 00	—
1·10	Camden No. 1 . . .	—	4 00	—
5·40	WILLESDEN JUNCTION .	9	10 56	58
8·05	Wembley	—	13 42	57½
11·40	Harrow	—	17 07	58
13·30	Hatch End . . .	—	19 03	59
17·45	WATFORD JUNCTION .	21	23 00	67
20·95	Kings Langley . . .	—	26 07	66
24·50	Hemel Hempstead . .	—	29 18	65
27·95	Berkhamsted . . .	—	32 28	64
31·65	TRING	35	35 57	63½
36·10	Cheddington . . .	—	39 30	84
40·20	Leighton Buzzard . .	—	42 27	82
46·65	BLETCHLEY . . .	47	47 10	81½/77½
52·40	Wolverton . . .	—	51 22	82
54·75	Castlethorpe . . .	—	53 05	—
59·90	ROADE	58	57 17	67½
62·85	Blisworth . . .	61	59 45	78½/77
69·70	Weedon . . .	67	65 00	78
75·30	Welton . . .	—	69 30	68½
80·30	Hillmorton . . .	—	73 45	74
82·55	RUGBY . . .	79	76 15	*40
			p.w.s.	*25
88·10	Brinklow . . .	—	85 09	63½
91·40	Shilton . . .	—	88 20	61
97·10	NUNEATON . . .	93	93 25	78
102·30	Atherstone . . .	—	97 27	75
106·50	Polesworth . . .	—	100 35	82
110·00	TAMWORTH . .	106	103 11	78½/81½
116·25	LICHFIELD . .	112	107 57	66
121·00	Armitage . . .	—	111 55	—
124·30	Rugeley . . .	119	114 30	70
127·15	Colwich . . .	123	118 02	*25/61
138·80	STONE . . .	137	131 18	58
141·35	Barlaston . . .	—	133 54	57
143·05	Trentham . . .	—	135 43	59
			sig. stop	*0
145·90	STOKE-ON-TRENT . .	146	142 50	—
1·15	Etruria	3	3 05	—
2·90	Longport	—	5 12	—
6·20	Kidsgrove . . .	9	8 40	62½
8·60	Mow Cop	—	10 57	—
11·85	CONGLETON . . .	—	13 37	73/75
15·20	North Rode . . .	19	16 23	70
17·50	Macclesfield Moss . .	—	18 25	64½
19·95	MACCLESFIELD† . .	27	22 15	—
4·30	Adlington . . .	—	5 40	64
6·45	Poynton	—	7 36	71
7·85	Bramhall	—	8 49	67
9·40	Cheadle Hulme . . .	12	10 20	*30
11·75	STOCKPORT . . .	16	13 50	—
3·55	Slade Lane Junction . .	—	5 00	64
5·90	MANCHESTER‡ . .	10	8 15	—

* Speed restriction.   † Hibel Road Station.
‡ London Road Station (now Piccadilly).

up the second, from Kings Langley to near Tring, it fell very gradually from 67 to 63½ m.p.h. From Cheddington to Wolverton 81½ to 84 m.p.h. was maintained, save for a brief fall to 77½ on the faint rise to Denbigh Hall, after Bletchley; then followed notably high minima of 67½ m.p.h. in Roade Cutting and 68½ at Kilsby Tunnel. So Rugby, 82·55 miles, was passed in 76 min. 15 sec. Just beyond here came the one and only permanent-way check of the journey; in the Trent Valley speed rose again to 81½ and 82 m.p.h. before and after Tamworth, and by Colwich the 'Comet' was 5 min. early. It might have been 6 to 6½ min. early at Stoke, but for a stop outside; net time for the 145·9 miles from Euston was 138 min.

Fine work continued; the top speed of 75 m.p.h. at Congleton was on practically level track, and the minimum of 64½ m.p.h. at Macclesfield Moss Box was after 3½ miles up at 1 in 176. So 4¾ min. were gained from Stoke to Macclesfield, 2¼ min. from there to Stockport, and yet another 1¾ min. to Manchester. Addition of the four actual or net times gives a total of 182¼ min. for the 183½ miles, including slowing down to and restarting from three intermediate stops. Such running would be regarded as first class even for a Class '8' Pacific of the 'Duchess' type, and was outstanding for a Class '7' 'Britannia'. The fastest time ever regularly scheduled in the past between Euston and Manchester, with one stop, by the much easier (if 5 miles longer) Crewe route, has been 195 min., and by this the excellence of *Byron*'s performance may be measured.

On the Western Region, as already mentioned, the Canton shed at Cardiff succeeded in mastering the handling of the 'Britannias', and has done some excellent work with them. Table VIII (E) sets out a run, timed by Roger Pope, with No. 70028 *Royal Star* from Newport to Paddington; the load was thirteen bogies, 445 tons tare and 475 tons gross. This is a substantial tonnage to have to lift out of the depths of the Severn Tunnel up the 20-mile climb to the summit at Badminton, even though it may be succeeded by 100 miles of relatively easy steaming from Badminton to Paddington.

The South Wales trains for the most part have very leisurely timings through the Severn Tunnel, to allow a margin in the event of freight train delays, and of this the driver of *Royal Star* took full advantage; up the 3¾ miles at 1 in 100 from the centre of the tunnel to Pilning speed dropped from 73 to 36 m.p.h., and, after a momentary recovery at Cattybrook, from 40 to 20½ m.p.h. up the ensuing 3¾ miles at the same grade to Patchway. Speed had recovered to a steady 49 m.p.h. up the long 1 in 300 from Stoke Gifford when there came a dead stand for a minute at Chipping Sodbury, due to a preceding freight train not having cleared into Badminton loop.

From the re-start, 44 m.p.h. was attained up the remainder of the 1 in 300 to Badminton. A higher speed might have been expected at Little Somerford than 72 m.p.h., but no doubt the boiler was being refilled after the hard climb. Onwards from Swindon, while the speed down the 1 in 754 to Didcot was kept mostly at 67–68 m.p.h., on the level from Didcot it rose to a steady 70–73 m.p.h., so that by Reading the train was 1½ min. early. After the Maidenhead signal check, there was another 72 m.p.h., at Southall, and with

TABLE VIII (E)
W.R. NEWPORT–PADDINGTON
Engine: Class '7' 4-6-2 No. 70028 *Royal Star*
Load: 13 coaches, 445 tons tare, 475 tons gross

Dist.		Sched.	Actual	Speeds
miles		min.	min. sec.	m.p.h.
0·00	NEWPORT . . .	0	0 00	—
3·75	Llanwern	—	6 47	54
7·40	Magor	—	10 25	64
9·80	SEVERN TUNNEL JUNC. .	13	13 18	*30
10·70	Severn Tunnel West . .	14½	14 59	52/73
15·60	Severn Tunnel East . .	—	19 46	40
16·75	Pilning	(†2)	21 39	36
18·15	Cattybrook . . .	—	24 01	40
20·25	Patchway	31½	29 24	20½
21·55	Stoke Gifford West . .	33½	31 26	38
24·95	Coalpit Heath . . .	—	36 01	49
28·85	Chipping Sodbury . .	—	{ 42 36 / 43 27	sig. } / stop }
33·40	BADMINTON . . .	49½	51 45	44
39·15	Hullavington . . .	—	58 07	63
43·65	Little Somerford . .	—	62 08	72
46·40	Brinkworth . . .	—	64 32	65
50·50	Wootton Bassett . .	67½	68 51	*53
56·10	SWINDON . . .	73	74 55	59
61·90	Shrivenham . . .	—	80 29	64
66·90	Uffington	(†2)	85 05	67
69·60	Challow	—	87 33	67
73·00	Wantage Road . . .	—	90 39	68
76·90	Steventon . . .	94	94 03	70
80·30	DIDCOT	97	96 54	71
84·95	Cholsey	—	100 54	70
88·65	Goring	—	104 04	72
91·85	Pangbourne . . .	—	106 44	73
94·75	Tilehurst	—	109 07	72
97·40	READING . . .	113	111 26	67
102·40	Twyford	117½	115 52	69
			sigs.	*25
109 15	Maidenhead . . .	123½	123 15	—
114·95	SLOUGH	129	130 26	66
120·15	West Drayton . . .	—	134 59	70
124·30	SOUTHALL . . .	138	138 30	72
127·70	Ealing Broadway . .	—	141 29	66
132·15	Westbourne Park . .	145	146 32	*25
133·40	PADDINGTON . .	149	149 25	—
133·40	Net time (min.) . .	149	140	—

* Speed restriction.   † Recovery time (min.).

a cautious approach to the terminus Paddington was reached in 149 min. 25 sec.; the net time of 140 min. showed a gain of 9 min. on schedule. From Chipping Sodbury the 104·55 miles to London had been run in 105 min. 58 sec. start to stop, or 101½ min. net; from Hullavington to Ealing Broadway the time over the 88·55 miles, pass-to-pass, was 83 min. 22 sec., or just under 79 min. net, a very sound performance with this 475-ton train.

It is a pity that the 'Britannia' Pacifics appeared on the scene so late in

British steam locomotive history. With reasonably good maintenance and in competent hands they might have established a notable reputation. In any event, the runs just described leave no doubt as to their outstanding capabilities.

7 – The 'Clans', Class '6'

ONE of the least distinguished in their performance of all the British standard locomotive types has been the 'Clan' class. In his paper on 'British Standard Locomotives' to the Institution of Locomotive Engineers, already mentioned, E. S. Cox stated that 'the smaller 4-6-2 provides a more powerful engine where such is required over the many routes that call for an axle-load of under 19 tons. It will, in general, run over nearly every route over which the Regional 4-6-0 mixed traffics run, and there are a number of duties for which it would seem to be specially suitable, as, for example, former Class "5X" working on the London Midland Region, the Great Central main line, and a variety of work in Scotland, where, in fact, the first ten of these engines are allocated.'

Why in any event it should have been thought necessary to supplement the large numbers of other Class '6' types, such as the L.M.S. 'Jubilee' 4-6-os (the former Class '5X') by a type of greater weight and cost, and, as it turned out, little if any greater tractive power, is a mystery. The 'Clans' never appeared in any regular working as replacements of the 'Jubilees' on the Midland Division of the L.M.R., nor on the Great Central line. No. 72009 *Clan Stewart* made a brief appearance on the Great Eastern line as a proposed substitute for the latter's 'Britannia' Pacifics, but after trial runs between Liverpool Street and both Clacton-on-Sea and Norwich the outcry raised by the prospect of so dubious a bargain resulted in a speedy return of the stranger north of the Border. It had been thought that the 'Clans' would take over the working of the Highland main line, and also the lines between Glasgow St Enoch and Stranraer and Stranraer and Carlisle, but this did not happen.

The first Class '6' 4-6-2, No. 72000 *Clan Buchanan*, left Crewe Works in December 1951. The chassis was generally similar to that of the 'Britannia', and many details, including the bogie, were interchangeable between the two types. The boiler, however, was smaller, in order to give the necessary reduction in weight; the total heating surface was 401 sq ft less, the super-heating surface 90 sq ft less, and the firegrate area 6 sq ft less than that of a 'Britannia'. With cylinders of 19½ in. instead of 20 in. diameter and a reduction in working pressure from 250 to 225 lb per sq in., the 'Clan' tractive effort of 27,520 lb, at 85 per cent of the boiler pressure, was thus 4,630 lb less than that of the Class '7' Pacific. The difference in weight was comparatively small – 88½ as compared with 94 tons for the engine, and 135¾ compared with 141¼ tons for engine and tender, the two tenders being identical, as also the length over buffers, 68 ft 9 in.

The 'Clans' have proved more tricky engines to handle than the 'Britannias'. They can steam, provided that they are worked fairly hard, but this means a heavy coal consumption. Also if the boiler pressure gets down, it is no easy matter to pull them round. The run from Symington to Carlisle set out in Table VIII (F), recorded by R. I. Nelson, who accompanied Driver N. Campbell and Fireman T. White of Polmadie on the footplate, is as good a one as I have seen with one of these engines. The fact that it began at Symington meant that the major part of the climbing to Beattock summit was over; after the falling start, to Lamington, there was only the gradual rise of the Upper Clyde Valley to negotiate, and the final 2 miles at 1 in 99 to the summit.

TABLE VIII (F)
SCOTTISH REGION: SYMINGTON–CARLISLE
Engine: Class '6' 4-6-2 No. 72002 *Clan Campbell*
Load: 11 coaches, 345 tons tare, 360 tons gross

Dist.		Sched.	Actual	Speeds
miles		min.	min. sec.	m.p.h.
0·00	SYMINGTON . . .	0	0 00	—
3·70	Lamington . . .	—	6 17	60/61½
6·50	*Wandelmill* . . .	—	9 20	55½
9·10	Abington	—	12 07	55/57½
11·65	Crawford	—	14 56	56/49
14·30	Elvanfoot	—	18 06	55½/58
17·20	Summit	21	21 42	41¼
21·50	*Greskine*	—	26 09	67
27·20	BEATTOCK . . .	31	31 36	69/72
32·40	Wamphray . . .	—	36 22	68½
35·20	Dinwoodie . . .	—	38 56	71
38·25	Nethercleugh . . .	—	41 31	72½
41·15	LOCKERBIE . . .	43	44 07	67
44·20	*Castlemilk* . . .	—	46 59	61
46·80	Ecclefechan . . .	—	49 20	73
50·20	Kirtlebridge . . .	—	52 07	76½
52·10	*Milepost 14¾* . . .	—	53 49	66
56·60	Quintinshill . . .	—	57 42	77¼
58·20	Gretna Junction .	58	59 03	72
60·75	Floriston . . .	—	61 08	75½
64·80	Kingmoor . . .	—	64 49	66¼
66·80	CARLISLE . . ˋ.	68	67 57	—

For all the uphill work full regulator was used; the start was on the first valve, with 70 per cent cut-off, reduced to 31 in the first mile, and then, after the movement of the regulator to full open, to 15 per cent down to the crossing of the Clyde beyond Lamington. Then came a gradual advance of cut-off to 26 per cent up the short climb from Crawford, and after a slight easing to 21 per cent on the 1½ miles of level past Elvanfoot, to 34 per cent before the summit was breasted. Speed fell from 61½ m.p.h. beyond Lamington to 49 m.p.h. beyond Crawford, and after a recovery to 58 m.p.h. past Elvanfoot, to 41½ m.p.h. at Beattock summit.

After drifting down Beattock bank without steam, which permitted the boiler pressure to rise from the 180 lb to which it had dropped to 225 lb, full regulator working was resumed over the undulating stretch beyond Lockerbie, which was covered at between 68½ and 72 m.p.h., with a fall to 61 on the final rise to Castlemilk; easy running then followed down the two long stretches at 1 in 200 to Floriston. Boiler pressure had varied between 225 and 200 lb until midway up the 1 in 99 to Beattock summit; after the fall to 180 lb already mentioned, it kept at between 200 and 225 lb on to Carlisle, with the steam-chest pressure about 10 lb below that in the boiler at all times when the regulator was full open. The schedule of 68 min. for the 66·8 miles from Symington to Carlisle was a sharp one, but it was only just kept, and with a moderate load of no more than eleven coaches of 345 tons tare and 360 tons gross the work, for a locomotive of these dimensions and weight, could not be regarded as anything outstanding.

Six months after the appearance of No. 72000 all ten engines of the class had been completed, and the intention to use them in Scotland was clear from their all being named after Scottish clans. After the summer of 1952 no more were built. It is surprising that in performance the 'Clans' have fallen so far short of the 'Britannias'. Indeed, a far better purpose might have been served had some of the rebuilt Southern 'West Country' Pacifics, which are on an altogether higher level of performance, been transferred to Scotland instead. It is highly interesting to speculate as to what capable Scottish crews might have done with the latter, if they had had the chance.

8 – The 'Duke of Gloucester', Class '8'

IF the trouble taken to design and build in 1951 a new type of light Pacific – the 'Clans' – was a surprise, even more mysterious was the emergence as late as 1954 of a brand-new Class '8' express passenger Pacific, No. 71000 *Duke of Gloucester*. It is true that in the papers to the Institution of Locomotive Engineers on British Railways standard locomotives, to which reference has already been made, a Class '8' design had been foreshadowed; but by now it was becoming abundantly clear that the writing was on the wall for steam. Only a year later the British Transport Commission's modernization and re-equipment plan was to be made public, and the fact that it included the substitution of diesel for steam power on an extensive scale obviously must have been with the knowledge and consent, well before this announcement, of the locomotive authorities.

Moreover, within the previous five years the Eastern and North Eastern Regions had added the fifty 'A1' express passenger Pacifics to their already extensive 4-6-2 stud; it was pretty certain that the Southern Region, with forty 'Merchant Navy' and 110 'West Country' Pacifics, would not want any more engines of this wheel arrangement, if, indeed, it was not already over-supplied; and the Western Region's attitude to the 'Britannia' Pacifics would hardly indicate any overwhelming desire to be supplied with bigger and more powerful standard Pacifics. This left only the London Midland Region, which could well have done with some addition to its fifty 'Princess Royal' and 'Duchess' Pacifics; but in view of the very limited need in the country for more Class '8' power, surely a modest addition to the well-tried and most capable Stanier series would have been a considerably more economical plan.

However, it was not so; and in the early months of 1954 No. 71000 *Duke of Gloucester*, destined to remain the one lone example of his class, emerged from Crewe Works. The design embodied some surprising features. It was the only standard design to be provided with three cylinders, of 18 in. diameter and 28 in. stroke, as compared with the two 20 in. by 28 in. cylinders of the 'Britannias'. Yet the boiler supplying them with steam was identical in all respects with the 'Britannia' boiler, save for its larger firebox and superheater. The firegrate area had gone up from 42 to 48·6 sq ft, and the firebox heating surface from 210 to 226 sq ft; but the superheating surface, rather curiously, had been reduced from 718 to 691 sq ft. A second surprise was the use, in a locomotive intended almost exclusively for express passenger service, of 6 ft 2 in. driving wheels; but experience with the Bulleid Pacifics on the Southern Region and the 'A2' Pacifics on the Eastern, North Eastern and Scottish Regions had shown that with modern front-end design a reduction from the former driving wheel diameter customary with British express passenger designs, of 6 ft 6 in. to 6 ft 9 in., had had little or no adverse effect on speed capacity.

But most surprising of all, without a doubt, was the decision to equip the *Duke of Gloucester* with poppet-valves of the Caprotti type in place of the customary piston-valves. The middle cylinder, forward of the outside cylinders, drove the leading coupled axle, and the outside cylinders the middle axle, each cylinder having separate inlet and exhaust valves, actuated by rotary cams, at both ends. Reversing the engine was effected by advancing or retarding the angular position of the cams relatively to the cam-shafts, and any desired cut-off was obtained by the angular adjustment of the inlet cams relatively to each other. The drive for the inside cylinder cam-box was taken from an extension of the worm-shaft of the left-hand cam-box through a right-angle bevel gearbox.

Unlike the 'Britannias', with the *Duke of Gloucester* a double blastpipe and double chimney were fitted. The firebox, 12 in. longer than that of a 'Britannia', was extended into the barrel to provide a combustion chamber. The firegrate had fourteen rocking sections, both of which could be operated separately from the footplate, and with two different travels, a full travel for dropping the fire over an ashpit, and a half travel to agitate the fire when running for the breaking up of clinker and disposal of ash. The tender was of a new type, with sides carried up to cab roof level and accommodating 10 tons of coal and 4,725 gallons of water, as compared with the 'Britannia's' 7 tons and 4,250 gallons; this put the tender weight up from 47¼ to 55½ tons. A steam-operated coal-pusher was installed, similar to that used on the L.M.S. 'Duchess' Pacifics.

By reason of the increased cylinder volume, the tractive effort at 85 per cent boiler pressure of the *Duke of Gloucester*, 39,080 lb, was 6,930 lb greater than that of *Britannia*; but it remained to be proved whether the former's boiler would be able to produce a proportionately increased weight of steam to make the higher tractive effort effective. The adhesion weight increased from 60¾ tons to 66 tons, the engine weight in working order from 94 to 101¼ tons, and the weight of engine and tender from 141¼ to 156¾ tons. Dimensionally, therefore, the *Duke of Gloucester* should have been considerably superior to a 'Britannia' and very nearly the equal of a London Midland 'Duchess' 4-6-2; but this has not proved to be the case.

The engine was subjected to the usual exhaustive tests, in this case on Western Region main lines and on the test plant at Swindon Works. The new 4-6-2 proved to have a very healthy appetite for coal. As compared with a Bulleid 'Merchant Navy' Pacific, which achieved a steam rate of 42,000 lb per hour, No. 71000, when fired at the same rate, was producing 34,000 lb only; this was with two firemen feeding coal at the tremendous rate of 7,000 lb (over 3 tons) an hour. Even a 'Britannia' had shown itself capable of steaming up to a rate of 37,560 lb per hour. It was estimated that when No. 71000 was called on for any exceptional power output, the engine was burning about 12½ per cent more coal than other 4-6-2 types that had been tested at Swindon or Rugby, and that at any firing rate above about 4,000 lb per hour coal was beginning to be thrown unburnt out of the chimney. The *Duke of Gloucester* could be worked in cut-offs as low as 5 per cent, and nothing above 20 per cent was used in the tests.

In the road tests a 459-ton train was attached to the new 4-6-2, and this was worked from Swindon by way of Didcot and the Reading West curve over Savernake summit to Westbury. On the level No. 71000 maintained 75 to 76 m.p.h. on a coal consumption of 3,139 lb per hour, producing steam at an average rate of 22,910 lb per hour. The drawbar pull on the level was mostly just over 5,000 lb, and rose to between 6,500 and 7,000 lb up the gradually rising grades of the Kennet Valley to Savernake, where the equivalent drawbar h.p. was between 1,215 and 1,280. A change was then made to a 586-ton train, which was worked at a steady 78 to 80 m.p.h. on the level between Wantage Road and Tilehurst, but this involved a coal consumption averaging 4,850 lb per hour (nearly 2¼ tons) and an average steam production rate of 30,000 lb per hour. On the rising gradients from Newbury to Savernake a steady drawbar h.p. of 1,530 to 1,545 was recorded, as compared with slightly under 1,500 on the previous level stretch.

The *Duke of Gloucester* has been stationed continuously since building at Crewe North shed, and from there has worked both southwards to Euston and northwards to Carlisle, Glasgow and Perth. Some engine-crews have been able to make nothing of the engine, and have lost time heavily; others have mastered handling totally different from that of a Stanier Pacific, and have done quite well, though in general on a coal consumption heavier than with a locomotive of the latter type. Maintenance costs, on the other hand, have been on the low side. One of the trains most frequently worked, up to

TABLE VIII (G)
L.M.R. EUSTON–CREWE
Engine: Class '8' 4-6-2 No. 71000 Duke of Gloucester
Load: 14 coaches, 453 tons tare, 485 tons gross

Dist.		Sched.	Actual	Speeds
miles		min.	min. sec.	m.p.h.
0·00	EUSTON	0	0 00	—
1·00	Milepost 1 . . .	—	3 16	24
5·40	WILLESDEN JUNCTION .	9	9 19	58½
8·05	Wembley	—	11 54	67½
11·40	Harrow	—	15 16	58
13·30	Hatch End . . .	—	17 18	56
17·45	WATFORD JUNCTION .	21	21 31	64
20·95	Kings Langley . . .	—	24 39	66½
24·50	Hemel Hempstead . .	—	28 33	59½
			p.w.s.	*15
27·95	Berkhamsted . . .	—	34 09	51
31·65	TRING	35	38 14	59
36·10	Cheddington . . .	—	42 07	75½/78
40·10	Leighton Buzzard . .	—	45 20	74
46·65	BLETCHLEY . . .	47	50 27	78/73½
52·40	Wolverton . . .	—	54 51	83
54·75	Castlethorpe . . .	—	56 44	74
59·90	ROADE	58	61 17	63/62
62·85	Blisworth	61	63 50	74/78½
			sigs.	*50
69·70	Weedon	67	70 21	70½
75·30	Welton	—	75 23	63
80·30	Hillmorton . . .	—	79 50	77
			sigs.	*22
82·55	RUGBY	80	83 47	—
0·65	Rugby No. 7 . . .	—	1 59	—
5·55	Brinklow	—	7 42	60/64
8·85	Shilton	—	10 47	60/59
10·95	Bulkington	—	12 49	67/77
			p.w.s.	*10
14·55	NUNEATON . . .	15	16 14	—
19·75	Atherstone . . .	—	23 19	61
23·95	Polesworth . . .	—	26 59	74½/76
27·45	TAMWORTH . . .	28	29 47	73/77
33·70	LICHFIELD . . .	34	34 58	68/65
38·45	Armitage	—	39 14	69/74
41·75	Rugeley	41	41 57	72½
44·60	Colwich	—	44 18	69
47·00	Milford	—	46 17	74
51·00	STAFFORD . . .	51	50 02	*50
54·30	Great Bridgeford . .	—	53 48	62
56·30	Norton Bridge . . .	57	55 49	58
60·85	Standon Bridge . .	—	60 28	59
65·10	Whitmore	66	64 39	61
67·50	Madeley	—	66 58	64½
70·70	Betley Road . . .	—	69 37	79
			sigs.	*30
75·45	CREWE	77	76 24	—

* Speed restriction.

the time when the train concerned was altered to a non-stop run with strictly limited load between Euston and Carlisle, was the down 'Midday Scot'. With the heavy load of this train, the timing of 80 min. only over the 82·55 miles from Euston to Rugby was one of the hardest on the London Midland Region, whereas 77 min. for the 75·45 miles on to Crewe was relatively easy.

By the courtesy of R. I. Nelson, who rode on the footplate with Driver J. Stevenson and Fireman J. Leigh of Camden, I am able to set out, in Table VIII (G), details of a good run on this train with a fourteen-coach load of 453 tons tare and 485 tons gross. Full regulator working was the order of the day throughout the run, save only for a moment or two after each start. Out of Euston 75 per cent and the first valve were used to get the train on the move, with the usual rear-end assistance; almost at once the regulator was opened to full as cut-off was brought back to 54, and then in stages to 40 and 27 per cent at milepost 1, where speed at the top of Camden bank had risen to 24 m.p.h. Cut-off was next reduced very gradually until it was down to 10 per cent at Brent Junction, speed here having risen to $67\frac{1}{2}$ m.p.h. From Wembley a gradual increase to 13 per cent by Hatch End could not prevent a fall in speed to 56 m.p.h. up the 1 in 330. With 10 to 12 per cent on the slight fall and level past Watford to Kings Langley came an acceleration to $66\frac{1}{2}$ m.p.h. before the bad permanent way slowing at Hemel Hempstead; in recovering from this 31, 25 and 18 per cent cut-offs were used in succession and resulted in an acceleration to 59 m.p.h. up the second 1 in 330 stage.

Then, on $7\frac{1}{2}$ and 8 per cent cut-off, the *Duke of Gloucester* quickly worked up to 78 m.p.h., and with a brief 10–11 per cent from Leighton up the slight rise through Bletchley to Denbigh Hall, followed by a reversion to 7–8 per cent, the top speed of the journey, 83 m.p.h., was attained through Wolverton. From here onwards, on cut-offs varying between 10 and 15 per cent, No. 71000 was doing no more than keep point-to-point times, and so reached Rugby $3\frac{3}{4}$ min. late; the checks, however, had more than accounted for the arrears, and the net time was not more than 78 min. Steam-chest pressures with full regulator averaged 10 lb less than the boiler pressure; the latter fluctuated from 250 lb at the start through 230–240 lb most of the way to Watford, after which there was an unaccountable drop to 195 lb at the Hemel Hempstead slowing, though by Tring 250 lb had been re-attained. But at no stage did there appear to be any trouble with steaming.

The handling of the locomotive over the Rugby–Crewe stage followed the same pattern. By No. 7 box at Rugby the cut-off was down to 19 per cent and soon after Brinklow to 12 per cent; 38 per cent was used in recovering from the Nuneaton 10 m.p.h., but by Atherstone No. 71000 was cutting off at 12 per cent, and from Polesworth to Tamworth at 8–9 per cent. After this the engine was worked slightly harder, to recover the lost minutes, yet even so with no longer cut-off than 18 per cent up the 1 in 330 past Lichfield, surmounted at a minimum of 65 m.p.h. Thus the 27·25 miles from Atherstone to Milford were covered in a shade under 23 min. With the train still behind time because of the late start from Rugby, a little more energy might have been expected from Stafford onwards, but as a signal check was experienced outside Crewe, an earlier approach to that junction might not have succeeded in securing a punctual arrival; actually the train was $3\frac{1}{4}$ min. late. The gross time for the 75·45 miles from Rugby was thus 76 min. 24 sec., but the net time was not more than $71\frac{1}{4}$ min., the two stages of the 158-mile run therefore having been run in a total net time of $149\frac{1}{4}$ min. The comment on the firing made by the recorder of the run was that 'if the coal consumption appeared to be very heavy, it was not disproportionately high in relation to the steam rates achieved'. An interesting feature of the handling was the marked susceptibility of the engine to the slightest changes in the cut-off positions.

TABLE VIII (H)
LEADING DIMENSIONS OF B.R. STANDARD PACIFICS

Class	7P6F 'Britannia'	8P	6P5F 'Clan'
Cylinders, diameter . . .	(2) 20 in.	(3) 18 in.	(2) 18 in.
,, stroke	28 in.	28 in.	28 in.
Driving wheels, diameter . .	6 ft 2 in.	6 ft 2 in.	6 ft 2 in.
Wheelbase, coupled . . .	14 ft 0 in.	14 ft 0 in.	14 ft 0 in.
,, total . . .	35 ft 9 in.	36 ft 4 in.	35 ft 9 in.
Heating surface, tubes and flues .	2,264 sq ft	2,264 sq ft	1,878 sq ft
,, ,, firebox . . .	210 sq ft	226 sq ft	195 sq ft
,, ,, total . . .	2,474 sq ft	2,490 sq ft	2,073 sq ft
Superheating surface . . .	718 sq ft	691 sq ft	628 sq ft
Firegrate area	42·0 sq ft	48·6 sq ft	36·0 sq ft
Working pressure, per sq in. .	250 lb	250 lb	225 lb
Tractive effort (85 per cent) . .	32,150 lb	39,080 lb	27,520 lb
Adhesion weight	60·8 tons	66·0 tons	56·4 tons
Engine weight (working order) .	94·0 tons	101·3 tons	88·5 tons
Engine and tender weight . .	141·2 tons	156·8 tons	135·7 tons
Length over buffers . . .	68 ft 9 in.	70 ft 0 in.	68 ft 9 in.

TABLE VIII (J)
NUMBERS, NAMES AND BUILDING DATES,
B.R. STANDARD PACIFICS

Class	No.	Name	Building date
7P6F ('Britannia')	70000	Britannia	1951
,,	70001	Lord Hurcomb . . .	,,
,,	70002	Geoffrey Chaucer . . .	,,
,,	70003	John Bunyan	,,
,,	70004	William Shakespeare . .	,,
,,	70005	John Milton	,,
,,	70006	Robert Burns	,,
,,	70007	Coeur-de-Lion . . .	,,
,,	70008	Black Prince	,,
,,	70009	Alfred the Great . . .	,,
,,	70010	Owen Glendower . . .	,,
,,	70011	Hotspur	,,
,,	70012	John of Gaunt . . .	,,
,,	70013	Oliver Cromwell . . .	,,

Class	No.	Name	Building date
,,	70014	Iron Duke	1951
,,	70015	Apollo	,,
,,	70016	Ariel	,,
,,	70017	Arrow	,,
,,	70018	Flying Dutchman . . .	,,
,,	70019	Lightning	,,
,,	70020	Mercury	,,
,,	70021	Morning Star . . .	,,
,,	70022	Tornado	,,
,,	70023	Venus	,,
,,	70024	Vulcan	,,
,,	70025	Western Star . . .	1953
,,	70026	Polar Star	,,
,,	70027	Rising Star	,,
,,	70028	Royal Star	,,
,,	70029	Shooting Star . . .	,,
,,	70030	William Wordsworth . .	,,
,,	70031	Byron	,,
,,	70032	Tennyson	,,
,,	70033	Charles Dickens . . .	,,
,,	70034	Thomas Hardy . . .	,,
,,	70035	Rudyard Kipling . . .	,,
,,	70036	Boadicea	,,
,,	70037	Hereward the Wake . .	,,
,,	70038	Robin Hood	,,
,,	70039	Sir Christopher Wren . .	,,
,,	70040	Clive of India . . .	,,
,,	70041	Sir John Moore . . .	,,
,,	70042	Lord Roberts	,,
,,	70043	Lord Kitchener . . .	,,
,,	70044	Earl Haig	,,
,,	70045	Lord Rowallan . . .	1954
,,	70046	Anzac	,,
,,	70047		,,
,,	70048	The Territorial Army, 1908–1958	,,
,,	70049	Solway Firth	,,
,,	70050	Firth of Clyde . . .	,,
,,	70051	Firth of Forth . . .	,,
,,	70052	Firth of Tay	,,
,,	70053	Moray Firth	,,
,,	70054	Dornoch Firth . . .	,,
8P	71000	Duke of Gloucester . .	,,
6P5F ('Clan')	72000	Clan Buchanan . . .	1952
,,	72001	Clan Cameron . . .	,,
,,	72002	Clan Campbell . . .	,,
,,	72003	Clan Fraser	,,
,,	72004	Clan Macdonald . . .	,,
,.	72005	Clan Macgregor . . .	,,
,,	72006	Clan Mackenzie . . .	,,
,,	72007	Clan Mackintosh . . .	,,
,,	72008	Clan Macleod . . .	,,
,,	72009	Clan Stewart . . .	,,

IX

BRITISH PACIFIC DESIGNS THAT WERE
NEVER BUILT

IN the first two decades of the present century, with 4-6-2 locomotives rapidly becoming standard express passenger power on the mainland of Europe and in other countries, it is not surprising that the eyes of British designers began to turn in the Pacific direction. Well before the appearance in 1922 of the first successful British Pacific prototype – Gresley's *Great Northern* – a number of Pacific designs had reached the drawing-board stage. The first Chief Mechanical Engineer to build a Pacific in this country, as we have seen already in Chapter I, was G. J. Churchward of the Great Western Railway in 1908, but the comparative failure of *The Great Bear*, and the restrictions placed on its use by the G.W.R. civil engineering department, may well have proved a deterrent to other British locomotive chiefs. Between 1908 and 1922, however, several other Pacific designs were prepared and seriously considered, though in the end nothing came of them.

The first of these was J. F. McIntosh's proposed Caledonian Railway Pacific of 1913. Ten years previously his first 4-6-0 express engines, Nos .49 and 50, had taken the road, and in 1906 they had been followed by the famous No. 903 *Cardean* and Nos. 904 to 907; these had done good work, but over the long and steep gradients of the West Coast main line they had their limitations, and with the smaller 4-4-0 locomotives piloting was frequent on the heavier trains. With East Coast motive power in view, no doubt, at one stage McIntosh had even thought of Atlantics for the Caledonian; then, after the exploits in 1910 of the Great Western Railway 4-6-0 *Polar Star* on the London & North Western line, a four-cylinder 4-6-0 type suggested itself. But in the end it was a four-cylinder Pacific which took his fancy, and the drawing reproduced below, signed by him over the date 8th October, 1913, shows what was proposed.

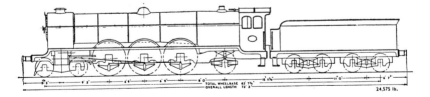

Four 16 in. by 26 in. cylinders would have been mated to 6 ft 6 in. driving wheels on a coupled wheelbase of 13 ft 6 in.; the parallel boiler barrel, of 5 ft 8 in. diameter and no less than 22 ft long between tubeplates, would have

227

provided 2,440 sq ft. of heating surface, while the firebox (which the drawing does not indicate to have been of the wide type) would have added 158 sq ft., and the superheating surface would have been 516 sq ft. For so large an engine a firegrate area of 37 sq ft. would have been on the small side. McIntosh would also have been content with a boiler pressure of 180 lb per sq in., which would have given a tractive effort, at 85 lb per cent of the working pressure, of 24,575 lb. The estimated weight of the engine was 90 tons, and of the bogie tender, accommodating 4,600 gallons of water and 6 tons of coal, 56 tons. Owing to the exceptional length of the boiler, the proposed 4-6-2 with its tender would have measured 72 ft 3 in. over buffers.

To start with, four only of these Pacifics were envisaged, two to be stationed at Kingmoor (Carlisle), one at Polmadie (Glasgow) and one at Perth. There is no evidence that the design was ever submitted formally to the Caledonian directors or their locomotive committee, and if any tentative proposals were made by McIntosh to individual directors, the assumption is that, if only on the grounds of needless expense, the designer was discouraged from pro-ceeding any further. But the proportions do not suggest that the design, which in effect was an elongated *Cardean* with four cylinders, would have achieved any great success.

Next in chronological order of British Pacific designs that were never built was that of Gresley for the Great Northern Railway in 1915; published details of this appeared for the first time in F. A. S. Brown's book *Nigel Gresley – Locomotive Engineer*, to which I have made reference previously. Soon after Gresley had succeeded Ivatt at Doncaster it was becoming evident that to cope with steadily increasing loads on the Great Northern main line greater adhesion would be necessary than was possible with any Atlantic design. A 4-6-0 would not be acceptable, for it could not incorporate the wide firebox needed for the most efficient burning of Yorkshire coal. The obvious alter-native, therefore, was a Pacific.

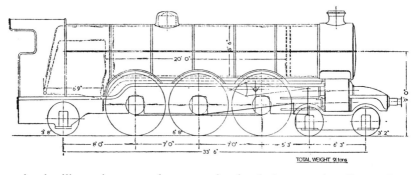

As the illustration seen above reveals, the design was, in effect, a long drawn-out Ivatt Atlantic with four cylinders, in this respect the exact counter-part of McIntosh's extended *Cardean*. The 5 ft 6 in. diameter Ivatt boiler barrel, parallel throughout its length, was retained, but to reduce the length between tubeplates to 20 ft the smokebox was recessed about 3 ft back into the barrel, rather than a combustion chamber being provided at the firebox end. The tube heating surface would have been 2,402 sq ft, the firebox heating surface 150 sq ft, and the superheating surface 730 sq ft; but the firegrate area of no more than 36 sq ft does not suggest that the steaming would have been of the highest order.

Four 15-in. cylinders would have been fitted, all driving the middle coupled axle, for which purpose the inside cylinders would have been steeply inclined; outside Walschaerts motion would have operated the piston-valves of the inside cylinders by rocking-shafts. By limitation of the working pressure to the 170 lb per sq in. then standard with the Ivatt Atlantics, the tractive effort on starting would have been no more than 21,130 lb. In working order, the engine weight would have been 91 tons, of which 54 tons would have been available for adhesion.

As a preliminary experiment, in 1915 Gresley rebuilt Ivatt Atlantic No. 279 with four 15 in. by 26 in. cylinders, and a front end similar to that which he proposed for the Pacific; also a twenty-four element superheater providing 427 sq ft of superheating surface was installed. But in practice, apart from a slight superiority in acceleration over the other Atlantics, No. 279 showed little justification for the change; probably the boiler was too small to provide sufficient steam for four cylinders of this size. So the first Gresley Pacific design never proceeded beyond the paper stage. For the sake of Gresley's reputation this is probably just as well, for the curious combination of Ivatt with Churchward was very unlikely to have achieved the outstanding success of his 'A1' Pacific design of seven years later, an entirely original conception throughout.

We come now to the early Pacific designs of the London, Midland & Scottish Railway. After its formation in 1923, for a little over two years George Hughes, former Chief Mechanical Engineer of the Lancashire & Yorkshire Railway (and of the London & North Western from the amalgamation of these two companies in 1922) was in charge of the locomotive affairs of the new group. His four-cylinder L. & Y. 4-6-0s took over some of the West Coast passenger work between Crewe and Carlisle, but without any marked superiority over the L.N.W.R. 'Claughtons'. As a result, and stimulated, no doubt, by the success of Gresley's 'A1' Pacifics on the L.N.E.R., he prepared a Pacific design based largely on his own 4-6-0s, but with 6 ft 9 in. in place of 6 ft 3 in. coupled wheels, a wide firebox, and a tractive effort of 33,600 lb. The L.M.S.R. operating authorities were resolutely opposed to large engines, however, and nothing came of the plan.

In 1925 Henry Fowler succeeded Hughes as Chief Mechanical Engineer of the L.M.S.R. Much impressed by the success of compound propulsion in France, he first toyed with the idea of a Midland compound enlarged to the 4-6-0 wheel arrangement, with one high-pressure cylinder 20¼ in. by 30 in., and two low-pressure 22¼ in. by 30 in., a 5 ft 3 in. diameter boiler with 1,965 sq ft heating surface and 529 sq ft superheating surface, 31·5 sq ft firegrate area and 220 lb pressure, which would have called for an engine weighing some 82 tons. Then, after converting Hughes 4-6-0 No. 10456 into a four-

230 *British Pacific Locomotives*

cylinder compound for experimental purposes, he designed the four-cylinder compound Pacific illustrated below.

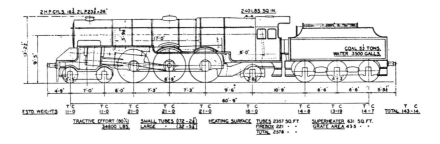

The low-pressure cylinders would have had the largest diameter of any ever mounted between the frames in a British locomotive – 23⅝ in. – and would have been the answer to the claim that compounding of a really powerful locomotive in this country was impossible because of the limits of the British loading gauge. The high-pressure cylinders, outside, would have been 16¾ in. diameter, and the common stroke of all four would have been 26 in. It was not intended to have independent cut-offs for the high- and low-pressure cylinders, as in French practice, because it was felt that the majority of British drivers would not have taken kindly to such a complication; the two sets of outside Walschaerts motion would have operated on all four piston-valves, with a fixed ratio between high- and low-pressure cut-offs, as in the Midland 4-4-0 compounds.

The boiler design was of considerable interest. In the first place, Fowler's proposed working pressure of 240 lb per sq in., again influenced, no doubt, by current French practice, would have set a new record for Great Britain at that time. Although the length of the 5 ft 9 in. diameter boiler barrel would have been 21 ft, the distance between tubeplates would have been shortened to 17 ft by the provision of a combustion chamber extending by no less than 4 ft from the firebox into the barrel. Evaporative heating surface would have totalled 2,578 sq ft, and superheating surface 631 sq ft, while the firegrate area would have been 43.5 sq ft. Out of an estimated engine weight of 101 tons in working order, 66 tons would have been available for adhesion.

It is a great pity that this Fowler design was never built, as it might have made possible a full-scale trial of compounding in Great Britain, with long-lap valves and a higher working pressure than ever previously. But once again the L.M.S.R. operating authorities refused to entertain the idea of locomotives of such size and weight. When at last they realized the inadequacy of their motive power on the West Coast main line, the need was met temporarily by the hurried design and construction of the first 'Royal Scot' 4-6-0s in 1927, and six years more were to elapse before the first L.M.S.R. Pacific, of Stanier's design, took the rails in 1933. But Stanier had a much freer hand than any of his predecessors.

The next British designer to turn his thoughts in the direction of the Pacific wheel arrangement was R. E. L. Maunsell of the Southern Railway. As mentioned already in Chapter VII, by the late 1920s the increasing weight of the Continental boat trains to and from Folkestone and Dover was beginning to overtax even the comparatively new 'Lord Nelson' 4-6-os; and double-heading of some of the services which were not worked by 'Nelsons' was proving expensive. A preliminary experiment by Maunsell in 1929 was the fitting of 'Lord Nelson' 4-6-0 No. 859 *Lord Hood* with 6ft 3in. instead of 6 ft 7 in. coupled wheels, with a view to improving acceleration and uphill work. but this made no perceptible difference in the performance of the engine. Nevertheless 6 ft 3 in. was the diameter decided on in the Pacific design, of which the outline appears below.

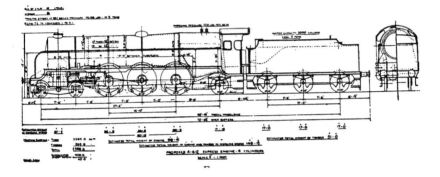

Apart from the smaller driving wheel diameter, the Pacific would have been practically identical with a 'Lord Nelson' from the front end to the rear coupled axle; it would then have had a wide firebox with a grate area of 40 sq ft. To keep the tractive effort at roughly the same figure as before – with the Pacific 33,190 lb – the four cylinders would have been reduced in diameter from 16½ in to 16 in, so balancing the 4 in. reduction in driving wheel diameter. The boiler barrel, 5 ft 7½ in. diameter for the first ring, would have tapered slightly to 5 ft 9 in. diameter through the second ring, and then more sharply over the third ring, from the dome backwards, to 6 ft 5 in. diameter at the firebox end. It would have had 2,303 sq ft tube heating surface, 205 sq ft in the firebox, and 400 sq ft superheating surface. The estimated total weight of the engine was 98¾ tons, including 60¾ tons on the coupled wheels; to keep the total length over buffers – 72 ft 6¾ in. – within the limits of turntable length on the Eastern Section, the tender would have been six-wheeled only, though its capacity of 5 tons of coal and 5,000 gallons of water would have been ample for the relatively short Eastern Section runs.

The idea behind the design was obviously to produce a variant of the 'Lord Nelson' with a greater steaming capacity rather than an entirely new design. But the obstacle this time was not the operating authorities, as on the L.M.S.R., but the civil engineering department, which at that time would have severely restricted the number of routes over which an engine of such length and weight would have been permitted to work. It may be added that after this, following on the outstanding success of Maunsell's three-cylinder 'Schools' 4-4-0 design, plans were roughed out for a Pacific with three 20 in. by 28 in cylinders and 6 ft 7 in. driving wheels, later amended to a three-cylinder 2-6-2 with 18 in. by 28 in. cylinders and 6 ft 3 in. wheels, but neither project came to anything owing to civil engineering objections to the weights involved. As we have seen already in Chapter VII, when under Bulleid the first Southern Pacifics at last did take the rails in 1941, it was only at the expense of extreme measures in weight reduction, some of which were eventually to prove troublesome by reason of failures in service.

In 1938 a Pacific design was prepared by Sir Nigel Gresley which never materialized as a locomotive. The popularity of the three London & North Eastern streamlined trains – the 'Silver Jubilee', 'Coronation' and 'West Riding Limited' – had increased to such an extent that it was nothing unusual for their seating to be booked to capacity and for last-minute prospective passengers to be turned away. Gresley realized that this tendency might call eventually for increased accommodation, which might overtax even the 'A4' Pacifics. A new design was therefore prepared for a streamlined Pacific with 275 lb pressure, which would have raised the starting tractive effort from 35,455 lb to 39,040 lb. But the onset of war in the following year caused this scheme to be shelved.

There have often been rumours of a Swindon Pacific, designed there during the middle 1940s, and I have actually seen an outline drawing of this engine. Like Maunsell's Southern Railway Pacific design, this Swindon machine would have closely resembled a 'King' 4-6-0 from the front end to the rear coupled axle, behind which there would have been a wide Belpaire firebox. A certain amount of work seems to have been done on the design, but this must have been unofficial, for F. W. Hawksworth, Chief Mechanical Engineer of the Great Western Railway and Western Region from 1941 to 1949, in a letter to me has dismissed the design as no more than 'a draughtsman's dream'.

Not so, however, the design prepared by the Chief Mechanical Engineer's Department of the London, Midland & Scottish Railway in 1938 – the same year as Gresley's Super-'A4' design – for an express locomotive which, if built, would have put any other design in the country completely in the shade. Strictly speaking, like No. 10000 of the L.N.E.R., it has no place in this chronicle, for it would have been a 4-6-4 and not a 4-6-2 locomotive. As on the East Coast main line, so on the West Coast the power demand was steadily increasing, and the idea in Sir William Stanier's mind was that eventually he might be required to produce a locomotive capable of working 500-ton trains between Euston and Glasgow on the same 6½-hour timing as the 300-ton 'Coronation Scot' of that period. The design, of which the general arrangement drawing, signed by Stanier in January, 1938, was first made public by E. S. Cox in his Presidential Address to the Institution of Locomotive Engineers in 1957, is seen in outline on page 233.

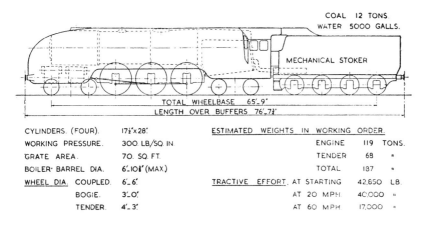

COAL 12 TONS.
WATER 5000 GALLS.

MECHANICAL STOKER

TOTAL WHEELBASE 65'-9"
LENGTH OVER BUFFERS 76'-7½"

CYLINDERS. (FOUR).	17⅞"x28"	ESTIMATED WEIGHTS IN WORKING ORDER.		
WORKING PRESSURE.	300 LB/SQ. IN.	ENGINE	119	TONS.
GRATE AREA.	70. SQ. FT.	TENDER	68	"
BOILER· BARREL DIA.	6'-10½" (MAX)	TOTAL	187	"
WHEEL DIA. COUPLED.	6'-6"	TRACTIVE EFFORT. AT STARTING	42,850	LB.
BOGIE.	3'-0"	AT 20 M.P.H.	40,000	"
TENDER.	4'-3"	AT 60 M.P.H.	17,000	"

The boiler barrel would have tapered to a maximum diameter of no less than 6 ft 10½ in., and for the first time in British locomotive history the firegrate would have expanded to an area of 70 sq ft. This would have been beyond the capacity of any fireman to fire manually, and mechanical stoking therefore would have been installed. The boiler pressure, 300 lb per sq in., would have created another British record. With 6 ft 6 in. driving wheels, the engine would have had a starting tractive effort of 42,850 lb; at 20 m.p.h. the estimated effort would have been 40,000 lb and at 60 m.p.h. 17,000 lb.

It had yet to be learned whether the Chief Civil Engineer would have agreed to axle-loads up to 24 tons, but the 72 tons of adhesion, coupled with a limitation in maximum cut-off to 65 per cent, would have ensured that the maximum power output would have been within normal adhesion limits. Total calculated weight of the 4-6-4 in working order was 119 tons; for adequate fuel (12 tons) and water (5,000 gallons) supplies, a departure from L.M.S.R. precedent would have been the provision of an eight-wheel tender, weighing full 68 tons. Engine and tender together would thus have weighed 187 tons; and the length of this mammoth over buffers would have been 76 ft 8 in. Alas, in this case also the outbreak of war put paid to this proposal for a locomotive of modern design which should have broken all British steam records for power output at speed.

So the ultimate in British Pacific or Baltic design was never actually reached, and now, in common with all other British locomotive types, the building of Pacifics has come to an end; moreover, the first scrapping of Pacifics has begun. Their disappearance can cause nothing but regret, for the principal Pacific classes have added one of the most distinguished of all chapters to British locomotive history.

APPENDIX

Some Recent Performances of Bulleid Pacifics

WHEN this book was at the proof stage, details reached me of some recent performances by rebuilt 'Merchant Navy' Pacifics of the Southern Region even superior to the best of those described in Section 10 of Chapter VII, and the times and speeds of two of these are set out in tabular form herewith. On the first of them, No. 35029 *Ellerman Lines* took the 'Atlantic Coast Express' from Waterloo down to Salisbury in an actual time of 73 min. 35 sec. with a 12-coach load of 395 tons tare and 420 tons full, and on the second, No. 35024 *East Asiatic Company* achieved almost exactly the same net time with one coach more, making a total of 430 tons tare and 460 tons gross.

The first run was timed by A. D. Nicholson, who rode on the footplate with Driver Britton and Fireman Watts of Salisbury, and so was able to watch how the engine was being handled. The reason for their outstanding work was a late start of 13 min. from Waterloo. By Hampton Court Junction speed had risen on the level to 75 m.p.h., and there was a further increase to 77 m.p.h. on the brief descent to Byfleet Junction. The long rise from there to milepost 31 lowered the speed no more than to 71 m.p.h., and then followed the continuous spell at 75 to 78 m.p.h. from Farnborough to Hook, and a brief 80 just beyond before the driver slackened to 65 m.p.h. for the speed restriction through Basingstoke.

It was then noteworthy that No. 35029 accelerated from 65 to 68 m.p.h. up the 1 in 249 to Battledown summit; next, after a maximum of 87 m.p.h. at Andover, there came the outstanding feat of climbing 1¾ miles at 1 in 264 and 2¾ miles at 1 in 165 to Grateley at a minimum of 75 m.p.h. – the highest speed I have ever known at this point with such a load. Finally, with no higher speed than 80 m.p.h. down Porton bank, *Ellerman Lines* brought the train to a stand at Salisbury in 73 min. 35 sec. from London, having regained 6½ min. of the late start.

Notwithstanding such times and speeds as these, the engine still had plenty of power in hand. Driver Britton's method was to drive on his regulator, which was never fully open; apart from starting, also, no longer cut-off was used than the 20 per cent to which it was set directly the train was well on the move. Over most of the stretches where the hardest steaming was being done the boiler pressure averaged 220 lb., and the lowest point to which it fell was 210 lb. after the tremendous effort up to Grateley; over the easier lengths about 240 lb. was the general figure. But the acceleration to Surbiton, the climb to milepost 31 and the brilliant climb to Grateley were all accomplished with no more than 180 lb. pressure in the steam-chest, the only time that the

S.R. WATERLOO–SALISBURY

Engine: Class 'MN' 4-6-2 No.: Load: Coaches/tons tare/tons gross			†35029 12/395/420		‡35024 13/430/460	
Dist.		Sched.	Times	Speeds	Times	Speeds
miles		min.	min. sec.	m.p.h.	min. sec.	m.p.h.
0·00	WATERLOO . . .	0	0 00	—	0 00	—
1·30	Vauxhall	—	3 07	—	3 27	34/51
3·90	CLAPHAM JUNCTION .	7	6 43	*43	Sigs. 7 22	*25 30
7·20	Wimbledon . . .	—	10 25	61	11 30	60
9·75	New Malden . . .	—	12 58	64	13 55	68
12·05	SURBITON . . .	—	14 54	70	15 50	70
13·35	Hampton Court Junction .	—	16 05	75	16 56	71
17·10	Walton	—	19 05	75	19 58	77
19·10	Weybridge . . .	—	20 49	72	21 32	78/81
21·65	West Byfleet . . .	—	22 56	77	23 27	77
24·30	WOKING . . .	26½	25 03	76	25 30	76
28·00	Brookwood . . .	—	28 05	74	28 28	74
31·00	Milepost 31 . . .	—	30 40	71	31 00	71
33·25	Farnborough . . .	—	32 29	75	32 50	75
36·50	Fleet	—	35 04	78	35 20	78
39·85	Winchfield . . .	—	37 41	77	37 55	77
42·20	Hook	—	39 25	78/81	39 37	81/84
47·80	BASINGSTOKE . .	—	44 03	*65	44 05	*65
50·30	Worting Junction . .	50	46 19	68	46 27	63
52·40	Oakley	—	48 10	75	48 15	72
55·60	Overton	—	50 33	81	50 47	78
59·20	Whitchurch . . .	—	53 20	84	53 27	82
61·10	Hurstbourne . . .	—	54 46	87/83	54 50	84/79
66·35	ANDOVER JUNCTION .	—	58 30	86	58 40	86
67·75	Red Post Junction . .	—	59 34	83	59 42	80
72·75	Grateley	—	63 15	75	63 38	67
75·60	Allington	—	65 16	75	65 55	82
78·25	Porton	—	67 51	80	67 48	86/90
82·60	Tunnel Junction . .	—	71 20	*48	71 35	*45
83·70	SALISBURY . . .	80	73 35	—	74 03	—
83·70	Net times (min.) . .	80	73½	—	73¼	—

* Speed restriction.   † *Ellerman Lines.*   ‡ *East Asiatic Company.*

steam-chest pressure reached 200 lb. being during the acceleration from Basingstoke to Battledown.

In view of the heavier load, the work of *East Asiatic Company*, as set out in the second column, was even finer; the driver was Roberts of Nine Elms and the recorder A. Swinburne. Once again the incentive was a late start out of Waterloo, though this time by 6½ min. only. As on the previous run, milepost 31 summit was breasted at 71 m.p.h., after 81 m.p.h. attained at Byfleet Junction, and then, after 77–78 m.p.h. along the level from Farnborough, 84 m.p.h. was touched beyond Hook, preceding the prescribed slowing to 65 m.p.h. through Basingstoke. Last of all came maxima of 86 m.p.h. at Andover and 90 down Porton bank, separated by a minimum of 67 m.p.h. over Grateley summit – again a notable figure.

On this run the 70·55 miles from Surbiton, where speed first reached the 70 m.p.h. mark, to Tunnel Junction, Salisbury, were reeled off in 55 min. 45 sec., at a mean speed of 76 m.p.h. throughout. Allowing for the slight signal check before Clapham Junction, *East Asiatic Company* achieved a net time of 73½ min. for the 83·7 miles from Waterloo, and so tied with the actual time of *Ellerman Lines* on the first run.

As things are at present, the Bulleid Pacifics, the newest express passenger steam power in the country – if the date of their complete reconstruction be regarded as the beginning of their career – are likely to be the last British steam locomotives that will continue to handle front-rank passenger trains. It is clear from such runs as those just described that they would have no difficulty in coping with a general acceleration of the services to and from both Bournemouth and the West of England, which might well be claimed today as overdue.

Index

Accidents and failures in service:
B.R. standard
broken piston-heads ... 203
broken engine-tender draw-
bar 208
slipping at speed 207
wheels shifting on axles ... 203
No. 70026, derailment, Mil-
ton 207
No. 70052, slidebars de-
tached, Settle 208
L.M.S.R.
No. 6202, turbine failures ... 130
No. 6224, boiler explosions
Cleghorn and Lamington 152
No. 6225, derailment, Gretna 152
No. 6231, collision, Eccle-
fechan 152
No. 6235, collision, Lam-
brigg Fell 152
No. 6244, derailment, Grendon 152
No. 6251, collision, Wins-
ford 153
No. 46202, collision, Weald-
stone 131, 153
No. 46242, collision, Weald-
stone 153
L.N.E.R.
fatality when taking water at
troughs 63
No. 2512, motion failure ... 60
No. 2512, derailment (of
train), Kings Cross ... 80
No. 2565, derailment, Cram-
lington 80
No. 2565, derailment, Gos-
wick 80
No. 2744, collision, Castle-
cary 80
No. 4469, destruction by
enemy action ... 80, 85
No. 60700, derailment,
Peterborough 41
Adhesion ... 97, 104, 166, 174, 175,
180, 195, 202, 207

Balancing ... 23, 51, 161, 197, 204
Bearings, roller ... 109, 115, 135,
195, 199, 203
Blast, Lemaître multiple-jet 160, 175, 177
Blastpipe, double ... 37, 40, 53, 66, 84,
97, 99, 109, 129, 132,
141, 198, 221

Boilers, all-welded 156, 157 et seq., 168
Brake-power 52, 55, 66

Cab comfort ... 52, 161, 199, 205
Coal consumption ... 27, 31, 32, 34, 39,
50, 63, 103, 104, 109, 119, 122,
145, 149, 173, 175, 202, 222
Coal-pusher, tender ... 133, 169
Comparative tests and trial running
Bulleid Pacifics before and after
rebuilding 174, 178
Bulleid Pacifics on Great East-
ern Line 165
Gresley and Raven Pacifics ... 16
Gresley Pacifics and G.W.R.
'Castle' 4-6-0s ... 28 et seq.
Gresley 180-lb and 220-lb
Pacifics 33
Locomotive exchanges, 1948 49,
74, 76, 83, 146, 165, 170, 196
Peppercorn 'A1' and 'A2' Pacifics 109
Standard 'Britannia' Pacifics ... 201
Standard Class '8' Pacific Duke
of Gloucester 222
Thompson 'A2/1' and 'A2/2'
and Gresley 'A4' Pacifics ... 103
Thompson 'A1/1' and Gresley
'A4' Pacifics 104
Compound propulsion ... 38, 229
Conjugated motion, Gresley 22, 81 et seq.
Cut-off, limitation 24, 233

Dimensions, leading, tabulated
B.R. Standard Pacifics... ... 225
G.W.R. The Great Bear ... 13
L.M.S.R. Stanier Pacifics ... 155
L.N.E.R. Gresley Pacifics ... 93
L.N.E.R. Peppercorn Pacifics... 116
L.N.E.R. Thompson Pacifics ... 105
N.E.R. Raven Pacifics 18
S.R. Bulleid Pacifics 194
Dome, banjo ... 36, 100, 106
Drive, divided or undivided 15, 97, 99,
106

Engineers, locomotive
Ahrons, E. L. 12
Bond, R. C. 130, 195
Bulleid, O. V. S. 94, 156 et seq.
Burrows, M. G. 168
Chapelon, André 50
Churchward, G. J. 11, 21, 25, 81,
119, 227, 229
Collett, C. B. 34, 119
Cook, K. J. 12, 83

Engineers, locomotive—*continued*
Cox, E. S.   120, 195 *et seq.*, 202, 218
Dalby, Professor W. E.   ...   38
Drummond, Dugald   158
Fletcher, Edward   114
Fowler, Sir Henry   229
Gresley, Sir Nigel   15, 19 *et seq.*, 94,
    100, 106, 109, 156, 227, 232
Harrison, J. F.   115
Holcroft, H. 11, 81
Holden, James   114
Hookham, J. A.   196
Hughes, George   229
Ivatt, H. A.   ...   20, 22, 25, 44,
    114, 195, 229
Ivatt, H. G.   135
Jarvis, R. G. 176, 191
Maunsell, R. E. L.   ...   156, 231
McIntosh, J. F.   227
Peppercorn, A. H   85, 89, 106 *et seq.*
Raven, Sir Vincen   12, 15, 21, 94,
    114
Riddles, R. A.   ...   137, 148, 195
Robinson, John G.   114
Spencer, B.   24, 32, 39, 49, 52, 81,
    94, 106
Stanier, Sir W. A.   ', 119 *et seq.*,
    196, 232
Stirling, Patrick   ...   ..., 114
Sturrock, A. 20, 114
Swift, H. H.   176
Thompson, Edward   ...   48, 79,
    94 *et seq.*, 106, 109, 156
Wallace, A. L.   168
Worsdell, Wilson   114
Exhaust, multiple-jet   160, 175, 177

Feed-water heating   35
Feed-water treatment, T.I.A.   ...   168
Feed-water treatment, S.R. system   169
Fire-door, pedal-operated ...   162, 178
Fore-and-aft motion   204

Hot-box detectors   82

Kylchap exhaust 37, 53, 133

Locomotives (other than Pacific)
Caledonian R. 4-6-0s   227
C.B. & Q. RR. 'Pioneer Zephyr'   42
German 'Fliegende Hamburger'   42
G.N.R. Ivatt Atlantics   20, 22, 228,
    229
G.N.R. 'K3' 2-6-0s   ...   19, 22
G.N.R. Stirling 4-2-2s   ...   20
G.W.R. 'Castle' 4-6-0s   17, 28 *et seq.*,
    127, 197, 207, 209
G.W.R. 'King' 4-6-0s   34, 75, 120,
    147, 170, 209, 232
G.W.R. 'Hall' 4-6-0s   170
Ljungström turbo-condensing...   128
L.M.S.R. Class '5' 4-6-0s   95, 120,
    170, 203

Locomotives (other than Pacific)—*cont.*
L.M.S.R. 'Jubilee' 4-6-0s   197, 218
L.M.S.R. 'Royal Scot' 4-6-0s   36, 75,
    121, 146, 170, 197, 213, 230
L.N.E.R. 'B1' 4-6-0s   95, 170, 211
L.N.E.R. 'B17' 4-6-0s...   ...   95
L.N.E.R. 'P2' 2-8-2s   ...   95, 157
L.N.E.R. 'V2' 2-6-2s   ...   99, 197
L.N.E.R. 'V4' 2-6-2   158
L.N.W.R. 'Claughton' 4-6-0s...   229
Pennsylvania RR. 'K4' Pacifics 22, 24
S.R. 'Lord Nelson' 4-6-0s   157, 160,
    231
S.R. 'Schools' 4-4-0s   232
U.P.RR. 'City of Portland'   ...   4

Mileages, high   ...   84, 115, 169, 206
Motion, poppet-valve   221

Names and numbers, notes on
B.R. Standard Pacifics 2 0
L.M.S.R. Stanier Pacifics   ...   15
L.N.E.R. Gresley 'A4' Pacifics   53,
    62, 65, 77
L.N.E.R. Peppercorn Pacifics...   11
S.R. Bulleid Pacifics   ...   , 04
Non-stop runs
Lond   sie   151
don–Edinburgh   ...   35
London–Glasgow   123
Names, numbers and building dates,
    tabulated
B.R. Standard Pacifics...   ...   225
L.M.S.R. Stanier Pacifics   ...   154
L.N.E.R. Gresley Pacifics   ...   90
L.N.E.R. Peppercorn Pacifics...   117
L.N.E.R. Thompson Pacifics ...   105
N.E.R. Raven Pacifics   18
S.R. Bulleid Pacifics   191

Oil-burning   107

Pacific designs never built
Caledonian R. (McIntosh)   ...   227
G.N.R. (Gresley)   232
G.W.R. (Swindon, unofficial)...   232
L.M.S.R. (Fowler)   229
L.M.S.R. (Stanier 4-6-4)   ...   232
L.N.E.R. (Gresley super-pres-
    sure)   232
S.R. (Maunsell)   230
Performance, exceptional
B.R. 'Britannia' type   ...   209 *et seq.*
B.R. 'Clan' type   219
B.R. *Duke of Gloucester*   ...   223
L.M.S.R. 'Princess Royal' type
    123 *et seq.*
L.M.S.R. 'Coronation' type 136 *et seq.*
L.N.E.R. Gresley
    original 'A1' type   25, 42, 69, 74
    'A3' type   ...   33, 46, 69, 71
    'A4' type   ...   48, 54, 59, 62, 64,
    71–73, 85, 89

Performance—*continued*
No. 10000 (rebuilt) ... 40
'P2' type (2-8-2) 95
L.N.E.R. Peppercorn
'A1' type 110
'A2' type 107
L.N.E.R. Thompson
'A2/2' type 97
'A2/3' type 101
S.R. 'Merchant Navy' type
171 *et seq.*, 182 *et seq.*, 234
S.R. 'West Country' type 185, 189
Performance, footplate experiences
B.R. 'Britannia' type ... 206, 214
B.R. 'Clan' type 219
B.R. *Duke of Gloucester* ... 224
L.M.S.R. 'Duchess' type ... 145
L.M.S.R. 'Princess' type ... 126
L.M.S.R. 'Turbomotive' ... 130
L.N.E.R. 'A1' type (original)... 26
L.N.E.R. 'A3' type 33
L.N.E.R. 'A4' type 75
S.R. 'Merchant Navy' type ... 180
S.R. 'Merchant Navy' type
(rebuilt) 181, 234
S.R. 'West Country' type ... 181
Performance records, tabulated
B.R. 'Britannias'
Euston–Manchester, *via*
Stoke 215
Ipswich–Norwich 211
Newport–Paddington ... 217
St Pancras–Leicester ... 212
B.R. 'Clans', Symington–Car-
lisle 219
B.R. *Duke of Gloucester*, Euston–
Crewe 223
L.M.S.R. 'Princesses'
Euston–Glasgow (non-stop) 124
Euston–Rugby 125
L.M.S.R. 'Duchesses'
Crewe–Glasgow (test runs) 140
Euston–Crewe (record runs) 138
L.N.E.R. 'A1'
(original), Kings Cross–
Leeds 45
(Peppercorn), Hitchin–Ret-
ford 111
(Peppercorn), York–Kings
Cross 113
L.N.E.R. 'A2',
Aberdeen–Dundee ... 108
L.N.E.R. 'A2/2',
York–Darlington ... 98
L.N.E.R. 'A2/3'
Edinburgh–Newcastle ... 101
York–Darlington 102
L.N.E.R. 'A4'
Doncaster–Kings Cross ... 86
Kings Cross–Peterborough
('Silver Jubilee' trial trip) 57
Newcastle–Edinburgh ... 88
Peterborough–Kings Cross 73

Performance—*continued*
S.R. 'Merchant Navy'
Salisbury–Sidmouth Junc.... 188
Southampton–Waterloo ... 184
Waterloo–Salisbury 186, 235
Waterloo–Southampton ... 183
S.R. 'West Country', Salisbury–
Waterloo 190

Rebuilt locomotives
L.M.S.R. 'Turbomotive' as 4-
cyl. Pacific 131
L.N.E.R. 'P2' 2-8-2s as Pacifics 95
L.N.E.R. No. 4470 as 'A1/1'
Pacific 99
S.R. 'Merchant Navy' Pacifics
176 *et seq.*
S.R. 'West Country' Pacifics ... 179
Reliability, locomotive 63, 68, 82, 84,
115, 169, 179, 195

Smoke deflection 36, 84, 129, 165, 177
Speed indicators 52, 59
Speeds, 100 m.p.h. and over
126 m.p.h., L.N.E.R. No. 4468 66
114 m.p.h., L.M.S.R. No. 6220 137
113 m.p.h., L.N.E.R. No. 2512 60
112½ m.p.h., L.N.E.R. No. 2509 56
112 m.p.h., L.N.E.R. (B.R.) No.
60007 87
109 m.p.h., L.N.E.R. No. 4489 64
108 m.p.h., L.N.E.R. No. 2750 47
102 m.p.h., L.N.E.R. No. 2512 60
101 m.p.h., L.N.E.R. (B.R.) No.
60526 109
100½ m.p.h., L.N.E.R. (B.R.)
No. 60140 112
100 m.p.h., L.M.S.R. No. 6220 139
100 m.p.h., L.N.E.R. No. 4472 44
100 m.p.h., L.N.E.R. (B.R.) No.
60007 87
100 m.p.h., S.R. (B.R.) No.
35012 187
Stability at speed 51, 55
Stoker, mechanical... ... 169, 223
Streamlining ... 38, 49, 61, 63,
132, 134, 233
Super-pressure locomotives ... 37
Syphons, thermic 158, 175

Tender, corridor 34
Turbine propulsion ... 127 *et seq.*

Valve-motion
chain-driven ... 156, 159 *et seq.*,
166, 177
derived ... 22, 38, 122, 132, 159
Valve-setting 23, 32, 94, 120, 198

Water-tube boiler 37
Water-tubes in firebox ... 12, 158
Wheels, 'B.F.B.' cast type 160